CW01500289

Contents

PART I

National Frameworks to Balance Fiscal Discipline and Local Investment Needs

Financing Cities

Financing Cities

Fiscal Responsibility and Urban Infrastructure in
Brazil, China, India, Poland and South Africa

Editors

**George E. Peterson
Patricia Clarke Annez**

THE WORLD BANK

A co-publication of The World Bank and Sage Publications India Pvt Ltd

First published in 2007 by

Sage Publications India Pvt Ltd
B1/I1 Mohan Cooperative Industrial Area
Mathura Road
New Delhi 110 044
www.sagepub.in

Sage Publications Inc
2455 Teller Road
Thousand Oaks, California 91320

Sage Publications Ltd
1 Oliver's Yard, 55 City Road
London EC1Y 1SP

Sage Publications Asia-Pacific Pte Ltd
33 Pekin Street
#02-01 Far East Square
Singapore 048763

Published by Vivek Mehra for Sage Publications India Pvt Ltd, typeset in 10/12 pt Garamond by Star Compugraphics Private Limited, Delhi and printed at Chaman Enterprises, New Delhi.

Library of Congress Cataloging-in-Publication Data

Financing cities: fiscal responsibility and urban infrastructure in Brazil, China, India, Poland and South Africa/editors, George E. Peterson and Patricia Clarke Annez.
    p. cm.
Includes bibliographical references and index.

1. Fiscal policy—Case studies. 2. Finance, Public—Case studies. 3. Infrastructure (Economics)—Case studies. I. Peterson, George E. II. Annez, Patricia Clarke.

HJ192.5.F56	336'.014—dc22	2007	2007001254

ISBN: 978-0-7619-3564-3 (HB)   978-81-7829-724-8 (India-HB)

Sage Production Team: Manidipa Mandal, Shweta Vachani and Santosh Rawat

List of Tables

List of Figures

List of Abbreviations

ANC	African National Congress
APHDC	Andhra Pradesh Housing Development Corporation
APUIFDC	Andhra Pradesh Urban Infrastructure and Finance Development Corporation
ARO	Anticipação de Receita Orçamentária (Revenue Anticipation Operations)
ATM	Automated Teller Machine
AUWSP	Accelerated Urban Water Supply Programme
BEA	Budget Enforcement Act
BESA	Bond Exchange of South Africa
BEST	Brihan-Mumbai Electric Supply and Transport Undertaking
BIS	Bank of International Settlements
BMC	Brihan-Mumbai Municipal Corporation
BOT	Build, Operate, Transfer
CDB	China Development Bank
CEC 4	'Major' Central European Countries (i.e., Czech Republic, Hungary, Poland and Slovakia)
CEE	Central and Eastern Europe
CESifo	Center for Economic Studies Information and Forschung
CFC	Central Finance Commission
CIDCO	City and Industrial Development Corporation
CIDE-Combustíveis	Contribuição de Intervenção no Domínio Econômico (Revenue from Federal Excise on Petroleum Derivatives)

CIT	Corporate Income Tax
CLIFF	Community Led Infrastructure Finance Facility
CMWA	Chennai Metropolitan Water Authority
CNG	Compressed Natural Gas
CRISIL	Credit Rating Information Services of India Ltd
CSO	Central Statistical Organisation
DBSA	Development Bank of Southern Africa
DDA	Delhi Development Authority
DFID	Department for International Development (United Kingdom)
DFV	District Financing Vehicle
DJN	Delhi Jal Nigam
DRU	Desvinculação das Receitas da União (a mechanism which frees from earmarking 20 per cent of federal tax revenue)
EAP	East Asia and Pacific
EBRD	European Bank for Reconstruction and Development
ECA	Europe and Central Asia
ECLAC	Economic Commission for Latin America and the Caribbean
EFC	Eleventh Finance Commission
EU	European Union
FCL	Fiscal Crimes Law
FDI	Foreign Direct Investment
FIRE (D)	Financial Institutions Reform and Expansion (Debt)
FPEx	Fundo de Compensação pela Desoneração das Exportações (Fund for the Compensation of Exports)
FPM	Fundo de Participação dos Municípos (Municipal Participation Fund)
FRA	Fiscal Risks Annex
FRL	Fiscal Responsibility Law
FSI	Floor Space Index
FUNDEF	Fundo de Manutenção e Desenvolvimento do Ensino Fundamental e de Valorização do Magistério (National Fund for Primary Education Development and the Improvement of the Teaching Profession)
GCIS	Government Communications and Information System

GDP	Gross Domestic Product
GNI	Gross National Income
GOI	Government of India
GSDP	Gross State Domestic Product
HDFC	Housing Development Finance Corporation Ltd
HIC	High Income Countries
HUDA	Haryana Urban Development Authority
HUDCO	Housing and Urban Development Corporation
IADF	International Association of Development Funds
IBAM	Instituto Brasileiro de Administração Municipal (Brazilian Institute of Municipal Administration)
IBGE	Instituto Brasileiro de Geografia e Estatística (National Statistics Bureau)
ICMS	Imposto Sobre a Circulação de Mercadorias e Prestação de Serviços (State-Level Value Added Tax)
IDA	International Development Association
IDASA	Institute for a Democratic Alternative in South Africa
IDFC	Infrastructure Development Finance Corporation
IDSMT	Integrated Development of Small and Medium Towns
IE	Investment Expenditure
IFC	International Finance Corporation
ILFS	Infrastructure Leasing and Financial Services Ltd
ILPES	Instituto Latinaméricano de Planificacion Económica y Social
IMF	International Monetary Fund
INCA	Infrastructure Finance Corporation
IOF-Ouro	Financial Transactions Tax on Gold
IPI	Imposto Sobre Produtos Industrializados (Federal Tax on Industrialised Products)
IPlexp	Federal Value Added Tax Levied on Exports
IPTU	Imposto Sobre Propriedade Territorial Urbana (Municipal Urban Property Tax)
IPVA	Imposto Sobre a Propriedade de Veículos Automotores (Vehicle Registration Tax)
IR	Imposto de Renda (Income Tax)
IRPF	Imposto de Renda de Pessoa Física (Personal Income Tax)

IRRF	Income Tax at Source
ISPA	Instrument for Structural Policies for Pre-Accession
ISS	Imposto Sobre Serviços (Municipal Services Tax)
IT	Information Technology
ITBI	Transfers Tax
ITR	Imposto sobre a Propriedade Territorial Rural (Federal Rural-Property Tax)
IWK	Indah Water Konsortium
JBIC	Japanese Bank for International Cooperation
KMC	Kolkata Municipal Corporation
KMDA	Kolkata Metropolitan Development Authority
KUIDFC	Karnataka Urban Infrastructure Development Finance Corporation
LAC	Latin America and the Caribbean
LDC	Less Developed Country
LDO	Lei de Diretrizes Orçamentárias (Budget Guidelines Law)
LIC	Low-Income Countries
LMIC	Lower-Middle Income Countries
LOA	Lei Orçamentária Anual (Annual Budget Law)
MENA	Middle East and North Africa
MDF	Municipal Development Fund
MHADA	Mumbai Housing and Area Development Authority
MIG	Municipal Infrastructure Grant
MMC	Mumbai Municipal Coropration
MMRDA	Mumbai Metropolitan Regional Development Authority
MOU	Memorandum of Understanding
MRDC	Mumbai Roads Development Corporation
MSWM	Municipal Solid Waste Management
MUDF	Municipal Urban Development Fund
MVRC	Mumbai Rail Vikas Corporation
NATO	North Atlantic Treaty Organization
NBER	National Bureau of Economic Research
NCMP	National Common Minimum Programme
NDMC	New Delhi Municipal Corporation
NSSF	National Small Savings Fund
O&M	Operating and Maintenance
OCC	Other Current and Capital Spending

OECD	Organisation for Economic Co-operation and Development
PIT	Personal Income Tax
PLANASA	Plano Nacional de Saneamento (National Water Supply and Sanitation Plan)
PNAD	Pesquisa Nacional por Amostragem de Domicílios (National Household Survey)
PNSB	Pesquisa Nacional de Saneamento Básico (National Survey of Basic Sanitation)
PPA	Plano Pluriannual (Multi-year Budget-Framework Law)
PPI	Private Participation in Infrastructure
PPIAF	Private Participation in Infrastructure Advisory Facility
PPP	Public–Private Partnership
PSIRU	Public Services International Research Unit
PWD	Public Works Department
RE	Revised Estimate
RMB	Renminbi (Chinese Local Currency, a.k.a. Yuan)
RSC/JSB	Regional Services Council/Joint Services Board
SABESP	Companhia de Saneamento Básico do Estado de São Paulo (Sao Paulo State water utility)
SAR	South Asia Region
SFC	State Finance Commission
SIDA	Swedish International Development Agency
SOE	State-Owned Enterprise
SPV	Special Purpose Vehicles
SUS	Sistema Único de Saúde (National Health System)
TDRs	Transferable Development Rights
TFC	Twelfth Finance Commission
TNUDF	Tamil Nadu Urban Development Fund
TNUIFSL	Tamil Nadu Urban Infrastructure and Financial Services Ltd
TUFIDCO	Tamil Nadu Urban Finance and Infrastructure Development Corporation
URIF	Urban Reforms Initiatives Fund
UDA	Urban Development Authority
UDIC	Urban Development and Investment Company
UDF	United Democratic Front

ULB	Urban Local Body
UMIC	Upper-Middle Income Countries
US	United States (of America)
USAID	United States Agency for International Development
VAT	Value Added Tax
WSS	Water Supply and Sanitation
WTO	World Trade Organization

Foreword

Cities are the engines that drive national economic growth. By clustering complementary economic activities, intellectual and financial capital, and entrepreneurial energy, they raise labour productivity and create the potential for sustainable growth through urbanization as low-productivity rural labourers move to the cities. The backbone of a well-functioning city is its urban infrastructure—the network of roads, distribution of electricity, water supply and waste removal—which allows residents and firms to work productively under high-density conditions. We in India have come to appreciate the critical nature of urban infrastructure. The floods in Mumbai reminded us that even as we frame fundamental economic reforms, the biggest gap in India's infrastructure remains urban infrastructure. The whole world envies the congregation of brilliant, entrepreneurial people in Bangalore, but the city is dying a slow death owing to a congested and dysfunctional infrastructural system. This growing 'urban infrastructure deficit' needs to be corrected as quickly as possible, because growing cities are India's future.

From one perspective, the urban infrastructure challenge is a challenge for public finance; in a federal system, it's a challenge also for intergovernmental finance. As this volume makes clear, large sums will be required in all countries to invest adequately in urban infrastructure and to operate and maintain systems once they are built. For some advocates of fiscal federalism, the only solution lies in transferring greater revenue-raising powers to local governments. However, what are needed are reliable revenue streams that can be dedicated to infrastructure support. Much of the financing for electricity distribution, water supply, sanitation and waste removal can appropriately come from user fees, shared federal tax revenues and well-designed property taxes.

More than a revenue challenge alone, urban infrastructure is a challenge in terms of institutional arrangements and management authorities. In India, no management team, no institution is clearly responsible for urban infrastructure and none can be held accountable when the system fails. A user-fee system for urban infrastructure finance may be easy to design in principle, but local governments may not have adequate incentives to implement such a system in practice. Accountability for results is perhaps the most essential element in an intergovernmental framework. Fiscal frameworks often have been erected in the shadow of a fear that local governments will irresponsibly overreach themselves through excessive borrowing or spendthrift operations. They are therefore filled with restrictions or prohibitions on local behaviour. However, local governments, like other economic agents, also respond to positive incentives and act most effectively (just as other agents do) when they have clearly assigned responsibilities for which they have management discretion and clear accountability for results. At all levels, governments are the agents of the people. We need to reach clarity on the infrastructure outcomes that are priorities and clarity as to how local governments will be rewarded for infrastructural success and how they will be held accountable for failure.

This book brings out how accountability for urban infrastructure outcomes and financing has been built into different countries' institutions, and assesses from each country's own perspective how well this aspect of the intergovernmental system is working within the overall fiscal framework. The chapters lay out an impressive range of successes and failures, with valuable lessons to be gleaned from these experiences. No country will want to blindly adopt institutions or intergovernmental frameworks from elsewhere. Each nation has the responsibility to design its own particular approach to urban infrastructure, consistent with its intergovernmental fiscal structure, institutional frameworks and the roles of local governments. It is here that this volume makes an important contribution by providing a much better menu of experience-tested institutional arrangements and financing strategies, and thus offering a much better-informed basis for making policy choices. This is knowledge-based policy making at its best.

One of the most important lessons from the outstanding essays of this volume is that capital markets are quite responsive. If institutional arrangements are clear, with transparent rules for accountability, and authorities are fiscally responsible, capital markets will provide adequate resources for overcoming the infrastructure deficit of the urban economy.

Vijay Kelkar
Chairman, IDFC Private Equity Co. Ltd
Mumbai

Preface

This book is based on a conference, the 'Practitioners' Conference on Mobilizing Urban Infrastructure Finance in a Responsible Fiscal Framework: Lessons from Brazil, China, India, Poland and South Africa'.[1] The conference sought to examine two potentially conflicting policy goals: the first, maintaining fiscal discipline, and the second, mobilizing adequate finance for infrastructure, needed both to support economic growth and to improve the quality of life in cities in developing countries. The participants in the conference were experienced in managing either or both objectives. Recognizing that both were worthy of attention, we sought to encourage a dialogue between different viewpoints. We emphasized case studies on different topics to look at the interactions of a range of variables and factors and to see how they fit together. Rather than require each case to follow the same format, the authors have structured their papers around the issues that matter most from their perspective in addressing the topic in hand.

The first part of this book presents case studies describing the framework established at the national level to promote urban infrastructure finance while ensuring fiscal discipline and reviewing recent experience as well as future challenges. The subjects covered include the impact of political and fiscal decentralization, limitations on borrowing, managing moral hazard, the role of the financial sector, the achieving of the right balance between stringent controls and encouragement of local governments taking responsibility for fiscal discipline coupled with market discipline. The cases featured include three of the world's largest decentralized nations; together the five countries featured in the conference account for nearly a third of the world's urban population. Part I includes case studies for each of the five countries featured in the conference: Brazil (Chapter 1), China (Chapter 2), India (Chapter 3), Poland (Chapter 4) and South Africa (Chapter 5).

Part II then shifts from the frameworks for fiscal discipline to urban infrastructure investments and the strategies used to mobilize investment funding. Chapters 6 and 7 examine the financing strategies for urban infrastructure in Shanghai and Brazil respectively. These two case studies, written from the perspective of practitioners, examine how different potential elements of a financing strategy were brought together in very different circumstances, including the national development priorities, fiscal rules and options offered by financial intermediaries. The next two chapters focus on specialized intermediaries offering urban infrastructure finance in cities. One is a fully private venture in South Africa (Chapter 9) while the other, in Tamil Nadu, India (Chapter 8), is a spin-off of a government fund with minority private ownership. The final two chapters examine experiences with two other mechanisms for mobilizing funding for infrastructure investments from the private sector, land leasing and sales (Chapter 10) and private participation in infrastructure operations (Chapter 11).

Note

1. Held on 6–8 January 2005 in Jaipur, India, and sponsored by the UK Department for International Development, the Caixa Econômica Federal of Brazil, the Council of Europe Development Bank, the Infrastructure Development Finance Corporation of India, the National Institute of Urban Affairs, the Private Public Participation in Infrastructure Advisory Facility, the United States Agency for International Development, and the World Bank. In addition, the Ministry of Finance, Government of India, and the Government of the state of Rajasthan supported and hosted the conference.

Acknowledgements

The editors are most grateful for the strong support, both financial and substantive, provided by the sponsors of the conference and this book: Aser Cortines and Rosane Maia of the Caixa Econômica Federal of Brasil, Krzsystof Ners of the Council of Europe Development Bank, Ian Curtis of the Department for International Development of the United Kingdom, Deepak Parekh of the Infrastructure Development Finance Company Limited of India, Usha Ragupathi of the National Institute of Urban Affairs of India, Jyoti Shukla and Bhavna Bhatia of the Private Public Participation in Infrastructure Advisory Facility, Rebecca Black and Nabaroon Bhattacharjee of the United States Agency for International Development, and Elio Codato, Vincent Gouarne, Sonia Hammam, Lili Liu and Maryvonne Plessis-Fraissard of the World Bank. We are much obliged to the Honourable Vasundhara Raje, Chief Minister of the Government of Rajasthan, for hosting the conference in Jaipur, and to Subhash Garg, then Joint Secretary of the Government of India and now Secretary of Finance of the Government of Rajasthan, who provided considerable support to the organization of the event and helpful advice regarding its content. We would also like to thank all the participants in the conference for their insights and engaging discussion at the conference and in subsequent interactions. A number of colleagues, in addition to those mentioned above, were particularly helpful in helping to conceive the project and offering advice and encouragement for the conference and this book. We thank especially Jan Brzeski, Robert Buckley, Sandra Cointreau, Mila Freire, Hu Jing, Barjor Mehta, Jack Stein and Roberto Zagha. Oscar Apodaca, Mamata Baruah, Margaret d'Costa, Laura De Brular, Constance Hope, Christianna Johnnides and Norma Silvera provided able administrative and logistical support to our efforts. Herschel Pant of the

London School of Economics provided expert research assistance in preparing the book for publication.

We would like to pay a special tribute to the late Messrs S.P. Gupta and Krzysztof Ners. Mr Gupta, Principal Secretary of Finance of the Government of Rajasthan, at the time of the conference played an invaluable role in ensuring a warm welcome to all the participants in Jaipur and for his very efficient arrangements for the conference. Mr Ners, Vice-Governor of the Council of Europe Development Bank, at the time of his death, supported and participated in the conference, and offered a valuable contribution to this volume. Their untimely demise was a great loss to their respective governments as well as family and friends. This volume is dedicated to their memory.

PART I

National Frameworks to Balance Fiscal Discipline and Local Investment Needs

Urban Finance: A Force for Development and Growth

Most policy makers would agree that fiscal discipline is a good thing for long-term growth. It is perhaps less widely understood that urban infra-structure finance is an essential element in growth and development. This may change as projected demographic projections become reality. Only 50 per cent of the world's population is now urban. In the two most populous countries in the world, the urbanization rate for India is only about 30 per cent and for China about 40 per cent. Over the next 25 years, India and China's cities alone will absorb a population increase greater than twice the entire current population of the United States. Successful policies must meet the demands for infrastructure and services to which this will give rise.

Jane Jacobs was of the view that 'Cities, not countries, are the constituent elements of a developing economy and have been so from the dawn of civilization'.[1] It is indeed difficult to argue with the proposition that cities are the loci of growth in most economies, even if this concept hasn't always figured in growth models. The performance of the world's fastest-growing economies also underscores the significance of solid urban infrastructure in a growth strategy. Two of the countries featured in this book, India and China, are amongst those identified as having grown faster than the United States for the last 20 years in a recent study by the World Bank (2005). Table I.1 illustrates clearly that the outstanding long-term rates of growth achieved in both countries are due to services and manufacturing rather than agriculture, even though over this period their agricultural growth has been respectable in comparison to many other countries. Looking beyond these two particularly strong performers, we find that in every country in which per capita income grew faster than in the United States over the period 1980–2002, growth in manufacturing and services both exceeded agricultural growth.[2] Without strong performance in urban activities, countries do not grow quickly. Gramlich (1994) has argued in the case of the United States that the capacity to make good infrastructure investment decisions and fund these projects when needed contributes powerfully to growth and improvements in the quality of life in cities.[3] It is precisely this capacity that is the valid policy objective this book explores.

Table I.1
Average Annual Growth Rates in India and China, 1990–2004

Average annual growth rates, 1990–2004	India	China
GDP	5.7%	9.7%
Manufacturing	6.1%	12.2%
Services	7.8%	8.9%
Agriculture	2.5%	3.1%
Ratio of manufacturing to Agriculture	2.5	3.9
Ratio of services to Agriculture	3.1	2.8

Source: Development Data Platform, World Bank. Data for 1990–2004. in Real 2000 $.

Decentralization: Reconciling Potentially Conflicting Objectives

Decentralization has taken place in a wide range of countries for a multitude of reasons, usually in response to demands for increased local involvement in the management of resources. These forces for decentralization, oftentimes political, trump economic and fiscal considerations alone. Many have pointed out that this shift has made fiscal management more difficult (for example, Rodden et al. 2003 and Ter-Minassian 1997). While decentralization affects the appropriate design of policies, it is only part of the context, and not the source of the potential policy conflict that is treated in this book. Addressing multiple investment needs for public services and productive infrastructure in a fashion that supports growth and development is a problem all governments must resolve. Centralized systems are easier to control; they usually have a harder time making good investment decisions.

Even the most centralized governments contend with competing investment demands, especially in large, diverse countries. Sometimes they fail to contain the pressures for more expansive government, and this causes problems for macroeconomic stability. When governments are highly centralized and unresponsive to local needs, they perform poorly in mobilizing public support to pay for services. Likewise, poorly designed decentralization efforts can undo the benefits that the principle of subsidiarity[4] offers in theory and can undermine fiscal discipline. In either case, bad investment decisions by a government have an opportunity cost and can reduce long-term growth.

Beyond the question of how much to invest, what to invest in, and where to invest, policy frameworks also affect investment efficiency and equity. For example, financing long-lived infrastructure projects out of current revenues imposes an undue burden on the current generation of beneficiaries in relation to later generations who can enjoy the 'free ride'. This approach is particularly costly when demands for long-lived assets such as urban infrastructure are growing rapidly, due to rapid economic growth and urbanization, as is the case in India and China. But even for countries, such as Poland, which has very little demographic growth but whose accession to the European Union has created significant demands for upgrading both environmental and economic infrastructure, this matters. The converse, abuse of borrowing for unproductive purposes, burdens future generations unduly and can burden the macroeconomy in the process.

The countries examined here use rather different tools to articulate the relationships across levels of government. In some cases, administrative controls will feature strongly—in India, China and Brazil, for example. In others, such as South Africa and Poland, a variety of institutions—including the financial sector, the courts and Constitutional prohibitions—are used to establish financial discipline in sub-national governments. Amongst those countries using administrative controls, there is considerable variation in the adaptability of their systems. India's federal system relies on the states to set the framework for city finance, while Brazil, Poland and South Africa treat cities more independently of the provinces. China's system relies heavily on the provinces to delegate to cities, but policy is more closely coordinated across levels of government through consultation and adaptation.

Taking the Risk of Empowering Cities

Each of the cases in this section discusses approaches to managing these issues in a specific context. These circumstances bring with them a whole set of risks beyond the economic realm. One of the interesting lessons from examining this particular set of cases is that decentralizing was a risk taken successfully, albeit quite differently in China, Poland and South Africa. In all three of these cases, this decentralization took place against the backdrop of major economic, social or political transitions, fraught with risks that went well beyond concerns about fiscal profligacy.

In the case of South Africa, discussed in Chapter 5 of this volume, decentralization was a key element of the transition from apartheid. Social unrest in cities had been a major driver of political compromise. Refusal to pay user charges had been one of the tools of choice of the populations of black townships. Non-payment was a means of voicing protest against the whole set of controls on residency and poor-quality services in black townships. In many respects, cities and their services were the 'ground zero' of the conflicts that the new government had to resolve. A number of cities were in weak financial condition, and private financial institutions were not keen to expand their exposure. The central government had established a track record of providing guarantees to assist local governments in financial difficulty, often because of political sensitivities.

Rather than centralize control to manage these risks, the new government was constituted with considerable financial powers in cities, and local governments were empowered to improve service delivery. South Africa had a number of factors in its favour. Its white cities had good services and a good taxation base. Amalgamating under-served black townships with these prosperous cities gave the local governments in the larger cities a revenue base for building up their services. These amalgamated cities were also well-endowed with the technical capacity to manage investment programmes, municipal accounting, and so on. Safeguards such as a Constitutional prohibition of intergovernmental guarantees sent out a strong signal regarding fiscal discipline both to the local governments themselves and the financial sector. Mobilizing finance from the banking sector and capital markets, discussed in more detail below, was an important element in the overall strategy and produced a unique private intermediary as well (see Chapter 9). As Chapter 5 illustrates convincingly, services have expanded dramatically in South Africa in the face of only moderate income growth, while the consolidated fiscal deficit has improved quite substantially. This risk-taking strategy, which played to the strengths of the political pact underpinning decentralization and existing institutional capacity, has produced tangible results.

Poland decentralized while reconstituting its government after the transition from communism and domination by the former Soviet Union. Thus, this process took place as the entire economic base was restructured, and Poland and its trading partners faced a serious economic downturn. Much of the productive base and the operation of the social welfare system that it provided devolved on local governments in the transition. This offered an asset base to cities on the one hand and exposed them to substantial economic and political risks on the other. These risks have been managed well on the whole, and relationships across the various levels of government have been quite disciplined. Credit should go to the local governments, who used the resources that they were endowed with well. The success of the national government in achieving relatively rapid growth and the healthy development of a private financial sector undeniably helped create conditions in which the well-managed local governments could perform.

As Chapter 4 discusses, there has been some significant deterioration of the fiscal accounts in recent years in Poland, but the imbalance did not come primarily from local governments. As decentralization proceeded, some issues related to the fragmentation of municipalities arose, driving service costs very high. A correction was required and was successfully completed in the reform of the early 1990s. Continued adaptation of the system has sought to address fiscal imbalances. The system of fiscal discipline shares macro risks across levels of government. Shared taxes constitute a significant revenue source for local governments. Transfers of tax revenues to them must be curtailed when consolidated public-debt thresholds are exceeded, thus mitigating the potential for contradictory fiscal stances at different levels of government. Preventive thresholds for government debt aid in making the adjustment process more gradual, and the measures for fiscal discipline have not interfered with resource allocation decisions. Fiscal adjustment continues to be challenging, but measures have been successfully implemented to maintain investment spending in spite of budgetary contraction. Clearly, relatively strong economic growth overall and the requirement that investment spending be maintained in order to be eligible for EU grants has played an important role in this outcome. Nonetheless, the collaborative and even-handed approach to fiscal risk management that has resulted from steady adaptation of the system also appears to have played a useful role.

China's shift of economic power to a decentralized government, described in Chapter 2, was a central tool for the overall economic reform programme started in the 1980s, but had no link to a discrete political transition as in the Polish and South African cases. There were risks involved in the economic transition, of course. The Chinese case study provided in Chapter 2 describes how managing fiscal risks was linked to the economic policy underpinning decentralization. The Chinese decentralization policy implemented in the early 1980s explicitly shifted fiscal risks upward to the national government in order to provide both incentives and flexibility at the local level to develop the regional economy, making, as it were, a 'bet' on the local governments. Local governments were given buoyant tax bases, and in turn made contractual commitments to transfer revenues up to the centre. Viewed in terms of the promotion of economic growth, the bet paid off and the programme was a tremendous success, as is well known.

From a fiscal perspective, the central government bore considerable costs and its ability to promote such national objectives as regional equalization was compromised. Local infrastructure investment has been a significant beneficiary of this reform as well, as the case study of Shanghai in Chapter 6 illustrates so vividly. The government took strong measures to reform the system in 1994, with a view both to increasing overall revenues and to securing revenue flows to the national government, and since then the system has been adapted from time to time. As local government capacity has shifted, the financial system has absorbed considerable borrowing on behalf of local governments in spite of an interdiction on direct borrowing by local governments, oftentimes collateralized with municipal assets. While there are significant risks in principle to the financial system using such an approach, due to strong growth (among other factors), the worst-case scenarios have been avoided. As indicated in Chapter 2, the current debate is examining, among others, whether the adaptations that shifted resources to the centre have also had impacts on the financial system that are not desirable in the long term.

The Indian decentralization process—at least as it concerns urban local governments,[5] as opposed to states—was an adaptation of the well-established federal system in India, and took place in a period of relative political and economic calm. The economic crisis of 1991 was under control and the economic reforms started in the 1980s and much intensified in the 1990s were well underway. The fiscal accounts, particularly at the state level, as discussed in Chapter 3, were in reasonably good shape. The state-level deficits have since deteriorated to close to 5 per cent of GDP, fuelled in part by reductions in federal government transfers and continuing pressures for current expenditure increases. In addition, liberalization of the financial system has made it more difficult to finance state-level deficits.

Hence, the decentralization of local governments in the early 1990s was a relatively small event; the risks taken in the implementation were insignificant, as little by way of resources or administrative autonomy were entrusted to urban local governments. The state governments, whose control of the process was left unchanged by the Constitutional Amendment Act, began to face sharp adjustments on their own account and did not cede control of resources in this context.

The debate in India on how and when to offer more autonomy and control of resources to urban local governments is typically characterized by a question of how to manage the risks of further devolution. Yet, as decentralization was to be implemented at the local level, the states were encountering mounting difficulties in managing their own finances. Fiscal pressures at the state level as much as fiscal management capacities at the city level were significant constraints to devolution. The response to the Constitutional Amendment Act was unlikely to be substantive as long as the states were facing the adjustments they did and could withhold resources from the cities, no matter how well or poorly the cities managed their meagre finances. Indeed, it is hard to imagine what local governments could have done to persuade the states in India to provide more resources when the state fiscal position was under such stress.

The Brazil case in Chapter 1 offers a rather different picture of risk management and its role among the federal government and sub-national governments. Management of debt, especially international obligations, has played a dominant role in fiscal policy in Brazil since the 1980s. Fiscal adjustment was driven by measures that could yield results quickly. Expenditure compression was achieved largely through successive cuts in investment spending, making future compression difficult. Revenue mobilization efforts were very strong, bringing levels of taxation (as a share of GDP) to OECD country levels. This included property tax yields at 1.5 per cent of GDP. A persistent and growing problem on the expenditure side, across all levels of government, was the wage and pension bill. Pensions alone currently account for about 11 per cent of GDP, nearly one third of the total government revenue. Tax earmarking—currently at 80 per cent of federal tax revenues, up from 60 per cent in the late 1980s—further adds to rigidity in spending decisions. Thus discretionary spending, including investment in infrastructure, is strongly constrained, and fiscal management is perceived as focusing on debt management rather than dampening the business cycle.

The Brazil case has come to be very well known for the repeated debt reschedulings provided by the federal government to sub-national governments. Poor fiscal discipline in some local governments is one of many factors that drove this result. Allowing sub-nationals to borrow in foreign currency meant that the central government ended up with a very important stake in avoiding local government defaults to protect its own position in international capital markets. Furthermore, the interest-rate shocks administered economy-wide to control inflation imposed rapid fiscal adjustment on sub-national governments. This, in turn, led to debt rescheduling that cheapened the cost of borrowing through interest payment caps (Rodden 2003) and thus made this debt more attractive as interest rates rose. Predictably, the financial sector did not discipline sub-nationals in such an environment. Ultimately, a reform process culminated in the Fiscal Responsibility Law (FRL) introduced in 2000;[6] mandating fiscal balance. This step was an important one in signalling a clean break with a pattern of increasing intergovernmental indebtedness. The FRL was supplemented with prohibitions on local government borrowing and limitations on the exposure of the banking system to sub-nationals. The result is that all the channels by which sub-national governments can incur debts have been blocked. These very tight regulations have constrained all local governments, even though only three municipalities are responsible for 70 per cent of the municipal debt. Looked at from the perspective of risk management, the Brazil case emerges as one where the macro strategy of monetary contraction and high interest rates made indebtedness very risky. This affected sub-national governments just as it did other players in the economy. Moreover, public expenditure was becoming increasingly difficult to compress as repeated fiscal adjustments combined with constitutionally-mandated revenue earmarking. The most attractive option for sub-nationals was to get help from the central government, which offered measures that cheapened credit to sub-nationals to avoid defaults. These steps both blunted the disciplinary effect that credit markets could exercise and made recourse to credit markets attractive. Perhaps shutting down the credit market for sub-nationals may have been the only means of putting an end to this vicious cycle. A number of measures were put in place, among them the FRL, and all of them were mutually aimed at getting municipal spending under control. Interestingly, the measures taken to achieve the targets for a high primary surplus may be a more significant constraint than the FRL, since the municipal debt stock in 2004 was one third of what the law would have allowed in terms of leverage and revenues ratios.

The most serious problem with the current solution is that while the vicious cycle has ended, many of the underlying causes of the problem remain unchanged. Expenditure is still inflexible and leaves little scope for discretionary spending, and access to the credit market bears little relationship to the quality of a local government's fiscal management. The main difference now is that no local government can fund investments efficiently through borrowing, no matter how well they manage or have managed their fiscal affairs. The heavily indebted municipalities will have to perform very well for years before they can borrow again. Specialized intermediaries have been closed down, thus losing valuable knowledge and capacity. As Chapter 1 argues, there may also be other reasons for the low levels of public infrastructure investment in Brazil, including lack of demand and coordination issues for large jurisdictions. However, where there are needs for local infrastructure investment, the current system is ill positioned to respond to them. Whatever selection process there is for allocating the very scarce funding available for urban infrastructure is unlikely to offer the efficiencies of a well-functioning financial market.

Using Financial Markets for Sub-National Fiscal Discipline

The Brazil case illustrates the most extreme of all of our cases in its treatment of municipal access to financial markets. There, the issues of government debt in the broader market repeatedly undermined both the financial sector and the conditions for municipal access to financial sector resources. That the outcome is one in which local governments are blocked from tapping private savings through capital markets is unfortunate. In a system with so many functions at the municipal level, well-managed local governments should be in a position to make good local investment choices. By charging and taxing properly for services, municipalities should be able to tap private savings to finance them. Inability thus far to break with the past practice of co-mingling sub-national and central government credit risk has kept a useful source of finance beyond the reach of municipalities. As a result, there is no scope for the extra fiscal discipline that capital markets and intermediaries could exercise with local governments, and institutional capacity in this area has declined.

South African experience stands in sharp contrast. As noted earlier, the central government made a clear break with the past practice of taking on bad local government debts in the post-apartheid period and the Constitution prohibited central government guarantee of sub-national debts. That strong stance did not waver during periods of fiscal stress. While the commercial banks were reluctant to risk their balance sheets on municipal debt immediately post-apartheid, they supported a very successful private intermediary dedicated to municipal borrowers (see Chapter 9). Amongst the factors that contributed to its success was a supportive legal framework, which permitted rapid action against defaulters, later enhanced by an explicit framework for addressing municipal bankruptcy. Strong technical capacity and a well-developed accounting system in the local government permitted lending against municipal balance sheets and encouraged municipal access to credit markets. Beyond the supporting institutional and legal environment, local governments had the wherewithal to borrow, derived from the strong revenue and asset base in the hands of local governments after the consolidation of the white cities with black townships. Both a government and a private specialized intermediary operated successfully in this market. Although both concentrated their portfolios on the better-financed municipalities, a large share of the urban population benefitted from this lending because these same borrowers were the largest cities. In recent years, the specialized intermediaries have played a less crucial role, as the commercial banks have increasingly lent to municipalities and, more recently, large intergovernmental grants are diminishing the aggregate demand for borrowing at the local level.

Poland's municipalities too benefitted from a balanced borrowing framework at the national level. The government restricted access to foreign-currency borrowing after Warsaw successfully issued a municipal bond in 1994. Municipalities have not defaulted on their debts as they have proven their capacity to mobilize resources, building on strong initial conditions post-transition. Directed credit programmes for the environment, in spite of their well-known distorting effects, appear to have been successful both in promoting environmental investment and in 'crowding in' commercial banks lending for these activities. (Hammam and Peterson 2005). Structuring the environment funds to encourage municipalities to seek complementary finance from private capital markets through partial grants rather than subsidized credit was important. Doubtless the presence in Poland of a strong group of commercial banks and good financial-sector policies also contributed to this result.

In this regard, India represents yet another contrast. Amongst the countries of the developing world, India has one of the deepest and most diverse financial sectors. Urban local bodies in India are allowed to borrow—with some regulatory constraints, but they do have access. Rating agencies have the capacity to assess urban local governments. Municipal bonds were pioneered 10 years ago, yet this has not been a growing source of finance for urban infrastructure. International agencies such as USAID and the World Bank have successfully supported transactions using new financial instruments for local infrastructure borrowing. Local intermediaries, specialized and unspecialized, have sought out ingenious means of tapping what could ultimately be an attractive municipal market (see Ravi 2005). These markets have had great difficulty moving beyond a handful of transactions, largely for reasons illustrated in Figure I.1. Capacity to lend, both technical and financial, and ingenuity to package products is hardly the constraint that binds in Indian municipal finance. The issue is the low revenue base of Indian municipalities combined with the strong administrative dependence on the states in decision making. The contrast with the other countries in this study striking, and the differences in revenues cannot be explained merely by differences in urbanization and responsibilities for functions delegated to the local level. Even more striking is the fact that this low expenditure and revenue figure in Indian cities have not noticeably changed since the decentralization process started 14 years ago (see Chapter 3). A substantial opportunity to mobilize finance for much-needed infrastructure can be opened up once the Government of India and the states find a means of endowing municipalities with more substantial revenues and the administrative autonomy to manage them.

Figure I.1
Municipal Government Expenditure
In Percentage of GDP

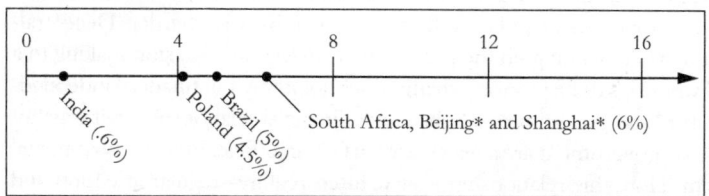

Source: Buckley (2005) based on IMF (2005: Chapter 3).
Note: *Urban infrastructure investment only as a share of regional GDP.

China has taken quite a different approach to the question of financial market access. Chapter 2 shows that local governments, while formally barred from borrowing, were able to establish companies that borrowed on their behalf. This capacity to borrow indirectly, coupled with the ability to raise funds 'off budget' through a variety of transactions (such as land leasing), offered a means of smoothing the adjustment to the intergovernmental fiscal reforms that were shifting the balance of revenues back to the centre without a corresponding shift of functions away from local governments. Impressive growth of the volume of infrastructure investments was achieved under this system, with the 9th Plan expenditures being two and a half times greater than under the 8th Plan, which had quintupled the level of the 7th Plan. Physical achievements, not just spending, have been impressive, as documented in Chapters 2 and 6. However, concerns are now arising about whether the borrowing and 'off budget' transactions can continue on past trends without undue risk to the banking sector. Until now, rapid growth, fundamental to the decentralization and urban finance strategy in China, has prevented some of the risks in the system from being realized. Meanwhile, the government has incrementally reined in some of the riskiest practices, such as using future land values as loan collateral. A protected banking system could absorb the risks of lending for urban infrastructure in the poorer regions. Now, with a World Trade Organization agreement allowing access of foreign banks to domestic lending, the government has ordered banks to adopt more prudent lending standards for local governments. If this shift from a 'permissive' to a more market-disciplined financial sector access can be completed successfully, China will offer an especially interesting, if somewhat heterodox, example of managing a substantial acceleration in urban infrastructure spending.

The cases covered in the following chapters offer interesting variants on a set of issues that all governments face and that don't ever go away.

All national governments must balance the risks of local governments' fiscal misbehaviour against providing opportunities to make more and better investments at the local level. All municipalities are faced with the risk that national government policy will make their jobs a lot harder. Decentralization, while opening up the possibility of delegating decision making to a level where it's done more efficiently, does not imply full financial independence for local governments. Substantive financial relationships with higher levels of government are a necessary part of an efficient intergovernmental system. How this relationship is structured requires regular attention and occasional recalibration to meet broader economic or social needs. Mobilizing the private capital markets and banks as part of the system of fiscal discipline has helped some countries achieve a good balance. On the other hand, the multiplicity of players involved is a complicating factor as well. Multiple levels of government and large diverse regions add complexity to the process of both finding and implementing the right balance in policies. Clearly, the presence of a 'provincial layer' makes a material difference in what can or even should be expected of a municipal government.

The case studies show that sometimes forces that have nothing to do with intergovernmental relations or finance can create opportunities or tensions in the framework for fiscal management. These cases also show that risks can be managed if the framework is well structured, and avoiding risk altogether can have a high opportunity cost. On the other hand, inability to adapt the set of relationships that make up a system of both decentralized fiscal responsibility and strong infrastructure finance to take account of a changing environment can be a risky strategy. All these cases show systems adapting to changed circumstances. Many of the successes described in this book offer heterodox approaches that worked in one country while having failed in others. None of them were arrived at with a 'one-off' reform, but emerged incrementally. One lesson from all of the cases is that finding the 'right' framework for balancing competing objectives may be less important than knowing when the current system needs to change and how to shift it in the right direction.

Notes

1. See Jacobs (1984), quoted in Martin Wolf's article in the *Financial Times* (2006).
2. World Bank (2006). Includes those countries for which total GDP and GDP in manufacturing, services and agriculture are available.
3. This comment was made in the context of a review of the econometric linkages between infrastructure investment and growth. Having reviewed studies with wide-ranging results

on this point, he suggested that these studies had perhaps received more attention than deserved for making decisions about investment policy.

4. The principle of 'subsidiarity' is defined in the *Oxford English Dictionary* (http://dictionary. oed.com) as 'the principle that a central authority should have a subsidiary function, performing only those tasks that cannot be performed effectively at a more immediate or local level'.

5. The 74th Constitutional Amendment Act in 1992 ensured relatively continuous elected local governments, placing limitations on the supercessions by the states that had been common practice. This is considered to be the start of decentralization in India. The Constitution had of course, from the start, established the rights and responsibilities of the states and the centre.

6. The provisions of the law are described in detail in Chapter 1.

References

Buckley, Robert. 2005. 'Macro Linkages with Municipal Finance: An Overview'. Paper presented at the Conference on Mobilizing Finance in a Fiscally Responsible Framework, 6-8 January, Jaipur. http://www.worldbank.org/uifconference.

Gramlich, Edward. 1994. 'Infrastructure Investment: A Review Essay', *Journal of Economic Literature*, 37 (3).

Hammam, Sonia and George E. Peterson. 2005. 'Environmental Funds'. Paper presented at the Conference on Mobilizing Finance in a Fiscally Responsible Framework, 6–8 January, Jaipur. http://www.worldbank.org/uifconference.

IMF (International Monetary Fund). 2005. *IMF Government Finance Statistics*. Washington, DC: IMF.

Jacobs, Jane. 1984. *Cities and the Wealth of Nations: Principles of Economic Life*. New York: Random House.

Ravi, P.V. 2005. 'Urban Infrastructure Investment in India: Mechanisms, Possibilities and Special Financing Vehicles'. Paper presented at the Conference on Mobilizing Finance in a Fiscally Responsible Framework, 6–8 January, Jaipur. http://www.worldbank.org/ uifconference.

Rodden, Jonathan. 2003. 'Federalism and Bailouts in Brazil', in Jonathan Rodden, Gunnar S. Eskeland and Jennie Litvack (eds), *Fiscal Decentralization and the Challenge of Hard Budget Constraints*, pp. 213–48. Cambridge, Massachusetts: Massachusetts Institute of Technology Press.

Rodden, Jonathan, Gunnar S. Eskeland and Jennie Litvack (eds). 2003. *Fiscal Decentralization and the Challenge of Hard Budget Constraints*. Cambridge, Massachusetts: Massachusetts Institute of Technology Press.

Ter-Minassian, Teresa (ed.). 1997. *Fiscal Federalism in Theory and Practice*. Washington, DC: International Monetary Fund (IMF).

Wolf, Martin. 2006. 'National Wealth on City Life's Coat Tails', *Financial Times*, 3 May.

World Bank. 2004. 'Development Data Platform'. Washington DC: World Bank.

———. 2005. *Economic Growth in the 1990s: Learning from a Decade of Reform*. Washington, DC: World Bank.

1

Fiscal Responsibility Legislation and Fiscal Adjustment: The Case of Brazilian Local Governments[1]

Luiz de Mello[*]

Introduction

This paper discusses trends in fiscal adjustment in Brazil since the 1990s, with particular emphasis on the strengthening of institutions for fiscal policy making, and its effect on local government finances and their ability to invest in infrastructure building and upgrading. Although fiscal adjustment, which is ongoing, has taken a toll on the government's ability to finance much-needed infrastructure investment, it is not the only culprit. A lack of budget flexibility, against a backdrop of increasing downward rigidities in current spending, also constrains the government's ability to invest. The paper argues that regulatory uncertainty in many sectors, particularly water and sanitation, in which the municipalities play a leading role, has discouraged private sector investment and that the financing of infrastructure building and upgrading goes beyond the municipal level of government.

[*] Luiz de Mello is Head of the Brazil/South America Desk of the Economics Department of the OECD.

Higher-level jurisdictions are responsible for financing investment in energy and transport infrastructure, for example.

Brazil's fiscal adjustment since the floating of the Real in 1999 has been impressive, even under adverse conditions. This has been of paramount importance in the consolidation of macroeconomic stability in the period and to ensure that the dynamics of public indebtedness are sustainable. But fiscal adjustment has taken place, piggy-backed on revenue hikes and, to a lesser extent, a compression of public investment rather than the retrenchment of current outlays. As a result, Brazil's tax-to-GDP ratio is now much higher than that of countries with comparable income levels, being close to the OECD average and nearly twice as high as that of the rest of Latin America. This suggests a quality problem: based on international experience, the composition of fiscal adjustment affects its likelihood of success in the sense of delivering a sustained reduction in indebtedness over time.

Against this background, this paper discusses trends in fiscal adjustment in Brazil since the 1990s, with particular emphasis on the strengthening of institutions for fiscal policy making, as well as its effect on local governments and their ability to invest in infrastructure building and upgrading. The main issues to be highlighted are as follows:

1. The strengthening of fiscal institutions has played an important role in instilling fiscal probity at all levels of government. Emblematic of developments in this area is the enactment of the Fiscal Responsibility Law in 2000. Market scrutiny also helps, and policy makers now appear to be responding more forcefully to changes in public indebtedness by delivering the primary budget surpluses needed to service their outstanding debt obligations.
2. Fiscal adjustment is ongoing and has taken a toll on the government's ability to finance much-needed infrastructure investment. But fiscal retrenchment is not the only culprit for a lack of investment. Regulatory uncertainty in many sectors, particularly water and sanitation, in which the municipalities play a leading role, has also discouraged private sector investment. It also needs to be recognized that the financing of infrastructure building and upgrading goes beyond the municipal level of government. Higher-level jurisdictions are responsible for financing investment in energy and transport infrastructure, for example.

This chapter is organized as follows: The first section reviews broad trends in fiscal adjustment since the early 1990s, focusing on debt sustainability. The second discusses the main provisions of fiscal responsibility legislation. The third section discusses trends in municipal finances, including investment. The fourth section serves to conclude the discussion.

Trends in Fiscal Adjustment: The Focus on Debt Sustainability

Brazil's fiscal performance has improved over the years at all levels of government, owing predominantly to the need to contain the rise in public indebtedness (Table 1.1).[2] Currently, at about 52 per cent of GDP, the consolidated net public debt is not only high but its composition, with relatively short maturities and a high share of securities paying floating interest rates, makes the debt dynamics overly sensitive to changes in market conditions. Exposure to foreign exchange risk has now been reduced considerably through

Table 1.1
Public Sector Fiscal Outcomes, 1995–2004 Budget Balance
In Percentage of GDP
(A Positive Ratio Indicates a Surplus)

	1995	1996	1997	1998	1999	2000	2001	2002	2003	2004[3]
Overall balance	**−7.3**	**−5.8**	**−6.1**	**−7.5**	**−5.8**	**−3.6**	**−3.6**	**−4.6**	**−5.2**	**−4.1**
Central government[1]	−2.4	−2.9	−2.6	−4.9	−2.7	−2.3	−2.1	−0.8	−4.1	−3.3
Regional governments	−3.6	−2.1	−3.0	−2.0	−3.2	−2.1	−2.0	−3.9	−1.8	−1.5
States	−	−	−	−1.8	−2.7	−1.8	−1.9	−3.3	−1.5	−1.3
Municipalities	−	−	−	−0.2	−0.5	−0.3	−0.1	−0.6	−0.3	−0.2
Public enterprises	−1.3	−0.8	−0.5	−0.5	0.1	0.7	0.6	0.0	0.7	0.7
Interest payment	**7.5**	**5.8**	**5.2**	**7.5**	**9.0**	**7.1**	**7.2**	**8.5**	**9.6**	**8.4**
Central government[1]	2.9	2.9	2.4	5.5	5.0	4.1	3.9	3.1	6.7	5.8
Regional governments	3.4	2.2	2.3	1.8	3.3	2.6	2.9	4.6	2.7	2.5
States	−	−	−	1.4	2.8	2.2	2.5	3.9	2.3	2.1
Municipalities	−	−	−	0.4	0.5	0.4	0.4	0.7	0.4	0.4
Public enterprises	1.3	0.7	0.5	0.2	0.6	0.3	0.4	0.7	0.2	0.1

Table 1.1 continued

Table 1.1 continued

	1995	1996	1997	1998	1999	2000	2001	2002	2003	2004[3]
Primary balance[2]	**0.3**	**−0.1**	**−1.0**	**0.0**	**3.2**	**3.5**	**3.6**	**3.9**	**4.4**	**4.3**
Central government[1]	0.5	0.0	−0.3	0.6	2.3	1.9	1.8	2.4	2.6	2.6
Regional governments	−0.2	0.1	−0.7	−0.2	0.3	0.5	0.9	0.8	0.9	0.9
States	−	−	−	−0.4	0.2	0.4	0.6	0.6	0.8	0.8
Municipalities	−	−	−	0.2	0.1	0.1	0.3	0.2	0.1	0.1
Public enterprises	−0.1	−0.1	0.1	−0.4	0.7	1.1	0.9	0.7	0.9	0.8

Source: Central Bank of Brazil.

Notes: 1. Includes the federal government, the social security system and the central bank.

2. Includes total revenue and expenditure minus interest payments.

3. Flows accumulated over 12 months to May 2004.

Figure 1.1
Brazil's Fiscal Performance, 1990–2003
In Percentage of GDP

Figure 1.1.1
Indebtedness and Fiscal Stance[1]

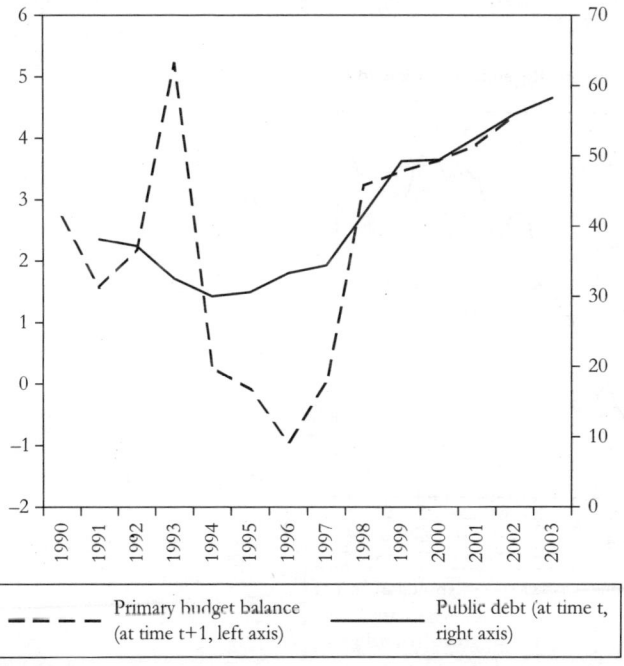

| - - - - | Primary budget balance (at time t+1, left axis) | —— | Public debt (at time t, right axis) |

Figure 1.1 continued

Figure 1.1 continued

Figure 1.1.2
Fiscal Stance Over the Business Cycle[2]

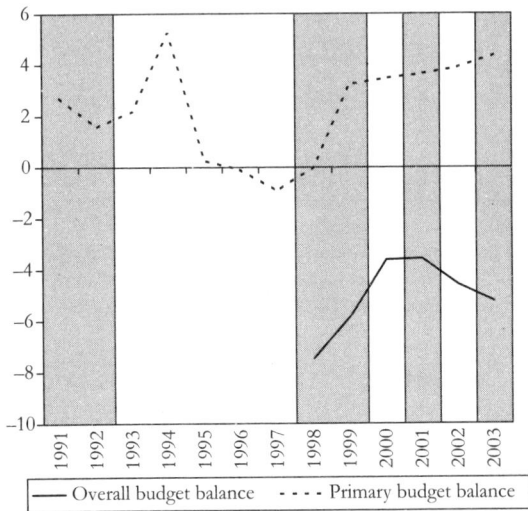

Figure 1.1.3
Central Government Revenue and Expenditure

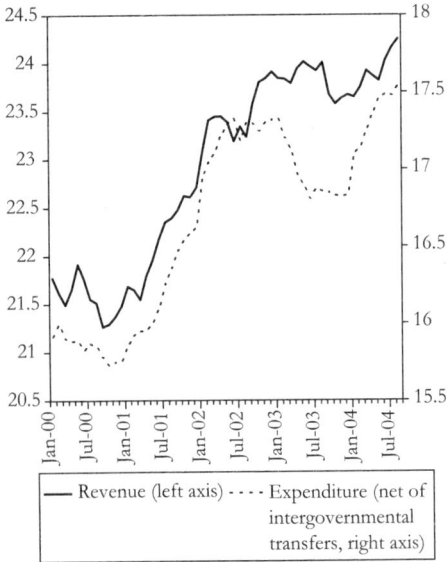

Figure 1.1 continued

Figure 1.1 continued

Figure 1.1.4

Central Government Outlays on Pensions and Discretionary Programmes

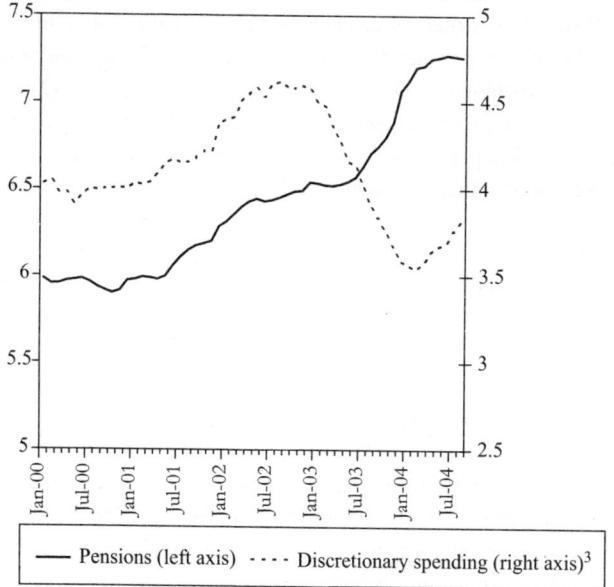

— Pensions (left axis) - - - - Discretionary spending (right axis)[3]

Source: National Treasury and author's calculations.

1. Refers to the consolidated public sector.
2. Refers to the consolidated public sector. The grey areas identify cyclical downturns, defined as the years in which changes in the output gap relative to the previous year are non-positive. The output gap is calculated as the per cent difference between actual and HP-filtered GDP.
3. Measured as 'other current and capital spending' (other OCC).

the gradual retirement of foreign exchange-indexed debt since 2003. Continued effort is, therefore, needed towards fiscal consolidation in countries such as Brazil, where public indebtedness is perceived as a source of vulnerability. Recent empirical evidence suggests that debt levels above 30–50 per cent of GDP may not be sustainable in emerging markets.[3]

Against this background, a few considerations are noteworthy:

1. Fiscal stance has responded swiftly to changes in the macroeconomic environment. The consolidated primary surplus—including the central and sub-national levels of government—has been raised over time to keep the debt-to-GDP ratio on a sustainable path (Figure 1.1).[4]

This has been the case even in periods of economic slowdown, making fiscal stance less counter-cyclical than desirable. Concern about the sustainability of public indebtedness calls for corrective action even in periods of below-potential growth. It makes fiscal consolidation, rather than short-term demand management, the overriding objective of fiscal policy making in indebted countries.[5] In fact, the OECD experience shows that a pro-cyclical fiscal stance is not uncommon in industrial countries, particularly when retrenchment is implemented to restore fiscal sustainability against a backdrop of high, or rising, indebtedness.[6]

2. Fiscal consolidation has been achieved predominantly by hiking revenue.[7] The ratio of tax revenue to GDP has risen to about 35 per cent in 2004 from about 28 per cent in 1995. The composition of revenue has also changed. At the federal level, while tax revenue has been broadly stable in relation to GDP, that of federal 'contributions' (i.e., levies whose revenue is earmarked for specific programmes, particularly in the social sectors, but not shared with the regional governments) has risen steadily. Contributions were originally levied on enterprise turnover and payroll, which had a detrimental effect on Brazil's trade competitiveness and encouraged informality in the labour market. The main federal contributions have now been converted into Value Added Taxes, somewhat mitigating this problem. The takings in subnational tax have also increased over time. Greater effort made towards fully exploiting local tax bases, which are often under-utilized even in the OECD area, has been a welcome development.

3. Downward rigidity in current spending has resulted in a compression of capital outlays in the course of fiscal adjustment. At the federal level, spending on investment came down from 0.6 per cent of GDP in 1995 to 0.4 per cent in 2003; it recovered somewhat in 2004. The state governments have compensated in part for this decline at the federal level. The existence of mandated minimum spending levels for several social programmes contributed to budget inflexibility.[8] At the same time, social security pressures have mounted and the creation of new expenditure commitments, particularly in assistance related to old age, has put additional upward pressure on current spending. Another source of budget inflexibility is revenue earmarking, which is widespread: it is estimated that about 80 per cent of federal tax revenues are earmarked, against less than 60 per cent in 1988.[9]

The Role of Fiscal Responsibility Legislation

An Overview of International Practices

Several countries have adopted fiscal responsibility legislation—encompassing a variety of fiscal rules and administrative or managerial processes—aimed at ensuring better discipline and efficiency at all levels of government. The scope of legislation varies a great deal across countries, and so does its coverage. The experience of OECD countries is illustrative of this diversity in institutional arrangements, although a few common elements can be highlighted:[10]

1. Administrative controls are possibly the crudest form of fiscal rule. This is more prevalent in developing countries and emerging market economies. In some OECD countries, sub-national borrowing is subject to central government approval (Ireland, Japan, Korea and the United Kingdom), but rules are becoming more flexible in others (e.g., the Czech Republic, Hungary, Finland, New Zealand and Norway). In Mexico, the states and municipalities, including their decentralized agencies and public enterprises, are prohibited from borrowing abroad and can only borrow domestically to finance investment up to the ceilings set by their respective legislatures.

2. More comprehensive fiscal rules include ceilings on public debt or debt service, expenditure or budget balances. These rules may be expressed in actual or cyclically adjusted terms. Among the OECD countries, the overall budget balance is capped in Austria, Belgium, Finland, Sweden and Spain. In other countries, including France, New Zealand and Norway, the operational, rather than overall, budget balance is capped, allowing borrowing for investment purposes. Golden rules (i.e., budgeted deficits must not exceed investment spending) are in place in Germany, Switzerland and the United Kingdom.[11] Ceilings on the public debt and/or debt-service outlays are also in place in some countries (Hungary, Poland and Portugal).

3. Markets appear to be a poor substitute for fiscal rules, particularly at the sub-national level of government, but have complemented these rules in many cases, such as in Canada and the United States. Prudential regulations on investors' exposure to sub-national government debt are often weak, and information disclosure requirements tend to be

more lenient on sub-national governments than on the central government and corporations.

4. To embed some flexibility in fiscal rules, escape clauses have been introduced in many countries, allowing for deviations from fiscal targets under exceptional circumstances (e.g., in Austria, Italy, Poland and some Canadian provinces, and the European Union's Stability and Growth Pact).

International experience suggests that more is needed to enhance the effectiveness of fiscal rules by broadening their coverage and giving them a medium-term focus. In particular:

5. It is sometimes easy to bypass fiscal rules through creative accounting. The expenditure ceilings in the United States' Budget Enforcement Act (in place up to 2002), for instance, could sometimes be circumvented by designating funds as emergency spending or by using advance appropriations to spread budget authority over a period of more than a year. Narrowing the coverage of legislation also creates problems.[12] Other mechanisms for circumventing fiscal rules include the channelling of expenditure through the tax system, off-budgetary funds, public–private partnerships and loan guarantees.

6. The future costs of current policies can be underestimated when the policy framework is not transparent. This is the case if policy decisions granting tax expenditures, creating off-budgetary funds or committing public resources to public–private partnerships and loan guarantees are not subject to standard budgetary oversight, and may be difficult to reverse. In this case, fiscal rules, even if well conceived, may fail to enhance fiscal probity.

The Case of Brazil[13]

Brazil's institutional framework for fiscal policy making has evolved considerably over time. Two important precursors to the current institutional set-up—enshrined in the Fiscal Responsibility Law of 2000—are: (*a*) the sub-national debt-restructuring programmes sponsored by the National Treasury in 1997–98, and (*b*) the introduction of ceilings on personnel spending at the sub-national level (Box 1.1). In particular:

1. The sub-national debt-restructuring programmes of 1997–98 were not a bail-out for the regional governments. They did, however, strengthen

federal control over sub-national finances through the introduction of explicit, legally binding sanctions for non-compliance and the use of shared revenue as collateral for the servicing of restructured debt. Continued enforcement of the debt-restructuring contracts and restricted access to market financing have required a considerable fiscal adjustment by the states and municipalities to generate the primary surpluses needed to service their outstanding debt obligations. A comprehensive sub-national privatization programme, particularly in the transportation and energy sectors, was subsequently put in place in support of fiscal adjustment.

2. The introduction of caps on personnel outlays was a first step towards the rules-based rationalization of sub-national spending. It was recognized that failure to retrench current expenditure would undermine any sustained effort towards fiscal consolidation, subsequently putting compliance with the debt-restructuring arrangements at risk. The growth of sub-national personnel spending would also further reduce the regional governments' ability to provide public goods and services adequately.

Box 1.1: The Evolution of Fiscal Institutions Over Time

Debt Restructuring

The debt restructuring arrangements between the National Treasury and the states (and the Federal District) date back to 1997. Similar arrangements were put in place in 1998 with over 180 municipalities (out of more than 5,500 municipalities), including most of the larger ones. Prior to these arrangements, federal credit lines could be extended to indebted states, provided they implemented comprehensive fiscal adjustment programmes, consisting primarily of the gradual reduction of personnel spending in relation to current revenue, stricter control of public enterprises (including their privatization) and the introduction of primary surplus targets. These consolidation efforts did not always bear fruit, due primarily to a lack of credible sanctions for non-compliance.

In the case of the 1997–98 arrangements, debt restructuring referred to outstanding liabilities incurred prior to 30 November 1995

Box 1.1 continued

Box 1.1 continued

(Credit Line I). Adjustment programmes aimed at reducing personnel spending could also be financed within the framework for debt restructuring (Credit Line II), as well as the conversion of short-term revenue anticipation operations (AROs), a de facto modality of budget financing, into debt to be restructured (Credit Line III).

These arrangements—formalized in bilateral contracts between the National Treasury and the sub-national jurisdictions—are legally binding. They called for the down payment of 20 per cent of the jurisdiction's outstanding debt liabilities, as well as a fixed repayment schedule based on below-market interest rates and revenue mobilization capacity, defined as the jurisdiction's total real net revenue, which includes own revenue and net constitutionally mandated transfers (i.e., mandated transfers from higher levels of government, net of mandated transfers to lower levels of government). Non-compliance is countered through the replacement of below-market interest rates by the nominal interest rate paid on the federal securitized debt plus a penalty of 1 percentage point per annum.

Ceilings on Personnel Spending

Ceilings on personnel spending were introduced in 1995 in support of sub-national fiscal retrenchment. Complementary Law No. 82 of 1995 (Camata Law I) set a ceiling of 60 per cent of a jurisdiction's net current revenue for personnel spending, including pensions. Net current revenue is calculated by excluding from the total current revenues all constitutionally mandated federal transfers, social security contributions of civil servants and the jurisdiction's net position relative to Complementary Law No. 87 of 1997 (Kandir Law) and FUNDEF.[1] Complementary Law No. 96 of 1999 (Camata Law II) maintained the same 60 per cent ceiling but broadened the definition of personnel spending to include several modalities of fringe benefits that had been excluded from Camata Law I.

1. Complementary Law No. 87 of 1997 created a mechanism for compensating the states for the revenue losses associated with the exemption of VAT from exports of primary and semi-manufactured goods. FUNDEF is a fund created in 1998 to

Box 1.1 continued

Box 1.1 continued

> equalize spending capacity among the states and municipalities in the area of primary and lower-secondary education. The federal government sets a floor for outlays per student and tops up spending in the sub-national jurisdictions that cannot afford the national spending floor. Please see de Mello (2001a, 2001b) for more information on FUNDEF, as well as Boxes 1.2 and 1.3.

The Fiscal Responsibility Law, enacted in May 2000, is at the core of the strengthening of fiscal institutions in Brazil. The FRL sets a general framework for budgetary planning and execution, applicable to all levels of government. Its main provisions are:[14]

1. On revenue, the FRL mandates: (*a*) the withholding of discretionary federal transfers to the states and municipalities that do not collect effectively their own taxes; and (*b*) the publication of the impact of tax exemptions on the budget when the exemptions take effect and in two subsequent budgets.

2. On expenditures, the FRL bans the creation of: (*a*) permanent spending mandates without a corresponding increase in permanent revenue or a reduction in other permanent spending commitments; and (*b*) new spending commitments that cannot be executed before the end of the incumbent's term in office, as well as the recording of these as unspent commitments in the two quarters prior to the end of the incumbent's term in office, unless there are sufficient cash balances to cover them at the end of the fiscal year.

3. The FRL contains a golden-rule provision for capital spending (i.e., annual credit disbursements cannot exceed capital spending).

4. The FRL sets separate ceilings for personnel spending at each level of government (including pensions and payments to sub-contractors) equivalent to 50 per cent of net current revenue for the central government and 60 per cent of net current revenue for the states and municipalities, as well as sub-ceilings for the executive, legislative and judiciary branches of each level of government. If in breach of the personnel ceilings, the jurisdiction will not be allowed to engage in new credit operations and sub-national governments will not be allowed to receive discretionary transfers or credit guarantees from the federal government. The FRL also bans voluntary intergovernmental transfers to finance personnel spending without an explicit budget allocation in the budget laws of the jurisdiction providing the grants and benefits.

5. The FRL contains stringent provisions on indebtedness and the issuance of public debt by the central bank. It also prohibits creditor debt-restructuring operations among the various levels of government. Debt ceilings were set by the Senate in 1998 and 2001 at, respectively, 200 and 120 per cent of net current revenue for the state and municipal governments. Although the ceilings on sub-national indebtedness are legally binding, those for the federal government are yet to be set by law. When in breach of the debt ceilings, new financing and discretionary transfers to sub-national governments are banned, including short-term revenue anticipation operations (ARO), other than those taken to refinance securitized debt.

6. The FRL also contains escape clauses. The time frame for reducing personnel spending or indebtedness in excess of the mandated ceilings can be lengthened if the economy contracts by 1 per cent or more during the previous four quarters or a national catastrophe is declared by the legislature, as well as in the case of a state of siege. These escape clauses can only be exercised with Congressional approval.

The FRL provides for more transparent fiscal reporting.[15] Budget outturns are to be presented in bi-monthly budget execution reports, as well as more comprehensive four-monthly reports on compliance with the FRL, including the statement of corrective measures if the relevant provisions are breached. The municipalities are required to report to the Ministry of Finance the fiscal outturn of the previous year by end-April and the states by end-May. The Ministry of Finance is required to publish a consolidation of the public finances of the previous year by end-June. The legislative branch of each level of government, aided by their respective Courts of Accounts, monitors compliance with the fiscal targets and ceilings.

The FRL strengthens the legal framework for medium-term budgeting.[16] It also requires the inclusion of a Fiscal Policy Annexe to the Multi-Year Budget Framework Law (PPA) of the federal government with multi-year fiscal targets and the inclusion of a Fiscal Targets Annexe to the Budget Guidelines Law (LDO) for all levels of government. The LDO is also required to include an annexe describing fiscal risks with an assessment of contingent liabilities. By introducing more stringent requirements on fiscal targets in the preparation of the LDO, the FRL strengthens its role in budget preparation and fiscal management in general. In particular:

1. The Fiscal Targets Annexe requires the assessment of compliance with the targets of the previous years and the analysis of the net worth of

the public enterprises, with emphasis on the use of resources from privatizations and asset sales in general. This is to avoid the use of capital revenues to finance current spending and the inclusion of these revenues above the line to generate higher primary balances.

2. The Fiscal Risks Annexe requires a detailed assessment of the government's contingent liabilities, including an evaluation of the likelihood of adverse outcomes in legal disputes. In the case of the central government, the Fiscal Risks Annexe provides a detailed assessment of the impact on revenues of changes in the macroeconomic framework, as well as deviations from the macroeconomic parameters based on which the annual budget law (LOA) is formulated.

3. The FRL strengthens the link between the LDO and the LOA. This is achieved by requiring the LOA to abide by the LDO's fiscal targets (detailed in the LDO's Fiscal Targets Annexe), the inclusion of a contingency reserve defined in per cent of net current revenues to be used for the settlement on unspent commitments (*restos a pagar*) of the previous year, as well as contingent liabilities that may materialize in the reference period, the reporting of tax expenditures and the inclusion in the LOA of debt service obligations in the reference period.

Complementary to the FRL is the Fiscal Crimes Law (FCL). The FCL applies to public officials of the executive, legislative and judiciary branches of the federal, state and municipal governments, as well as their decentralized agencies and public enterprises. Among other provisions, the FCL provides for detention of up to four years for public officials who: (*a*) engage in credit operations without prior legislative authorization (or in breach of the credit or indebtedness ceilings), (*b*) incur expenditure commitments in the last two quarters of his/her term in office that cannot be paid within the current fiscal year or without adequate cash balances, (*c*) incur unauthorized expenditure commitments, (*d*) extend loan guarantees without equal or higher-value collateral, (*e*) increase personnel expenditures in the 180 days prior to the end of his/her term in office, or (*f*) issue unauthorized unregistered public debt.

Prudential regulations limiting the exposure of financial institutions to government debt, including that of sub-national levels of government, have been complementary to the FRL. Financial institutions' exposure to the government (all levels of government, public enterprises and decentralized agencies combined) is limited to 45 per cent of their net worth, including all credit operations and loan guarantees. These institutions also face stringent provisioning requirements, at 150 per cent of the value of loans to the public sector. More recently, it has been recognized that these constraints have restricted access to finance by some regional jurisdictions that were compliant with the debt and debt service ceilings set under the FRL. Prudential regulations were, therefore, introduced in 2003, setting aggregate caps on credit operations with the municipalities to finance investment in water and sanitation, subject to the observance by each individual borrower of the debt service ceilings set under the FRL. These aggregate caps are consistent with the government's target for aggregate spending on these programmes. The option of introducing similar aggregate caps for investment in transport infrastructure is under discussion, pending an assessment of the measures introduced for water and sanitation against the expected increase in government spending on these programmes.

Municipal Finances and Infrastructure Investment

Local Government Spending and Economic Performance: A Word of Caution

Although a case can be made for increasing local government investment in search of stronger economic performance, often—through the reassignment of these expenditure functions across the different levels of government—a few considerations are noteworthy. In particular, an increase in local government spending, particularly on infrastructure, need not enhance economic performance for the economy as a whole. Empirical evidence on the link between fiscal decentralization and economic growth is mixed. For example, Davoodi and Zou (1998) show that local government spending is growth-reducing in developing countries, but no causal link is found in the case of developed countries.[17] Likewise, Zhang and Zou (1998) report a negative correlation between post-reform decentralization and economic growth in a sample of Chinese provinces. On the other hand, in a somewhat different strand of literature, Glaeser et al. (1995) report a positive impact of local investment in sanitation on population growth in a panel of 260 cities in the United States. In the case of Brazil, de Mello (2002) provides evidence based on a panel of 26 state capitals in the period 1985–94, suggesting that municipal spending on healthcare, sanitation, housing and urbanization are important growth determinants at the municipal level. General infrastructure investment and municipal spending on transport services are also reported to be strongly correlated with growth.

The scope for enhancing economic performance by boosting local government spending on infrastructure depends on how these outlays are financed. Overlapping responsibilities across the different levels of government, reliance on open-ended grants for financing service delivery and weak accountability can create an upward bias in sub-national spending, with adverse macroeconomic consequences. Conversely, central governments may transfer spending functions without taking full account of their costs, and these unfunded mandates may force the sub-national authorities to cut back investment or raise taxes to keep their own accounts in balance. The empirical evidence reported by de Mello (2002) for Brazilian state capitals suggests that municipal borrowing is detrimental to growth. This is not surprising, since borrowing increases indebtedness and debt servicing tends to displace resources that could otherwise be used to finance growth-enhancing expenditures.

It is believed, as elsewhere in Latin America, that Brazil suffers from an 'infrastructure gap', which is an obstacle to faster growth, and that financial resources are needed to close the gap.[18] While there is considerable demand for infrastructure building and upgrading in developing countries, it should also be noted that not all public investment is productive and that a reduction in public capital spending need not necessarily be disruptive. This is particularly the case where local government spending is financed in a fiscally unsustainable manner. Evidence reported by Devarajan et al. (1996) for a panel of 43 developing countries suggests that the investment component of public expenditure may turn out to be unproductive when financed by instruments that misallocate government spending at the expense of current expenditures.

The association between fiscal decentralization and performance indicators in the infrastructure sector is not clear-cut. It is difficult to find unequivocal empirical evidence in this area. For example, the cross-country evidence reported by Estache and Sinha (1995) suggests that more decentralized countries tend to spend more on infrastructure projects, particularly in the developing world. This is possibly due to the fact that differences in local preferences are taken into account better in more decentralized countries. But, at least as gauged by the cross-country empirical evidence reported by Humplick and Estache (1995), the performance of several projects, including roads, electricity and water, does not seem to improve significantly as a result of greater sub-national spending on infrastructure development.

The claim that fiscal rules tend to reduce the ability of local governments to invest may not necessarily be correct. Evidence for developing countries is not readily available; but the experience of the United States, where the states have had a variety of balanced budget rules for a relatively long period, suggests that rules may indeed induce some pro-cyclicality in the sub-national fiscal stance, which may nevertheless be mitigated through the accumulation of rainy-day funds in good times. These funds can be used not only for the purpose of short-term demand management, which tends to be of a limited scope at the sub-national level, but also, and more importantly, to avoid disruption in the financing of public investment in bad times.[19] In this regard, evidence provided by Sorensen et al. (2001) suggests that the states that have relatively tight balanced-budget rules seem to have less pronounced swings in both revenue and expenditure over the business cycle than the states with less stringent fiscal rules.

Overview of Brazilian Municipal Finances: A Focus on Infrastructure Investment[20]

There are several constraints on the ability of Brazilian local governments to boost spending on infrastructure investment. They range from institutional provisions—on the assignment of expenditure functions across and within the different levels of government—to a lack of budget flexibility against a backdrop of increasing downward rigidities in current spending and on-going fiscal adjustment.

Regarding institutional constraints, the Brazilian Constitution empowers the local governments to delegate to the private sector, often through concessions, the provision of local services such as urban transportation, water and sanitation. These services, along with housing and urbanization, are provided primarily by the municipalities (Table 1.2). Other services requiring considerable infrastructure investment, such as intermunicipal transport and gas distribution, are under the purview of the states, whereas energy, telecommunications and interstate transportation, among others, are assigned to the federal government.[21]

The municipalities are becoming more active in the provision of social services. This is essentially the case with healthcare, with the decentralization of the national health system (SUS) in the early 1990s, and education, particularly after the implementation of FUNDEF in 1997–98 (Box 1.2). These two functions account for almost half of the municipal spending, but outlays are financed predominantly through revenue sharing and earmarked revenue.

In some cases, municipal governments are also involved in the provision of conditional income transfers to poor households, a social expenditure more often financed by the central government.

Table 1.2
Composition of Public Social Spending, 2002
In Percentage of GDP

		Levels of government		
	Total	Central government	States	Municipalities
Total public social spending	**24.4**	**13.3**	**5.8**	**5.2**
Social asistance	0.9	0.5	0.1	0.2
Social security	10.7	9.2	1.2	0.3
Healthcare	4.7	1.9	1.3	1.5
Sanitation	0.4	0.0	0.2	0.2
Labour	0.7	0.6	0.0	0.0
Education	5.4	1.0	2.6	1.8
Culture	0.2	0.0	0.1	0.1
Civil rights	0.2	0.0	0.1	0.0
Housing	0.1	0.0	0.1	0.1
Urbanization	1.0	0.0	0.1	0.9
Land reform	0.1	0.1	0.0	0.0

Source: Ministry of Finance.

Box 1.2: FUNDEF

FUNDEF is a fund (created in 1996 and implemented in 1997–98) to finance sub-national spending on primary and lower-secondary education. While primary spending is assigned to the municipalities by the Constitution, the states were the main providers of services until the late 1990s. FUNDEF changed the mechanism for financing sub-national spending on education in two main ways. First, a national spending floor was introduced per student enrolled in primary and lower-secondary education (1st to 8th grades), coupled with a framework for the allocation of funds between the state and municipal public-school networks. Second, FUNDEF requires the federal government to top up spending in those states that cannot afford the national spending floor. Since 2000, different floors have been set for primary education (1st to 4th grades) and for lower-secondary education (5th to 8th grades), the latter being 5 per cent above the value for primary education.[1]

Box 1.2 continued

Box 1.2 continued

FUNDEF is financed by earmarking 15 per cent of (*a*) the state and municipal allocations in the revenue-sharing funds with the federal government, (*b*) revenue from the state Value Added Tax (ICMS), (*c*) revenue from the federal Value Added Tax levied on exports (IPIexp) and (*d*) federal transfers to the states associated with ICMS revenue insurance (i.e., a mechanism for compensating the states for the revenue losses associated with the exemption of Value Added Tax on the exports of primary and semi-manufactured goods). FUNDEF resources are allocated within each state according to the number of students enrolled in the state and municipal public-school networks. At least 60 per cent of FUNDEF allocations must be spent on personnel, with the remaining share being spent on operations and maintenance. Within FUNDEF, the municipalities are required to spend at least 25 per cent of their revenue on education (at least 15 per cent on primary education).

FUNDEF is associated with a rapid increase in enrolment rates in primary and lower-secondary education. Although this increase cannot be attributed solely to FUNDEF, there appears to be a strong association between changes in enrolment rates and in the composition of enrolment between the state and municipal school networks, which has been changing over time in favour of the municipal school network. Based on evidence for a data set including 26 state capitals in the period 1991–94 and 1998–2001, enrolment rates were estimated to have risen by more than 2 per cent faster per year after the introduction of FUNDEF.[2]

1. See de Mello (2001a, 2001b); Afonso and de Mello (2002); and Ministry of Education (2003) for more information.
2. See de Mello and Hoppe (2005) and OECD (2005) for empirical evidence.

The municipalities face downward rigidities in their budgets, constraining their ability to reallocate funds to investment. The existence of minimum spending levels for education and healthcare impose downward rigidity on current spending. This is also the case with the federal government, although revenue earmarking is less pervasive at the federal level. The Constitution requires the municipalities (as well as the states) to earmark 25 per cent of revenue (18 per cent for the federal government) to finance spending on education and 15 per cent (12 per cent for the states) on healthcare. At the same time, spending on personnel, including pensions to retired civil servants, places a heavy burden on municipal budgets (Figure 1.2). Outlays on debt service, consistent with continued compliance with the debt restructuring arrangements with the National Treasury, reduce the room for manoeuvre in indebted jurisdictions.

The municipalities' ability to finance infrastructure investment is also constrained by their revenue-raising capacity, which tends to be lower than at the state and federal levels. The municipalities' tax services (except for communications and interstate or intermunicipal public transportation) levy

Figure 1.2
Trends in Municipal Expenditure, 1998–2003
In Percentage of Municipal Current Expenditure, Weighted Averages[1]

Figure 1.2.1
Investment

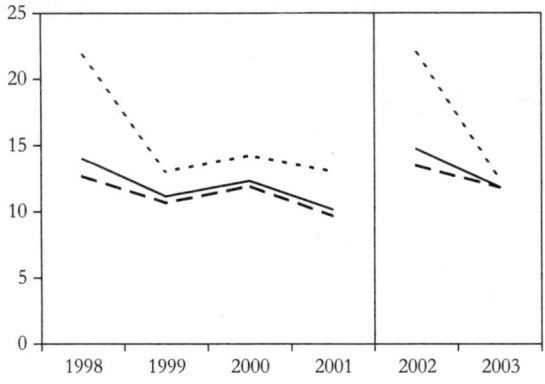

Figure 1.2.2
Personnel

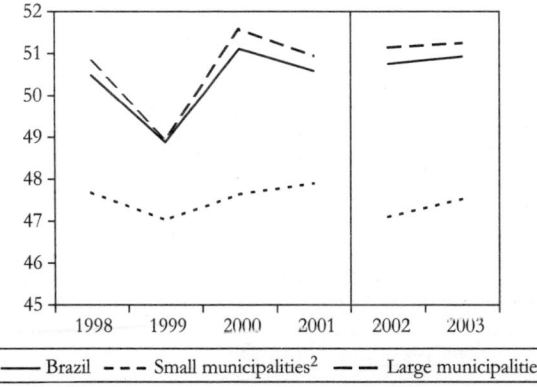

—— Brazil   - - - Small municipalities[2]   — — Large municipalities[3]

Figure 1.2 continued

Figure 1.2 continued

Figure 1.2.3
Transport

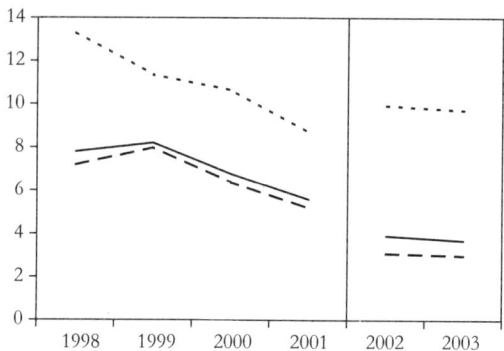

Figure 1.2.4
Debt Service: Interest and Amortization

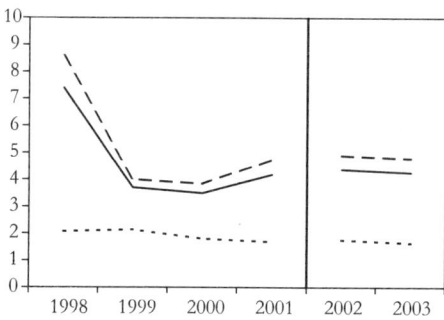

Figure 1.2.5
Healthcare and Sanitation

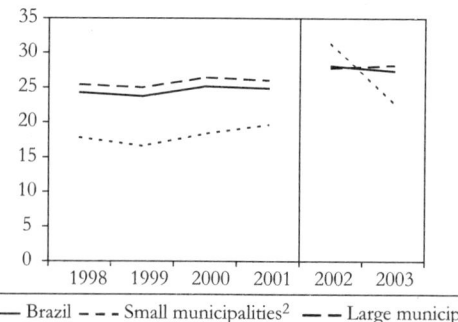

—— Brazil - - - Small municipalities[2] — — Large municipalities[3]

Figure 1.2 continued

Figure 1.2 continued

Figure 1.2.6

Housing and Urbanization

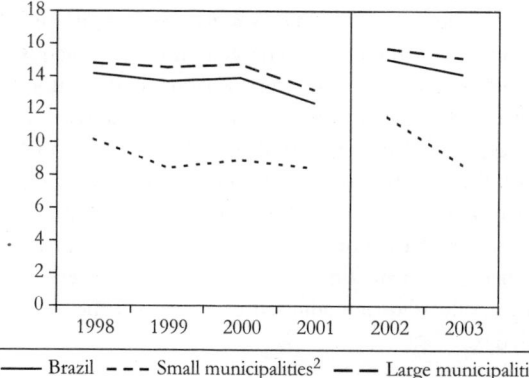

| —— Brazil   - - - Small municipalities² — — Large municipalities³ |

Source: National Treasury and author's calculations.

1. The number of municipalities varies between 3,807 (in 1998) and 4,881 (in 2001).
2. Refers to the municipalities with a population of less than 5,102 inhabitants in 2000, which are in the lowest quartile of the distribution.
3. Refers to the municipalities with a population higher than 22,425 in 2000, which are in the highest quartile of the distribution.

property taxes and, to a lesser extent, raise revenue through user fees and charges (Box 1.3). Revenue sharing is another important source of revenue at the municipal level, particularly for the smaller municipalities, which have a low revenue-mobilization capacity (Table 1.3).[22] However, the formula for allocating shared revenue among the municipalities in a given state favours smaller municipalities to the detriment of larger jurisdictions and metropolitan areas, where the demand for public provision may be strongest.[23]

Box 1.3: Municipal Revenue

Municipal Taxes

The main municipal taxes are those on services (ISS) and urban property (IPTU). In particular:

1. ISS rates are set by the municipalities, subject to the ceilings introduced by the federal government. Rates can vary considerably across

---

Box 1.3 continued

Box 1.3 continued

sectors. Tax legislation is designed to avoid overlapping with federal corporate income and state Value Added Taxes. In the banking sector, for example, ISS is levied on non-lending services such credit card and ATM fees but not on the interest charged on loans, which is taxed by the federal government. In the case of land transportation, ISS is levied on intramunicipal transport but not on intercity or interstate transport, which are subject to the state Value Added Tax.

2. IPTU is levied on the capital value of land and buildings in legally designated urban areas. Property valuations are based on the physical characteristics of each property, converted to an estimate of market value using construction-cost parameters and surveys of land prices. These valuations are adjusted each year on the basis of an inflation index.

Revenue Sharing

Based on Constitutionally mandated revenue sharing (Box 1.3, Table 1), the municipalities are entitled to: (*a*) 25 per cent of revenue from the state Value Added Tax (ICMS), (*b*) 50 per cent of revenue from the state tax on motor vehicle registration (IPVA), (*c*) 22.5 per cent of revenue from the federal value-added (IPI) and income (IR) taxes, (*d*) all revenue from the income tax held at source (IRPF) and paid by the municipalities or by their decentralized agencies, (*e*) 70 per cent of revenue from the federal financial-transactions tax levied on transactions with gold (IOF-Ouro) and (*f*) 50 per cent of revenue from the federal rural-property tax (ITR).

Constitutional Amendment No. 42 of 2003 increased the municipal revenue sharing rate by 1 percentage point, to 23.5 per cent of IPI and IR, leaving the rate unchanged for the states; introduced the sharing of revenue from the federal excise on petroleum derivatives (CIDE-*Combustíveis*) with the municipalities (25 per cent of state share in revenue); and increased the revenue-sharing rate for ITR to 100 per cent if the municipality opts for collecting this tax.

Box 1.3 continued

Box 1.3 continued

Box 1.3, Table 1
Intergovernmental Transfers to Municipal Governments, 2002
In Percentage of GDP

	All municipalities
Total	**4.9**
Constitutional transfers	**3.9**
Revenue sharing	**3.0**
of which:	
FPM (municipal participation fund)	1.2
ICMS (value added tax)	1.5
IPVA (tax on motor vehicles)	0.3
Compensatory transfers	**0.8**
of which:	
ICMS revenue insurance	0.1
FUNDEF (fund for education)	0.7
Non-Constitutional transfers	**0.9**
of which:	
Healthcare	0.5
Capital	0.3
Other	**0.2**

Source: Afonso and Araujo (2004).

Compensatory Transfers

Compensatory transfers include: (*a*) the Fund for the Compensation of Exports (FPEx), consisting of 10 per cent of the total collection of IPI, proportional to the value of exports of industrialized goods,[1] (*b*) royalties for the exploitation of petroleum and natural gas, hydroelectricity and other mineral resources in their territory or on the adjacent maritime platform, (*c*) ICMS revenue insurance, consisting of compensation for the exemption of ICMS from the export of primary and semi-manufactured goods[2] and (*d*) FUNDEF allocations.

Box 1.3 continued

Box 1.3 continued

Other Transfers

The main additional transfers refer to healthcare and voluntary transfers, associated primarily with investment programmes.

1. It is distributed to the states and, in turn, to the municipalities. The states have to share 25 per cent of this transfer with the municipalities.
2. The municipalities are entitled to 25 per cent of the ICMS revenue insurance.

Table 1.3
Composition of Municipal Revenue, 2002
In Percentage of GDP

	All municipalities	*Metropolitan areas*	*Non-metropolitan areas*
Total revenue	**7.9**	**4.0**	**4.0**
Own sources	**1.5**	**1.2**	**0.4**
Local property tax (IPTU)	0.5	0.4	0.1
Services tax (ISS)	0.6	0.5	0.1
Transfer tax (ITBI)	0.1	0.1	0.0
Other taxes	0.1	0.1	–
User charges and fees	0.2	0.1	0.1
Shared revenue	**3.2**	**1.3**	**1.9**
Municipal Participation Fund (FPM)	1.2	0.2	1.0
ICMS	1.5	0.7	0.8
Motor vehicle registration tax	0.2	0.1	0.1
Federal income tax (IRRF)	0.2	0.1	0.0
Other	0.1	0.0	0.1
Specific grants and compensatory transfers	**2.2**	**0.9**	**1.2**
Healthcare	0.5	0.2	0.2
FUNDEF	0.7	0.2	0.5
Other current transfers	0.7	0.4	0.3
Capital grants	0.3	0.1	0.2
Other revenues	**1.0**	**0.6**	**0.4**

Source: Rezende and Garson (2004).

Municipal borrowing is low in comparison with higher levels of government, reflecting their lower debt-repayment capacity, ongoing fiscal adjustment and limited access to markets. The municipal fiscal stance, as gauged by the primary budget balance (excluding municipal enterprises), has fluctuated over time (Figure 1.3). The municipalities of São Paulo, Rio de Janeiro

Figure 1.3
Municipal Indebtedness and Primary Budget Balance, 1998–2004
12-month Flows in Percentage of GDP

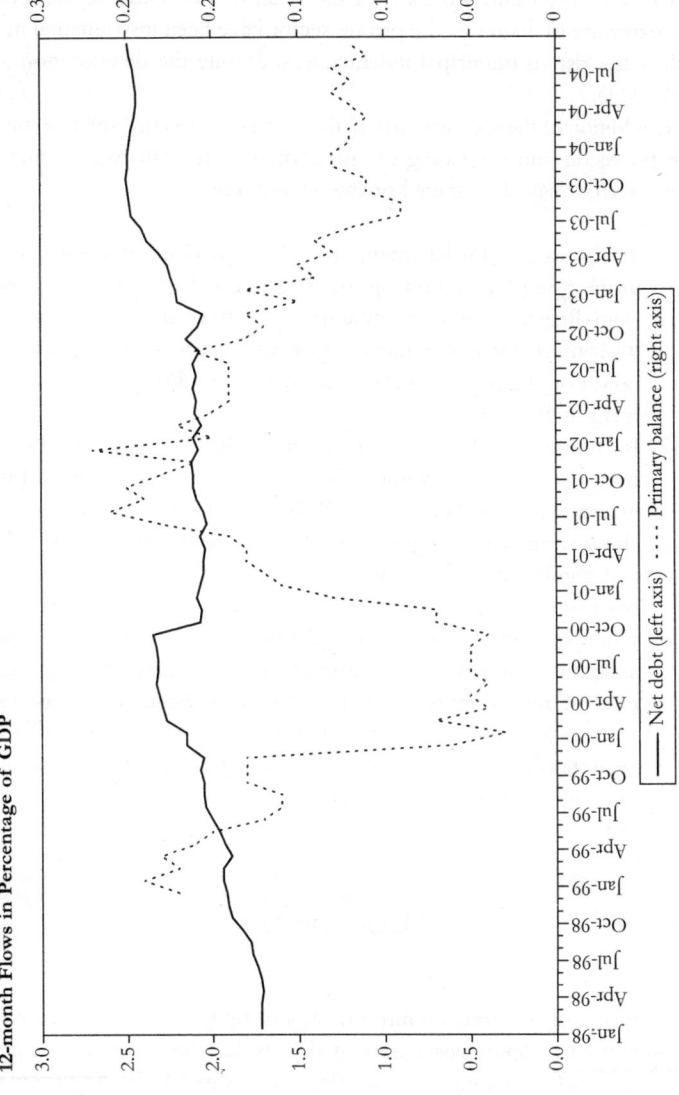

— Net debt (left axis)   · · · · Primary balance (right axis)

Source: Central Bank of Brazil.

and Salvador account for about 75 per cent of outstanding municipal debt. The debt restructuring arrangements discussed above, the introduction of debt ceilings in the context of fiscal responsibility legislation, and the issuance by the Central Bank over the years of prudential regulations on the exposure of banks to the private sector have been instrumental in curtailing the rise in municipal indebtedness, despite the deterioration since early 2003.

In addition to these constraints on the local governments' ability to finance the provision and upgrading of infrastructure, regulatory uncertainty in some sectors has discouraged private investment:

1. The private sector has traditionally been involved in service delivery in the case of urban transportation, predominantly through concessions. Regulatory uncertainty and constraints on pricing that simultaneously meets the requirements of private investors and the purchasing power of the population has deterred greater Private-Sector involvement in other areas.
2. In the case of water and sanitation, public investment has been cut back over the years without being offset by an increase in private investment. This can be attributed predominantly to a lack of clarity about which level of government is responsible for service delivery and regulation in the sector.[24] Investment, both public and private, has also been discouraged by the externalities associated with the provision of sewerage and water treatment services. In addition, water and sanitation networks are costly, investment maturities are long and rates of return are relatively low. This is particularly the case in the metropolitan regions, which straddle municipal borders. These trends are noteworthy because, despite progress in expanding access to drinking water, connection rates to sanitation and, in particular, to wastewater treatment remain low.[25]

Conclusion

The provision of infrastructure investment by local governments is constrained by the lumpy costs associated with these programmes, as well as spillovers and economies-of-scale effects. Costs may be prohibitive in view of local governments' limited revenue-mobilization capacity, including access to finance. But there are options for overcoming these difficulties. For example, cross-border joint ventures have been encouraged in many countries to maximize economies of scale and to internalize the externalities associated with the provision of regional public goods. The OECD experience is illustrative. In France, for instance, small communes contract out service delivery to private regional water companies, and contiguous municipalities often create regional associations to manage services such as waste disposal. Municipalities in Norway frequently cooperate in such sectors as waste disposal, water supply and energy (through the joint ownership of power plants). In Latin America, Peru attempted to decentralize much of its road networks to provincial and municipal governments, but then failed to provide financing for operations and maintenance (Gutman 1999). This resulted in widespread deterioration of the network and, ultimately, recentralization (Burki, Perry and Dillinger 1999; Humplick and Moini-Araghi 1996). In Brazil, there are intermunicipal water and sanitation companies, particularly in large metropolitan areas, where the networks straddle local government borders.

Another option for mobilizing the private sector to finance infrastructure investment is through public–private partnerships. At the core of PPP operations is the need to achieve an appropriate balance of risk taking between the government and its Private-Sector partners. In Brazil, new legislation has been approved, creating instruments for providing Private-Sector partners with guarantees that the financial commitments entered into by the government in these projects will be honoured. The government will be able to create fiduciary funds in a financial institution to honour these commitments. These funds can be capitalized with resources from the budget, non-tax credits, non-financial assets and real estate, among others. Revenues from PPP projects accruing to the government can also be earmarked to finance the settlement of contractual obligations. Several state governments have also passed PPP legislation (i.e., Goiás, Minas Gerais, Rio Grande do Sul, Santa Catarina and São Paulo). Options for the provision of financial guarantees vary across the states: Minas Gerais, Santa Catarina and Rio Grande do Sul have opted for the creation of fiduciary funds along the lines of federal legislation, whereas São Paulo and Goiás have created public companies linked to the state treasuries to manage state guarantees.

While there are options for boosting local government spending on infrastructure, when deemed cost-effective and growth-enhancing, it is important to safeguard fiscal responsibility. To this end, the Brazilian legislation on PPPs calls for the accounting and reporting of commitments entered into by the governments in PPP contracts in line with the provisions of fiscal responsibility legislation for all levels of government. In this regard, care must be taken to avoid the possibility of misclassification of debt-creating commitments as current spending, as a means of bypassing the debt ceilings set by law. The introduction of a ceiling on government outlays related to PPP projects—possibly defined as a share of net current revenue, such as the debt service ceilings already provided for by the FRL—is therefore welcome. Consistency between long- and short-term budgetary objectives should also be preserved, given the long-term duration of PPP contracts. However, the assessment of risks and transparency is complicated by heterogeneity in reporting, as required by the different audit courts within and across different levels of government. Therefore, the Treasury has an important role to play in standardizing accounting and reporting requirements. State legislation also requires PPP contracts to be in line with budget legislation, requiring the assessment of the budgetary impact of projects prior to contracting. It is expected that limits will be set through prudential regulations on the exposure of public financial institutions to PPP projects.

Notes

1. The views expressed in this paper are the author's own and do not necessarily reflect those of the OECD. The author is indebted to José Roberto Afonso, Silvana Malle, Nanno Mulder, and the Conference participants for useful comments and discussions, in particular Sol Garson; and to Anne Legendre, for statistical assistance.
2. See de Mello (2006) and OECD (2005) for more information.
3. The argument is that a typical emerging market may not be able to repay and refinance its debt obligations due to its lower revenue ratio, its more volatile tax bases and its higher, more volatile spending on debt service. Budget financing is also affected by supply-side constraints in emerging markets, given their imperfect access to international capital markets and shallow domestic financial markets. Many emerging markets also face more 'debt intolerance' than more mature economies, in the sense that credit ratings are often worse in some countries for the same level of indebtedness, reflecting individual countries' record in external debt repayment and macroeconomic stability. Reinhart et al. (2003) show that external debt intolerance is a good predictor of domestic debt default.
4. See de Mello (2006) for the estimation of a fiscal reaction function for Brazil. However, policy reactivity tends to be stronger in more mature economies. Recent research suggests that primary balances tend to have lower sensitivity to indebtedness in emerging markets than in industrial countries, controlling for other determinants of fiscal stance. This sensitivity is also affected by the level of indebtedness: it is estimated to be lower in emerging markets as the debt-to-GDP ratio rises (and not statistically significant when debt exceeds 50 per cent of GDP) than in industrial countries (IMF 2003).
5. The example of Latin America is illustrative. According to ECLAC analysis, in 13 out of the 17 cases in which GDP growth was above trend, the change in the cyclically adjusted public-sector balance was negative, reflecting an expansionary fiscal policy. There are

also episodes in which the budget balance, adjusted for the cycle, exhibited little variation despite significant changes in the output gap, such as in Chile (1992–98), Brazil (1990–94) and Mexico (1995–97). See Martner and Tromben (2004) for more information.

6. The OECD experience suggests that public indebtedness is a key determinant of whether fiscal stance is pro-cyclical during downturns. But it is important to note that fiscal consolidation in a downturn need not be destabilizing so long as it restores confidence by putting the debt dynamics on a sustainable path. For example, Giavazzi et al. (2000), as well as Alesina and Ardagna (1998), among others, show that fiscal contractions may be expansionary in indebted OECD countries and that the composition of adjustment, via tax increases and/or expenditure cuts, affects the expansionary potential of fiscal retrenchment. See also OECD (2003a), chapter IV, for more information.

7. Empirical evidence for OECD countries suggests that fiscal adjustments are more successful when based on the retrenchment of current expenditure, rather than on hiking revenue and/or cutting back public investment. Governments that are able to cut the more politically sensitive components of the budget (public employment, social security and welfare programmes, for example) may signal that they are more committed to sustained fiscal adjustment (Alesina and Perotti 1997; McDermott and Wescott 1996). Fiscal consolidation based on expenditure cuts, especially transfers and government wages, are more likely to succeed in reducing the debt ratio. Evidence for Latin America is limited, but using Alesina and Perotti's (1997) methodology, Rocha and Picchetti (2003) show that Brazil's fiscal consolidation in 1994 was likely to be unsuccessful as it was achieved on the back of investment cuts, while wages and transfers remained unchanged.

8. The introduction in 1996 of a minimum spending level per student (primary and lower-secondary education) has been instrumental in increasing school enrolment rates and reducing pay disparities at the regional government level. The Constitutional amendment of 2000 setting a floor for aggregate federal spending on healthcare has also exacerbated downward rigidities.

9. An arrangement is currently in place for withholding federally earmarked revenues (DRU), mitigating in part the budget rigidity associated with revenue earmarking. Accordingly, 20 per cent of federal revenue (net of intergovernmental transfers) are withheld by the federal government. Discussions are underway to implement a comparable arrangement at the state level. See Ministry of Planning and Budget (2003) and OECD (2005) for more information.

10. See OECD (2002, chapter IV; 2003a, chapter V) for more information.

11. The United Kingdom introduced in 1997 a golden rule and a debt rule ('sustainable investment rule'), capping the ratio of net debt to GDP over the cycle at 40 per cent. In Switzerland, an expenditure rule was introduced at the federal level in 2003, aiming at keeping the budget balance close to zero over the cycle and setting a ceiling for expenditure which cannot exceed cyclically adjusted revenue.

12. For example, the provision in the United States' BEA that legislated changes affecting revenue or mandatory spending programmes (i.e., healthcare, unemployment benefits and farm price support) be budget-neutral did not apply to pensions.

13. This section draws from de Mello (2005) appendix 2.

14. See Nascimento and Debus (2001) and IMF (2001) for more information.

15. Municipalities with less than 50,000 inhabitants face less stringent provisions on budget reporting.

16. There are three integrated budget framework horizons in Brazil. First, a four-year budget framework (PPA) is defined by the federal government to allocate its projected budgetary

resources over the following years to different programmes and activities, consistent with the medium-term macroeconomic framework, fiscal targets and revenue forecasts. Second, a three-year Budget Guidelines Law (LDO) sets targets for the main budget aggregates (expenditure, revenue, budget balance and debt) for the current year and indicative targets for the following two years. Third, an annual budget law (LOA) allocates budget resources to the programmes and activities defined in the PPA and consistent with the targets set in the LDO. Programmes and activities, as well as their costs, are clearly identified in the preparation of the PPA and in the LOA.

17. Davoodi and Zou (1998) analyse the relationship between fiscal decentralization and economic growth from a cross-country perspective, using a sample of 46 countries over the period 1970–89. Emphasis is placed on sub-national governments as a whole, and not only on local government spending.

18. See Tanzi (2005) for more discussion on the 'infrastructure gap' in Latin America. See also Prud'homme (2004) for more information.

19. This is consistent with the evidence reported by Bohn and Inman (1996), which, although sensitive to the cyclical indicator used to gauge fiscal responsiveness, indicates that stringent fiscal rules encourage precautionary savings in good times, which can be used subsequently to finance counter-cyclical measures in bad times. By contrast, also using US state data, Alesina and Bayoumi (1996) argue that fiscal rules have indeed reduced flexibility in state-level fiscal policy making without, however, having a bearing on the cyclicality of state fiscal policy.

20. The source of data on municipal finances is the National Treasury. The data refer to the balance sheets of the municipalities, excluding their decentralized agencies (*autarquias* and *fundações*) and off-budget funds (including pension funds). The number of municipalities in the sample, which spans the period 1998–2003, varies between 3,807 in 1998 and 4,881 in 2001. Due to methodological constraints, intertemporal comparability is ensured within the periods 1998–2001 and 2002–03. The National Statistics Bureau (IBGE) also publishes municipal data based on the national accounts, but the coverage is less comprehensive and data are typically available only after a two-year lag.

21. This assignment of expenditure functions across the different layers of government in consistent with the principle of subsidiarity, whereby services should be delivered by the lowest level of government capable of internalizing the externalities associated with public provision. In principle, the assignment of expenditure functions to sub-national governments is constrained by the ability of smaller jurisdictions to make the most of economies of scale in service delivery. The other important constraints are spillover effects, by which the inhabitants of adjacent jurisdictions can benefit from spending in the neighbouring one, which may result in the underprovision of services or stretch local budgets beyond their means.

22. The distribution of population is unequal across Brazil's 5,560 municipalities. In the sample of municipalities used in this paper, three-quarters of the municipalities had a population less than 22,405 in 2000. See IBAM (2001) and Souza (2004) for more information.

23. According to Rezende and Garson (2004), the 10 main metropolitan areas, accounting for 30 per cent of the population and 50 per cent of GDP, received only 12.7 per cent of FPM funds in 2002.

24. According to the 1988 Constitution, the municipalities are in charge of granting concessions for 'local' public services, while the federal and state governments should

guarantee efficient and well-regulated water supply and sanitation services. The 1995 Concession Law provided more guidelines for private concessions, but did not clarify which level of government is in charge of water and sanitation provision. The Concession Law challenged the monopolies that state companies enjoyed for 25 years, stating that the municipalities also have the right to grant concessions or enter into licensing agreements for 'local' services or provide these services themselves. Prior to 1994, a decline in the inflation-adjusted value of user charges contributed to lower investment capacity. See Parlatore (2000) for more information.

25. While about 80 per cent of households have access to piped water, less than two-thirds are connected to public sewerage networks or septic tanks. Moreover, there are large regional disparities in connection rates between the northern and south-eastern states, large and small municipalities, and rich and poor households. In 2000, connection rates to public sewerage and non-rudimentary septic tanks for urban households were 56 and 16 per cent respectively, while for rural households they were 3 and 10 per cent respectively. Urban sewerage coverage reached 70 per cent in the south-east, but only 2 per cent in the north. Only 9 per cent in poor rural areas had access to piped water in 2000, although some had access to wells and springs. Of all households earning less than two minimum wages, two-thirds had access to piped water and one-third to sewerage. See OECD (2005) for more information.

References

Afonso, J.R., and E.A. Araújo. 2004. 'Local Government Organisation and Finance'. World Bank. Unpublished manuscript.

Afonso, J.R., and L. de Mello. 2002. 'Brazil: An Evolving Federation', in E. Ahmad and V. Tanzi (eds), *Managing Fiscal Decentralization*. London: Routledge.

Alesina, A., and R. Perotti. 1997. 'Fiscal Adjustments in OECD Countries: Composition and Macroeconomic Effects', *IMF Staff Papers*, 44 (2): 210–48.

Alesina, A., and S. Ardagna. 1998. 'Tales of Fiscal Contractions', *Economic Policy*, 27: 489–543.

Alesina, A., and T. Bayoumi. 1996. 'The Costs and Benefits of Fiscal Rules: Evidence from US States', *NBER Working Paper*, No. 5614.

Bohn, H. and R.P. Inman. 1996. 'Balanced-Budget Rules and Public Deficits: Evidence from the U.S. States', *Carnegie-Rochester Conference Series on Public Policy*, 45: 13-76.

Burki, S.J., Perry, G.E., and Dillinger, W.R. 1999. *Beyond the Center: Decentralizing the State, World Bank Latin American and Caribbean Studies.* Washington, DC: World Bank.

Davoodi, H. and H.F. Zou. 1998. 'Fiscal Decentralization and Economic Growth: A Cross-Country Study', *Journal of Urban Economics*, 43 (1998): 244–57.

Devarajan, S., V. Swaroop and H.F. Zou. 1996. 'The Composition of Public Expenditure and Economic Growth', *Journal of Monetary Economics*, 37 (2): 313–44.

Estache, A. and F. Humplick. 1995. 'Does Decentralization Improve Infrastructure Performance?' in A. Estache (ed.), *Decentralizing Infrastructure: Advantages and Limitations*, World Bank Discussion Paper 290. Washington, DC: World Bank.

Estache, A., and S. Sinha. 1995. 'Does Decentralization Increase Spending on Public Infrastructure?', in Policy Research Working Paper Series 1457. Washington DC: World Bank.

Giavazzi, F., T. Jappelli and M. Pagano. 2000. 'Searching for Non-Linear Effects of Fiscal Policy: Evidence from Industrial and Developing Countries', *European Economic Review*, 44 (7): 1259-89.

Glaeser, E.L., J.A. Scheinkman and A. Shleifer. 1995. 'Growth in a Cross-Section of Cities', *Journal of Monetary Economics*, 36 (1): 117–43.

Gutman, J. 1997. 'Decentralizing Roads: Matching Accountability, Resources, and Technical Expertise', in S.J. Burki, G. Perry, and W. Dillinger (eds), *Beyond the Center: Decentralizing the State*, Latin American and Caribbean Studies, Viewpoints No. 19636. Washington, DC: World Bank.

Humplick, F. and A. Moini-Araghi. 1996. 'Decentralized Structures for Providing Roads: A Cross-Country Comparison.' Policy Research Working Paper No. 1658. Washington, DC: World Bank.

IBAM. 2001. 'Evolução do quadro municipal brasileiro no período entre 1980 e 2001', *Série Estudos Especiais*, (20). Rio de Janeiro: IBAM.

IMF (International Monetary Fund). 2001. *Brazil: Report on Observance of Standards and Codes*. Country Report No. 01/127. Washington DC: IMF.

———. 2003. *World Economic Outlook*. Washington DC: IMF.

Martner, R., and V. Tromben. 2004. 'La Sostenibilidad de la Deuda Pública, el Efecto Bola de Nieve y el "Pecado Original"', *Serie Gestión Pública*, (46). Santiago: ILPES/ECLAC.

McDermott, J., and R.F. Wescott. 1996. 'An Empirical Analysis of Fiscal Adjustments', *IMF Staff Papers*, 43 (4): 725–53.

de Mello, L.R. 2001a. 'Social Spending in Brazil: Education and Health Care', in *Brazil: Selected Issues and Statistical Appendix*. Washington DC: IMF.

———. 2001b. 'Social Spending in Brazil: Recent Trends in Social Assistance', in *Brazil: Selected Issues and Statistical Appendix*. Washington DC: IMF.

———. 2002. 'Public Finance, Government Spending and Economic Growth: The Case of Local Governments in Brazil', *Applied Economics*, 34: 1871–83.

———. 2005. 'Estimating a Fiscal Reaction Function: The Case of Debt Sustainability in Brazil', OECD Economics Department Working Paper No. 423. Paris: OECD.

———. 2006. 'Estimating a Fiscal Reaction Function: The Case of Debt Sustainability in Brazil', *Applied Economics* (forthcoming).

de Mello, L. and M. Hoppe. 2005. 'Education Attainment in Brazil: The Experience of FUNDEF', Economics Department Working Paper No. 424. Paris: OECD.

Ministry of Education. 2003. *Relatório Sobre a Fixação do Valor Mínimo Nacional por Aluno/ano*. Brasília: Ministry of Education.

Ministry of Planning and Budget. 2003. *Vinculações de Receitas dos Orçamentos Fiscal e da Seguridade Social e o Poder Discricionário de Alocação dos Recursos do Governo Federal*. Brasília: Federal Budget Secretariat.

Nascimento, E.R., and I. Debus. 2001. 'Entendendo a Lei de Responsabilidade Fiscal'. Unpublished manuscript.

OECD. 2002. *Economic Outlook*, (72). Paris: OECD.

———. 2003. *Economic Outlook*, (74). Paris: OECD.

———. 2005. *OECD Economic Survey of Brazil*. Paris: OECD.

Parlatore, A.C. 2000. 'Privitização no Setor de Saneamento no Brasil', in A.C Pinheiro and K. Fukasaku (eds), *A Privatização no Brasil: o Caso dos Serviços de Utilidade Pública*. Rio de Janeiro: OECD/BNDES.

Prud'homme, R. 2004. 'Infrastructure and Development'. Paper prepared for the Annual Bank Conference on Development Economics, 3–5 May, World Bank, Washington, DC.

Reinhart, C., K. Rogoff and M. Savastano. 2003. 'Debt Intolerance', *Brookings Papers on Economic Activity*: 1–62. Brookings Institution.

Rezende, F., and S. Garson. 2004. 'Financing Metropolitan Areas in Brazil: Political, Institutional, Legal Obstacles and Emergence of New Proposals for Improving Coordination'. Unpublished manuscript.

Rocha, F., and P. Picchetti. 2003. 'Fiscal Adjustment in Brazil', *Revista Brasileira de Economica*, 57 (1): 239–52.

Sorensen, B.E., L. Wu and O. Yosha. 2001. 'Output Fluctuations and Fiscal Policy: US State and Local Governments 1978–94', *European Economic Review*, 45 (7): 1271–310.

Souza, C. 2004. 'Governos locais e gestão de polícitas sociais universais'. Unpublished manuscript.

Tanzi, V. 2005. 'Building Regional Infrastructure in Latin America', Inter-American Development Bank. Unpublished manuscript.

Zhang, T. and H.-F. Zou. 1998. 'Fiscal Decentralization, Public Spending, and Economic Growth in China', *Journal of Public Economics*, 67: 221–40.

2

China: Fiscal Framework and Urban Infrastructure Finance

Su Ming and Zhao Quanhou*

Introduction

Since its economic reform and opening up to the outside world, China has experienced impressive economic development. Between 1978 and 2004, China's annual GDP growth rate averaged 9.4 per cent, far greater than the world average of 2.8 per cent. Economic growth has been accompanied by rapid urbanization. In 1978, only 17.9 per cent of China's population lived in urban areas; by 2003, the urbanization rate was 40.5 per cent.

Although the capital stock for urban infrastructure also has expanded swiftly—probably faster than anywhere else in the world—it has not kept pace with the rate of industrialization and urbanization. Until recently, China's urban infrastructure financing was heavily dependent on the fiscal budget. Fiscal capacity constraints, especially in the lower levels of government, have forced governmental authorities to make greater use of borrowing, introducing a new degree of risk into intergovernmental finance; but urban infrastructure construction continues to lag behind the rate that many experts believe is required to sustain China's extraordinary economic growth.

To analyse the impact of the fiscal framework on urban infrastructure financing, we need to first understand China's fiscal system. This chapter

* Su Ming works at the Research Institute for Fiscal Science (RIFS) under the Ministry of Finance of China, and is also Chancellor and member of the Standing Council, China's Institute for Urban Finance.

Quanhou Zhao is a researcher at the RIFS.

summarizes the principal reforms that have led to today's fiscal framework, then considers the current situation and future options for urban infrastructure finance.

China's Fiscal System and the Change of Fiscal Policy

China's market-oriented economic reforms started in 1978. The nation gradually phased out the planned economic system, and shifted economic power to decentralized levels of government and locally-owned companies. Reform of the fiscal system thus underlaid national economic reform.

The Pre-Reform Fiscal Pattern

The pre-reform fiscal regime of China was adapted to the highly concentrated planning economy. Not only did the government do everything, but sub-national governments were totally dependent on the central government. It was a typical regulated fiscal regime, in which all taxes and profits were remitted to the Centre and then transferred back to the provinces, and from there to the local level.[1] Policy makers in the central government decided what type of revenues should be collected and how these revenues were to be reallocated for national and sub-national public goods.

The pre-reform fiscal regime had the merit of generating broadly equal fiscal capacities across different regions. However, it provided no incentives for sub-national governments to promote economic growth or collect budgetary revenues.

The Fiscal Contracting System: 1980–93

China began its fiscal decentralization reform in earnest in 1980, with the goal of giving sub-national governments more and more power to finance their own needs, subject to a budgetary constraint. The initial strategy involved a variety of contracting methods, whose basic spirit was to apportion revenues and expenditures between the central and local authorities while holding the latter responsible for their own profits and losses. The fiscal contracting system gradually evolved into six contracting categories by 1988—(*a*) contract sharing of incremental revenues; (*b*) proportional sharing of base revenue; (*c*) proportional base sharing plus incremental sharing; (*d*) contractually designated incremental remittance amounts; (*e*) fixed remittance; and (*f*) fixed central subsidy.

The fiscal contracting system gave sub-national governments a certain amount of space to decide their own affairs (a kind of fiscal deregulation), encouraging them to develop the regional economy and collect revenues. From a national perspective, the system had two principal drawbacks. First, it caused the central government's share of fiscal revenues to decline steeply. This phenomenon was due in part to the fact that provincial and municipal governments 'gamed' the system by producing just enough on-budget shared revenue to satisfy their contract obligations, while shifting further revenue generation to off-budget and other revenue sources that did not have to be shared. Central government revenue as a percentage of total fiscal revenue, fell from 34.8 per cent in 1985 to 22 per cent in 1992. Second, the different contracting methods were complicated and inequitable, enlarging the fiscal differentials between regions. Rich provinces (such as Guangdong) had more bargaining power and benefitted from more favourable fiscal contracts. In addition, under the contracting system, the central government fell into an inefficient rut of constantly bargaining with sub-national governments over revenue-sharing terms.

The 'Tax Assignment System Reform' of 1994

In 1994, China undertook a fundamental intergovernmental fiscal reform called the 'tax assignment system reform'. The objectives of the reform package were to: (*a*) simplify and rationalize the tax structure by reducing tax categories and tax rates, thereby unifying the tax burden on taxpayers and cutting down tax exemptions; (*b*) raise the overall fiscal revenue-to-GDP ratio; (*c*) raise the central government's share of total fiscal revenues; and (*d*) put central–local revenue sharing on a more transparent, objective basis by shifting from revenue-sharing contract negotiations to a tax and revenue assignment system.

Expenditure Assignments between the Central and Sub-National Governments

The 1994 reforms concentrated solely on the revenue side of public budgets. No expenditure assignments were made. In fact, there is still no legislation in China that codifies the expenditure responsibilities of different tiers of government, either differentiating the central and provincial levels, or the provinces and the local level. Leaving intergovernmental expenditure responsibilities undefined has given upper-tier governments more flexibility in offloading responsibilities to lower tiers without compensatory transfers of revenue or fiscal autonomy.

Table 2.1 identifies the key expenditure functions commonly understood to be sub-national functions. The list is extensive and costly. Most of the service delivery functions, along with the corresponding investments in urban infrastructure, are the responsibilities of local governments. The local level is also responsible for economic development and economic planning—which involves ensuring a pro-active direction in the local enterprise sector. Local governments in China also have much greater responsibility for poverty alleviation and social protection of displaced workers than is true in the West, where these functions are assumed primarily by the central governments.

Table 2.1
Sub-National Expenditure Responsibilities

1. Sub-national government administration
2. Local capital construction
3. Basic local services, including water supply and distribution; local and regional roads and highways; wastewater collection and treatment; garbage collection and disposal; urban gas supply; mass transit systems
4. Maintenance, repair and operation of urban infrastructure
5. Management of local state-owned enterprises (SOEs)
6. Support for agricultural production
7. Primary and secondary schooling; large portion of higher education
8. Healthcare and hospitals
9. Price subsidies
10. Poverty alleviation
11. Protection of laid-off workers from SOEs
12. Cultural and heritage protection
13. Environmental protection
14. Local and regional economic development
15. Physical planning

Source: Authors.

Revenue Assignment

The principle of revenue assignment between the central and sub-national governments is that taxes concerning national interest or macroeconomic adjustment belong to the central government and those with regard to local economic development are under the jurisdiction of sub-national governments. Table 2.2 shows the specific situation after the 1994 reform.

Table 2.2
Revenue Assignment between Central and Sub-National Governments, 1994

Central revenues	1. Import tariffs
	2. Consumption taxes
	3. Income taxes and profits of SOEs under the jurisdiction of the central government
	4. Import-related consumption taxes and VATs
	5. Taxes imposed on banks, non-bank financial institutions and insurance companies (including business taxes, income taxes and the urban maintenance and development tax)
	6. Taxes on railroads
Sub-national revenues	1. Business taxes (excluding banks, non-bank financial institutions and insurance companies, and railroads)
	2. Company income tax (excluding local banks, foreign banks, and non-bank financial companies)
	3. Profits of locally owned SOEs
	4. Personal income tax
	5. Urban land use tax
	6. Urban maintenance and development tax (excluding banks, non-bank financial institutions and insurance companies, and railroads)
	7. Fixed assets capital gains tax
	8. House property taxes
	9. Stamp taxes
	10. Agriculture and related taxes
	11. Tax on contracts
	12. Land-value increment taxes
Shared revenues	1. VATs 75 per cent central–25 per cent sub-national governments
	2. Stamp taxes on security exchange (50–50 per cent)
	3. Resource taxes

Source: Authors.

A distinctive characteristic of this revenue assignment was that, while it initially boosted the central government's share of total revenue significantly, as will be discussed later, it assigned to sub-national governments all or part of what turned out to be the fastest-growing major revenue sources—100 per cent of the personal income tax, most of the company income tax, and 25 per cent of VAT.

Central-to-Provincial Transfer System

The intergovernmental fiscal reform also defined a new intergovernmental transfer system. What is called 'tax rebating' from the central to sub-national governments is actually a kind of transfer payment, a grant paid to provinces in relation to the growth in certain tax revenues since the last pre-reform year, 1993. Revenue increments from the consumption tax and Value Added Taxes collected in a province are received by the central government, then up to 30 per cent is 'rebated' to the province in the form of a tax-related return grant.

A second type of transfer from the centre was also introduced. This is a formula-based grant depending on the gap between a province's 'standardized' fiscal expenditure and its 'standardized' fiscal revenue. All central transfers are made to provincial governments. The provinces then transfer revenues to the local level, generally following grant arrangements modelled after the central-to-provincial design.

General Tax Reform

These changes in the intergovernmental fiscal system were made within the context of a general overhaul of the tax system. The most dramatic changes were establishment of a VAT-dominated turnover tax system and a unification of the various elements of domestic income tax. The tax changes had the objective of increasing total fiscal revenues, assuring future growth of fiscal revenues in line with economic growth, and increasing the central government's share of fiscal revenues. To ensure effective collection of the central government's portion of the revenues, the central and sub-national governmental tax collection bureaus were separated. The National Tax Collection Bureau is now in charge of collecting revenues from tax sources that are the exclusive domain of the central government as well as revenues from shared taxes, while the local tax bureaus are in charge of collecting sub-national tax revenues.

Changes in Revenue Rules after 1994

After 1994, further changes in the intergovernmental revenue system have been made, but gradually. Most of the changes have taken the form of increasing the central government's portion of shared revenues, increasing tax rates on centrally collected taxes or eliminating various sub-national taxes and fees.

First, in 1997, the sharing proportion between the central and local governments of the revenue from stamp taxes on security exchanges was changed from 50:50 to 88:12 per cent. Later, the sharing ratio was again adjusted, moving gradually from 88:12 to 97:3 per cent.

Second, the company tax rate on the finance and insurance industry was increased from 5 to 8 per cent, with all of the increase going to the central government. (The tax rate was reduced to the original level of 5 per cent between 2001 and 2003 because of the economic slowdown.) Third, income-tax revenue sharing was introduced in 2002. Except for some special industries and companies (such as banks, the China Gas Company and the China Oil and Chemical Company), the tax-sharing arrangement provided that the central and sub-national governments would in future share the combined revenues of company (business) income taxes and personal income taxes. The local governments would keep the income tax revenues collected in 2001 as a base, but increases would be shared between the central and local governments. In 2002, the central government's share was introduced at 50 per cent. From 2003 to now, the central government's share has been 60 per cent. This change has had the effect of converting the fastest-growing significant sources of tax revenue—company and personal income taxes—from sub-national taxes to shared taxes, the majority of whose revenue goes to the central government.

Fourth, in 2004, the government announced that China would progressively abolish the agriculture tax system over the next five years in order to lighten the farmers' tax burden. Several provinces have already eliminated the agricultural tax totally, while other provinces have lowered the agriculture tax rate from 3 per cent to 1 per cent. To partially compensate for the lost sub-national revenue, the central government increased special transfer payments by RMB 9.1 billion as budget-gap coverage.

Finally, from 1997 until now, the central government has issued a series of documents to cancel, regulate or limit the fees and user charges that can be collected at the sub-national (mostly urban) level.

Generally speaking, tax assignment reform established a new fiscal framework for China. It set up a better-defined and rational arrangement of intergovernmental financing. The new system enables all levels of government to have their own exclusive revenue sources, clarifying the boundaries of revenue allocation between different levels. A formula-based transfer system has been introduced. As was intended, the tax assignment system gives sub-national governments more power to develop their economies and to collect their own taxes.

The reforms carried out since 1994, however, have caused sub-national governments a great deal of fiscal difficulty. The government has recentralized fiscal revenues without cutting back on the sub-national governments' expenditure responsibilities.

The Revenue Impact of Fiscal Reform

The 1994 fiscal reform had the desired effect of accelerating fiscal revenue collection. Before 1994, the total fiscal revenue was growing between RMB 20 and 30 billion annually. After 1994, the annual fiscal revenue growth increased to more than RMB 150 billion on average. Figure 2.1 shows the trend of China's fiscal revenue.

Figure 2.1
China's Fiscal Revenue and its Structure

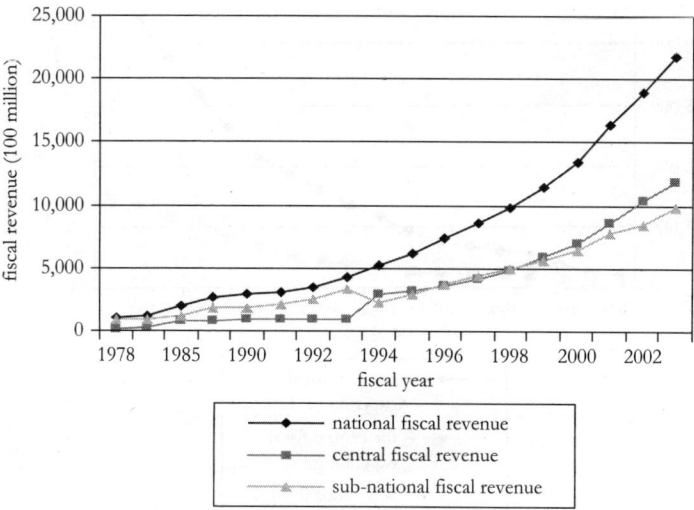

Source: Authors.

The 1994 reform also had the intended effect of shifting fiscal revenues from sub-national governments to the central government. This impact can be seen clearly in Figure 2.1, where central revenues jump ahead of sub-national revenues for the first time in 1994. Subsequent changes in revenue-sharing rules have assured that the central government's fiscal revenues continue to grow faster than sub-national fiscal revenues. Under the fiscal contracting system, the sub-national share of total fiscal revenue was very high, reaching a peak of 78.9 per cent in 1993. After 1994, due to the newly introduced tax assignment system and subsequent increases in the central portion of shared taxes, the sub-national governments' revenue share steadily declined from 78 per cent in 1993 to 45 per cent in 2002. The tax assignment system has cut sharply into sub-national governments' own revenues and their share of fiscal revenue distribution.

On the expenditure side of budgets, however, the share of the sub-national governments' spending in the total fiscal expenditure has stayed stable, at roughly 70 per cent (see Figure 2.2).

Figure 2.2
National Fiscal Expenditure and its Structure

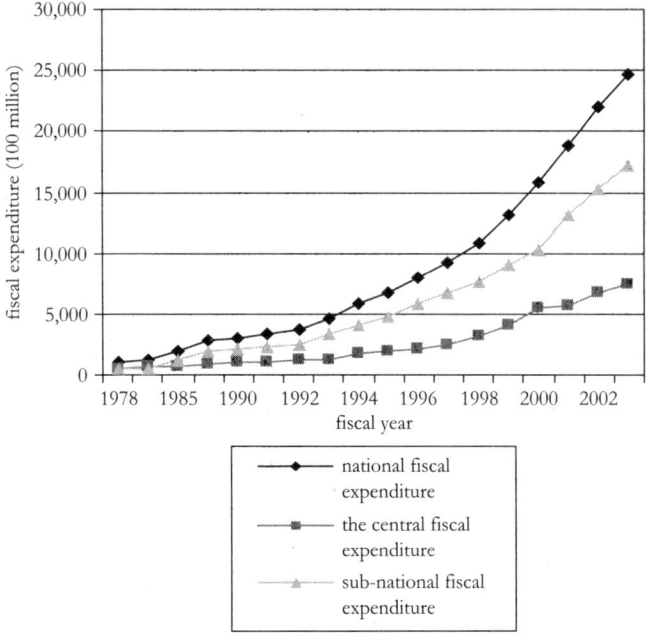

Source: Authors.

The widening fiscal gap between sub-national expenditure and sub-national fiscal revenue is shown dramatically by Figure 2.3. As a result of these trends, sub-national governments have grown more and more dependent on the central government fiscally. The tax rebating system has become a type of universal grant, which all sub-national governments need to receive. At the same time, regional disparities in income, fiscal revenue and self-financing capacity have grown. Figure 2.4 shows that the sub-national 'self-support' rate ranges from almost 90 per cent in Beijing to less than 40 per cent in Qinghai (Tibet may be viewed as an exceptional case.)

Figure 2.3
Sub-National Fiscal Revenue and Expenditure

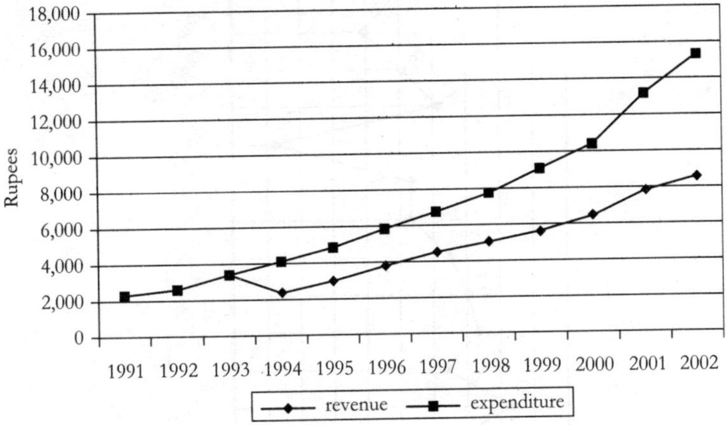

Source: Authors.

The Transfer System: From Central to Sub-National Level

Under the present fiscal system in China, transfer payments from central to sub-national governments are important, but they do not quantitatively offset the widening disparity in own-source revenue collection and they do not qualitatively incorporate the new norm of a formula-based standardized system fully. Reforms in the transfer system have been hampered by the political and economic power of high-growth regions. The largest part of intergovernmental transfers is still based on incremental revenue sharing (tax rebating) relative to 1993 base-year receipts.

The Tax Rebating System

After the 1994 reform, in order to compensate sub-national governments' revenue losses, the central government introduced the tax rebating system. The tax revenue rebating scale is decided thus: first, upward transfer of the amount that was transferred by sub-national governments to the centre in 1993; second, computation of the overall incremental revenue growth of

Figure 2.4
**The Sub-National Governments' Self-Support Rate
In Percentage of Total**

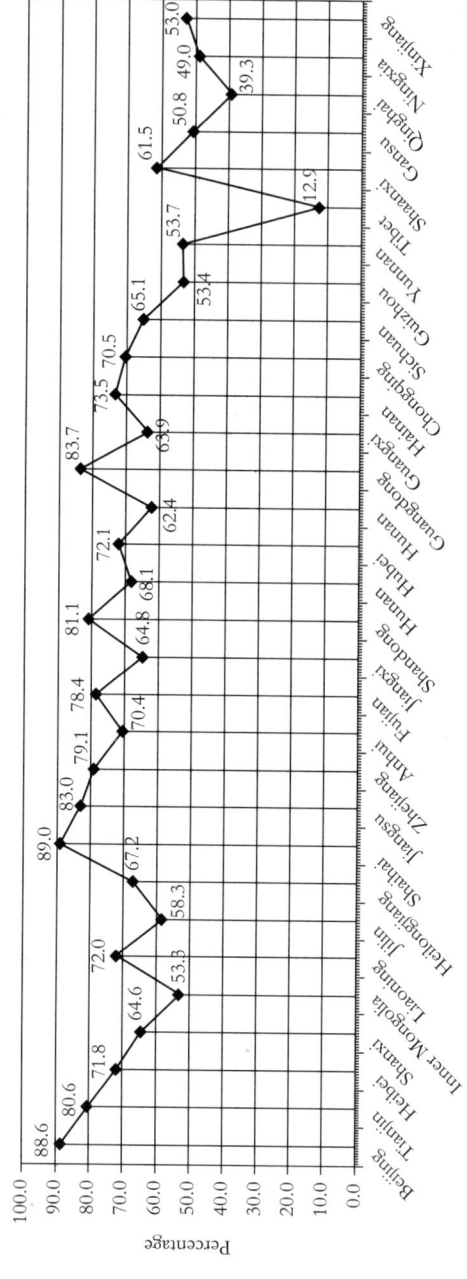

Source: Authors.

Note: The fiscal self-support rate is the share of own-source revenue in total revenue.

VAT and consumption tax revenue; third, whether or not revenue collected within a particular province is at least as large as in 1993. Provinces that meet this hurdle receive tax rebates. The rebate system is scaled so as to enable the richer provinces to get more tax rebates, expanding fiscal disparities among regions.

The 'Standardized' Fiscal Transfer System

In 1995, a new 'standardized' transfer system was introduced in addition to this rebate system. Based on a formula, the new system aimed to establish an objective, normative transfer mechanism. The amount of funds disbursed under the standardized transfer system has grown continually, from RMB 2.1 billion in 1995 to 74.5 billion in 2004, but the transfer amount under this method is still small compared to the magnitude of tax rebating.

Up to now, the formula for the standardized fiscal transfer has been simple but unstable. For example, the formula in 2002 was:

The volume of transfer payment of province N = (the N regional standardized expenditure – the N regional standardized revenue) × the transfer coefficient of province N.

Only when the standardized expenditure is larger than the standardized revenue could the province N obtain fiscal aid (net transfer payment).

Standardized revenues are calculated according to the regional tax base and the tax rates for sub-national and shared taxes. Since all tax rates are set at the national level, differences in standardized revenue reflect differences in tax-base capacity. Standardized expenditure is mainly the sum of a province's expenditures for government employees, education and administration, all calculated at 'standardized' rates (e.g., a standard number of public employees per 1,000 of population.) The transfer coefficient for a particular province is calculated by taking account of the regional standardized expenditure, standardized revenue, the situation of the fiscal deficit and the overall pool available for transfer payments. So the transfer coefficient is flexible from year to year. Provinces cannot accurately project their transfer receipts in advance, nor can they calculate the impact on transfers of the budget adjustments they make. Municipalities and other sub-provincial governments are subject to the same type of transfer formula calculations at the provincial level, and the same uncertainty surrounding the amount of transfer.

Earmarked Grants

Aside from the two transfer systems, there are still earmarked grants. In 1999, a transfer for income distribution adjustment was introduced when the central government decided to increase the middle and the lower classes' income. The transfer was earmarked for income distribution and excluded some rich areas, such as Beijing, Shanghai, Jiangsu, Zhejiang, Guangdong, Fujian and Shandong. The transfer amount in 1999 was RMB 10.8 billion doubled in 2000, and reached 40.3 billions in 2001.

Further earmarked grants were introduced in conjunction with China's Western Economic Development Programme. For example, the transfer payment earmarked for minority areas in order to support the minority areas' economic development was established in 2000. Similar grants are now being earmarked for redevelopment of China's rustbelt region in the north-east. Table 2.3 summarizes the overall transfer payment structure in China in recent years.

To recapitulate: the present transfer system consists mainly of the tax rebating programme and earmarked grants. The general transfer payment that was intended to narrow the standardized fiscal gap between provinces accounts for only about a quarter of total transfers, though its relative importance has been growing since it was introduced in 1995. Taken as a whole, the present transfer system does not fulfil the fundamental purpose of reducing fiscal disparities while providing effective incentives to responsible local fiscal management. Future reforms should expand the size of the standardized transfer relative to tax rebating and earmarking.

Fiscal Disparity in China

In recent years, a big problem that has emerged is the increasing fiscal disparity among regions. Regional inequalities have hindered harmonious economic development. Table 2.4 shows the situation in six provinces, ranging from the eastern coastal zone to the western areas of China. Fiscal disparities among the six areas have been continually growing. For example, in 2001, the wealthiest province (Shanghai) had a per capita fiscal capacity of RMB 3,776; the lowest (Guizhou) had only RMB 262.6. In 2003, the highest one (Shanghai) had a fiscal capacity of RMB 5,180 per capita; the lowest one (Guizhou) had 321.8. In other words, the fiscal disparity between the wealthiest and poorest province was more than 15 times. The overall

Table 2.3

Transfer Payments from Central to Sub-National Level, 1995–2004

In RMB 100 Million

Fiscal year	1995	1996	1997	1998	1999	2000	2001	2002	2003	2004
Total	2,449	2,655	2,784	3,228	3,931	4,588	5,893	7,348	8,656	10,17
Tax rebating and fixed subsidy amounts	1,982	2,060	2,124	2,196	2,234	2,326	2,431	3,328	4,196	4,33
Transfer payments for fiscal capacity	91	107	143	155	336	506	1,108	1,586	1,884	2,61
Of which: Standardized fiscal transfer	20	35	50	61	75	85	138	279	380	74
Earmarked for minority areas						25	35	39	55	7,
Income distribution adjustment					108	217	631	817	901	99
Grant for 'fees and tax reform' in rural area							80	245	305	30
Grant for abolition of agriculture tax										21
Special transfer payments	375	489	518	878	1,360	1,756	2,355	2,434	2,577	3,22

Source: National Bureau of Statistics, China, 1996–2005.

Note: Sub-items do not add to category total because of exclusion of minor items.

Table 2.4
Fiscal Disparity among Provinces
In RMB per Person

Year\\Province	1995	1996	1997	1998	1999	2000	2001	2002	2003
Guangdong	525.90	659.50	748.20	881.40	1,053.90	1,252.50	1,491.09	1,528.97	1,653.90
Shanghai	1,489.60	1,902.80	2,255.50	2,582.70	2,849.10	3,292.90	3,776.16	4,362.78	5,179.59
Jiangxi	148.40	182.20	209.00	229.60	248.50	263.90	315.29	332.89	395.32
Hunan	165.60	199.60	210.00	240.00	254.90	271.00	311.42	348.69	403.19
Guizhou	104.60	133.30	150.60	176.10	200.20	229.70	262.57	282.20	321.85
Yunnan	234.60	310.10	358.80	401.30	411.90	431.20	446.19	477.18	523.31
Disparity coefficient	1.069	1.104	1.133	1.134	1.131	1.153	1.16	1.21	1.24

Source: National Bureau of Statistics, China, 1995–2004.

Note: The disparity coefficient is the standard deviation divided by the arithmetic mean.

fiscal disparity coefficient grew steadily between 1995 and 2003. Most of the economically developed and fiscally strong provinces are now located in the eastern coastal area.

Mismatch of Governmental Function and Fiscal Capacity Across Levels

Another type of fiscal disparity is that between higher levels of government and lower tiers. The reform of 1994 and its aftermath shifted fiscal revenues upward to the Centre. At the same time, higher levels, such as the central and the provincial governments, managed to shift expenditure responsibilities down to the basic levels, such as counties and townships. This has caused a mismatch between function and fiscal capacity at different levels.

In China, sub-provincial governments include city, county and township governments. The sub-provincial fiscal situation outside of the big cities has become very difficult. The fiscal problems at basic levels of government have been exacerbated by the tendency of provincial governments to retain a high share of the revenues generated within the province. For example, the per capita fiscal revenue of the Yunnan provincial government is on average 11 times greater than the per capita revenue of the county governments. Guangdong's per capita provincial revenue is seven times greater than the counties'—despite the fact that much of the burden for service delivery and social welfare protection falls on the counties.

From a national perspective, the two highest levels of sub-national government (provincial governments and city or administrative regions) account for about 70 per cent of all sub-national fiscal revenue, while the lower two levels (county and township) only have 30 per cent. Meanwhile, the sub-provincial transfer payment system still is not efficiently established. Because of this skewed fiscal revenue distribution, the fiscal capacity of the base levels of local government outside the biggest cities has worsened and worsened.

Currently, the county and township governments undertake too many responsibilities. Some of these functions—such as compulsory education, militiaman training, social security, agricultural support, family planning, environmental protection and poverty alleviation—should be assigned to higher-level governments, especially the central government. Because of their excessive functional responsibilities, the basic levels of local government lack enough money to do the essential things that they should do.

Fiscal Management and Local Autonomy

Thus far, we have considered the fiscal flows resulting from tax sharing and transfer arrangements. At least as important to the fiscal framework, and with an impact on urban infrastructure finance, are the systems of intergovernmental hierarchy and the policies of central fiscal management.

Limited Sub-National Autonomy

At present, China maintains a multi-layered budgeting system, in which each level of government is responsible for its own budget. The People's Congresses at each level are formally responsible for budgetary legislation and approval. Budgets are not submitted to higher-level governments for approval. Each level of government does, however, report its budget and budget execution to the next level, and is responsible for conforming to budget rules.

In practice, the intergovernmental fiscal system is a blend of rules-based decentralization and hierarchical oversight that is a legacy of centralized planning. The budget law establishes fiscal limits for each tier of sub-national government. All sub-national governments are prohibited from having deficits, issuing bonds and borrowing. Tax rates for all sub-national taxes are established at the central level; sub-national governments do not have the flexibility of modifying tax rates or introducing new forms of taxation.

A detailed reporting system is applied upward through the governmental hierarchy. The Economic Development and Reform Commission (formerly the Planning Commission) at each level specifies in each five-year plan the physical development targets that the government will achieve, along with targets for local investment, economic growth rates and revenue collection. These targets reflect goals established at the national level and communicated downward to sub-national governments. Progress toward targets is closely monitored, both within the governmental system and within the parallel Communist Party hierarchy. The political system abundantly rewards local leadership for achieving or exceeding goals, especially those referring to investment levels, physical development and economic growth reflected in fiscal revenue.

Layered on top of this hierarchical structure and limited local autonomy is a countervailing tendency—distinctive to China—that is a legacy from the contracting period of decentralization (from the 1980s and 1990s up to the reforms started in 1994). This is represented by the 'off-budget fiscal fund' and a variety of other off-budget local resources. The 'off-budget' thrust gained momentum during the period of contractual revenue sharing, when local and provincial governments had to share their budgetary revenues with higher levels of government according to contractual terms. Sub-national governments, especially those at the local level, responded by introducing a large number of special fees, special charges and revenues realized from land leasing, which were not shared with, and often not reported to, higher-level governments. It is difficult to obtain exact information on the scale of these off-budget and other revenues, since one of the purposes behind the arrangement is to carve out revenue sources for which local authorities are not upwardly accountable. However, a special study of Beijing's revenue structure illustrates the scale of the problem.

Table 2.5
Structure of Beijing's Municipal Revenue

Year	1998	1999	2000
On-budget revenue	39.4%	45.2%	47.4%
Formal 'off-budget' revenue	18.2%	18.0%	20.3%
Other revenues	42.4%	36.8%	32.3%

Source: Cited in Zhang Rufei (2005).

The national government has sought to cut back the amount of non-reported revenues, first by greatly restricting the variety of fees that local governments can impose (on the grounds that many of the fees were 'illegally' adopted and interfere with predictable business investment) and second, by requiring local governments to report revenues from the list of authorized fees and some land leasing under a formal category of 'off-budget revenue'. These initiatives have reduced the magnitude of unaccounted-for local revenue, but not eliminated it. Table 2.5 shows the modest progress being made toward reducing 'other', largely unreported revenues.

The question of budget organization and restructuring is especially important to infrastructure financing, given that the largest part of financing has come from the proceeds of land leasing, fees and asset incomes, which lie outside the regular local budget. The category 'fees' is a composite of user fees for services such as water supply and a wide variety of more arbitrary fees imposed by local governments to generate revenue. At least until the most recent round of reforms, service-related user fees were a small part of the total.

From Pro-active to Prudent Fiscal Policy

Macroeconomic fiscal policy is established at the national level, under the guidance of the Ministry of Finance. An important shift in policy occurred in 2004, which has affected all parts of China's economy, but especially infrastructure finance.

After years of implementing a 'proactive' fiscal policy—i.e., one of fiscal stimulus and economic development financed by borrowing—China in 2004 formally adopted a 'prudent' fiscal policy—one of greater fiscal restraint, with less reliance on borrowing. The proactive policy was adopted largely in response to the Asian financial crisis, for the purpose of stimulating national growth. As the economy shook off the shadow of economic recession and entered the rising phase of a new cycle, certain stresses became apparent in the latter half of 2003, such as over-investment in some sectors, such as steel, and inflationary pressures.

The content of the new 'prudent' fiscal policy, announced at the National People's Congress, can be summarized as (*a*) controlling deficits and national borrowing; (*b*) focusing fiscal resources on sectors that have critical bottlenecks or have lagged behind in the emphasis on general economic growth—these include agriculture, environmental protection and social protection of laid-off workers from SOEs (*c*) devoting more attention to the fiscal impact on income distribution, including income differences between regions and between the rural and urban sectors; and (*d*) reinforcing tax collection and budgetary management in order to finance these initiatives within more closely balanced budgets.

In terms of economic development strategy, this programme has been called one of 'five balances'—that is, the need to balance urban and rural development, to balance the development of different geographical regions, to balance economic and social development, to balance the development of man and nature (environment), and to balance domestic development with international trade. One of the first steps in implementing this 'prudent' national fiscal policy was to lower the target for the 2005 central deficit.

Identifying and Managing Fiscal Risk

The move to a 'prudent' macroeconomic fiscal policy reflects the judgement that the greatest fiscal risk to China's sustained development now is public-sector debt, as reflected both in the balance sheets of the government and in the balance sheets of banks and the financial sector. The national (central government) debt has grown to some RMB 2.1 trillion, or about 60 per cent of GDP, in 2005.

Non-performing loans threaten the domestic banking sector. The government has already relieved the banking sector of a large volume of non-performing loans by forming special asset companies to assume these loans and the underlying assets. Still, the government estimates that some RMB 3.3 billion of non-performing loans remain, and some outside analysts project that the share of non-performing loans is considerably higher. A large part of the bad debt consists of loans to sub-national governments and to local SOEs.

There is no exact information on the aggregate volume of bad debt owed by sub-national governments.[2] However, the total of direct non-performing loans plus uncovered contingent liabilities is likely to lie somewhere between RMB 800 billion and 1.2 trillion. This makes sub-national governments a very large part of the banking sector's aggregate debt problem. The issue of banks' bad debts takes on special urgency because of the WTO agreement allowing entry of foreign banks into domestic lending, which will bring well-financed new entrants into competition with China's domestic banks. In addition to offloading some of the banking sector's bad loans, the government has hence ordered banks to adopt much stricter lending standards for local governments and locally owned SOEs.

Finally, under current intergovernmental expenditure responsibilities, sub-national governments will have to absorb a large part of the unfunded social security liability, which is estimated at some RMB 2.5 trillion. In all, public debt might account for more than 280 per cent of GDP in 2005, threatening China's future economic development if not handled prudently.

All of these factors point to the macroeconomic risk involved in increasing sub-national governments' debt by financing the large volume of urban infrastructure investment that is needed through borrowing. This is especially true if infrastructure investment is to be focused on lagging regions and on counties and townships whose capacity to repay debt is limited.

Impact of the Fiscal Framework on Urban Infrastructure Investment

Ever since the early 1990s, China's urban public infrastructure has drawn great attention from all levels of governments. Investment has been climbing at a rapid rate. Total urban infrastructure investment during the period of the 'Eighth Five-Year Plan' was RMB 260 billion, five times as much as in the 'Seventh Five-Year' period; while during the 'Ninth Five-Year' period, ending in 2000, the investment total grew to RMB 700 billion, 2.7 times the amount of the previous five years. The high rate of growth has continued through the Tenth Five-Year period.

China has a comprehensive physical reporting system, which makes it possible to track urban infrastructure capacity along various dimensions. Table 2.6 shows that the growth in most measures of urban infrastructure provision (and urbanization) has been remarkable.

Table 2.6
Basic Statistics on Urban Infrastructure Coverage

Item	1990	1995	2000	2002	2003
Developed areas (sq km)	12,856	19,264	22,439	25,973	28,308
Population density of urban districts (persons/sq km)	279	322	442	754	847
Total floor space of buildings (100 million sq m)	39.8	57.3	76.6	131.8	140.9
Per capita water consumption for residential use (tonnes)	67.9	71.3	95.5	77.8	77.1
Percentage of population with access to tap water	48	58.7	63.9	77.9	86.2
Percentage of population with access to gas	19.1	34.3	45.4	67.2	76.7
Area of paved roads per 1,000 population (sq m)	3.1	4.4	6.1	7.9	9.3
Length of sewer pipelines per capita (m)	3.9	6.0	6.8		
Density of sewer pipelines (km/sq km)	4.5	5.7	6.3	6.7	7.0
Percentage of treated sewerage	14.9	20.0	34.2	36.5	
Number of public transportation vehicles per 100 population	2.2	3.6	5.3	6.7	7.7
Per capita public green areas (sq m)	1.8	2.5	3.7	5.4	6.5
Volume of garbage disposal (10,000 tonnes)	6,727	10,671	11,818	13,650	14,857

Source: National Bureau of Statistics, China, 1995–2004.

Despite this growth, many Chinese experts and policy officials believe that urban infrastructure investment lags behind the rate appropriate to the country's growth in urbanization, industrialization and income levels and that urban infrastructure investment will have to accelerate in the future.

One key element in this argument is China's commitment to urbanization as the primary domestic growth strategy. Although China has more cities with a population of at least 1 million than any other country in the world (171 in 2002), it remains largely a rural nation. Moreover, as a report of the Research and Development Center of the State Council (Xie Fuzhan 2004) points out, China has industrialized to a far greater extent than it has urbanized, and has urbanized faster than it has invested in urban infrastructure. China's degree of urbanization today corresponds to that of England in 1950, the United States in 1911 and Japan in 1950. If the worldwide correspondence between industrialization and urbanization were to hold true in China, the country would now be 60 per cent urbanized, instead of just over 40 per cent.

China's economic growth strategy rests on continued rapid urbanization to absorb surplus rural labour. As Chen Yuan, Governor of the China Development Bank, has written (Chen Yuan 2005):

> Urbanization is the most important and enduring motive force in stimulating consumption and investment in China's domestic economy today; it is also the engine to simultaneously propel our economic and social development.

Rapid, and even accelerating, urbanization will require very high rates of urban infrastructure investment to accommodate cities' population growth while at the same time improving coverage and service standards.

By some measures, China's rate of urban infrastructure investment to date has been less robust than it may first seem. The World Bank's (1994) World Development Report found that infrastructure investment in developing countries tended to average about 50 per cent of total government investment, 20 per cent of total national investment and about 4 per cent of GDP. 'Urban' infrastructure investment—i.e., infrastructure investment serving the municipal level—averaged about 3–4 per cent of urbanized GDP. Table 2.7 shows that urban infrastructure investment levels in China have been rising rapidly over time, but remained a relatively modest share of total national investment in 2000. The most successful cities have made much greater commitments to urban infrastructure investment. Over the period of the Ninth Five-Year Plan (ending in 2000), Shanghai devoted 12.5 per cent of total investment to urban infrastructure, or 5.9 per cent of regional GDP. In Beijing, 13.7 per cent of total investment went to urban infrastructure, which corresponded to 6.3 per cent of regional GDP, more than triple the share in earlier years.

Table 2.7
Urban Infrastructure Investment Ratios

Year	Ratio to total fixed asset investment (%)	Ratio to GDP (%)
1980	1.2	0.2
1985	2.5	0.7
1990	2.7	0.7
1995	4.0	1.4
2000	5.8	2.1

Source: Construction Industry of China (2002).
Note: Urban infrastructure investment ratios are calculated relative to total national investment and total national GDP.

Government experts have estimated that approximately 20–30 per cent of the spending on urban infrastructure construction during the Tenth Five-Year Plan (period ending in 2005) will be expended by local, provincial and central governments directly from budget (fiscal) resources. The remainder will be financed by a combination of domestic loans, foreign and multilateral loans, revenue from asset earnings and asset sales, and various forms of market-based financing.

The Fiscal Framework and Infrastructure Financing Options

Perhaps the best way to examine the linkage between the national fiscal framework and national fiscal policy, on the one hand, and urban infrastructure financing, on the other, is to look individually at the three broad channels that are responsible for the bulk of urban infrastructure financing. These are: direct budget investment from fiscal resources, borrowing, and market-based financing.

Direct Budget Expenditures

Direct budget expenditures on urban infrastructure investment include spending at the central, provincial and local levels from fiscal resources. Because urban capital construction is a local (sub-provincial) responsibility, the vast majority of spending is done by local governments. Before 1990, the main funds for urban infrastructure construction came from the local urban maintenance and construction taxes and from public utilities surcharges. Now, local infrastructure investment can in principle be financed from general resources in the local budget, although for budget presentation purposes, revenue from the urban maintenance and construction taxes is typically allocated to infrastructure investment.

As described earlier, sub-provincial governments have been placed in a fiscal squeeze stemming from a downward shift of expenditure responsibilities, an inadequate intergovernmental tax-sharing and tax-transfer system and the tendency of provincial governments to hold on to revenues rather than return them to the local level. One result has been strong pressure on local governments' budgets, which in turn has diminished the share of local budgets available to finance capital construction.

These trends have led to a steady decline in the proportion of urban infrastructure investment that is financed from the direct budget spending or operating surplus. Figure 2.5 shows that the proportion of total urban infrastructure construction financed by budgetary funds decreased from 50 per cent in 1991 to 29 per cent in 2001. The decline has continued thereafter, and is projected to continue into the future.

Figure 2.5
Share of Urban Infrastructure Investment Financed from the Budget

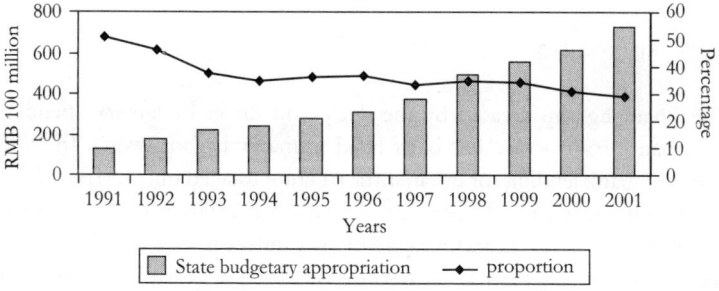

Source: Authors.

A second source of direct public financing is off-budget fees. As noted earlier, the central authorities have vigorously sought to rein in local fees, marked by periodic initiatives since 1994 (e.g., in 1996 and 2001) to limit the number of authorized fees to a restricted list and bring them within the formal revenue-reporting system. Most of these fees did not take the form of service charges or user fees for service consumption which have been increasing at the central government's urging, but were arbitrary fees levied on such items as construction permits and various 'authorizations' for domestic and international business operations. Nonetheless, they provided a source of unrestricted local income that often was channelled into infrastructure investment. The growth of fees used for infrastructure finance up to the 1994 intergovernmental fiscal reform and the subsequent sharp fall-off is shown in Figure 2.6.

Figure 2.6
Share of Urban Infrastructure Investment Financed by Fees and Charges

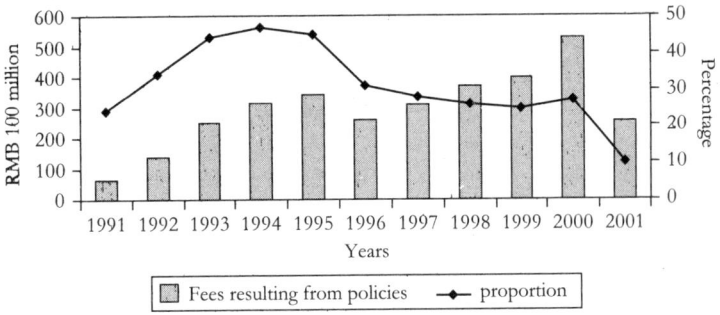

Source: Authors.

Debt Financing

The financing gap created by the decline in direct budgetary spending on urban infrastructure has been filled primarily by borrowing. In 1986, domestic-bank lending for urban infrastructure totalled only RMB 0.32 billion, accounting for just 2.4 per cent of total urban infrastructure investment. As Figure 2.7 makes clear, the share of investment financed by borrowing declined up to the 1994 fiscal reform, then began to explode. Although exact figures for the period after 2001 are not available, it is clear that borrowing volumes have continued to rise rapidly thereafter. By 2001, more than 60 per cent of the cities in China had infrastructure loans from banks or outstanding loan applications. The total banking-sector debt of local governmental units for urban infrastructure stood at RMB 74.2 billion in 2001, up 23 fold in just a decade. Use of the banking sector to finance urban infrastructure investment was encouraged by national policy, which identified the urban infrastructure sector as a top priority for lending by banks, all of which were then owned by the state.

Figure 2.7
Share of Urban Infrastructure Investment Financed by Loans

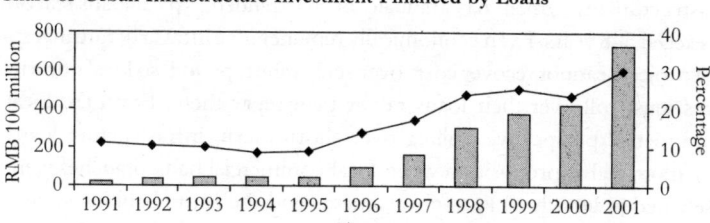

Source: Authors.

Central Government Borrowing and On-Lending to Local Governments for Infrastructure Investment

Bank borrowing has not been the only the type of debt financing. The national government also issued so-called infrastructure bonds and passed on the proceeds to provincial and local governments as a blend of 'on-lending' and grants. From 1998 to 2004, the Chinese government issued bonds to finance construction projects of RMB 910 billion, of which RMB 131.7 billion (roughly US$ 16 billion)[3] was for urban infrastructure financing. The money was used to complete almost 2,000 projects, including sewage and garbage disposal, water supply, and gas and heating facilities in 28 provinces. Funds were steered toward poorer regions, especially those in the western development area, and toward projects (especially those involving environmental protection) that could not recover costs through service charges or attract investment financing from the market.

Under the newly announced 'prudent' fiscal policy, national government will substantially reduce debt issuance for urban infrastructure investment purposes. In fact, funds from national debt are now supposed to be used only to complete constructions in progress and not to finance new projects. This change in national policy will severely affect the financing capacity of many local governments, especially those in the underdeveloped provinces of western China, where market-based financing is difficult to mobilize.

Structural Problems with Debt Financing

The risks created by debt financing go beyond the sheer volume of subnational debt. The bulk of bank loans have been provided by commercial banks. Although the maturity period of commercial bank loans for local infrastructure investment has gradually been extended, typical loans still do not exceed 5–8 years. Even economically remunerative infrastructure investment projects cannot recover costs over such a short period, so local governments must roll over their loans rather than repay them. From the local governments' perspective, rolling over shorter-term infrastructure loans was a more viable proposition when local commercial bank branches were closely tied politically to local governments and the entire banking system had planning targets for urban infrastructure investment to fulfil. Now, as part of financial deregulation, the People's Bank of China no longer establishes sectoral lending plans for banks. Banks have been required to heighten credit standards and prodded to clean up non-performing loans. Local governments' political control over local loans has been somewhat weakened in the effort to strengthen banks' balance sheets. Thus, the risk to local governments— in that old loans cannot be rolled over and that debt financing for new projects cannot be obtained—is greater than before. From the banking side, the fact that local government loans were routinely rolled over rather than required to be repaid, has hidden the true degree of non-performing loans, which is only now coming to light..

The China Development Bank (CDB), as a long-term policy bank, stands out against this sectoral backdrop. CDB regularly makes urban infrastructure loans of 15–20 years, or even longer periods, and has been a leader in identifying new types of revenue streams that can enhance local creditworthiness.

Central government on-lending for infrastructure investment from nationally issued bonds has been subjected to a variety of abuses, which the Ministry of Finance recognized in deciding to cut back the programme. Local and provincial governments often obtained financing on the premise that it would be invested in environmental projects and other social projects unable to generate a full economic return, then would switch to economic development projects once the financing was in hand. Public tendering was circumvented. Provinces (and the local governments that received funds from them) would obtain funds as 'loans', then plead inability to repay and succeed in getting repayment waived (Fu Tao 2004; Wang et al. 2003).

In part because of the legacy of state planning and state-directed financing of plans, the distinction between 'loans' that must be repaid and grants or transfers that are not to be repaid has not been fully established at the subnational level. Provincial and local governments, especially in lagging regions, continue to treat loan repayment to the central government as a matter of political negotiation rather than commercial obligation. This injects an element of endemic risk into sub-national debt that central authorities are now trying to eliminate.

Fear of the inability to control sub-national debt risk has also made the central government unwilling to allow rule-based issuance of municipal bonds. All proposed local bonds must be individually approved, both by the next higher level of government and by the State Development and Reform Commission. Most such proposals are denied or simply not acted upon. Local governments with strong economic bases, such as Shanghai, have sought bond approvals for years, but these have been approved only intermittently.

Marketization

'Marketization' is the term used in China for mobilizing capital from the private or social sector to invest in urban infrastructure. National planning calls for generating larger shares of financing from this mode to replace the declining share of direct fiscal investment and in recognition of the prudential constraints on borrowing.

In the first generation of 'marketization', emphasis was placed on land leasing—i.e., the sale to private developers of land development and leasing rights owned by local government. Leasing rights, though good for a specified time period (typically 50 years in the case of commercial property), are sold up-front in a cash transaction. Proceeds from land leasing have been used primarily to finance infrastructure construction. In some cities, land sales have been able to finance more than 100 per cent of all infrastructure investment, year in and year out, over a period of many years. (see Chapter 10). In fact, during the last decade and a half, land leasing has been the principal source of urban infrastructure investment finance in larger cities. However, its importance has declined of late in those cities that were the first to enter the market, because of the decline in the supply of land available for lease.

'Marketization' strategy is now moving toward a greater focus on infrastructure assets. This may take the form of selling existing assets (such as water treatment plants and bridges) to the private sector for specific periods of ownership, but more significantly involves attracting private capital to finance new construction of assets. A July 2004 policy pronouncement by the central government's State Council, 'Decision on Investment and Organizational Reform', formally reiterated the policy of approving social (private) capital investment in infrastructure and public utilities, and endorsed specific measures that would be necessary for implementing this broad policy, such as moving toward tariff rates that include an adequate return to capital and coverage of debt service, providing preferential tax treatment for private investment in urban infrastructure, and giving private investors in network systems (such as wastewater collection and treatment) preferential rights to use the network capacity for their own industrial and commercial projects.

Public policy has, in the short run, been motivated by a straightforward desire to mobilize financing for urban infrastructure investment. However, the marketization movement has opened up a broader discussion of how the urban infrastructure sector should be organized and how infrastructure services should be paid for.

Role of Urban Development and Investment Companies

According to public goods theory, the government should explicitly classify infrastructure into three different categories: infrastructure that can be operated profitably, quasi-profitable infrastructure and infrastructure that is inherently non-profitable because of its 'public goods' nature. Moreover, the scope of profitable infrastructure—i.e., infrastructure that can be operated on a profitable basis through service charges or other financial means—should be expanded as the market economy grows and as consumer ability to pay increases. For non-profitable infrastructure, the government will remain the main financing body and investor. However, for profitable and quasi-profitable infrastructure, business enterprises should become the main builders and operators. Profitable infrastructure can stand on its own with appropriate service pricing; quasi-profitable infrastructure will need targeted government subsidies to become competitive.

The present urban infrastructure management system in China runs together these three infrastructure categories. Profitable infrastructure is combined with non-profitable infrastructure under the management of a single, monopoly-holding SOE, without clear guidelines differentiating the way the different types of infrastructure will be operated or financed. Each city has an UDIC whose function is to (a) mobilize financing for new infrastructure construction of all kinds, (b) carry out construction of new infrastructure and (c) oversee the operation of existing infrastructure assets, running the gamut from mass transit systems to wastewater treatment plants, from water supply to trash collection and disposal.

This monopoly-holding company is the juridical person that acts on behalf of the government to borrow funds from banks and other sources, issue bonds when allowed to do so, raise capital from trusts and other special purpose vehicles, enter into joint ventures with private companies for infrastructure development, sell local infrastructure assets, assemble land packages for sale and development, serve as the implementing body for international loan programmes, and oversee actual service delivery from the assets it owns, typically drawing upon complex cross-subsidization arrangements to keep all of its activities afloat.

UDICs were established in most cities at the end of the 1990s, or even later, in response to a central government directive that responsibility for asset and liability management should be taken away from municipal governments and placed in the hands of specialized local enterprises. However, further unbundling is required. Potentially profitable and quasi-profitable infrastructure functions can be operated on a standalone basis that allows competition from private suppliers and can attract private capital for new ventures. UDICs will continue to have responsibility for the overall physical development of the city and for the financing and infrastructure strategies that are necessary to accomplish planning objectives. However, in changing from the plan-oriented economy to the market-oriented economy, a fundamental requirement is to eliminate the UDICs' monopoly over all phases of infrastructure development and operation and all types of infrastructure. The UDIC's job, in addition to overall infrastructure development strategy, should be to operate and upgrade those infrastructure services that are inherently unprofitable because of their 'public goods' nature, while spinning off profitable and quasi-profitable infrastructure to other institutions that can participate in market-based competition.

Some UDICs have begun the unbundling process. The Shanghai Municipal UDIC, for example, has spun off a separate institution to invest in development of water and wastewater assets and to negotiate agreements with private investors for new projects in the sector. Additional unbundling is in progress (see Chapter 6).

Infrastructure Revenue Streams

Whether capital funds are mobilized in the form of direct private investment or market-based loans, the economics of infrastructure investment is based on the revenue streams that are generated. Over the past 15 years, the most prolific and dependable revenue streams have been those attached to land. Special requirements or incentives for land developers to invest in associated off-site infrastructure have been another important source of infrastructure investment. The economic value of urban land is widely recognized in China and the conversion of land-leasing rights or land development rights into infrastructure finance is widely practised (see Chapter 10).

It has proved more difficult to implement market-based reforms of infrastructure service tariffs, such as water tariffs, wastewater treatment charges and garbage collection and disposal fees. The State Development and Reform Commission, in October 2002, issued a circular on urban tariffs, stating that 'cities with existing wastewater and garbage treatment facilities shall start to immediately charge a treatment tariff', and that all other cities should do so before the end of 2003. Cities that had water, trash collection, wastewater treatment and trash disposal tariffs were given a strict timetable for moving to tariff schedules that 'shall cover operations cost and a reasonable investment return'. The purpose of the circular was specifically to make these urban infrastructure sectors attractive to private capital, so that investors could earn a satisfactory profit and lenders could have an adequate margin for payment of debt service.

In practice, almost all cities have failed to adopt full cost-recovery pricing for these basic services. Even the national government has backtracked. In 2004, it issued another circular prohibiting cities from raising service fees, as an inflation-fighting measure. Political reluctance to increase basic service fees has caused cities to look to private developers and larger commercial activities for alternative revenue streams that could be capitalized into investment financing. In its effort to clean up the Suzhou River, for example, the Shanghai Municipal Government granted project implementing agencies the right to collect a special drainage assessment charge from those who discharged into the river, creating a revenue stream that served as collateral for a large loan from the CDB.

Conclusion: A Policy Agenda for the Future

In looking to the future, it will be necessary to establish a more supportive fiscal framework for urban infrastructure investment that serves both economically strong and weaker local governments. The basic elements of such a reform package are:

1. **First, better matching between expenditure responsibilities and fiscal ability.** Along with development of the market-oriented economy, the marketability of urban infrastructure investment has been

enhanced greatly, but local governments cannot withdraw from the infrastructure construction domain completely. They require fiscal resources commensurate with their expenditure obligations. In China, the vertical fiscal imbalance has not been resolved. Fiscal revenues are centralized upward, so that outside of the biggest cities, fiscal resources for infrastructure construction at the local level are extremely limited. Addressing this problem will require enlarging the scope of general transfers aimed at narrowing differentials in fiscal capacity, supplemented by special subsidies to meet specified standards for city infrastructure construction.

Even before implementing new fiscal transfers, however, it is imperative to distinguish more precisely the responsibilities of each level of government in infrastructure provision and finance. At present, weaker local governments are being asked to handle more functions than they can possibly manage with existing resources.

2. **Second, the local governments' fiscal autonomy should gradually be strengthened.** Legislative power over local taxes now rests with the central government. The power to establish tax rates and modify the local tax and fee structure should be gradually released downward to local governments, within centrally determined limits, so that they can generate their own revenues according to the local development level and the local development strategy. This policy will primarily benefit rapidly growing cities with strong economic bases.

3. **Third, the national budget law should be modified to allow local governments (or the UDICs acting on their behalf) to raise finances from the capital market through bond issuance.** At present, the intergovernmental systems of budget surveillance and control are inadequate for permitting generalized access to a municipal bond market. However, certain cities whose economies, fiscal revenues and management experience are stronger (such as Beijing and Shanghai) should be allowed to issue bonds for city construction, subject to general rules rather than case-by-case approval, as an experiment that, if successful, could be broadened to other cities.

4. **Fourth, the rules for converting land assets into infrastructure finance should be standardized.** For the last decade and a half, land leasing has been the principal source of urban infrastructure financing in China's big cities. However, the municipalities' manipulation of land markets has led to important development distortions, as municipalities began to act like profit-maximizing land monopolists.

The national government must continue to clarify the rules for land acquisition and land disposition by municipal authorities.

5. **Finally, the framework for mobilizing capital from the social or private sector needs to be solidified.** The present level of marketability in China has made it possible for private capital to access the city infrastructure domain. However, if private capital is to play the expansive role projected for it in the future, service tariffs for infrastructure must be increased to include capital costs and revenue streams must become fully reliable. Special incentives, such as tax breaks for infrastructure investment, can help at the margins, but private investment on the scale envisioned will require that a significant portion of the urban infrastructure 'industry' be placed on a routinely profitable basis, supported by service charges.

Notes

1. In China, the term 'local' is commonly used to describe all sub-national units of government. In this chapter, 'local' refers to sub-provincial units, including municipalities, townships and counties.
2. Local governments are technically prohibited from borrowing. Borrowing is done on their behalf by special enterprises wholly owned by the local government, called urban development and investment companies (UDICs), which are the juridical holders of all local development assets and liabilities. However, these companies execute municipal government policy, report to the municipal government and are owned by the municipal government. Banks typically require a municipal 'comfort letter' backing UDIC loans. This states that the municipal government will do whatever it can to ensure that the UDIC is able to repay its loans.
3. Exchange rate used is $1 = Yuan 8.23.

References

Budget Department, Ministry of Finance, People's Republic of China (ed.). 2003. *China's Inter-Governmental Fiscal Relationship*. Beijing: China Fiscal and Economic Press.

Chen Yuan. 2005. 'Development Financing and China's Urbanization', Shanghai: China Development Bank. www.cdb.com.cn/english/NewsInfo.asp?NewsID=1174. Accessed in March 2006.

China Investment Academy. 2004–2005. 'Study on Establishing Financing Platform for Urban Infrastructure', No. 157.

———. 2004–2005. 'The Research on the Innovation of Financing Mechanism for Urbanization', No. 164.

Construction Industry of China. 2002. *Study on Urban Infrastructure Investment and Finance in China.* Beijing: Construction Industry of China.

Fu Tao. 2004. 'Local Credit Systems for Urban Environmental Infrastructure in China'. Paper Prepared for OECD.

Ming Su and Quanhou Zhao. 2004. 'China's Fiscal Decentralization'. Paper Presented at the International Symposium on Fiscal Decentralization in Asia Revisited, 20–21 February, Hitotsubashi University, Tokyo.

National Bureau of Statistics, China. 1995–2004. *China Statistic Yearbook.* China Statistics Press.

Wang, Y.X., Z. Fang, M. Ji, J.L. Huang and L. Tan. 2003. 'A Study on the Multi-Channel Investment in China: Urban Environmental Infrastructure Construction in China'. Report of the Task Force on Financial Mechanisms for Environmental Protection, CCICED (China Council for International Cooperation on Environment and Development).

World Bank. 1994. *World Development Report 1994:Infrastructure for Development.* New York: Oxford University Press.

Xie Fuzhan. 2004. 'Speeding Up City Infrastructure Development Should Have a Sense of Urgency'. *Chinese Economic Times,* 23 December. www.china.org.cn/chinese/OP-c/466537. htm.

Zhang Rufei. 2005. 'Shanghai Case Study, Report Prepared for Fiscal Systems and Subnational Growth Project.' World Bank. Unpublished Manuscript.

3

Overview of Urban Infrastructure Finance in India

Subhash Chandra Garg[*]

Introduction

India has a large urban population of 300 million living in 3,700 urban areas, including 27 million-plus cities. While urban local bodies have been in existence for a long time, the Constitution allocates primary responsibility for urban infrastructure in India to the states. The municipal tier has very Limited Resource Raising authority and can provide only those services that are delegated to them by the states. A separate list of subjects for the municipalities was incorporated into the Constitution in the 1990s, but it was left to the states to decide which of these functions to delegate. Not much delegation has since taken place. Consequently, the responsibility for urban infrastructure still lies mainly with the states. Municipal bodies depend upon the states for the assignment of taxation powers, and fiscal transfers (including loans), and resort to market borrowing (albeit in a few cases), largely with state guarantee, for infrastructure responsibilities that are allocated to them. The tradition of levying user charges to cover even operating costs for infrastructure services has not yet developed in the country.

[*]Subhash Chandra Garg served as Joint Secretary (State Finance), Department of Expenditure, Ministry of Finance, Government of India.

A study conducted by the Twelfth Finance Commission (TFC) reported that municipalities' share in own taxes is around 3 per cent and their total revenue is less than 0.75 per cent of GDP. The fiscal situation of states is also quite precarious, with their aggregate revenue deficit amounting to over 2 per cent of GDP for several years now, leaving little room for capital expenditure. All of these factors have contributed to low expenditure on the provision of urban infrastructure. The states have felt resource-constrained to do so either on their own or through municipal bodies. Low Private-Sector investment demand, observed since 2000, has re-emerged in 2005, enabling governments to run large fiscal deficits without any visible crowding-out effect. In fact, interest rates have decreased and banks are regularly lending to the Central Bank in reverse repos. The financial position of the municipalities is not consolidated and made available in the public domain.

Increasing urbanization and income in urban areas, on account of greater service-sector incomes, have raised the demand for larger and better quality infrastructure networks. Completing fiscal consolidation, restructuring state governments' finances and defining a clear role for the municipalities, with financial empowerment, are essential to meet this demand. The states have not been, in general, very keen to delegate the responsibility of providing urban infrastructure and other services to the municipal bodies.

The Government of India has initiated some measures and schemes for fiscal reform and consolidation at both the state and municipal levels. The TFC has also recommended an incentive-based policy reform initiative to encourage the states to adopt fiscal responsibility laws.

Given the general reluctance of the states to grant authority and functions to municipal bodies, it is necessary for the centre to take a more proactive role. The centre can either create incentives for states to delegate the Constitutional mandate to municipalities and make them financially strong or introduce another Constitutional amendment for granting legislative and executive authority to municipalities, like the states have, with an independent list of subjects and assignment of specific taxes.

India, still predominantly rural, has a larger urban population than the entire population of the United States. With urban India growing at double the rate of rural India, the demand for urban services and infrastructure is expected to increase quite sharply in the years to come. Out of the total population of 1.027 billion as on 1 March 2001, 285 million—150 million males and 135 million females—were living in urban areas. This reflects an increase of 70 million (from 216 million to 285 million) or 31.2 per cent within a decade. Statewise details of urban, rural and total population, divided into male and female, are provided in Annexure 3.1.

There are 27 cities which were over the 1 million population mark as per Census 2001.[1] There were 35 such urban agglomerations when municipal and rural areas in the urban agglomeration limits of the cities were also considered. These 27 million-plus cities are located across 13 states and union territories, with a combined population of 7.3 million, which is 25.6 per cent of the total urban population of the country. The Municipal Corporation of Greater Mumbai is the most populous in the country, with 11.9 million people, accounting for 16.3 per cent of the total population of the 'million-plus' cities in the country. It is followed respectively by the Delhi Municipal Corporation with 9.8 million people (13.4 per cent) and the Kolkata Municipal Corporation with 4.6 million people (6.3 per cent). At the state level, Maharashtra has the largest number of 1 million-plus cities (seven of them)—Greater Mumbai, Pune, Nagpur, Thane, Kalyan-Dombivili, Nashik and Pimprichinchwad—and accounts for 28.8 per cent of the total population of 1 million-plus cities. Uttar Pradesh, the most populous state in the country, has only five such cities—Kanpur, Lucknow, Agra, Varanasi and Meerut—that account for 11.2 per cent of the population in the 1 million-plus cities.

The highest decadal growth of population among these 1 million-plus cities was recorded for Pimprichinchwad Municipal Corporation (94.6 per cent) in Maharashtra. The lowest growth, of 4.1 per cent, was observed in the Kolkata Municipal Corporation in West Bengal. Among these 27 cities, Chennai registered the highest sex ratio,[2] of 951 as per Census 2001. Ludhiana is at the bottom, with a sex ratio of 766, preceded by Surat with 774.

Census India follows a different classification system for identifying urban areas. There are more than 5,000 urban areas in the country in terms of the census. However, urban areas organized in any of the forms of urban corporatized entities are over 3,700, organized into 109 municipal corporations, 1,432 municipal councils and over 2,100 Nagar Panchayats, i.e., city 'rural bodies'.

States Have Primary Responsibility for Urban Infrastructure

Urban infrastructure in India is primarily the responsibility of the state governments as per the Constitution. Legislative authority in relation to most types of urban infrastructure is vested in the state governments. Please refer to Annexure 3.2 for the list of urban infrastructure subjects allocated to the states. Vesting of legislative authority in state governments makes them responsible for creating the legal framework. Executive authority in India is co-terminal with legislative authority. This makes state governments responsible for deciding whether these infrastructure services are provided by the state itself, municipalities, specialized local bodies created by state governments, the private sector (directly or in public–private partnerships) or through a combination of the foregoing mechanisms. The duty to ensure that the legislative and executive frameworks and structures created take care of the legitimate interests of both the suppliers of services and the consumers thereof is cast upon the state governments.

Local government in India is also a subject assigned to the states under Entry Five of the State List (GOI). The entry is as under:

Local government, that is to say, the Constitution and powers of municipal corporations, improvement trusts, districts boards, mining settlement authorities, and other local authorities for the purpose of local self-government or village administration.

The 74th Amendment to the Constitution in 1992 sought to bring about a major change in the institutional arrangements for urban local governments by developing a sound political and institutional framework for municipal bodies. Additionally, the amendment sought to create a guiding framework for state governments to empower municipalities in their states by incorporating a list of 18 subjects or functions under the Twelfth Schedule of the Constitution for transfer to them under Article 243W. These 18 subjects describe all functions that modern and fully empowered city municipalities should undertake—namely, urban planning; regulation of land use and the construction of buildings, roads and bridges; water supply for domestic, industrial and commercial purposes; public health, sanitation, conservation and solid waste management; fire services; protection of the urban environment; slum improvement and upgradation; provision of urban amenities and facilities such as parks, gardens, playgrounds and public amenities (including street lighting, parking lots, bus stops and public conveniences). However, it is still entirely up to the state governments to empower the municipalities in their states to perform any or all of these functions, as Article 243W, in line with Entry Five of the State List of the Seventh Schedule, requires a law to be passed by the legislature of a state to endow municipalities with powers and responsibilities with respect to the performance of functions enumerated in the Twelfth Schedule and implementation of other schemes as may be entrusted to them, including those in relation to matters listed in the Twelfth Schedule.

The states are primarily responsible for the provision of and/or for the creation of the necessary legal and regulatory framework for private provision of urban infrastructure in India. There are some types of infrastructure that are the responsibility of the central government, such as airports and 'urban railways'. States may choose to entrust a part or most of the responsibility to their urban bodies or deliver the services directly through their own departments and agencies, or even create agencies for specific areas and functions.

Limited Resource Raising Authority of Urban Bodies

All taxation powers on the usual urban tax bases, as listed in Annexure 3.2, are vested in the state governments. State legislatures can, however, empower municipalities to levy, collect and appropriate such taxes, duties, tolls and fees, in accordance with such procedures and subject to such limits as the legislature may decide. Similarly, the legislature of a state is empowered to assign taxes, duties, tolls and fees levied and collected by state governments and to make such grants-in-aid from the Consolidated Fund of the state. Thus, whether a municipality would have any taxation power with respect to any of the local tax bases mentioned above depends entirely on state governments. The state legislatures can transfer the power to tax any of these tax bases to municipalities in the broadest sense, i.e., both in terms of defining the tax base and of deciding the rate of taxation. The state legislature can also confer the power to tax in different degrees, i.e., in a different mix of levying authority, collection authority and appropriation authority. The same applies to non-tax revenues such as duties, tolls and fees. In short, the fiscal domain of local bodies is entirely in the hands of state legislatures.

Under the Constitution, the legislatures of states will also make provision by law for the maintenance of accounts by municipalities and the auditing of such accounts. Consequent to the 74th Amendment, the Constitution provides for a finance commission to be established at the state level every five years to review the financial position of municipalities and to make recommendations to the state governor in the following matters:

1. Distribution between the state and municipalities of the net proceeds of the taxes, duties, tolls and fees leviable by the state and the allocation between the municipalities at all levels of their respective shares of such proceeds;

2. determination of taxes, duties, tolls and fees that may be assigned to or appropriated by municipalities; and
3. grants-in-aid to Panchayats[3] and municipalities from the Consolidated Fund of the state.

The commission is also required to discharge the same duties in respect of Panchayats. Municipal bodies are empowered to charge for the services they deliver, including charges for the use of the municipalities' assets by private persons. Additionally, municipal authorities may borrow from financial institutions and banks or raise resources from the capital markets, subject only to the provisions of a state's municipal legislation. There is no Constitutional bar on municipalities borrowing outside the territory of India, as is the case with the state governments under Article 293 of the Constitution. This article does not apply to municipalities and, furthermore, there is no such disabling provision in Part IX of the Constitution, dealing with urban local bodies. Municipal bodies may also take loans from banks since they are corporate bodies (there are regulatory restrictions on bank loans to state governments, but not on municipalities).

Municipal Political Framework in Place, but not Empowerment

As per the Constitution, it is mandatory to constitute municipal bodies, i.e., city Panchayats, municipal councils and municipal corporations, depending upon whether an urban area is in transition from rural to urban habitation or on the size of the area. In instances where industrial establishments provide urban services, the Constitution excludes such industrial townships from municipal bodies. The Constitution also provides for district and metropolitan-area planning bodies, but their jurisdiction is mainly limited to producing plans for the development of the entire area for which such bodies have coordination responsibilities, and are confined to the functions that a state legislature entrusts to municipalities.

It has been more than a decade since the 74th Constitutional Amendment was enacted. However, a uniform model of empowering or entrusting urban infrastructure functions to municipal bodies has yet to emerge in India. Thus, the various states continue to follow different models. In some states, municipalities are entrusted with only the very basic and traditional functions of maintenance of birth and death records, street cleanliness and lighting, and that too without any fiscal empowerment. State-government departments continue to provide the majority of urban services and are responsible for urban infrastructure directly or through undertakings under their control, such as water and sewerage boards. Some states, such as Tamil Nadu, Maharashtra and Gujarat, entrust certain municipal infrastructure and urban services such as water supply, primary education, bus services and electricity to municipal bodies. Almost all states have separate institutional arrangements for area development within municipal limits, or wider urban agglomeration limits for a city.

Mumbai has two specialized area development agencies: the Mumbai Metropolitan Region Development Authority (MMRDA) for Bandra–Kurla and the City and Industrial Development Corporation (CIDCO) for New Mumbai. Mumbai also has a separate development agency for roads, the Maharashtra Roads Development Corporation (MRDC), and a separate development agency, the Mumbai Rail Vikas Corporation (MVRC), for railroad transport. Delhi has a separate Delhi Development Authority (DDA) for area development. Non-metropolitan major cities have urban development authorities or urban improvement trusts. Additionally, the development of sub-cities is entrusted to para-state boards or corporations in most states. Rajasthan, for example, has a housing board, Haryana has the Haryana Urban Development Authority (HUDA), Andhra Pradesh has the AP Housing Development Corporation (APHDC), Maharashtra has the Mumbai Housing and Area Development Authority (MHADA), and so on. In some major cities, specialized urban SPVs were created before and after the 74th Constitutional Amendment, such as the Chennai Metropolitan Water Authority (CMWA) for water supply in Chennai or the Delhi Jal Nigam (DJN) in Delhi.

Electricity supply in municipal areas exhibits all the models present today. The Brihanmumbai Electric Supply and Transport Undertaking (BEST), a part of the Mumbai Municipal Corporation (MMC), supplies electricity to the island city; Delhi has four private distribution licensees; the rest of Mumbai as well as Surat and Kolkata have old private licensees continuing to provide electrical services; and in most other urban areas, state electricity boards or corporations provide electricity services.

Very little additional empowerment of municipal bodies consequent upon the 74th Constitutional Amendment has been observed in the country so far. The Ministry of Urban Development and Poverty Alleviation has developed a model municipal law to assist states with much-needed reform to their existing municipal laws in order to establish strong local governance and service delivery organizations in cities. The model law seeks to classify municipal functions into three categories: core functions, which include water supply, drainage and sewerage, solid waste management and roads; functions assigned by the government; and other functions. The model law also provides for establishing a State Municipal Regulatory Commission that will determine user charges and standards for services and will suggest avenues for Private-Sector participation. The model law has thus far not been acted upon by any state.

Government Sector and Municipal Finance in India

Healthy Growth of the Economy and Reasonable Savings Rates

The Indian economy has grown at a healthy average rate of over 6 per cent for more than two decades. In particular, the service sector has been reporting robust growth rates, as reflected by the figures in Table 3.1.

The majority of service-sector GDP originates in urban areas and goes to the factors of production residing in urban areas. A decade of high service-sector growth in India has considerably increased the size of the urban middle-class and is reflected in their consumption expenditure, especially on motor cars and means of communication. The consequence is a massive spurt in demand for urban infrastructure. Infrastructure services that are in the private sector—such as telecommunications—are expanding quite rapidly and adequately to meet this upsurge in demand. Services with adequate competition—e.g., banking—are also growing at a good rate. However, urban infrastructure services that are essentially managed by the government or municipal sector—such as water, electricity, sewerage and roads—have not responded to the growing demand, either in terms of quantity or in terms of quality of service.

India's gross domestic savings are reasonably healthy at 24 per cent, but the public sector continues to be a net dissaver. Public sector dissavings peaked at –2.7 per cent of GDP at market prices in 2001–02. Household savings are quite robust at over 22.5 per cent. Households are, however, increasing their savings in physical assets to a greater extent than in financial assets. Increasing dissavings by the public sector, coupled with the fact that households are also investing more of their savings in physical assets, has

Table 3.1
Growth Rates of the Indian Economy

Sector	1996–97	1997–98	1998–99	1999–2000	2000–01	2001–02 (Provisional)	2002–03 (Quick)	2003–04 (Advance)
GDP at factor cost	7.8	4.8	6.5	6.1	4.4	5.8	4.0	8.1
Industry	7.1	4.3	3.7	4.8	6.5	3.4	6.4	6.5
Services, of which	7.2	9.8	8.4	10.1	5.5	6.8	7.1	8.4
1. Trade, hotels, transport and communications	7.8	7.8	7.7	8.5	6.8	8.7	7.0	10.9
2. Financial services	7.0	11.6	7.4	10.6	3.5	4.5	8.8	6.4
3. Community, social and personal services	6.3	11.7	10.4	12.2	5.2	5.6	5.8	5.9

Source: GOI (2003–2004).

brought down the financial savings available for investments. The gross domestic investment rate of the public sector has decreased notably from 7.7 per cent of GDP in 1995–96 to 5.7 per cent in 2002–03, further affecting infrastructure investments, along with capital expenditure in the public sector. Further details on savings and investments are given in Table 3.2.

Another notable macroeconomic change is that India is no longer a capital-deficient country as there is more domestic savings than investment. India had a positive savings–investment gap of 0.3 per cent and 0.9 per cent of GDP in the fiscal years 2001–02 and 2002–03. The same trend is likely to continue in the fiscal years 2003–04 and 2004–05.[4]

General Government Finance Presents Grim Fiscal Situation

The consolidated position of general government finance in India is summed up in Annexure 3.3. Some noteworthy features are:

1. Tax receipts have hovered around 15 per cent of GDP at market prices, for the centre and states together, with central government tax receipts accounting for 9 per cent of GDP and the remaining 6 per cent being directly collected by the state governments. After tax transfers from the centre to the states, the share of the states in the total tax revenues increases marginally, to over 8 per cent, whereas the central government's share decreases to a little less than 7 per cent.

2. Non-tax receipts for the combined general government are around 4 per cent of GDP. The central government's non-tax revenues approximate 2.7 per cent of GDP, while the states' non-tax revenues—inclusive of grant transfers from the centre—are approximately 3.5 per cent of GDP.

3. Total general government revenue, at approximately 19 per cent of GDP, is grossly inadequate to support the general government expenditure of approximately 30 per cent of GDP. After accounting for receipts from the recovery of debts and other non debt-creating capital receipts such as disinvestment receipts, the general government's fiscal deficit has been around 10 per cent of GDP for the past several years.

4. The general government's consolidated expenditure of around 30 per cent of GDP is largely revenue expenditure. Revenue expenditure of governments at both central and state levels is approximately

Table 3.2
Public and Private Savings and Investment in India

	1995–96	1996–97	1997–98	1998–99	1999–2000	2000–01	2001–02	2002–03
Gross domestic savings	25.1	23.2	23.1	21.5	24.2	23.7	23.5	24.2
Public	2.0	1.7	1.3	–1.0	–1.0	–2.3	–2.7	–1.9
Private-household, of which	18.2	17.0	17.6	18.8	20.9	21.9	22.7	22.6
Financial	8.9	10.4	9.6	10.4	10.6	10.7	11.1	10.3
Physical	9.3	6.7	8.0	8.4	10.3	11.3	11.6	12.3
Gross domestic investment	26.9	24.5	24.6	22.6	25.3	24.4	23.1	23.3
Public	7.7	7.0	6.6	6.6	6.9	6.3	5.8	5.7

Source: GOI (2003–2004).

25 per cent of GDP, with state governments together making revenue-expenditure disbursements of around 14 per cent. The central government's expenditure is around 13 per cent, but 11 per cent of GDP if transfers to states are excluded.

5. The revenue deficit at the aggregate level accounts for more than two-thirds of the fiscal deficit, leaving very little for capital expenditure. As the general government provision of loans and advances is at 1 per cent of GDP, on an average, the capital expenditure by both levels of government is only around 3.5 per cent of GDP. The general government's capital expenditure in India in 2002–03 was only Rs 880 billion.[5]

6. The state governments in India collect 40 per cent of the taxes, but have a 56 per cent share in the revenue expenditure of the general government and 58 per cent of the total government expenditure.

The fiscal position of the states was reasonably comfortable when India embarked on market economy reforms in 1991, with the states running a nominal revenue deficit and a gross fiscal deficit of about 3 per cent. Deregulation of interest rates in the economy, coupled with the GOI's decision to stop borrowing from the Reserve Bank of India directly, led to a massive increase in rates of interest from the middle of the 1990s. Consequently, the interest burden for the states started rising.

The continued fascination of the states with increasing plan sizes—in terms of expansion of existing scale and introduction of new services—forced them to borrow more, despite increasing interest rates. As most of the additional plan expenditure was of a revenue nature—expansion of schooling, poverty reduction, employment expenditures, etc.—expenditure growth continued to outpace revenue growth. The finances of the states received the sharpest shock when states decided to grant hefty pay increases to their employees along the lines of the pay increases granted by the central government to employees in 1996–97. By the end of the 1990s, the states confronted an unsustainable situation, with their fiscal deficit at 4.72 per cent and revenue deficit at 2.79 per cent of GDP in 1999–2000.

The worsening fiscal position of the states affected the municipalities adversely. To add to their woes, octroi abolition also picked up pace in the 1990s. Compensatory grants to offset the abolition of octroi had a buoyancy of less than 1. Pay Commission benefits were also extended to municipalities in most of the states. Deteriorating state finances, along with a variety of other political and non-political factors, ensured that the states did not provide any notable increases in either the assignment of taxes or in the sharing of taxes with municipalities or in terms of providing enhanced grants, even after the 74th Constitutional Amendment came into effect. Consequently, municipal expenditures relative to GDP remained at less than 0.85 per cent of GDP. The states tried to escape the constraints of fiscal deficits by providing guarantees to their corporations and municipalities to borrow directly from financial institutions, which many did. However, as most of these borrowings were for financially non-viable projects, the GOI and the Reserve Bank of India tightened the regulatory regime to contain the same. In sum, the worsening fiscal position of the states in the 1990s led to a major reduction in infrastructure spending at both state and municipal levels.

Low Private-Sector Investment Demand since 2000

As the combined government is running a deficit of around 10 per cent of GDP, most of the financial savings are pre-empted by the general government. There has been a lack of investment demand from the private sector since around 2000. This has enabled the government to not only finance their deficits easily, but there has been a sharp reduction in interest rates also. The yields on government borrowings eased out by as much as 3 per cent in the last two years. Corporates have also been able to refinance most of their debts at lower rates and raise new finances at low spreads to government paper. There has not been any evidence of crowding out in the last three years.

Municipalities' Financial Position not Available in a Consolidated Account

The accounts of local bodies in India are not consolidated at either the state or national level. While a common accounting framework exists for the centre and the states, there are no common standards for account maintenance at the local level. Therefore, the consolidated finance position for the general government is only available for the central and state governments. However, even at the central and state levels, consolidation is possible only for the Consolidated Funds of the centre and the states. The transactions in the public accounts of the states and the centre, and their non-commercial enterprises, remain unconsolidated. The Auditor and Comptroller General of India appointed a task force to recommend a system of accounting and budgeting for local bodies, following the recommendations of the

Eleventh Finance Commission (EFC) in this regard. The recommendations outlined in the task force's report have been generally agreed to be implemented by the states, but the pace of adoption of the recommendations has varied.

Accumulated Debts and Liabilities Constrain Infrastructure Financing

Large deficits have led to large debt stocks. The central government's liabilities, at Rs 17.2 trillion at the end of 2003–04 have crossed 60 per cent of GDP. State governments' outstanding debt stocks have crossed 30 per cent of GSDP. Inclusive of their guaranteed obligations, the same crossed 37 per cent of GDP at the end of 2003–04. Crossing out central government loans and NSSF liabilities, the aggregate central and state liabilities are over 80 per cent of GDP.

A large part of the true revenue base[6] of the states is being spent on meeting interest obligations and retirement payments. If we classify[7] the states on the basis of the percentage of their true revenue base used for currently unproductive payments of interest and pensions, the statewise position as it emerges on the basis of 2002–03 and 2003–04 figures is presented in Annexure 3.4. Almost half the states use more than 50 per cent of their true revenue base for meeting these liabilities and there is no state in the 'debt stress-free' category.

In summary, general government finances in India are quite precarious. Governments at the central and state levels are running large revenue deficits, and fiscal deficits at atrociously high levels near 10 per cent are chiefly financing these revenue deficits. In addition, there are several new and competing demands on government revenues, which will perhaps require more debt financing. There is a commitment from the current government to bring in employment guarantee legislation. The National Common Minimum Programme's (NCMP) implementation cost has been variously assessed. Most of the NCMP projects are meant for rural areas. In such a situation, expecting state governments to increase their outlay on urban infrastructure dramatically (to meet large-scale requirements) would be quite unrealistic.

Meagre Taxation Resources of Municipalities

The municipal system in India acquired a definite personality for the first time when Lord Ripon adopted a resolution in 1882 to grant non-official majorities in all municipalities which provided for a non-official chairman in place of the district collector. Additional functions also devolved on the municipalities. The Government of India Act, 1919, broadened the scope of municipal taxation to include tolls, a land tax, a tax on buildings, a tax on vehicles and boats, a tax on menial and domestic servants, a tax on animals, octroi, a terminal tax, a tax on trade, professions and callings, a tax on the private market, and a tax on municipal services such as water supply, lighting, drainage and public conveniences. However, the Government of India Act, 1935, drastically altered the position and provided a structure that was later adopted by the Constitution and is, by and large, prevalent to this day. The subject of local self-government was assigned to the states and they were empowered to take decisions on taxation and other financial powers of municipalities, besides deciding which functions to assign to municipalities. The position has not been significantly altered by the 1992 Constitutional Amendment, except by bringing some more moral suasion on states to empower municipalities.

The various states in India have followed different practices with respect to endowing municipal bodies with taxation powers, as we shall now discuss.

Octroi Has Been Generally Abolished

Octroi has been the principal revenue source for most municipal bodies in India. However, very legitimate concerns regarding the deleterious effect of octroi collection processes has caused octroi to be perceived as a harmful tax, and therefore resulted in its abolition in most states. Andhra Pradesh was the first state to abolish octroi as far back as 1966, followed by Madhya Pradesh in 1976 and Karnataka in 1979. In the late 1980s, only the states of Gujarat, Goa, Haryana, Himachal Pradesh, Jammu and Kashmir, Maharashtra, Nagaland, Orissa, Punjab, Rajasthan and Uttar Pradesh were levying octroi. Presently, Maharashtra,[8] Punjab, Orissa, Manipur, Goa and Gujarat allow municipalities to levy octroi, with others having abolished the same in the 1990s. Punjab has also decided to abolish octroi, but this decision was recently overturned by the Supreme Court. The Gujarat government has also decided to abolish octroi in principle. Some states—such as Rajasthan, Uttar Pradesh, Karnataka and Madhya Pradesh—'compensate' municipalities for the loss of octroi revenues in different measures by collecting entry tax or surcharge on sales tax or simply a share from their revenues.

Property Tax Is the Principal Source of Tax Revenues

In principle, all states allow municipalities to collect property tax on houses and commercial buildings, although the tax base, tax rates and method of assessment are determined by state legislatures. Kerala, Tamil Nadu and Rajasthan levy additional land and building tax or property tax in specified cities, in addition to permitting municipalities to collect property tax, although receipts from this tax are very small. Kerala receives a revenue of approximately Rs 300 million, Rajasthan approximately Rs 250 million and Tamil Nadu Rs 150 million annually from this source. The land and building tax has now been abolished in Rajasthan. Property tax, a classical local tax, is the only tax in India that can be described as a municipal tax, though much of the policy decisions and legislation for this tax is also in the states' hands.

Profession Tax Is Mostly Levied by States or not at All

The Constitution permits states and their authorized municipalities to collect profession taxes not exceeding Rs 2,500 per annum on professions, callings, trades and occupations. As many as 16 states are levying and collecting the profession tax themselves. Six states do not levy or allow their municipalities to levy and collect profession tax. Only six states—Goa, Haryana, Kerala, Madhya Pradesh, Maharashtra and Uttar Pradesh—have assigned tax proceeds or allowed their municipal bodies to collect and appropriate the profession tax. The states were budgeted to collect an amount of Rs 37.7 billion from profession tax in the fiscal year 2003–04, as against the previous years' collections of Rs 30 billion and Rs 32.9 billion respectively.

Entertainment and Advertisement Taxes Levied and Collected by State Governments; Some Share Passed on to Municipalities as Grants

Entertainment tax is levied by all states except Kerala and four small states in the north-east. Kerala permits this tax to be collected by local bodies. Some states, such as Uttar Pradesh and Chattisgarh, transfer a part of their entertainment tax revenues to local bodies.

Minor Taxes/Non-Taxes Assigned to Urban Bodies

Minor taxes such as water tax, lighting tax, animal tax, boat tax and toll tax have been assigned to municipalities in many states.

State Finance Commissions' Different Approaches for Devolution of Taxes to Urban Bodies

A statement of tax receipts from property tax, professions tax and entertainment tax for the states (not municipalities) is provided in Annexure 3.5.

As finance can only follow the entrustment of functions, the SFCs have felt constrained by the fact that the states have not transferred functions and schemes to municipalities in accordance with the letter and spirit of the 74th Constitutional Amendment and Twelfth Schedule. Thus, SFCs have mainly followed a slow and incremental approach to enhancing the resources of municipalities. The recommendations of the SFCs have also not been treated as having the same authority and importance as those of the Central Finance Commission (CFC), resulting in the failure of most states in implementing their recommendations.

The first set of SFCs appointed by the states used different approaches for tax devolution to urban bodies and allocated different shares to urban bodies, largely reflecting the current state of municipal empowerment in respective states. Assam and Andhra Pradesh provide examples of SFCs that have used the widest definitions for determining the share of the municipalities. These two SFCs, along with Goa, used 'total revenues of the state' as the divisible pool, whereas many states (such as Kerala, Madhya Pradesh, Uttar Pradesh and the second Andhra Pradesh SFC) used 'own revenues of the state' for determining the share of local bodies. The narrowest definition (of 'states own taxes') was used by Tamil Nadu and West Bengal. Karnataka's SFC used 'non-loan own revenue' as the basis. The share of the divisible pool so defined allocated to municipalities and rural local bodies varied substantially across the states, but most SFCs recommended very small shares. The share of urban local bodies has reflected the share of the urban population in that state, with the highest share of 42 per cent being recommended by the SFC of Tamil Nadu.

As mentioned earlier, the SFCs have not acquired the respect and acceptability which the CFC has been able to command. Almost all the financial recommendations of the CFC have usually been accepted by the central government, even when the CFC proposed drastic changes. However, the states have moved slowly, if not at all, in implementing the recommendations of the SFCs. A major reason for this is that the SFCs have been considered by many states to be extensions of their administrative machinery. These commissions have not been staffed with persons of eminence in most cases.

An amendment to Article 280 of the Constitution in 1992 provides for CFCs to recommend measures for augmenting the consolidated funds of the states in order to manage additional financial resources required for implementing the recommendations of the SFCs. The states have tried to use this provision to shift the cost of functions transferred to municipalities for persuading the EFC—the second central commission after the Constitutional Amendment of 1992—to recommend additional grants from the centre to the states for covering the cost of these functions.[9] The EFC did not agree and argued that transfer of functions, functionaries and finances does not translate into additional costs as the additional financial requirement of local bodies consequent upon transfer would provide corresponding savings to the states in direct expenditure.

Government of India (GOI) Grants Transferred via State Governments

The central government provides grants for urban local bodies based on the recommendations of the EFC. For the five-year period 2000–05, the EFC recommended an annual grant of Rs 4 billion for urban local bodies, totalling Rs 20 billion. Concerned about the non-availability of fiscal data for local bodies, the EFC recommended that a database on the finances of municipalities be developed at the district, state and central levels. Data would be made easily accessible electronically, and computer systems with this data would be linked. Work has commenced on this initiative, for which the EFC has earmarked Rs 29.3 million. The TFC has continued with the grant framework of the EFC.[10] A total grant of Rs 50 billion has been recommended for urban local bodies. These grants are untied, except that a certain portion is earmarked for urban local bodies of cities with a population of more than 100,000, which will be used to encourage urban sanitation projects implemented through public–private partnerships.

State Government Grants Are Multiple but Nominal

There are three primary ways in which state governments transfer grant resources to municipal bodies: compensation in lieu of octroi, block grants for general purposes and grants for specific purposes.

User Charges and Public–Private Partnerships

Constrained by the abolition of octroi and limited revenues from other tax sources, some municipalities have started levying user charges. *Urban Finance*, a quarterly newsletter of the National Institute of Urban Affairs (2004), has reported innovative user charge levies—such as the Pay and Park Scheme of the Bangalore Municipal Corporation, where fees are based on the duration of parking, as well as an 'eco fee' for people using the municipal gardens. The Delhi Government is planning to impose a 'pollution cess' on industries operating in the capital, to generate funds to implement anti-pollution and environment-related programmes. Municipalities have started focusing on conservation and solid-waste management projects using the public–private partnership model, while the TFC has earmarked a part of urban local bodies' grants for developing urban sanitation projects along similar lines as well.

GOI Measures for Fiscal Reform and Consolidation at State and Municipal Levels

The states in India are free to borrow on the strength of their Consolidated Fund within limits, if any, fixed by their legislatures. As none of the state legislatures have passed laws placing any type of limit on borrowing, the states have very little statutory fiscal discipline. With no laws pertaining to balanced budgets either, the states can borrow for revenue expenditure as well. The institutional interface between the GOI and the states also encourages fiscal indiscipline. States are required to get their annual plans approved from the Planning Commission. Equating increasing plan expenditures with increasing investments, the Planning Commission used to be quite happy to encourage states to borrow progressively larger amounts. Since suppliers of loan funds to states were banks and financial institutions owned by the GOI, the states had no difficulty in obtaining loans from them, irrespective of their fiscal situation. The GOI also became a large direct supplier of plan loans to states. These loans, coupled as they were with grants, contributed to the build-up of state debt. Thus, while the GOI was constitutionally charged with the responsibility of seeing that the states did not borrow indiscriminately, its institutional set-up and lending practices facilitated the build-up of state debt. By the late 1990s, however, the situation had got out of hand, with the accumulated debt of the states crossing 30 per cent of GDP and interest payments consuming about one-fourth of their own revenues.

When the GOI finally woke up to this situation, it initiated several measures to help states consolidate their finances and reduce their fiscal deficits.

Fiscal Reforms Facility

The Fiscal Reforms Facility was launched in 2000 to encourage states to reduce their revenue deficits. States were promised grants if they brought about a 5 per cent reduction in the ratio of their revenue deficits to their revenue receipts within a year and 25 per cent over a five-year period, coinciding with the award period of the EFC. Rs 106 billion was provided in the incentive fund created for this purpose. The experience during the last four years has been quite mixed, with states having on average succeeded in reducing the ratio of revenue deficit to revenue receipts from 26 per cent to 22 per cent only by March 2004. More than 50 per cent of the states could claim incentives for all or some years, and more than Rs 50 billion was disbursed as incentives. A few states' fiscal indicators also deteriorated. A system of medium-term fiscal frameworks was instituted as part of this facility.

Cap On Borrowing by States

In 2002–03, the GOI started using its authority to put in place an arrangement to control the overall borrowings of states. Although a debt sustainability analysis was conducted for determining the states' borrowing limits, the overall borrowing ceilings decided by the GOI brought down the growth rate of state debt to less than 5 per cent in nominal terms. By 2004, five states had passed their own fiscal responsibility legislation, providing for restrictions on fiscal deficit and elimination of revenue deficits over a defined period of time. The government needs to refine its system of capping borrowings and bring them in line with the fiscal deficit constraint recommended by the TFC.

Debt Swap and Other Measures

In 2002, the GOI initiated a measure to help states swap costlier GOI loans by accessing cheaper market and small-savings loans. The states' debt of over Rs 1 trillion was swapped under this arrangement, bringing down interest costs to the states by about Rs 50 billion per annum, i.e., 0.15 per cent of GDP. The states have also been encouraged to swap costlier institutional loans and have been offered the option to discontinue GOI loans in exchange for market loans. All these measures are expected to result in state borrowing becoming more market-oriented.

Discontinuance of Loans from the Centre

The GOI, acting on the recommendations of the TFC, has discontinued the practice of providing plan loans to states from the fiscal year 2005–06.

This has decoupled the centre's grants from loans. The GOI has been, in fact, very proactive in this respect. The TFC recommended a phased dismantling, whereas the GOI decided on a single swoop. The measure has been successfully implemented. This should lead to increased market orientation in the states' borrowing, as they will be required to raise their borrowing requirements from the market.

Fiscal Consolidation and Restructuring of State Governments' Finances Essential

The TFC has proposed a significant plan that has the potential to create fiscal discipline in the states and to provide additional resources for capital expenditure. This plan provides for consolidation of outstanding central government debts on the states at lower interest rates and waiver of debt servicing for the next five years. However, this is dependent on the states enacting fiscal responsibility laws, eliminating revenue deficits by 2008–09 and restraining fiscal deficits to 3 per cent of GSDP. If the states are successful in doing so, it should be possible to increase capital spending to 3 per cent of GSDP from the current level of less than 1.5 per cent, leading to greater investment in infrastructure. The states appear to be quite motivated by this incentive, as there has been a flurry of activity since the announcement. State after state is now passing fiscal responsibility laws. Buoyant revenues, reduced interest rates in the economy and the prospect of substantial debt relief by the centre should help in consolidation and restructuring of state finances. It is hoped that this will also encourage states to empower their municipal bodies.[11]

Current Arrangements for Financing Urban Infrastructure in India

Responsibility for Urban Infrastructure Services Across States and Municipalities

There is wide variation from state to state in the assignment of responsibility for urban infrastructure services. Additionally, there are variations amongst municipalities within a state, depending upon the class of municipality concerned. A comparison across states for six major kinds of urban infrastructure—water and sewerage; electrical services; bus services; area and roads development; development of new housing areas/sub-cities; cleanliness; and street lighting—is provided in Annexure 3.6.

Central Government Grants for Infrastructure Investments Are Small

The GOI runs several schemes for assisting states and municipalities to undertake infrastructure projects in urban areas. These schemes are either implemented as central plan schemes (including centrally sponsored schemes), with the Ministry of Urban Development and Ministry of Urban Employment and Poverty Alleviation as the implementing ministries, or in the state sector as central grants to states for their plan schemes. Central plan schemes include financing for the National Capital Region (NCR), integrated development of small and medium towns, infrastructural development of mega cities, urban water supply and sewerage, solid waste management near airports, hospital waste management, and resettlement of slums in Dharavi, a major slum in Mumbai. All these schemes have small outlays and the total allocation is quite small; in consequence the impact expected is also marginal. Table 3.3 presents actual expenditures during 2003–04 and revised expenditure for 2004–05, with budget outlays for 2005–06 on these schemes.

Table 3.3
Central Government Expenditure on Schemes for Urban Infrastructure in the Central Sector
In Rs Million

Scheme	2003–04(RE)[1]	2004–05(RE)[1]	2005–06(BE)[2]
National Capital Region (NCR)	500	550	700
Integrated development of small and medium towns	1,090	1,990	1,000
Infrastructural development of mega cities	1,200	2,200	1,500
Urban water supply and sewerage schemes	1,460	1,560	960
Solid waste management near airports	50	400	550
Hospital waste management			10

Table 3.3 continued

Table 3.3 continued

Scheme	2003–04(RE)[1]	2004–05(RE)[1]	2005–06(BE)[2]
Total	4,300	6,700	4,720
GDP at factor cost	25,197,850	28,304,650	31,710,210
Proportion of GDP (%)	0.0171	0.0237	0.0149
GOI's plan expenditure	1,315,900	1,373,870	1,720,000
Proportion of GOI's plan expenditure (%)	0.33	0.49	0.27
Grants for rural employment programmes	96,400	64,080	90,000
Urban programme grants as a proportion of grants for rural employment programmes (%)	4.46	10.45	5.24

Source: GOI (2005–2006): Table 3.
Notes: Exchange rate: Rs 44 per US$.
   1. RE: Revised estimate.
   2. BE: Budget estimate.

It is interesting that the GOI's investment in the Delhi Metro Corporation, at over Rs 30 billion, during these three years is larger than the outlays of all the above schemes put together. A brief description of the GOI schemes is presented in Annexure 3.7.

The GOI also had two programmes in the urban sector assisted as state plan schemes—the Slum Development Programme and the Urban Reforms Initiatives Fund (URIF) with total outlays of Rs 6.43 billion and Rs 1.5 billion respectively during 2004–05 (RE). Both these programmes have been replaced with a set of two recast Urban Renewal Missions on Slum Development and Infrastructure[12] and Transport, with enhanced outlays of Rs 19.89 billion and Rs 34.77 billion. These two programmes also subsume some of the programmes earlier implemented through the Ministry of Urban Development. These programmes, if properly developed, should be able to provide significant increases in urban spending on infrastructure.

Large Departmental Expenditures by States on Urban Services

State governments incur both capital and revenue expenditure on urban development, inclusive of urban water-supply schemes and housing. State expenditure directly on these services is quite large in comparison to what is provided as transfers to municipalities.

HUDCO as Primary National Financing Agency in Urban Infrastructure

The Housing and Urban Development Corporation (HUDCO), a 100-per cent central government-owned non-banking finance company, is a specialized financial institution that funds state governments and their specialized agencies such as housing boards and urban development corporations, as well as municipal bodies for urban infrastructure projects. In particular, HUDCO has been financing urban infrastructure projects in water and sewerage, roads, area development and housing in a big way.

HUDCO averaged new sanctions for the three-year period 1999–2002 at Rs 80 billion. New sanctions dramatically soared to Rs 156.3 billion. A major part of the new loans and other investments were in the area classified as urban infrastructure, at Rs 111.3 billion. HUDCO has sanctioned total assistance amounting to Rs 290.3 billion, classified under 'urban infrastructure', up to 2002–03 as per Table 3.4.

HUDCO has primarily financed state government agencies such as the housing boards and municipalities on the strength of state government guarantees. As much as Rs 171.5 billion of the loans outstanding on 31 March 2003, out of the total outstanding loans of Rs 215.4 billion, was given for various projects against state government or bank guarantees. Going by anecdotal evidence, most of these projects were financially non-viable and state governments would need to provide for their servicing from their budgets in times to come. In addition, HUDCO lent Rs 14.3 billion directly

Table 3.4
HUDCO's Financing for Infrastructure Projects
In Rs Million

Infrastructure segments	No. of projects		HUDCO assistance	
	2002–03	Cumulative	2002–03	Cumulative
Water supply	35	367	27,143.1	88,720.7
Sewerage, drainage and solid waste management	11	88	2,630.0	15,721.4
Transportation and roads	36	160	42,167.0	88,588.3
Area development	3	101	1,052.8	11,958.2
Social infrastructure	31	131	7,135.1	19,987.7
Others, including commercial	33	154	31,200.7	60,224.6
Sanitation	5	1034	14.1	5,128.6
Total	154	2035	111,342.8	290,329.5

Source: Balance sheets of HUDCO (2003).
Note: Exchange rate: Rs 44 per US$.

to state government departments. HUDCO was fully secured by way of mortgages for loans outstanding an amount of Rs 26.0 billion.

HUDCO raises finance from banks and the capital market, with most of its resources coming from the banking sector.

IDFC and ILFS Identify Urban Infrastructure as Their Principal Infrastructure Financing Area

The Infrastructure Development Finance Corporation (IDFC) has been set up by the central government with equity participation from the State Bank of India and others to finance infrastructure projects including urban infrastructure. Until the end of March 2004, IDFC's gross approvals for urban infrastructure for a total of 15 projects exceeded Rs 6.4 billion.[13] IDFC has disbursed Rs 660 million only and has a long way to go in developing its urban infrastructure portfolio.

The Infrastructure Leasing and Financial Services Limited (ILFS) is another major player in the infrastructure sector, which seeks to provide concept-to-end solutions for urban infrastructure projects. ILFS' present activities in the area of urban infrastructure include the development of projects in water supply and sanitation, solid waste management and traffic management, i.e., bus terminals, flyovers and parking areas. Additionally, ILFS offers services in implementing institutional capacity-building and financial strengthening, i.e., revenue enhancement measures, accounting practices, municipal rating and municipal bond issue. Some of the major urban infrastructure projects where ILFS is involved are the Tirupur water supply, the Visakhapatnam Industrial Water Supply Project and an integrated parking infrastructure project in Jaipur.

State-level Municipal Finance Agencies

The Karnataka Urban Infrastructure Development and Finance Corporation (KUIDFC) was set up in 1993 to assist urban agencies in the state in planning, financing and providing expertise to develop urban infrastructure. KUIDFC is the nodal agency for externally aided projects and the centrally sponsored Mega City Scheme. Its objectives include project preparation for infrastructure development in urban areas of the state, particularly land development, sanitation, road management, transportation and inter-connected subjects, as well as extending financial assistance by way of loans and advances to urban bodies such as corporations and municipalities, urban development authorities, other local bodies and institutions, as notified by the state government from time to time for their developmental schemes.

The Tamil Nadu Urban Infrastructure Financial Services Limited (TNUIFSL) is a public limited company incorporated on 7 November 1996 under the Indian Companies Act, 1956, with a paid-up share capital of Rs 10 million. TNUIFSL is a public–private partnership in the urban sector between the government of Tamil Nadu and three all-India financial institutions, namely ICICI Bank Limited, Housing Development Finance Corporation Limited (HDFC), and ILFS. TNUIFSL undertakes fund management on the basis of management contracts and is also engaged in fee-based activities.

Similar corporations have been set up in some other states also, but their role has been essentially marginal. In many states, the financing of urban infrastructure projects is also combined with other financing such as financing for industrial infrastructure or the social sector.

The World Bank and Some Other External Assistance Agencies

The World Bank, Asian Development Bank, Japanese Bank for International Cooperation (JBIC), French International Development Agency and some other bilateral aid agencies have funded several urban infrastructure projects, especially in the urban water supply and sanitation sector. The World Bank has assisted in water supply and sanitation schemes in Chennai, Bangalore and Mumbai. Recently, the Bank adopted an urban reform-based funding approach, and programmes to this effect have been taken up in Karnataka and Tamil Nadu. The Karnataka programme seeks to develop a long-term vision for the urban water sector in the state, thus creating high-quality, sustainable services in the urban water sector through all urban local bodies. The strategy for achieving this vision is to implement a phased programme towards full service coverage and quality service provision in a sustainable manner. The components of the Karnataka Urban Water Sector Improvement Project are:

1. Assisting the state government in finalizing its policy reform agenda and executing initial implementation steps for staged sector reforms, and preparing the business model and private sector participation processes for service provision.

2. Seeking to improve service provision and attaining continuous service in select demonstration zones; generating credibility for the overall programme and learning lessons on the challenges faced in the demonstration zones for scaling up continuous service provision; and simultaneously improving the efficiency of bulk supply operations and distribution networks, attaining initial improvements in water service provision to all state residents.

3. Financing the project's incremental operational costs and studies related to project management and implementation, including incremental, short-term consultants for the KUIDFC; preparation and establishment of a monitoring and evaluation system; meeting costs related to the financial management systems within KUIDFC; staff training within the KUIDFC project management unit; and providing for the incremental operating costs at KUIDFC, including supervision costs.

The World Bank is becoming more reform-oriented in the urban sector.

New Financing Mechanisms for Municipal Infrastructure and Programmes for Promoting Municipal Reforms

Municipal Bond Issues and Pool Finance Structures at Municipal Level

Municipal bonds first appeared in India when the Bangalore Municipal Corporation raised Rs 1.25 billion by issuing secured, redeemable, non-convertible municipal bonds in 1997. This issue was, however, backed by a government guarantee and not secured by any specific source of revenue for servicing debt. The Ahmedabad Municipal Corporation came out with a bond issue of Rs 1 billion in 1998 for financing capital works of water supply and sanitation projects without any government guarantee support. Octroi from 10 octroi-collection points were earmarked for servicing the bond. The issue had a public component of 25 per cent. CRISIL rated both these issues, which were followed by bond issues from the Nashik Municipal Corporation (Rs 1 billion), Calcutta Municipal Corporation (Rs 500 million), Ludhiana Municipal Corporation (Rs 100 million), Nagpur (Rs 500 million), Madurai (Rs 290 million) and Hyderabad (Rs 825 million). Ahmedabad is the only corporation that came up with a second issue of Rs 1 billion. These issues have been trendsetters, yet not many municipal corporations have raised funds from the capital market by issuing bonds.

The Tamil Nadu Urban Development Fund (TNUDF) has pioneered pooled finance structures to enable smaller municipalities to raise finance from the capital markets. Pooled finance structures allow municipalities to get together to make the issue of a reasonable size and save on costs of bringing out an issue, as individual documentation, marketing and other costs are avoided. The portfolio of projects helps in spreading risks as well. There have been a few such issues in Tamil Nadu and Karnataka. Municipal bond markets and pool finance structures have been promoted by USAID as part of its FIRE (D) project.

Government of India Scheme to Help Municipal Bodies Pool Finance from Capital Markets

The Ministry of Urban Poverty Alleviation and Employment has framed a 'Pool Finance Scheme' to promote bond banks, to enable smaller municipal bodies to tap the capital market through a state-level intermediary or by forming a consortium. Existing corporations for urban infrastructure development finance at the state level are expected to act as intermediaries. States that do not have such corporations will be assisted to establish the same. The central government also proposes to share the cost of raising funds from the capital market.

Loan Financing from Banks Directly without State Government Guarantee

Municipalities have raised direct finance from banks in the form of loans for their capital investment projects, without state government guarantees, in the state of Maharashtra and elsewhere.

Community-based Urban Infrastructure Financing

The Community Led Infrastructure Finance Facility (CLIFF), a financial mechanism created with funding from the Department for International Development (DFID), Swedish International Development Agency (SIDA) and Homeless International, is providing venture capital in India through CLIFF-I to help communities of the urban poor to seek and avail of finance from banks to provide community-driven infrastructure, housing and other urban services. CLIFF-I is working with banks and regulatory authorities to bring about necessary changes in the mindset and processes of the formal banking system in order to finance infrastructure projects undertaken directly by communities of poor people. If successful, municipal bodies may join with such community organizations to help them complete projects and also raise finance from banks for undertaking the capital expenditure that municipalities have to incur.

GOI's Urban Reforms Incentive Fund (URIF)

The GOI launched URIF during the fiscal year 2002–03 as part of its central assistance to state plans. This programme has 100 per cent grant support to provide reform-linked assistance to states so as to stimulate and accelerate the process of urban reforms identified and agreed upon by the GOI and state governments. An outlay of Rs 5 billion per annum has been provided for this purpose. The states select reforms out of a menu of seven identified reforms, which have been assigned appropriate individual weights, and enter into an MoU with the GOI. The identified reforms in the first tranche include repeal of the urban land ceiling law; rationalization of stamp duty in phases to reduce it to no more than 5 per cent by 2007–08; reform of rent control laws, to remove rent control so as to stimulate private investment in rental housing; introduction of an electronic process of registration of property transfer; reform of property tax so as to make it the major source of revenue for urban local bodies, and arrangement for its effective implementation so that collection efficiency reaches 85 per cent by 2007–08; levy of reasonable user charges by urban local bodies with the objective that the full costs of operation and maintenance are collected by 2007–08; and introduction of the double-entry system of accounting in urban local bodies.

States have been allocated funds in proportion to their urban population, and 50 per cent of the agreed incentive is available on signing the MoU while the rest is released on completion of the agreed-upon reform action.

The GOI has signed such MoUs with most states and union territories. Some states can also claim a partial second instalment of incentive upon completion of the promised reforms. There has been good movement towards certain key components such as reduction in stamp duty, abolition of urban land ceilings and adoption of the accrual basis of accounting.

URIF has been discontinued from 2005–06 and replaced with an investment-cum-reforms programme called Urban Renewal Mission for Urban Infrastructure and Transport. The Renewal Mission has substantially enhanced outlay. It is expected that the reform content of the Renewal Mission will be implemented seriously, so as not to allow the mission to only fund the investment without reforms actually being implemented.

GOI Contemplates Creating City Challenge Fund

The GOI has been planning to introduce a new centrally sponsored scheme entitled the City Challenge Fund to encourage institutional, fiscal and financial reforms for making cities creditworthy and accountable, so that they may raise finance for funding the infrastructure gap. The scheme proposes to meet transition costs such as preparing reform plans, setting up regulatory bodies, financing the gradual phasing of tariff rebalancing, financing safety nets for the poor, financing potential labour adjustment costs, and other like costs. The programme would operate at the city level. However, the state governments would need to play a major role as these kinds of reforms can only be brought about by state governments. The City Challenge Fund is unlikely to be accepted as a separate programme for now.

USAID FIRE (D) Project Plays Catalytic Role

The Indo-USAID programme on Financial Institutions Reform and Expansion (Debt) for developing a long-term debt market for viable urban infrastructure projects was launched in 1994. The programme envisages development of a viable urban infrastructure finance system that could support the development of the debt market in India by using the Urban and Environmental Credit Guaranty Funds—earlier known as the Housing Guaranty Funds—for contemplating the issuing of debt instruments to finance urban infrastructure projects. The mission of the FIRE (D) programme is to institutionalize the delivery of a commercially viable urban-environmental infrastructure service to urban residents, with particular focus on the poor.

Besides providing technical assistance, USAID also facilitates access to the Urban and Environmental Credit Guaranty Funds for a period of 30 years to develop an urban infrastructure finance system. HUDCO and ILFS act as financial intermediaries to channel the funds, along with a matching amount of locally raised funds going to municipalities or Private-Sector entities to finance select, commercially viable urban infrastructure projects relating to water supply, sewerage, solid waste management and area development.

FIRE (D) kickstarted and demonstrated novel ways of financing urban infrastructure in India. It advocates concepts such as commercial viability of urban infrastructure projects, financing by accessing the debt market, credit rating of municipal and urban infrastructure entities, and private participation for the provision of urban infrastructure projects. Steps have been taken to develop projects in a number of cities, which are now in progress. Positive spinoffs of FIRE (D) have been substantial even in non-project cities. The most important impact is the motivation and interest created in other cities in different states to think of alternative ways of financing urban infrastructure, beyond the traditional methods of plan and budgetary allocations that have built-in aberrations hindering effective and efficient management. An equally important impact of the programme has been the interest created among financial institutions for funding urban infrastructure projects. The programme has also led to innovative urban management practices in some cities, in terms of public–private partnerships, accessing of the capital market and sprucing up of financial management practices.

Another substantive impact of the programme has been in changing the mindset of planners, urban managers and policy makers in relation to the commercial viability of infrastructure and services such as water supply, sewerage and solid waste management. These were regarded as social welfare services that could not be structured on a commercial format. It has now been demonstrated that it is feasible to develop commercially viable and bankable projects for such urban infrastructure. Furthermore, there is a realization of the production costs of such infrastructure being akin to other economic goods, and hence the need to recover costs through ingenious project structuring and development, targeted subsidy and effective financial administration.

An important contribution of FIRE (D) has been that its concepts and tools have attracted other international donor agencies, financial institutions, project development boards and the private sector.

Major Issues in Financing Urban Infrastructure in a Fiscally Sustainable and Responsible Manner

Can State Governments Invest Adequately to Meet the Growing and Large Need of Urban Infrastructure?

The Constitutional division of responsibility and authority places the onus for creating urban infrastructure on state governments. The states can entrust municipal bodies and other forms of local institutions to do the same. However, barring Tamil Nadu, Delhi and Maharashtra (in the case of Mumbai and some other major cities) to some noticeable extent, the states have generally not enabled municipal corporations to emerge as strong institutions with clear mandates to provide urban services and create urban infrastructure to do so. The 74th Constitutional Amendment has also not altered the situation much. The states, therefore, are primarily responsible for undertaking and finding resources for municipal infrastructure investments.

The investment requirements for urban infrastructure are enormous, running into billions of dollars. The states are neck deep in debt, with their explicit debts and liabilities having crossed 35 per cent of GDP. Inclusive of pensions and other unrecognized liabilities, the states' real liabilities have crossed over 60 per cent of GDP in the aggregate. The states are running fiscal deficits of over 4–5 per cent of GDP,[14] largely to finance their revenue deficits. Today, there are more than 13 states that have to use more than 50 per cent of their true revenue base to discharge only pensions and interest payments. The states are in no position financially to undertake such massive investments. The municipalities have so far not been exposed to substantial direct borrowings. Their indebtedness to markets is quite low today in India. When the states undertake infrastructure investments in their cities, consideration for dividing the investment kitty among most or all municipalities is predominant, making the situation still worse as meagre resources get even more thinly spread. It does not appear feasible that the states can directly invest in the cities to match the resource requirement for urban infrastructure in India.

The TFC's recommendations for bringing about revenue balance are likely to help improve the financial position of the states. If the states succeed in restoring the revenue balance, the space created would certainly help them in raising capital expenditure, including expenditure on urban infrastructure. However, there is no possibility of the states or municipalities being able to meet the demand for infrastructure spending. Increased central financing has already begun through the Urban Renewal Mission, but will need to be raised; and public–private partnerships are the only other way to meet the requirement.

Can Cities become Major Drivers of Economic Growth and Better Local Governance?

India has 35 urban agglomerations of more than 1 million inhabitants. Cities such as Mumbai, Delhi, Kolkata, Chennai and Hyderabad are bigger than many countries in the world. Delhi is the only city-state in India. The record of Delhi since its conversion into a state has demonstrated that there has been a much sharper focus on issues of city infrastructure and governance than earlier, resulting in a substantial improvement in the city's infrastructure. The metro rail project, privatization of power and lowering of pollution by requiring buses to use compressed natural gas (CNG) as well as by banning diesel in other means of public transportation demonstrate that a city government[15] is much more sensitive to people and can be far more focused on urban infrastructure. Similarly, Mumbai's electricity and bus services have performed well since they came to be managed by the municipal authorities. In contrast, the local train service has not been upgraded because it is being run by the monolithic Indian Railways. Cities have shown that they are capable of delivering better services to their people and investing in infrastructure with greater involvement from the private sector. This is because city governments are nearest to the people and most directly accountable.

City governments without any access to ways and means such as overdraft facilities from the Central Bank would be far more careful in designing capital expenditure projects in such a way that user charges or dedicated sources of revenue pay for debt service. Cities can be entrusted with this responsibility and this is in accordance with the Constitutional mandate. Indian cities should, therefore, be delegated far more authority and responsibility for urban services.

Should the Central Government Be Very Proactive in Nudging States to Delegate Powers to Municipalities?

The 74th Constitutional Amendment was a result of the initiative of the central government that envisioned municipal bodies as the real third tier of governance and development. Parliament, however, stopped short of actually conferring the mandate envisaged in the Twelfth Schedule on municipalities and left it to the state governments to delegate these functions to the municipalities. However, the states have not translated the Constitutional vision into reality and there may be a need for the central government to step in to complete its unfinished agenda. The central government can do so through another Constitutional amendment, creating a municipal/Panchayat list along the lines of the state list in order to entrust legislative and executive authority for such subjects to municipalities. Additionally, independent taxation powers could be assigned. This would make municipalities independent of states[16] just as the states are from the centre for subjects in the state list. This has been suggested by a Constitutional commission appointed by the previous government.[17] Alternatively, the central government could design a conditional grant programme that would be effective in encouraging states to endow the municipalities with functions enumerated in the Twelfth Schedule and also strengthen municipalities into powerful institutions to carry out this mandate. However, as the Constitutional amendment option is more difficult and may not actually succeed, as not all municipalities can be expected to effectively take up such a large mandate, it would be preferable to adopt a large fund-based, centrally sponsored scheme to create incentives for states. Also, given that the states are at different stages of urbanization, it might be better to provide effective support to the states that are more urbanized and more favourably disposed toward strengthening city governments. Successful transition in such states would serve as a demonstration to other states.

Is Privatisation of Urban Infrastructure and Increased Resort to Public–Private Partnership the Answer?

Many urban infrastructure services such as electricity supply, bus transportation, water supply, airports, bridges, stadia and parks are private goods. These services are easily subjected to user charges, with safety nets for the poor wherever there is a 'merit goods' dimension. These services could, thus, be privatized or provided for through public–private partnerships, or could be housed in SPVs for clear determination of costs and charges. The experience of the Delhi Metro, Delhi Vidyut Board privatization and Tirupur water supply projects show that these services can be provided and managed by a SPV, privatized entity or public–private partnerships reasonably well and with good cost recovery. There are also massive efficiency gains. These models can be replicated elsewhere and offer good potential for the provision of urban infrastructure services. This reduces the dependence on government finance substantially. Therefore, municipalities need to be put in charge of these initiatives. Municipalities with hard budget constraints would be far more motivated to design appropriate formats for these services.

Should Mumbai and Other Major Municipalities Be Empowered to Use TDRs for Urban Infrastructure Development?

The Maharashtra government has used transferable development rights (TDRs) for catalysing private investment to create housing for the urban poor, who have been squatting on governmental lands, in exchange for permitting developers to raise floor space index (FSI) restrictions. The same method can be used for encouraging investment in urban infrastructure. Governments can empower urban local bodies to auction FSI space for generating capital resources for financing infrastructure. Quite contrarily, there are many who believe that the concept of TDRs as such is against public policy and advocate its abolition altogether. However, abolition of TDRs would lead to tremendous discrimination between those who got additional FSI on payment for TDRs and those who would simply get the same benefit without paying for it. It would not be possible to charge different property taxes for additional space built on the basis of TDRs and without TDRs. If, therefore, TDRs have to continue, why not use them more aggressively to make the maximum use of them in the short-term and use the proceeds for urban infrastructure?

Conclusion

India has been evolving over the centuries from an agricultural–tribal society to an urban–rural tribal society. Cities have grown as marketing centres for agriculture produce first, as social and financial/marketing infrastructure providers for industrial development second, and only recently as major services providers. Only a few new cities developed as organized cities.

The diversity of India and its history made the authors of the Constitution of India opt for a model with a strong centre and states as the primary providers of infrastructure and other development services. City governments did not have any significant role in this scheme of things. The development and institution-building strategies of the GOI and the states reflected the same mindset. Many city-level power companies existing in pre-Independence India were merged in the parastatal power utilities. Similar was the fate of bus services and quite a few other infrastructure services.

There has been an increasing realization now that cities need to be placed at the forefront of infrastructure and service delivery, though this view is still not shared by many state governments and state legislators. The direction of change is, however, quite discernible.

Municipal corporations have no debt overhang on them. Many of the municipal-level services are quite amenable to good cost recovery also. If strong city governments are placed in charge of urban services by appropriate Constitutional amendments or a national consensus, implemented by the states with due support and encouragement from the centre, urban infrastructure can be financed in a major way and without compromising fiscal responsibility.

Annexure 3.1
Rural–Urban Distribution of Population in Indian States/Union Territories, 2001

Territory	T/R/U	Population Persons	Population Males	Population Females	Urban population (per cent)
INDIA	T	1,027,015,247	531,277,078	495,738,169	27.8
	R	741,660,293	381,141,184	360,519,109	
	U	285,354,954	150,135,894	135,219,060	
State/Union Territory					
Jammu & Kashmir	T	10,069,917	5,300,574	4,769,343	24.9
	R	7,564,608	3,925,846	3,638,762	
	U	2,505,309	1,374,728	1,130,581	
Himachal Pradesh	T	6,077,248	3,085,256	2,991,992	9.8
	R	5,482,367	2,754,251	2,728,116	
	U	594,881	331,005	263,876	
Punjab	T	24,289,296	12,963,362	11,325,934	34.0
	R	16,043,730	8,500,647	7,543,083	
	U	8,245,566	4,462,715	3,782,851	
Chandigarh*	T	900,914	508,224	392,690	89.8
	R	92,118	56,837	35,281	
	U	808,796	451,387	357,409	
Uttaranchal	T	8,479,562	4,316,401	4,163,161	25.6
	R	6,309,317	3,143,380	3,165,937	
	U	2,170,245	1,173,021	997,224	
Haryana	T	21,082,989	11,327,658	9,755,331	29.0
	R	14,968,850	8,017,622	6,951,228	
	U	6,114,139	3,310,036	2,804,103	
Delhi*	T	13,782,976	7,570,890	6,212,086	93.0
	R	963,215	533,219	429,996	
	U	12,819,761	7,037,671	5,782,090	
Rajasthan	T	56,473,122	29,381,657	27,091,465	23.4
	R	43,267,678	22,394,479	20,873,199	
	U	13,205,444	6,987,178	6,218,266	
Uttar Pradesh	T	166,052,859	87,466,301	78,586,558	20.8
	R	131,540,230	69,096,765	62,443,465	
	U	34,512,629	18,369,536	16,143,093	
Bihar	T	82,878,796	43,153,964	39,724,832	10.5
	R	74,199,596	38,510,686	35,688,910	
	U	8,679,200	4,643,278	4,035,922	

Annexure 3.1 continued

Annexure 3.1 continued

| Territory | T/R/U | Population | | | Urban population |
		Persons	Males	Females	(per cent)
Sikkim	T	540,493	288,217	252,276	11.1
	R	480,488	255,386	225,102	
	U	60,005	32,831	27,174	
Arunachal Pradesh	T	1,091,117	573,951	517,166	20.4
	R	868,429	453,560	414,869	
	U	222,688	120,391	102,297	
Nagaland	T	1,988,636	1,041,686	946,950	17.7
	R	1,635,815	846,651	789,164	
	U	352,821	195,035	157,786	
Manipur	T	2,388,634	1,207,338	1,181,296	23.9
	R	1,818,224	923,428	894,796	
	U	570,410	283,910	286,500	
Mizoram	T	891,058	459,783	431,275	49.5
	R	450,018	233,718	216,300	
	U	441,040	226,065	214,975	
Tripura	T	3,191,168	1,636,138	1,555,030	17.0
	R	2,648,074	1,359,288	1,288,786	
	U	543,094	276,850	266,244	
Meghalaya	T	2,306,069	1,167,840	1,138,229	19.6
	R	1,853,457	939,803	913,654	
	U	452,612	228,037	224,575	
Assam	T	26,638,407	13,787,799	12,850,608	12.7
	R	23,248,994	11,983,157	11,265,837	
	U	3,389,413	1,804,642	1,584,771	
West Bengal	T	80,221,171	41,487,694	38,733,477	28.0
	R	57,734,690	29,606,028	28,128,662	
	U	22,486,481	11,881,666	10,604,815	
Jharkhand	T	26,909,428	13,861,277	13,048,151	22.3
	R	20,922,731	10,660,430	10,262,301	
	U	5,986,697	3,200,847	2,785,850	
Orissa	T	36,706,920	18,612,340	18,094,580	15.0
	R	31,210,602	15,711,853	15,498,749	
	U	5,496,318	2,900,487	2,595,831	
Chhattisgarh	T	20,795,956	10,452,426	10,343,530	20.1
	R	16,620,627	8,290,983	8,329,644	
	U	4,175,329	2,161,443	2,013,886	
Madhya Pradesh	T	60,385,118	31,456,873	28,928,245	26.7
	R	44,282,528	22,975,256	21,307,272	
	U	16,102,590	8,481,617	7,620,973	
Gujarat	T	50,596,992	26,344,053	24,252,939	37.4
	R	31,697,615	16,289,423	15,408,192	
	U	18,899,377	10,054,630	8,844,747	

Annexure 3.1 continued

Annexure 3.1 continued

| Territory | T/R/U | Population | | | Urban population |
		Persons	Males	Females	(per cent)
Daman & Diu*	T	158,059	92,478	65,581	36.3
	R	100,740	63,576	37,164	
	U	57,319	28,902	28,417	
Dadra & Nagar Haveli*	T	220,451	121,731	98,720	22.9
	R	169,995	91,887	78,108	
	U	50,456	29,844	20,612	
Maharashtra	T	96,752,247	50,334,270	46,417,977	42.4
	R	55,732,513	28,443,238	27,289,275	
	U	41,019,734	21,891,032	19,128,702	
Andhra Pradesh	T	75,727,541	38,286,811	37,440,730	27.1
	R	55,223,944	27,852,179	27,371,765	
	U	20,503,597	10,434,632	10,068,965	
Karnataka	T	52,733,958	26,856,343	25,877,615	34.0
	R	34,814,100	17,618,593	17,195,507	
	U	17,919,858	9,237,750	8,682,108	
Goa	T	1,343,998	685,617	658,381	49.8
	R	675,129	339,626	335,503	
	U	668,869	345,991	322,878	
Lakshadweep*	T	60,595	31,118	29,477	44.5
	R	33,647	17,196	16,451	
	U	26,948	13,922	13,026	
Kerala	T	31,838,619	15,468,664	16,369,955	26.0
	R	23,571,484	11,450,785	12,120,699	
	U	8,267,135	4,017,879	4,249,256	
Tamil Nadu	T	62,110,839	31,268,654	30,842,185	43.9
	R	34,869,286	17,508,985	17,360,301	
	U	27,241,553	13,759,669	13,481,884	
Pondicherry*	T	973,829	486,705	487,124	66.6
	R	325,596	163,586	162,010	
	U	648,233	323,119	325,114	
Andaman & Nicobar Islands*	T	356,265	192,985	163,280	32.7
	R	239,858	128,837	111,021	
	U	116,407	64,148	52,259	

Sources: Registrar General Census (2001).

1. The total rural and urban population of India includes the estimated total rural and urban population of the entire Kachchh district; Morvi, Maliya-Miyana and Wankaner *taluks* of Rajkot district; Jodiya *taluka* of Jamnagar district of the state of Gujarat; and the estimated total rural and urban population of the entire Kinnaur district of Himachal Pradesh, where population enumeration by the Census of India, 2001, could not be conducted due to natural calamities.

Annexure 3.1 continued

Annexure 3.1 continued

2. The figures of total rural and urban population of the state of Himachal Pradesh have been arrived at after including the estimated total and rural population of the entire Kinnaur district, where population enumeration by the Census of India, 2001, could not be conducted due to natural calamities.

3. The figures of total rural and urban population of the state of Gujarat have been arrived at after including the estimated total rural and urban population of the entire Kachchh district; Morvi, Maliya-Miyana and Wankaner taluks of Rajkot district; and Jodiya taluka of Jamnagar district, where population enumeration by the Census of India, 2001, could not be conducted due to natural calamities.

4. T = total; R = rural; U = urban.

Note: * Union territory.

Annexure 3.2
**Urban Infrastructure and Taxes Allocated to the States
in List B of the Seventh Schedule**

Subject	Entry
A. Infrastructure subjects	
Public health and sanitation; hospital and dispensaries	6
Roads, bridges, ferries and other means of communication, including municipal tramways, ropeways and traffic	13
Water supplies, drainage	17
Land	18
Industries	24
Gas and gas works	25
Markets and fairs	28
Theatres, cinemas, entertainment and amusements	33
B. Taxation powers	
Lands and buildings	49
Entry of goods into a local area for consumption, use or sale therein	52
Consumption or sale of electricity	53
Advertisements	55
Tolls	59
Vehicles	57
Animals and boats	58
Professions, trades, callings and employment	60
Luxuries including taxes on entertainment, amusements, betting and gambling	62
Stamp duty on documents	63

Source: From the State List in the Seventh Schedule of the Constitution (GOI).

Annexure 3.3

Combined Receipts and Disbursements of the Central and State Governments

	1990–91	1998–99	1999–2000	2000–01	2001–02	2002–03(RE)[1]	2003–04(BE)[2]
				In Rs million			
Total receipts	1,523,980	4,597,460	5,427,010	5,979,440	6,496,860	7,467,600	8,165,070
Revenue receipts	1,057,570	2,876,860	3,437,410	3,788,170	4,003,050	4,717,350	5,216,910
Tax receipts	875,640	2,330,690	2,749,740	3,053,740	3,139,740	3,666,800	4,134,820
Non-Tax receipts	181,930	546,170	687,670	734,430	863,310	1,050,550	1,082,090
Interest receipts	249,950	161,750	182,020	180,500	171,410	201,180	184,270
Capital receipts, of which	466,410	1,720,600	1,989,600	2,191,270	2,493,820	2,750,250	2,948,160
1. Disinvestment proceeds	—	63,790	17,240	21,250	36,460	33,600	132,000
2. Recovery of loans and advances	43,360	71,150	59,050	104,660	145,140	112,980	80,760
Total disbursements	1,636,730	4,632,650	5,458,130	5,955,980	6,531,110	7,519,500	8,236,420
Revenue	1,296,280	3,992,370	4,651,350	5,176,200	5,596,550	6,376,870	6,823,090
Capital	221,770	460,140	591,660	602,110	670,480	885,820	1,193,100
Loans and advances	118,680	180,140	215,120	177,670	264,080	256,810	220,230
Revenue deficit	238,710	1,115,510	1,213,940	1,388,030	1,593,500	1,659,520	1,606,180
Gross fiscal deficit	535,800	1,570,530	1,848,260	1,998,520	2,264,250	2,488,850	2,592,650

Annexure 3.3 continued

Annexure 3.3 continued

	1990–91	1998–99	1999–2000	2000–01	2001–02	2002–03(RE)[1]	2003–04(BE)[2]
			As per cent of GDP				
Total receipts (A+B)	26.8	26.4	28.0	28.6	28.5	30.2	29.6
Revenue receipts (1+2)	18.6	16.5	17.7	18.1	17.5	19.1	18.9
Tax receipts	15.4	13.4	14.2	14.6	13.8	14.8	15.0
Non-tax receipts, of which	3.2	3.1	3.6	3.5	3.8	4.3	3.9
Interest receipts	4.4	0.9	0.9	0.9	0.8	0.8	0.7
Capital receipts, of which	8.2	9.9	10.3	10.5	10.9	11.1	10.7
Disinvestment proceeds	0.0	0.4	0.1	0.1	0.2	0.1	0.5
Recovery of loans and advances	0.8	0.4	0.3	0.5	0.6	0.5	0.3
Total disbursements (a+b+c)	28.8	26.6	28.2	28.5	28.6	30.4	29.9
Revenue	22.8	22.9	24.0	24.8	24.5	25.8	24.8
Capital	3.9	2.6	3.1	2.9	2.9	3.6	4.3
Loans and advances	2.1	1.0	1.1	0.9	1.2	1.0	0.8
Revenue deficit	4.2	6.4	6.3	6.6	7.0	6.7	5.8
Gross fiscal deficit	9.4	9.0	9.5	9.6	9.9	10.1	9.4

Source: GOI (2003–2004).
Notes: The ratios to GDP at current market prices for 2003–04 (BE) are based on CSO's advance estimates released in February 2004.
Rs 10 million crores equals 1 crore, Rs 1 billion equals 100 crores, and so forth.
1. RE: Revised estimate.
2. BE: Budget estimate.

Annexure 3.4
Debt Stress Levels of States Based on Interest and Pensions
in Per cent of the True Revenue Base

States	2002–03 Actuals	2003–04 RE[1]	Category
Andhra Pradesh	46.66	46.25	Severely debt stressed
Arunachal Pradesh	38.22	43.29	Severely debt stressed
Assam	47.82	55.73	No debt capacity
Bihar	54.71	50.93	No debt capacity
Chhattisgarh	26.64	25.54	Debt stressed
Goa	45.27	44.13	Severely debt stressed
Gujarat	51.87	50.97	No debt capacity
Haryana	42.61	41.91	Severely debt stressed
Himachal Pradesh	76.78	104.98	No new debt capacity
Jammu & Kashmir	42.37	43.95	Severely debt stressed
Jharkhand	26.57	27.46	Debt stressed
Karnataka	36.37	34.93	Severely debt stressed
Kerala	51.58	48.82	Severely debt stressed
Madhya Pradesh	36.75	41.20	Severely debt stressed
Maharashtra	38.19	40.36	Severely debt stressed
Manipur	62.88	67.77	No new debt capacity
Meghalaya	30.76	33.23	Debt stressed
Mizoram	44.88	44.85	Severely debt stressed
Nagaland	39.33	39.67	Severely debt stressed
Orissa	59.23	64.73	No new debt capacity
Punjab	64.97	67.76	No new debt capacity
Rajasthan	60.10	58.27	No new debt capacity
Sikkim	33.36	36.24	Severely debt stressed
Tamil Nadu	42.92	45.54	Severely debt stressed
Tripura	63.29	56.28	No new debt capacity
Uttar Pradesh	41.16	51.56	No new debt capacity
Uttaranchal	51.61	66.69	No new debt capacity
West Bengal	77.19	84.71	No new debt capacity

Source: Reserve Bank of India (2003–2004).

Note: Level of debt stress is based on interest and pension as per cent of true revenue base. If states fall in different categories in the two years, their classification is based on 2003–04 numbers.

1. RE: Revised Estimate.

Annexure 3.6 continued

Infrastructure service	Metropolitan areas	Municipal corporation areas/major cities	Other urban areas
	KMC in Kolkata for tram services Indian railways for metros in Kolkata and Mumbai and Delhi Metro Rail Corporation in Delhi	Some municipalities in Gujarat run bus services	
Area and roads development	Most of the metros have specialized area development agencies such as MMRDA in Mumbai, DDA in Delhi, Hyderabad Urban Development Authority in Hyderabad, Bangalore Development Authority in Bangalore and Chennai Metropolitan Development Authority in Chennai. Roads are developed and maintained in a metro area depending upon which agency owns it— the state Public Works Department (PWD), a specialized agency, or the municipal corporation. In addition, there are special arrangements for road development such as the Maharashtra Roads Development Corporation in Mumbai and other major towns for roads and bridges etc.	Urban improvement trusts or specific municipal area/ agglomeration area development authority/state PWDs	Municipalities for municipal roads
Development of new housing areas/ sub-cities	In addition to city-specific/metro area-specific agencies, statewide housing development agencies such as housing boards, corporations, etc.	In addition to city-specific (wherever constituted) agencies, statewide housing development agencies such as housing boards, corporations, etc.	Statewide housing development agencies such as housing boards, corporations, etc. (generally neglected) or municipal bodies
Street cleaning and lighting	Municipal authorities	Municipal authorities	Municipal authorities

Source: Compiled by author.

Annexure 3.5 continued

States	Taxes on professions, trades, callings and employment			Urban immovable property tax			Entertainment tax		
	2001-02 Actual	2002-03 RE[1]	2003-04 BE[2]	2001-02 Actual	2002-03 RE	2003-04 BE	2001-02 Actual	2002-03 RE	2003-04 BE
Meghalaya	08.9	05.4	06.7	0	0	0	08.6	08.4	09.9
Mizoram	36.3	37.4	37.5	0	0	0	0	0	0
Nagaland	120.0	128.4	150	0	0	0	0	0	0
Orissa	398.6	450.0	464.9	0	0	0	276.2	60	46.0
Punjab	0	0	0	0	0	0	91.9	118.0	120
Rajasthan	0	0	0	239	250	300	222.9	321.0	353.5
Sikkim	0	0	0	0	0	0	04.2	05.0	05.5
Tamil Nadu	0	0	0	141.1	130	135	880	762	802.1
Tripura	115.9	140.0	154	0	0	0	13.4	13.5	14.9
Uttar Pradesh	145.3	48.1	53.5	0	0	0	54.7	934.5	1,066.3
Uttaranchal	21.8	18.2	40	0	0	0	56.9	45.2	59.8
West Bengal	2,158.7	2,374.5	2,730.7	09.4	10.4	11.9	502.8	599.2	679.3
NCT	0	0	0	0	0	0	466.5	450	600
All states	29,974.3	32,975.2	37,746.6	840.2	815.6	882.3	7,986.6	8,636.6	9,213.1

Source: Reserve Bank of India (2003–2004).
Notes: Receipts are not for municipalities and are from three major sources of tax revenues generally considered as municipal taxes.
1. RE: revised estimate.
2. BE: budget estimate.
3. NCT: national capital territory.

Annexure 3.6

Assignment of Responsibility for Providing Six Urban Infrastructure Services

Infrastructure service	Metropolitan areas	Municipal corporation areas/major cities	Other urban areas
Water and sewerage	Brihan Mumbai Municipal Corporation (BMC) in Mumbai Chennai Metropolitan Water Authority in Chennai Delhi Jal Nigam/New Delhi Municipal Corporation (NDMC) in Delhi Kolkata Municipal Corporation (KMC) in Kolkata Bangalore Municipal Corporation in Bangalore Hyderabad Water and Sewerage Board in Hyderabad	State departments and state/regional water and sewerage boards generally	State departments and state/regional water and sewerage boards generally
Electrical service	BEST/Bombay Suburban Electricity Supply BSES (now Reliance Energy) in Mumbai CESC in Kolkata Privatized distribution companies in Delhi Municipal Corporation (DMC) areas/NDMC in Central Delhi State electricity board/corporation in Bangalore, Chennai and Hyderabad	State electricity boards/ corporations in all cities except Surat in Gujarat Energy departments in north-eastern states except Assam and J&K	State electricity boards/corporations in all cities except Surat in Gujarat
Bus, metro and tram services	BEST in Mumbai and state/regional transportation corporation in the other five metros for buses	State transport corporations in almost all states, except Haryana and Punjab, where it is departmentally provided	State transport corporations in virtually all states, except Haryana and Punjab, where it is departmentally provided

Annexure 3.6 continued

Annexure 3.5
Receipts of States from Tax Revenues
In Rs Million

States	Taxes on professions, trades, callings and employment			Urban immovable property tax			Entertainment tax		
	2001–02 Actual	2002–03 RE[1]	2003–04 BE[2]	2001–02 Actual	2002–03 RE	2003–04 BE	2001–02 Actual	2002–03 RE	2003–04 BE
Andhra Pradesh	11,371.7	13,480.4	15,172.8	54.3	80	80	674.4	888.9	924
Arunachal Pradesh	0	0	0	0	0	0	0	0	0
Assam	732.7	802.9	883.4	04.1	04.7	05.4	315.9	261.6	287.7
Bihar	00.1	00.1	00.1	0	0	0	151.9	169.1	186.0
Chhattisgarh	476.2	562.7	612.5	0	0	0	11.4	82.2	90.5
Goa	0	0	0	0	0	0	27.2	44.0	350.0
Gujarat	933.1	1,000.0	1,000.0	07.9	15	20	648	600	600
Haryana	12.4	08.2	09.0	0	0	0	79.9	93.5	103.0
Himachal Pradesh	0	0	0	0	0	0	03.9	00.2	0
Jammu & Kashmir	0	0	0	22	05.5	05.0	25	12.5	15
Jharkhand	0	0	0	0	0	0	188.1	210.8	212.3
Karnataka	1,672.3	1,785.8	2,176.4	0	0	0	489.3	421.5	450.4
Kerala	0	0	0	362.4	320	325	02.4	04.4	04.9
Madhya Pradesh	1,821.8	1,999.9	3,105.0	0	0	0	319.6	198	217
Maharashtra	9,819.8	10,000.0	11,000.0	0	0	0	2,471.5	2,333.1	2,330
Manipur	128.7	133.2	150.1	0	0	0	0	0	0

Annexure 3.5 continued

Annexure 3.7: Summary of Urban Infrastructure Schemes of the Government of India

Mega City Scheme

A centrally sponsored scheme for infrastructure development in mega cities was initiated during 1993–94 to undertake infrastructure development projects of citywide/regional significance, covering components such as water supply and sewerage, roads and bridges, city transport, solid waste management and the like in the five largest cities of India except Delhi—i.e., Mumbai, Kolkata, Chennai, Bangalore and Hyderabad. This scheme operates through the mega city nodal agency. Funds are shared in the ratio of 25 per cent (central government), 25 per cent (state government) and 50 per cent (raised by the nodal agency/implementing agency from the capital market/financial institutions) and placed in the Revolving Fund. The central and state government support is in grant form, but the Fund is expected to approve project financing with a mix of loans and grants such that 75 per cent of the central and state shares are recovered and ploughed back into the Revolving Fund. The following agencies have been designated as the nodal agencies for the scheme:

Mumbai: Mumbai Metropolitan Region Development Authority (MMRDA)
Kolkata: Calcutta Metropolitan Development Authority (CMDA)
Chennai: Tamil Nadu Urban Finance and Infrastructure Development Corporation (TUFIDCO)
Hyderabad: Andhra Pradesh Urban Infrastructure and Finance Development Corporation (APUIFDC)
Bangalore: Karnataka Urban Infrastructure Development Finance Corporation (KUIDFC)

An amount of Rs 2.9 billion was allocated during the Eighth Plan and Rs 4.2 billion during the Ninth Plan under the scheme. The Tenth Plan has a provision of Rs 10.5 billion under the scheme. The state-level

Annexure 3.7 continued

Annexure 3.7 continued

sanctioning committees in all the five mega cities have approved 620 projects at an estimated cost of Rs 62.9 billion by 31 March 2004. An amount of Rs 29.4 billion was reportedly spent on these infrastructure schemes. An amount of Rs 12.5 billion was mobilized from HUDCO and other sources. The budget provision for 2004–05 is Rs 2.2 billion.

Integrated Development of Small and Medium Towns (IDSMT)

This is the oldest urban infrastructure scheme being supported by the GOI with grants. This scheme is aimed at developing select regional growth centres with infrastructure and service facilities, so as to enable such towns to emerge as regional centres of economic growth and employment. The scheme also aims at arresting migration from rural areas and small towns to large and metropolitan cities.

The scheme prescribes a certain portion of finance required to be raised from institutional sources, ranging from 20 per cent to 40 per cent, depending upon the size of the town. The remaining cost is shared between the centre and state in the ratio of 2:1. Annual GOI support to the scheme is approximately Rs 1 billion. There is a substantial step-up to Rs 2 billion for the fiscal year 2004–05.

Urban Water Supply

The Accelerated Urban Water Supply Programme (AUWSP), a centrally sponsored grants-funded programme, was initiated in 1994 to assist states to address the problem of drinking water in towns with populations of less than 20,000 as per the 1991 Census. The states are expected to provide 50 per cent of the cost of scheme from their resources. As of 31 March 2004, water supply schemes for 1,037 such towns have been approved at an estimated total cost of Rs 14 billion. The central government has released assistance of Rs 6.2 billion for this purpose.

Annexure 3.7 continued

Annexure 3.7 continued

All the states have taken assistance under the programme, but the biggest beneficiaries have been Uttar Pradesh (367 schemes; outlay Rs 2.9 billion) and Madhya Pradesh (128 schemes; outlay Rs 1.3 billion). A total amount of Rs 7.3 billion has been reportedly spent, with 365 schemes fully or partially commissioned.

Other Minor Schemes

A minor scheme of solid waste management and drainage in airfield towns, with an outlay of Rs 990 million, has been approved, with 100 per cent grant funding from the central government.

Notes

1. (Registrar General Census 2001) Counting the population confined to the statutory limits of the respective municipal corporations only.
2. Number of females for every 1,000 males.
3. Panchayats are rural local bodies in India, forming a three-tier structure corresponding to the districts (excluding areas under municipal bodies), blocks (rural areas of districts divided into development blocks, with a population of approximately 100,000 in 1961) and villages (rural areas notified as villages in revenue records).
4. The ratio of domestic savings to GDP further improved to 28.1 per cent in 2003–04 and the current account turned negative in 2004–05 after being in surplus for three years, suggesting investment pick-up.
5. Exchange rate at the time of writing this paper was US$ 1 = Rs 44.
6. The true revenue base comprises of own taxes, shares in central taxes, revenue deficit grants from the centre, revenues from mining and other concessions, and investment income.
7. 'No new debt capacity' if the ratio exceeds 50 per cent; 'severely debt stressed' if between 33.3 per cent and 50 per cent; 'debt stressed' between 25 per cent and 33.3 per cent; and 'debt stress-free' only with less than 25 per cent.
8. Municipal corporation towns only.
9. Punjab's State Finance Commission also left an explicit gap to be filled by the CFC.
10. Finance Commissions are appointed every five years to recommend the shares of the states in central taxes and grants-in-aid to their revenues. Finance Commissions have been referred to for advice on issues of sound public finance as well.
11. The introduction to VAT by most states has also helped.
12. Since launched as the Jawaharlal Nehru National Urban Renewal Mission Programme (the erstwhile mega cities programme has also been merged with the new programme).

13. Approvals net of cancellations being Rs 208 crore.
14. There has been consolidation of the states' fiscal deficits in the last two years. The states are estimated to have brought down their fiscal deficits to 3.8 per cent of GDP in 2004–05.
15. The Delhi Government is virtually a city government.
16. As cities are in Brazil.
17. Coalition government of 1998–99 led by the Bharatiya Janata Party with Atal Behari Vajpayee as the prime minister.

References

GOI (Government of India). 2003. *Balance Sheets, Housing and Urban Development Corporation*, New Delhi.

———. 2003–2004. *Economic Survey*. New Delhi.

———. 2005–2006. Union Budget (Expenditure Volume I). New Delhi.

———. Constitution of India, Seventh Schedule, State List. New Delhi.

National Institute of Urban Affairs. 2004. *Urban Finance*, 17, (3): 4. New Delhi.

Registrar General Census. 2001. *Census Report*. New Delhi: Census of India.

Reserve Bank of India. 2003–2004. *Study of State Budgets*. Mumbai.

4

Infrastructure Development in Poland: The Issues at Stake

Krzysztof Ners*

Introduction

Poland is a middle-income country situated in Central Europe. It is an OECD country, a member of NATO and, as of May 2004, a EU member state. As a result of its EU membership, Poland's economic and policy discussions at the national level have been somewhat distorted by an EU agenda skewed toward the more mature economies of western Europe. Further, as a middle-income country, Poland shares more problems with countries at a similar level of development, such as some Latin American countries, than the higher-income countries of western Europe.[1] Since the 1990s, Poland has undergone significant political, economic and social transformation. It has changed from a centrally planned economy to a market economy and from single-party rule to a pluralist democracy.

Table 4.1 outlines some basic data on Poland. Important indicators include the fact that Poland has the largest population in Central and Eastern Europe (CEE), of which approximately 62 per cent lives in urban areas.

---

* Krzysztof Ners served as Deputy Minister of Finance, Government Plenipotentiary for EU Funds.

Table 4.1
Basic Indicators 2003

Land area	312,685 sq km		
Population	38.6 million		
Main towns	Warsaw (capital)	Population	1,632,500
	Lodz	Population	812,300
Climate	Continental		
Language	Polish		
GNI/capita	5,273 US$		
Currency	Zloty		
Agriculture/forestry	3% of GDP		
Industry/construction	31% of GDP		
Services	66% of GDP		

Source: World Bank (2004a).

Issues Affecting Infrastructure Development in Poland

Although it is methodologically difficult to establish links between economic growth and the demand for infrastructure investment, Poland's policy makers respond to consumer and producer demand for infrastructure as a means to facilitate growth. Some of the factors that influence infrastructure investment are the following:

1. Density effect and cost of infrastructure services
2. Stage of development—the importance of infrastructure varies at different stages of development; returns on investment tend to be higher in low-income countries
3. Investment composition, which differs across income groups
4. Level of private investment in infrastructure
5. Size and depth of the private sector
6. Level of public investment in such sectors as telecommunication, sanitation and heating

History

When Poland was reunited in 1918, after being divided for more than 120 years between three empires—Russian, Prussian and Austro-Hungarian—it inherited three different infrastructure systems. Poland's economy was also badly damaged by two World Wars and 40 years of Communism.

During the Communist period, Polish participation in international trade was limited to the Soviet Bloc. Consequently, in 1989, when the transition to an open economy began, Poland's infrastructure was in a deplorable state compared not only to other OECD countries, but also to other post-Communist states.[2] The 2004 OECD economic survey on Poland reveals that only 600 kilometres of high-quality roadway existed in a country of 313,000 square kilometres. The report also indicates serious bottlenecks in improving the railway systems. As less than 25 per cent of the railway is in satisfactory condition, rail users face lengthy commutes and high costs.

According to the OECD, Poland invests just 0.50–0.70 per cent of GDP for infrastructure, less than half the average rate for other OECD economies (OECD 2004a). Relatively weak infrastructure is one of the main reasons why the foreign direct investment (FDI) in Poland is lower than in other post-Communist countries. Firms today choose locales based on an enabling environment in the host country, good governance, proximity of markets, quality of labour force, and production and transport costs.

Providing Infrastructure for Trade

As a member of the EU, Poland has increased its participation in the European production and distribution system. Hence, it has increased and diversified exports. Rising exports of manufactures, especially semi-finished goods and components as well as zero-inventory/just-in-time production systems, have increased demands on both the reliability and the quality of infrastructure. Since on-time delivery requires motorways and high-speed roads, dense railways networks are less crucial. However, as the service industry grows and Poland competes for outsourcing allocations, new types of infrastructure—such as telecommunication, IT facilities, modern office spaces and investment in human capital—are also required.

Two important political factors drive infrastructure development in Poland:

1. The need to connect Poland to its new markets (70 per cent of exports have been re-oriented to western Europe).
2. The need to reduce regional discrepancies within Poland.

Better-developed infrastructure will allow Poland to take advantage of its prime geographical location at the centre of the East–West European axis and between Scandinavia and southern Europe.

EU Accession

EU pre-accession programmes such as the Instrument for Structural Policies for Pre-Accession (ISPA)[3] and growing EU financing following accession have been vital in infrastructure development, such as constructing links to the Trans-European Networks, one of the major trans-port corridors across Europe.

Environmental Infrastructure

As a member of the EU, Poland must invest more in environmental infrastructure than it would otherwise; environmental awareness increases with GDP. Environmental investment in Poland started in earnest at the beginning of the transition and was supported by the EU's ISPA programme. Existing estimates of the required expenditure on the environment suggest a figure of 26–60 billion US$, or 1.2–2.7 per cent of GDP (OECD 2004b). Since the beginning of the 1990s, approximately 95 per cent of the total has come from domestic sources on a 'pay as you pollute' basis. In recent years, the issues of modernization, rehabilitation and better maintenance of existing housing have also gained in importance.

Policy Debate on Infrastructure Development

In his study on Latin America, Antonio Estache (2004) suggests that during the last 10–15 years, fiscal adjustment and privatization (actual and expected) have led to a 40–50 per cent drop in public expenditure on infrastructure in Latin America. Poland may have experienced a similar trend.

In Poland, as in other countries in transition, the policy debate on infrastructure investment is highly politicized. There are disputes on the direction investment should take, sometimes literally. This is illustrated by two competing motorways projects: the A2 motorway linking Warsaw and Berlin east to west, as opposed to the north-to-south A1 linking Scandinavian countries to Warsaw through Gdansk and then to southern Europe. Similarly, policy makers disagree on the relative merits of and the need for 'hard' versus 'soft' infrastructure investments, the former being more capital-intensive. The experience of Ireland over the past two decades has triggered a growing realization among policy makers that increasing public investment in education (soft infrastructure) is vital for a successful growth strategy and for convergence with EU averages for social and economic indicators.

It is important to stress that infrastructure investment involves increased short-term costs and provides long-term returns when accompanied by operations and maintenance (O&M) expenditure (see Table 4.2). Further, small-scale investments such as the fragmentary motorway system and the single metro line in Warsaw offer limited returns. This is because these investments fail to reach the critical mass necessary to achieve the benefits of a comprehensive network.

Table 4.2
Expected Annual Investments for Operation and Maintenance Needs, 2005–10
In Percentage of GDP

	Investment needs	*O&M needs*	*Total*
Middle-income countries	2.8–3.8	2.7–3.2	5.5–7.0
Low-income countries	3.2–4.2	3.3–3.5	6.5–7.7

Source: Estache (2004).

Urban Issues

As a middle-income OECD country, Poland is currently engaged in two simultaneous processes:

1. Convergence: Poland must try to meet OECD benchmark figures for GDP and other social indicators. According to its composite infra-structure index, the Economist Intelligence Unit has rated Poland at 5 out of a maximum of 10; Germany received a 9 (government of Poland 2004).
2. Modernization: Poland must improve basic infrastructure (including urban infrastructure) and housing conditions.

Poland supports both these processes fairly well. The country is quite urban-ized, with 62 per cent of the population already living in urban areas and over a third of that in big cities.[4] However, just 6.8 per cent of the urban population (4.2 per cent of the total population) lives in the capital, Warsaw, by far the most important city (see Table 4.3). The demographic trend at the national level is slightly negative but stable. Similarly, at the city level, the decline in population between 1990 and 2000 was less than 2 per cent for the 20 largest cities.

The urban population in Poland has grown from 9 million in 1950 to approximately 24 million today, with 6 million emigrating from rural areas.

Table 4.3
Urban Population Living in Polish Cities (by City Size)

City size	Population (in 1000s)	Per cent of total population
>5,000	883	3.7
50,000–100,000	11,556	48.4
100,000–200,000	3,012	12.7
>200,000	8,801	35.2
Total urban population	23,876	–

Source: Central Statistical Office, Poland (2005).

However, housing shortages and lack of urban infrastructure have significantly slowed down urban development in Poland. This has been accompanied by a pattern of limited migration from the countryside to big cities. In fact, the recent restructuring of heavy industry and the environmental crisis in some regions have caused net outflows from urban areas. Further, the present pattern of urbanization is in part a legacy of Poland's Communist era, when industries were widely dispersed across the country. Thus, many large companies are now located in small cities and use the local labour force.

Another pattern in Polish urban development is the outflow from urban centres to the urban periphery. Most urban migration consists of relocation to suburban areas or nearby cities. People who have moved out of central urban areas maintain their links with the cities, where they continue to work, shop and enjoy cultural activities.

The literature suggests that one reason for the lack of urban growth in Poland may be the housing situation.[5] Even in comparison to countries at a similar level of development, the ratio of dwellings to people is still low.[6] Further, privatization of housing has reduced the share of rented housing from 52 per cent in 1990 to the present 25 per cent of the total housing stock.

Decentralization and Economic Development, Fiscal Adjustment and Fiscal Rules: Implications for Infrastructure Financing

Economic Development, Fiscal Adjustment and Fiscal Rules

Beginning in 1976, Poland experienced a long period of economic crisis. The crisis brought on 1989's hyperinflation and the subsequent economic stabilization plan of January 1990. After an initial period of 'transition depression',

Poland entered a phase of economic recovery. By mid-1996, it was the first transition country[7] to reach its pre-transition level of output. After an initial period of 'transition depression', Poland entered a phase of economic recovery, as shown in Figure 4.1.

Figure 4.1
GDP Growth in Poland, 1993–2004

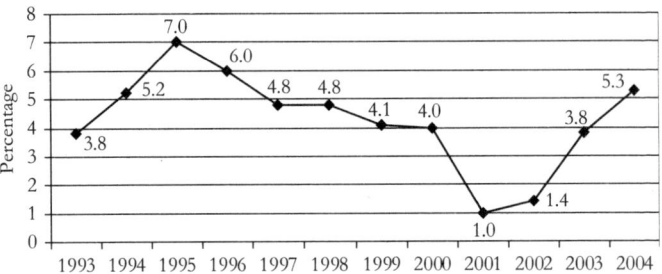

Source: World Bank (2004a).

However, macroeconomic reforms were not accompanied by a social equivalent of the Balcerowicz economic reform package.[8] Poland started its transition, but the share of non-discretionary expenditures remained at pre-transition levels. Between 1998 and 2004, however, the share of non-discretionary expenditure in the central budget had increased from approximately 54 per cent to about 67 per cent.[9] The increase occurred as these expenditures were determined by law and inherited from the previous system; they remained excessive and poorly targeted.[10] Further, the share of social transfers in budgetary expenditure remained higher in Poland than in other OECD countries. The growing budgetary costs inflated deficits and siphoned away resources from infrastructure development, human capital building and private sector development.

Between 1994 and 1999, Polish economic growth was the highest in the CEE. However, during that period, the budgetary deficit remained relatively high, suggesting that fiscal policy was pro-cyclical. A subsequent slowdown between 2000 and 2003 led to a further deterioration in public finances and a growing deficit (see Figure 4.2). The increasing budgetary deficits contributed to high interest rates, with adverse consequences for investment.

Additionally, Poland has a relatively low share of gross fixed capital formation to GDP compared to other middle-income countries or even some developing countries (see Figure 4.3). A two-digit growth rate of gross fixed capital formation was recorded between 1995 and 1998; the growth rate decreased considerably between 1998 and 2000, and became negative between 2002 and 2003. The share of investment to GDP decreased from 24 per cent in 1999 to below 19 per cent in 2003.

Figure 4.2
Cyclically Adjusted Deficit, 1995–2004

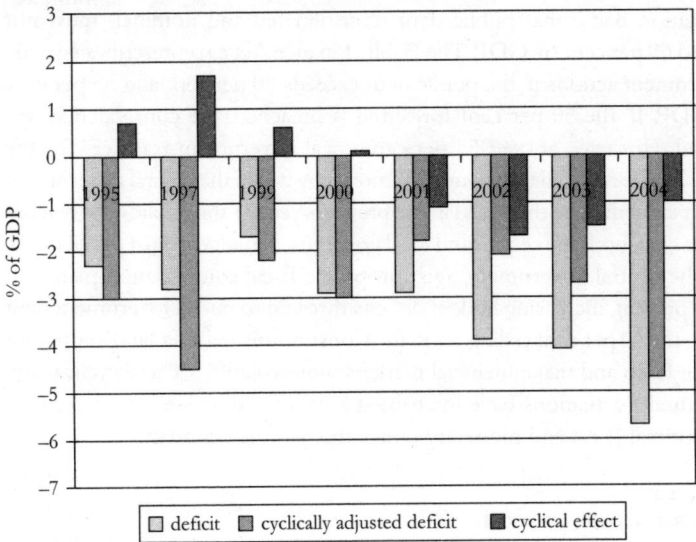

Source: OECD (2004a).

Figure 4.3
Gross Fixed Capital Formation, 2000–03

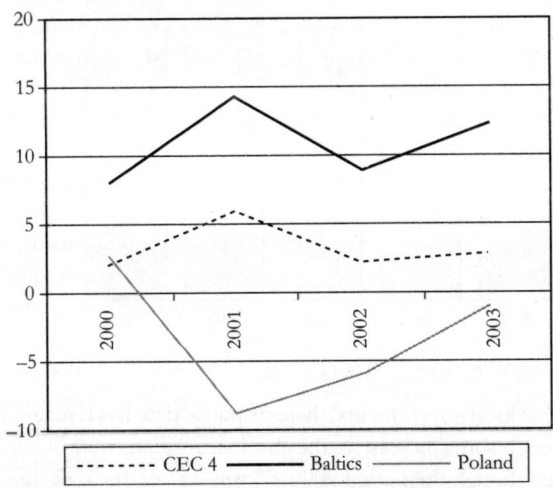

Source: IMF (2004).
CEC 4: The Czech Republic, Hungary, Poland and the Slovak Republic.

The guiding rules on fiscal policy and public debt management are set out in the Polish Constitution and the Public Finance Act, the relevant stipulation being that public debt (consolidated and nominal) must not exceed 60 per cent of GDP. The Public Finance Act also prescribes specific government actions if the public debt exceeds 50 per cent and 55 per cent of GDP. If the 50 per cent threshold is breached, the consequences are limited. However, at over 55 per cent, local government transfers for the next year are reduced to recoup the amount by which the central government deficit exceeded the threshold in the previous year. If the public debt reaches 60 per cent, both the central and local government budgets must be balanced, and the central government must propose a fiscal consolidation plan.

At present, increasing budget deficits threaten to push Government debt above the 60 per cent ceiling set in the Constitution, delay Poland's adoption of the Euro and make financial markets more volatile.[11] These cyclical and structural fluctuations have intensified a national discussion to determine the optimal fiscal and monetary policy mix for the country.

Figure 4.4
Gross Public Debt, 1999–2004

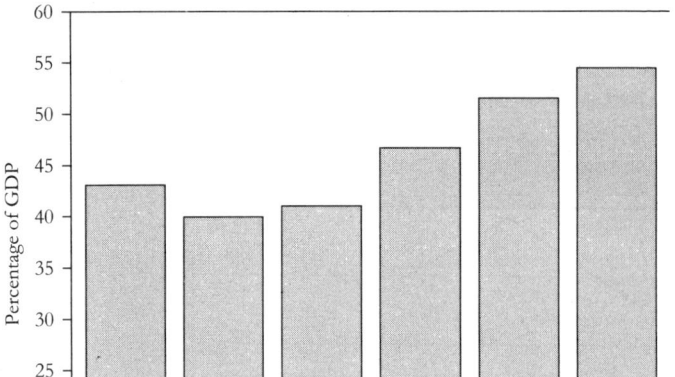

Source: OECD (2004a).

Table 4.4 shows that local governments' share of public debt has remained low and stable, although some increase in the absolute amounts may be observed. Further, even though the period 2000–03 was one of fiscal decline (see Figure 4.2), the local governments have limited responsibility for the increasing public debt.

Table 4.4
Distribution of Public Debt between Central and Local Governments,
31 December 2003
In PLZ* (Polish National Currency) Billions (bn)
and as a Percentage of Total

Year	2000		2002		2003		2004	
	PLZ bn	%	PLZ bn	%	PLZ bn	%	PLZ bn	%
Central government	271.1	96.7	338.5	96.0	392.1	96.0	413.9	95.7
Local government	9.2	3.3	14.1	4.0	16.5	4.0	18.4	4.3
Total	280.3	100	352.6	100	408.6	100	432.3	100

Sources: OECD (2004a).
Note: * The average exchange rate for the period 2001–2004 was 4.01 PLZ per US$.
   Source: Bloomberg data service.

Concerns about the rapid increase in public debt have forced the government to draw up a politically sensitive programme of spending cuts for 2004–07. Many of the cuts are due to take effect in an election year (2005). Thus, they are likely to be watered down by parliamentary debate, leaving most of the fiscal adjustment to the next government. A major reduction in the budget deficit will probably have to wait until the second half of this decade.

In the meantime, to address the challenge of growing public debt, Deputy Prime Minister Jerzy Hausner has offered a medium-term fiscal consolidation plan to stabilize the debt ratio in accordance with the Constitutional limit of 60 per cent. The plan suggests that efficient absorption of EU transfers should make reductions in infrastructure investment less likely.

The following factors created a need for the fiscal reform embodied in the Hausner Plan:

1. The economic consequences of breaching the limits set in the public Finance Act.
2. The fast-approaching 60 per cent public debt threshold.
3. Continuous pressure from the Central Bank to reduce fiscal deficits so that interest rates may be lowered.
4. The influx of EU funds.
5. The prerequisite of fiscal stability necessary for entry into the Euro zone .

The fiscal consolidation plan is not designed to reduce infrastructure investment at the central or local level. Instead, it aims to create more investment in infrastructure by reducing poorly chosen social and administrative expenditure. Data contained in Table 4.5 clearly demonstrate the government's efforts to protect investment expenditure. In a period of economic con-traction, investment expenditure as a share of central and local governments' overall expenditure remained relatively stable in both central and local governments' budgets, despite the decrease in the general government spending (see Figure 4.5).

Figure 4.5
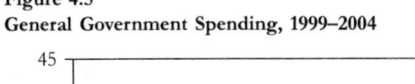
General Government Spending, 1999–2004

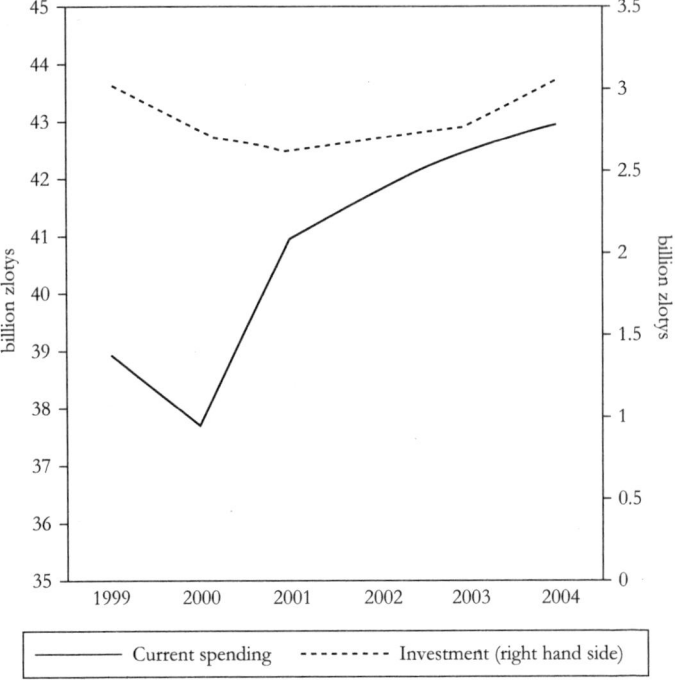

Source: Government of Poland (2004).

Even though the share of investment expenditure in total expenditure is almost three times higher for local than for central government, a comparison reveals that the central government's investment expenditure plays a significant role in overall development. In absolute terms, the value of local governments' investment expenditure was one-third to two-thirds higher than the central government's investment expenditure in 2000–04.

Poland has experienced high economic growth in recent years. In 2003, real GDP growth was 3.8 per cent, fuelled mainly by private consumption and exports; in 2004, it exceeded 5 per cent. Despite these positive economic

Table 4.5
Investment Expenditures (IE) in Central and Local Governments' Budgets
In PLZ Billions and as a Percentage of Total

	2000	2003	2004
Central government			
Total PLZ	151.1	189.2	197.7
Investment expenditure[1] PLZ	7.3	8.53	11.08
Share of IE in total (%)	4.9	4.5	5.6
Local government			
Total PLZ	75.75	80.95	91.39
Investment expenditure PLZ	13.21	12.31	14.83
Share of IE in total (%)	17.44	15.21	16.23

Source: Central Statistical Office, Poland (2005) (years presented as in the original source).
Note: 1. Including allocations for the investment tasks of local governments.

achievements, it is estimated that at an annual growth differential of 3 per cent between Poland and the EU, 100 per cent convergence of income per capita will be achieved in 32 years, 75 per cent in 22 years, and 50 per cent in 8 years (Pissarides 2003).

Decentralization and Infrastructure Development

In Poland, the impact of decentralization on infrastructure investment is a matter of continuing debate. Does decentralization increase both total as well as sub-national spending on infrastructure? Does locally financed infrastructure spending reflect better preferences for the quality and quantity of infrastructure? Is decentralization contributing to lower public spending? These questions are relevant for many countries beyond Poland.

Decentralization Framework

In Poland, the central government is responsible for most infrastructure services, namely motorways, the national roads network, railways and power. Telecommunications and part of district heating are privatized. Services linked to urban infrastructure and local service delivery that offer few economies of scale have remained within the remit of local governments. These are listed below:

1. Urban transportation
2. Water supply and sewage
3. Local roads

4. Solid waste management
5. Environmental protection
6. Heating
7. Housing

A major reform introduced in 1991 established a three-tiered local government system. A subsequent territorial reform and restructuring of financial decentralization took place in 1999. The following structure emerged:

1. 2,489 municipalities (*gminas*)
2. 373 counties (*powiats*), of which 65 are urban and 308 rural
3. 16 regions (*wojewodztwos*)
4. The capital city of Warsaw has a special statute and is divided into 11 city districts (*dzielnice*).

Financial Sources for Local Authorities

Local governments have three basic revenue sources:

1. Share of state taxes, including personal income tax (PIT) and corporate income tax (CIT), and local taxes
2. Non-tax revenues
3. Central government grants, including general subsidies and special-purpose grants (appropriated allocations)

Targeted grants from the national budget have proved to be ineffective. These grants are earmarked for predetermined purposes and have to be returned to the central government if not used accordingly.

In response to these weaknesses, the central government proposed several reforms to replace targeted grants with more independent revenues for local governments, thus increasing their financial independence and responsibility. The law of November 2003 on local administration revenues[12] had several important objectives:

1. Decentralizing and increasing the role of local governments in managing public financial resources.
2. Increasing the share of local resources in total revenue and thereby increasing local governments' economic responsibility.
3. Introducing counter-cyclical measures in central-to-local government transfers

4. Facilitating absorption of EU funds (the law of November 2003 stipulates that any debt created to co-finance EU grants—structural and cohesion funds—be excluded from the debt calculation).
5. Develop instruments to promote entrepreneurship, human capital and development.

Table 4.6
Structure and Dynamics of Local Government Revenues, 2000–04
In PLZ Billions and as a Percentage of Total

	Structure of revenues in the first semester					
	2000		2003		2004	
	PLZ	%	PLZ	%	PLZ	%
Own revenue—of which:	29.6	40.7	33.2	42.0	47.9	50.2
Share of corporate income tax receipts from State budget	0.9	1.3	0.8	1.0	4.9	5.4
Share of personal income tax receipts from State budget	9.1	12.5	9.5	12.0	15.1	16.5
Local taxes and fees	9.4	12.9	12.4	15.7	13.5	14.7
Revenue from property	5.1	6.9	3.4	4.2	3.8	4.2
Appropriated allocations from State budget	16.5	22.7	13.0	14.4	13.1	4.3
General subsidies from State budget*	25.9	35.6	31.7	40.1	31.3	34.2
Additional financing	0.7	1.0	1.2	1.5	1.1	1.2
Total	72.6	100	79.1	100	91.5	100

Source: Central Statistical Office 2005.
Note: *Approximately 80 per cent is a subsidy for educational responsibilities.

The central government's share of subsidies and appropriated allocations to local government has remained over 55 per cent since 1999, when the government introduced the new territorial reform and financial decentralization. By 2004, the law of November 2003 had produced an increase of own resources for local governments (to over 50 per cent) and a concomitant decrease in the share of state transfers (Table 4.6).

The changes in revenue structure reveal important information about urban infrastructure finance in cities with *powiat* status (see previous page). In the years 2000 to 2004, revenues for cities with *powiat* status grew more quickly (145.8 per cent) than for all other local government entities (126 per cent). Own resources grew even more rapidly (193 per cent) as a result of the law of November 2003. Transfers of personal and corporate income taxes from the state budget, especially in 2004, accounted for a share of own resources in these cities 10 per cent larger than for other local government entities. As a part of this evolution, the share of real-estate tax

Table 4.7
Structure of Revenue in Cities with *Powiat* Status, 2000–04
As a Percentage of Total

	2000	2003	2004
Own revenue, of which:	47.9	55.7	63.9
Transfer of personal income tax receipts from state budget	15.7	17.8	24.5
Transfer of corporate income tax receipts from state budget	1.5	1.8	3.3
Real estate tax	10.9	14.9	14.0
Property revenues	8.9	5.9	6.0
Other own revenues	11.6	15.3	16.1
Appropriated allocations from state budget	20.3	11.8	11.0
General subsidies from state budget	31.2	31.9	24.8
Other financing	0.6	0.6	0.3

Source: Central Statistical Office, Poland (2005) (years presented as in the original source).

decreased in total own revenues, but still remained the second highest source of own revenue (21.8 per cent). Personal income tax from the state budget (38.2 per cent) in 2004 was the largest single source of income for these local governments (see Table 4.8).

Table 4.8
Structure of Own Resources in Cities with *Powiat* Status, 2002–04
As a Percentage of Total

	2002	2003	2004
Transfers of corporate income tax receipts from state budget	3.1	3.2	5.2
Transfers of personal income tax receipts from state budget	33.4	31.7	38.2
Real estate tax	27.3	26.5	21.8
Property revenues	9.8	10.6	9.3
Other own revenues	26.4	28.0	25.5

Source: Ministry of Finance 2005.

Fiscal Issues at the Local Level

The Public Finance Act has introduced several restrictions on borrowing by local authorities. It stipulates that the total amount of debt at the end of the budget year cannot be higher than 60 per cent of the local actual revenue (and cannot exceed 60 per cent of yearly projected revenues at the end of any quarter). Further, the cost of servicing the debt cannot be higher than 15 per cent of the revenue projection for a given budget year.

Table 4.9
Deficits of Local Governments, 2002–04
In Percentage of Revenues

	2002	2003	2004
Planned budgets	–7.8	–6.1	–5.8
Executed budgets at end of year	–3.9	–2.3	0.1

Source: Ministry of Finance (2005).

The number of local governments with more than 60 per cent indebtedness has decreased from 17 in 2003 to 8 in 2004.[13] Urban *powiats*, on the other hand, are more indebted as the number of *powiats* with a debt-to-revenue ratio more than 30 per cent has increased from 19 to 33 (out of a total of 65 urban *powiats*) between 2002 and 2004. Over the past few years, more than three-quarters of all local governments have kept their debts below 30 per cent. Even as the central government deficit has grown over time (as discussed earlier), the local government deficit has remained stable—indeed, it has decreased from 4.3 per cent in 2000 to 2.3 per cent in 2003 and even reached a surplus in 2004 of 0.13 per cent of revenue. A factor in the decrease may be that local governments with debts above 50 per cent face serious cash-flow problems.

Table 4.10
Level of Indebtedness of Local Governments in 2002 and 2004
In Percentage of Total Number of Units

	<10		10–30		30–60	
	2002	2004	2002	2004	2002	2004
Gminas (first tier)	3.4	30.1	41.0	46.4	13.9	18.2
Urban *powiats*	22.7	13.8	47.0	50.8	28.8	35.4

Source: Ministry of Finance (2005).

Local governments are distinguished in the shrinking size of their annual deficits. In the period from 2002 to 2004, 41–45 per cent of local governments finished the budgetary year with a surplus. As mentioned earlier, in 2004, the local governments as a whole had a budgetary surplus for the first time. Still, it is unclear whether better economic growth is contributing to higher revenues through personal and corporate income tax, or whether there is more efficient expenditure management due to the declining share of tied grants. Barely a year since the introduction of new rules, it is still premature to draw firm conclusions about economic growth and decentralization.

Box 4.1: The example of Warsaw

Poland's capital Warsaw illustrates how fiscal issues and urban infrastructure investments are managed at the level of a big city. Even though Warsaw is the biggest city in Poland, its share of central government financing, at 14 per cent, is almost exactly the same as the national average.

Financing of Urban Investment in Warsaw
In Million PLZs

	2003	2004	2005 (projected)	2006 (projected)
Own income	329.9	291.6	295.2	205.2
EU grants	0	59.3	216.8	315.9
Central budget	113.8	151.3	150.3	151.3
Loans	368.6	891.4	793.6	527.1

Source: Warsaw City Hall 2005.

Most of Warsaw's investment has been financed by long-term loans on floating interest rates; however, only 3 per cent was financed using foreign currency loans. Decreasing interest rates and lower banking margins, due to a more competitive banking environment and increased cooperation with international financial institutions, have made local loans very attractive over the past few years.

In 2005, the city expects to obtain an international rating that will allow it to follow other Polish cities (Poznan, Krakow) in issuing bonds. Such bond issues have been on fixed interest rates, allowing diversification of instruments—for instance, in loans and bonds on fixed and floating interest rates. According to indicators from the Public Finance Act, the city is fiscally sound; the ratio of debt-to-own-income has been at 37 per cent, well below the 60 per cent threshold. The ratio of debt servicing-cost-to-own-resources is approximately 5 per cent, once again below the 15 per cent threshold.

Debt indicators
In percentage

	2003	2004	2005 (projected)	2006 (projected)
Debt-to-own income	37.0	37.7	38.5	41.7
Debt servicing to own income	4.7	5.2	5.7	5.6

Source: Warsaw City Hall 2005.

The prudential indicators in the Public Finance Act may restrict local government spending, as they employ 'own income' as a reference point or denominator. While the debt indicators above do not signal any difficulties in the immediate future, the growing debt of the central government is a source of uncertainty. When the 50 per cent and 55 per cent thresholds for consolidated government debt in relation to GDP are breached, the central government is forced to reduce its expenditure. Since reducing social transfers is difficult for Constitutional and political reasons, public expenditure on infrastructure and maintenance may have to be reduced to avoid breaching the guidelines. The limited role of the central government in financing urban infrastructure means that any decrease can be offset by increased local government borrowing. However, this will increase the total cost of finance as municipalities cannot borrow on the same conditions as the sovereign. It is likely that costs would be increased further due to high levels of uncertainty concerning the central government's financing contributions to projects already underway.

Although local governments must reconcile their own budget deficits, most investment expenditure must be implemented in accordance with the Public Procurement Act. In cases of extreme financial difficulty, a board of commissioners may be appointed to restore balance.

Local Governments' Role in Financing Infrastructure

Fiscal decentralization has ensured that local governments assume a growing role in funding infrastructure investment. Yet their involvement is relatively limited because current expenditures absorbed roughly 84 per cent of total spending in the period 2002–04. Additionally, over 60 per cent of local government expenditure goes to public administration, social welfare and education (Table 4.11).

The sectoral pattern of investment expenditure differs because the division between current and investment expenditure varies across sectors. There are clearly three sectors that absorb most of the local governments' investment expenditure: transport and communication (almost 33 per cent in 2003 and almost 35 per cent in 2004); urban economy and environment (19 per cent and almost 18 per cent, respectively); and education (approximately 13 per cent for both years) (Table 4.12).[14]

Poland's local governments have three sources of financing investment expenditure: own resources; transfers from the central budget; and other

Table 4.11
Structure of Local Government Expenditure, 2002–04
In Percentage of Total

	2002	2003	2004
Transport and communication	12.8	12.0	12.7
Housing	2.7	2.9	3.1
Public administration	10.1	10.5	9.9
Public order	6.0	2.3	2.2
Welfare	18.2	19.2	16.7
Education	32.5	35.0	36.6
Health	2.4	2.3	2.3
Communal and environment	5.9	5.9	5.7
Culture	3.1	3.3	3.3
Other	6.3	6.6	6.6

Source: Ministry of Finance (2005).

Table 4.12
Structure of Local Governments' Investment Expenditure by Sectors, 2003–04
In Percentage of Total

	2003	2004
Water, gas, energy	0.7	0.6
Transport and communication	32.9	34.9
Housing	4.9	4.9
Education	13.3	12.5
Health	5.5	4.9
Urban economy and environment	19.0	17.7
Other	23.7	24.5

Source: Ministry of Finance (2005).

para-budgetary financing (including Polish investment funds, of which the National Environment Fund is the most important) (Table 4.13).

Table 4.13
Financial Sources for Local Governments' Investment Expenditure, 2003–04
In Million PLZs and as a Percentage of Total

	2003		2004	
	PLZ	%	PLZ	%
Investment expenditure total	12,305.6	100	14,834.4	100
Own resources	9,846.6	80.0	12,421.9	83.7
Central budget transfers	1,810.3	14.7	1,725.8	11.6
Other financing	648.7	5.3	686.7	4.6

Source: Ministry of Finance (2005).

The 2003 local finance reform has already resulted in decreased dependence on central government revenues. The share of financing from own revenue increased by almost 4 per cent, while the share of central budget transfers decreased by 3 per cent. It is important, however, to realize that the importance of these transfers varies significantly among different sectors.

Table 4.14
Share of Central Budget Transfers in Financing Local Government Investment by Sector, 2003–04
In Percentage of Total

	2003	2004
Water, gas, energy	0.2	0.4
Transport and communication	14.6	8.9
Housing	1.0	1.4
Education	3.6	7.9
Health	62.3	44.0
Urban economy and environment	5.7	2.4
Total average	14.7	11.6

Source: Ministry of Finance (2005).

Table 4.14 reflects the pattern of Polish decentralization and territorial reforms, and should not be used as a basis for further generalization. For instance, as local governments are responsible for education, the share of central government transfers has been relatively limited, albeit doubled between 2003 and 2004. Conversely, the two sectors that rely most on central budget transfers are health and transport and communication (Table 4.15). This is reflected in the relatively large transfers to finance local governments' investment expenditure in these sectors. Between 2003 and 2004, the total average of central government transfers to finance investment expenditure by local governments has decreased from 14.7 per cent to 11.6 per cent.

Table 4.15
Sectoral Distribution of Central Government Transfers to Finance Local Governments' Investment Expenditure
In Percentage of Total

	2003	2004
Transport and communication	32.7	26.8
Health	21.1	18.4
Urban economy and environment	7.3	3.7
Education	3.3	8.5
Other	35.6	42.6

Source: Ministry of Finance (2005).

Infrastructure plays an important role in socio-economic development, especially in less-developed countries. In that context, how can infrastructure investment be increased within a responsible fiscal framework? There are three possible responses:

Increase expenditure in spite of the weak fiscal position of a country, including high levels of deficit and public debt

Countries with fiscal problems are often particularly keen to protect infrastructure investment during a macroeconomic adjustment, in order to protect the base for long-term growth. Some have suggested that public investment should be excluded from gross public debt calculations, on the grounds that financing productive investments in infrastructure can lead to temporary fiscal deficits that are self-correcting.[15] A similar discourse is taking place within the Euro zone regarding the relevance of the 3 per cent deficit limit of the Stability and Growth Pact.[16]

Create a 'fiscal space' for infrastructure investment without worsening the macroeconomic position

Some of the approaches for creating this 'fiscal space' include:

1. Increasing budgetary revenues either through tax increases or better tax collection.
2. Reducing other budgetary expenditures such as defence or 'social transfers'.
3. Reducing demands on government funding for infrastructure by increasing private involvement. This may be achieved through public–private partnerships, which may in turn improve borrowing conditions.

Increase efficiency of expenditures and operation of infrastructure

Some of the principle means of achieving such efficiencies are:

1. Decentralization, which can reduce volatility of expenditure, since local economic cycles may differ from economy-wide macroeconomic fluctuations. Local decision making may have the added benefit of more accurately reflecting local needs and preferences.
2. Privatization, which may improve the efficacy and efficiency of investments.
3. Administrative or institutional improvements that can make the regulatory framework more effective and reduce corruption.

4. Measures to encourage economies of scale in decentralized infrastructure-service delivery.

This list is not exhaustive; moreover, these approaches can often complement each other when adopted in combination.

Conclusion

Forty years of Communism have left a legacy of poor infrastructure in Poland. Underdeveloped infrastructure prevents Poland from taking full advantage of its strategic geographical location and hampers economic development.

It is argued that more than one source of investment in infrastructure (central as well as local governments) may address infrastructure needs in a more comprehensive manner and also diversify sources of investment funding. In spite of differing investment priorities, fiscal regulations can ensure the economic and financial viability of the choices made at both local and central levels.

Several specific observations may be drawn from the experience of Poland, a post-Communist country in transition and a new EU member:

1. Rapid growth over a relatively long period does not eliminate the risk of growing budgetary deficits and public debt. Cyclicality in the economy and its impact on the government's budgetary balance is not sufficient to explain Poland's experience over the last several years.
2. The size of local government units is important in securing a balance between fiscal capacity and fiscal responsibility. A three-tier approach that delegates most of the financial management to the lowest level has proven efficient in Poland.
3. Financial decentralization could, and probably should, be deeper. The aim would be to transfer more tasks and accompanying resources to the local level, to improve the effectiveness of decision making.
4. Increasing the share of local government revenue derived from the shared national tax income is a counter-cyclical measure that reduces pressure on central government transfers during the economic cycle.
5. The central government should provide most of the transfers to local authorities on a non-discretionary basis to limit volatility during downturns in the economic cycle.

6. Local governments have thus far shown an impressive level of fiscal responsibility by keeping their share of total public debt well below 5 per cent.

7. Local governments can borrow and issue bonds in the local currency. Thus the exchange-rate risk is limited, even though the cost may be higher than in the case of sovereign borrowing. Local governments may borrow in other currencies only from international financial institutions, with the consent of the Ministry of Finance.

8. Local governments, including municipalities, have demonstrated a strong borrowing capacity, as there have thus far been no defaults. Local governments have also proved that they can raise their own revenues. As a result, interest rates have decreased as inflation has been brought under control. Poland continues its steady convergence on EU standards. Moreover, EU accession has brought with it increased competition in the banking sector, leading to reduced margins and a wider range of financial products becoming available to local governments as well as downward pressure on interest rates.

9. Institutional and Constitutional regulation of fiscal exposure, such as the 60 per cent consolidated public-debt-to-GDP threshold, has proven effective by providing disciplinary measures while not interfering directly in the allocation of funds. Preventive thresholds, namely the 50 per cent and 55 per cent thresholds, have created an efficient institutional framework for fiscal adjustment and provided the central government with mechanisms to manage the impact of local transfers on its own fiscal balances. Local authorities are subject to stricter rules—for instance, a 15 per cent limit on the ratio of debt servicing to annual income—than the looser constraints imposed on the central government.

10. The disciplinary measures affecting the central government can nonetheless potentially penalize even the most disciplined local government if the Constitutional thresholds are breached.

11. Although multi-annual budgeting is not a panacea for the cyclical volatility of central budget transfers to local authorities, it would improve the predictability of financial flows.

12. Since public expenditure already constitutes a large share of GDP, further tax increases may undermine tax compliance.

13. Social expenditures should be structured to create 'fiscal space', secure mid-term fiscal sustainability and increase infrastructure investment. A new EU member's fiscal status is greatly improved

by EU transfers for infrastructure investment if the member state can supply co-financing.

14. Maintaining a constant level of infrastructure investment expenditure is now a condition for receiving 'additional' transfers from the EU. Thus the government cannot simply replace domestic investment with EU transfers.

15. The telecommunication sector disappeared from the public investment list following privatization. Other forms of private sector participation in infrastructure investment are very limited as private–public partnership legislation has not yet been adopted.

16. Commercialization of public utilities into municipal companies is common. Although it is not a full privatization, it separates these companies from the municipalities' books. There is, however, a risk that certain companies' liabilities may become a burden to their former owners.

Notes

1. The Polish GDP in 2003 was just 41 per cent of the EU average in terms of purchasing power parity (PPP).

2. Such as the other countries in the CEC 4: the Czech Republic, Slovakia and Hungary.

3. The ISPA is designed to address environmental and transport infrastructure priorities identified in the Accession Partnerships with the 10 applicant countries of the CEE for the period 2004–06. ISPA programmes allocated 50 per cent of funds to transport and 50 per cent to environment.

4. A big city is defined as one with a population of over 200,000.

5. In 1999, Poland had a ratio of 304.3 dwellings per 1,000 people, well below the EU average of 450 dwellings per 1,000.

6. In 1999, the number of dwellings per 1,000 people was 450 in Hungary, 374 in the Czech Republic and 349 in Romania.

7. Here we refer to the transition from non-democratic, single-party political systems and centrally planned economies, towards democracy and open market economies that took place in Eastern Europe starting in the late 1980s.

8. The essence of the Balcerowicz macroeconomic reforms were structural adjustment, convertibility of the currency, price and trade liberalization, and fiscal reform.

9. Data from the Ministry of Finance, Poland.

10. Social transfers constituted 25.9 per cent of GDP in 2003, of which 3 per cent was paid to non-poor families (World Bank 2004b).

11. As shown in Figure 4.2, the deficit rose in 1999 and continued to grow despite the growth recovery observable from mid-2003 onwards (see Figure 4.1). The fiscal situation fuelled an increase in public debt, particularly since 2000 (see Figure 4.4).

12. Act on Incomes of Local Self-Government Entities, 13 November 2003.

13. These constitute less than 0.3 per cent of all local governments. All eight entities in 2004 belong to the group of *gminas*—the lowest tier of local government.
14. Although agriculture and forestry has 15 per cent of total investment expenditure, it is not pertinent to urban infrastructure investment and is therefore not analysed.
15. See, for example, Blanchard and Giavazzi (2004).
16. The Stability and Growth Pact is an agreement by EU member states related to their conduct of fiscal policy, meant to facilitate and maintain the economic and monetary union of the EU.

References

Blanchard, Olivier, and Francesco Giavazzi. 2004. 'Reforms That Can Be Done: Improving the SGP through a Proper Accounting of Public Investment', Centre for Economic Policy Research: Discussion Paper Series (UK), (4220): 1–19.

Central Statistical Office, Poland. 2005. *Concise Statistical Yearbook of Poland*. Warsaw.

EBRD. 2005. *Transition Report Update*. EBRD publications.

Estache, Antonio. 2004. 'Emerging Infrastructure Policy Issues in Developing Countries', Policy Research Working Paper Series No. 3442. Washington, DC: World Bank.

Eurostat Database. 2004. Statistical Office of the European Communities. www.epp.eurostat. cec.eu.int. Accessed in November 2004.

Government of Poland. 2004. 'Convergence Program'. April 2004. Warsaw.

IMF (International Monetary Fund). 2004. *Staff Report for the 2004 Article IV Consultation Republic of Poland*.

Ministry of Finance, Poland. 2004. *Informacja o Stanie Zobowiazan Wedlug Tytulow Dluznych*. Warsaw: Government of Poland.

———. 2005. *Informacja o Skutkach Obowiazywania Ustawy z 13 Listopada 2003 Roku o Dochodach Jednostek Samorzadu Terytorialnego*. Warsaw: Government of Poland.

OECD. 2004a. *Economic Survey for Poland*. Paris: OECD Publishing.

———. 2004b. *Environmental Survey*. Paris: OECD Publishing.

Pissarides, Francesca. 2003. 'Economic Developments and Outlook in CEE'. Paper presented at the Central European Initiative Conference on European Bank Reconstruction and Development, 19–21 November, Warsaw.

Warsaw City Hall. 2005. *Informajca*. Warsaw.

World Bank. 2004a. 'Development Data Platform'. Washington DC: World Bank. www.devdata.worldbank.org/data-query.

———. 2004b. *Poland: Growth, Employment, and Living Standards in Pre-Accession Poland*. Washington, DC: World Bank.

5

Fiscal Decentralization and the Financing of Urban Infrastructure in South Africa

Philip van Ryneveld*

Introduction

South Africa held its first democratic elections in 1994, marking the end of three-and-a-half centuries of racially-based minority rule. The elections took place in accordance with an interim Constitution negotiated between the former apartheid regime and various movements and political parties unbanned in 1990.[1] The elected representatives formed the new parliament and functioned as a Constituent Assembly for the first two years, and in 1996, passed a new Constitution based on a set of pre-agreed constitutional principles.

The apartheid system entailed a systematic channelling of opportunity and resources towards the white minority and away from the majority black population. A key mechanism for achieving this was through the creation of sub-national territories and segregated residential areas for the different racial groups.

The mobilization of urban infrastructure finance in the decade since 1994 thus took place against a backdrop of very substantial Constitutional and administrative changes, which affected the running of the sub-national governments in particular. Also at issue was the need to address severe services backlogs amongst the majority urban (black) population.

* Philip van Ryneveld was Chief Financial Officer of the Cape Town Municipality.

While many difficulties remain, South Africa has made significant progress over the decade in addressing urban service backlogs in poor areas. At the same time, it has greatly improved the macroeconomic fundamentals. There are three levels—or 'spheres'—of government in South Africa, and most urban infrastructure is the responsibility of local governments. The process of Constitutional change has enabled considerable attention to be directed towards the creation of a sound, overall framework of decentralization and towards addressing infrastructure needs via the establishment of autonomous, financially stable local governments.

While the overall system has not yet been properly bedded down, the important elements are in place. Despite the fact that national government guarantees for local government debt are illegal, there is fairly significant lending by private financial institutions to metropolitan municipal governments in particular. In 2004, the city of Johannesburg successfully floated a general-obligation municipal bond, unsecured by any revenue intercept or national government guarantee.

South Africa is a middle-income country with a 2004 GDP of approximately R 1,350 billion.[2] It has a population of 43 million, which, while being relatively small, is highly diverse. This paper will attempt to sketch some of the main characteristics of the current approach to mobilizing urban infrastructure finance. It will place emphasis on describing the overall framework, since this—rather than the description of a specific city—is likely to be of more interest.

Key Relevant Developments and Achievements since 1994

Achievements in the Provision of Urban Services

Much of the emphasis since 1994 has been on the extension of services to poor areas. This has been relatively successful. Between 1996 and 2001, access to clean water was provided to approximately 9 million people, increasing coverage from 60 per cent to 85 per cent of all households. In the same period, electricity provision increased from 50 per cent to 70 per cent. Between 1994 and 2003, 1.6 million houses were built for low-income families through a state subsidy scheme[3] (Government Communications and Information System [GCIS] 2003).

A composite index relating to the provision of housing, water and sanitation, electricity and telephones has increased from 0.46 to 0.60 between

1995 and 2002, where full provision to all would be indicated by a score of 1.00. (GCIS 2003).

Independent surveys[4] from 2003 indicated that public approval rates with regard to basic services stood at 75 per cent and housing at 64 per cent (up from 30 per cent in 1996). Between 1994 and 2002, housing as a key concern dropped from 46 per cent to 22 per cent.

Government spending has been substantially redistributive since 1994. Of the total population of 43 million, the number of recipients of welfare grants increased from 2.6 million in 1994 to 6.8 million in 2003. The poorest quintile now receives two-thirds of its income from grants. A 2000 Gini coefficient of 0.59, when transfers to poor households are not taken into account, is transformed to 0.35 after these transfers. In 2003, independent surveys showed approval on welfare grants stood at 78 per cent (GCIS 2003).

Demographic and Economic Changes

These improvements have taken place against a background of significant economic and demographic changes. Key trends have included significant urbanization, with the metropolitan areas and key cities expanding by between 21 per cent and 40 per cent between 1991 and 2001. There has been a large increase in the number of households, accompanied by a decrease of average household size from 4.5 to 3.8 between 1996 and 2001 (Patel 2004).

Currently, 40 per cent of the urban population are regarded as 'poor'; 54 per cent of the unemployed are located in urban areas; of the latter, 38 per cent live in the nine largest cities and more than 25 per cent live in informal settlements (Patel 2004).

The change in the employment profile is of great significance. The net number of people in employment rose from 9.6 million to 11.2 million between 1995 and 2002. However, there was an even larger increase in the number of unemployed, from 1.9 million to 4.3 million, during the same period. The increase in unemployment can be attributed to people from rural areas seeking work, especially women entering the labour market (GCIS 2003).

The Macroeconomic Environment

Over the last decade, the macroeconomic environment has improved significantly. Economic growth has been steady, albeit unspectacular, improving from negative per-capita real growth in the decade prior to 1994 to an average of 3 per cent, equivalent to just over 1 per cent positive per-capita growth, in the decade since then. The country is currently experiencing the longest period of uninterrupted growth since the 1960s and the rate appears to be set to move beyond 4 per cent on a sustained basis.

In the financial year 1993–94, the year immediately prior to the first democratic elections, the fiscal deficit of the general government stood at 9.5 per cent of GDP. By 2002–03, this had been reduced to 1 per cent, rising to 2.8 per cent in 2003–04.

Taxes of all spheres of government combined have been held at about 26 per cent of GDP for a few years.

Inflation has been reduced from approximately 15 per cent in 1994. At the end of 2004, it had remained within its targeted band of between 3 per cent and 6 per cent for the previous 18 months, and this was expected to continue in the foreseeable future.

Political Background to the Decentralization Framework

The Emphasis on Local Government

During the apartheid period, there was considerable dissatisfaction with the very poor urban services in black areas in contrast to high service levels in white areas. Much of the opposition to apartheid in the 1980s was rooted in protests linked to the appalling local services.

The banning of the main opposition movement, the African National Congress (ANC), from 1960, meant that political activity in the late apartheid period was based, to a significant degree, on a coalition of local organizations called the United Democratic Front (UDF). The UDF addressed mainly local issues, but also cooperated around a national agenda for fundamental democratic change. One of the key slogans of the time was 'One city—one tax base', essentially a call to unite cities across racial lines and amalgamate the separate, racially based municipalities while enabling local redistribution of resources.

With the unbanning of the ANC, many activists from these organizations became ANC office-bearers and were closely involved in Constitutional negotiations, taking a strong focus on local government into these negotiations.

The Motivation for Provincial Governments

Significant interest groups, largely on the side of the old apartheid regime, supported the creation of strong provincial governments. A number of political entities with regional ethnic power-bases saw provinces as a means to control political power in their own territories, or at least to weaken the national government, which they were unlikely to control. Thus, while the creation of local governments had strong support from elements within the majority ANC, the creation of the provinces was regarded by many as a compromise which threatened to promote ethnic division. Attempts to increase the provinces' powers to tax were resisted on the grounds that key resources needed to be raised and distributed nationally to facilitate redistribution.

The Resultant Framework

Nine provinces and 284 municipalities were created under the new dispensation. The latter were created in a two-stage process, which initially entailed the formation of approximately 850 municipalities, subsequently reduced by means of a demarcation process.

The call for 'One city—one tax base' resulted in widely drawn local boundaries. There was a strong emphasis on having bodies that could govern urban functional areas in an integrated manner. In the metropolitan areas, a two-tier metropolitan government system was initially created. However, this proved complex and was replaced in the final process of local redemarcation in late 2000 with single-tier metropolitan governments fully incorporating each of the major metropolitan areas.

Drawing from the assignment of responsibilities to regional governments during the apartheid period, the new provinces were given responsibility 'concurrently' with the national government for primary and secondary education and health. Over 80 per cent of their budgets are allocated to these services. They were also given responsibility for the distribution of welfare grants; however, by the end of 2004, this was gradually being shifted to a single national welfare agency.

Local governments were given traditional municipal service responsibilities, including water, sanitation, electricity, refuse removal and a range of community services. This last category includes sports facilities, traffic, emergency services and the like.

The Constitution has two lists of functions set out in Schedule 4 and Schedule 5. Each schedule is divided into Part A and Part B. Schedule 4 contains functions for which national and provincial governments have concurrent legislative responsibility, while Schedule 5 contains functions for which provincial governments have exclusive legislative responsibility. But local governments have 'executive responsibility ... and the right to administer' all functions listed in Part B of each of these schedules. Moreover, national and provincial governments 'must assign to a municipality, by agreement and subject to any conditions' matters listed in Part A of each of these schedules 'which necessarily relates to local governments, if a) that matter would most effectively be administered locally; and b) the municipality has the capacity to administer it' (Section 156 of the Constitution of the Republic of South Africa). Thus there is a Constitutional commitment to the concept of 'subsidiarity' in respect of the functions listed in the two schedules. This is discussed further in the section on realignment of functions towards the end of the chapter.

The Intergovernmental Fiscal Structure

The Distribution of Revenue-raising Powers

Most of the power to raise revenue lies with the national government. However, municipalities have significant tax powers, including property taxes and a local business tax based on a combination of a small levy on turnover and total employee remuneration by the firm. An investigation was underway towards the end of 2004 regarding a possible reform of this second general source of local business tax revenue.[5]

User charges play a very important role in financing local government.

Table 5.1 shows a breakdown of the main tax sources between different spheres of government. To demonstrate their significance and for comparative purposes, user charges levied by municipal governments are also shown at the bottom of the table.

Fiscal Transfers

Such an approach to the allocation of tax sources results in significant vertical fiscal imbalances at the provincial level, which in turn leads to the need for a major grant or transfer system. Table 5.2 shows the flows of revenue between the different spheres.

Table 5.1
Proportion of Revenues Raised by Each Key Tax Source for All Spheres of Government, 2003–04 (Revised Estimate)

Tax type	Amount (R million)	Proportion of total tax revenues
Total taxes raised by national, provincial and local government combined	317,992	100
Net taxes raised by national government	294,593	92.6
Personal income tax	98,200	30.9
Corporate income tax	72,250	22.7
VAT	81,000	25.5
Excise duties	12,715	4
Fuel levies	16,350	5.1
Customs	8,800	2.8
Other	15,000	4.7
(less SA Customs Union payments)	–9,722	–3.1
Taxes raised by provincial governments	3,531	1.1
Taxes raised by local governments	19,868	6.3
Property tax	14,343	4.5
RSC/JSB levies	5,525	1.7
User charges and other non-tax own recurrent revenue raised by local governments	45,300	14.3*

Source: South Africa (2004a).
Note: *Amount raised by local governments in user charges and other non-tax own recurrent revenue shown as a percentage of total taxes raised by the three spheres of government combined.

Table 5.2
Own Revenue versus Grant Revenue for the Three Different Spheres of Government, 2003–04
In R Billions

Sphere	Own revenue generated	Borrowing	Transfers from national government	All budgeted spending	Actual expenditure (excluding interest payments)
National	300.3	27.1	–173.9	157.8	110.5
Provincial	6.6	0	161.5	168.1	170.8
Local	64.8	2.4	12.4	86.0	79.9
Total	371.70	29.5	0	411.9	361.2

Source: South Africa (2004a).

It also shows that local governments do receive fiscal transfers from the national government. However, they collect a substantial proportion of their own revenue and also borrow to finance part of their capital spending. The six metropolitan municipalities are largely self-financing. They receive just 3 per cent to 6.7 per cent of their budgets in grants. On the other hand, smaller and rural municipalities with weaker tax bases are much more dependent upon transfers; they receive up to 87.3 per cent of their resources from transfers.

According to the Constitution, each local government and each province is 'entitled to an equitable share of revenue raised nationally to enable it to provide basic services and perform the functions allocated to it'. The Constitution specifies broadly what needs to be taken into account in determining the transfers. A permanent, independent Financial and Fiscal Commission, created in accordance with the Constitution, gives advice on all aspects of intergovernmental fiscal relations. The division of revenue has been surprisingly uncontentious since 1994.

The objective has been to ensure that transfers are formula-driven, based on objective criteria, well-publicized and determined well in advance. All transfers from the national government have to be legislated. Thus, each year, a Division of Revenue Act is passed along with the national budget. This Act explains the basis for the transfers and sets out grants to each province and municipality for the forthcoming three financial years. The outer years can be adjusted in subsequent budgets, but such adjustments are minimal.

Grants to Local Governments

Transfers to local governments are divided into 'equitable share' (unconditional) and conditional grants, the latter including grants for capital purposes. Grants to local governments have been increasing significantly in real terms in recent years, as indicated in Table 5.3.

Table 5.3
Conditional and Unconditional Transfers from National to Local Governments, 2000–05
(R Millions)

Year	2000–01	2001–02	2002–03	2003–04	2004–05
Equitable share and related	3,201	3,876	4,887	7,352	8,536
Conditional	2,336	2,642	3,820	5,038	5,709
Total	5,536	6,517	8,706	12,390	14,245

Source: South Africa (2004a).
Note: Totals and components of totals do not add exactly because of rounding.

These grants are essentially aimed at eliminating infrastructure backlogs in poor residential areas and financing the operating costs of the provision of basic services to poor households.

In 2003–04, R 4,137 million of the conditional grants provided were used to address infrastructure backlogs. This excludes transfers provided for low-income housing. R 901 million was provided conditionally for capacity building.

In metropolitan municipalities in particular, as well as in the richer non-metropolitan cities, there is in addition considerable cross-subsidization of poor households out of locally generated revenue.

Overall Framework and Philosophy for the Financing of Urban Infrastructure

Subsidization through Grants, Rather than Cheap Loans

The broad goal in financing municipal infrastructure, both urban and rural, has been to create autonomous, financially stable, self-financing municipalities, able to borrow from the private financial sector on a sound basis.

A parastatal development bank, the Development Bank of Southern Africa has lent to municipalities alongside the private sector. However, the emphasis has been on subsidization via the grant system and not through the provision of cheap loans.

As indicated, there are formula-based, unconditional recurrent grants provided to assist in financing the operating costs of service provision to poor households. At the same time, significant resources are being provided in capital grants to help overcome infrastructure backlogs.

It is envisaged that poorer municipalities will remain largely dependent upon grants, while metropolitan and other wealthier municipalities will be largely self-financing for both operating and capital expenditure.

Building Conditions for Financing Infrastructure through Borrowing

Avoiding National Government Guarantees

If municipalities are to be able to borrow from the private financial sector at reasonable rates, lenders need to be assured of being repaid. This can be achieved either by the national government guaranteeing repayment of loans, or by ensuring that the finances of local governments are sufficiently rigorous that such guarantees are not required. The South African approach has been to avoid guarantees. Strong antagonism to that arises from the experience of the late apartheid period. The system created 'independent homelands'—territories in which black South Africans were intended to exercise their political rights, leaving whites in control of the core of the country. These homelands were, in effect, able to borrow with repayment implicitly or explicitly guaranteed by the main South African government. This was a major contributor to the very high fiscal deficits inherited in 1994.

Section 218 of the Constitution thus states that:

Government Guarantees

(1) The national government, a provincial government or a municipality may guarantee a loan only if the guarantee complies with any conditions set out in national legislation.

(2) National legislation referred to in sub-section (1) may be enacted only after any recommendations of the Financial and Fiscal Commission have been considered.

(3) Each year, every government must publish a report on the guarantees it has granted.

In essence, legislation now prevents the national government from guaranteeing repayment of municipal loans.

Ensuring Sound Municipal Financial Management

Sound municipal financial management is dependent upon an overall sound local-government framework.

The framework for municipal governments has been built over the last decade through a number of processes. The Constitution underpins the framework. Flowing from this, there has been:

1. legislation on municipal structures, which establishes different types of municipal government;
2. a demarcation process in terms of a new Demarcation Act;
3. Municipal systems legislation, outlining the functioning of municipal systems;
4. new legislation on municipal property rates (i.e., property tax);
5. redesigning of the grants systems;
6. significant capacity-building initiatives;

7. modernization and standardization of municipal accounting; and
8. a Municipal Finance Management Act.

Work on building the system continues in a number of areas, including the design of a second general source of tax revenue for local government to replace the local Regional Services Council and Joint Services Board (RSC/JSB) business levies.

Municipal Finance Management Act

The Municipal Finance Management Act, passed in 2003, is important legislation aimed at fostering sound municipal financial management.

The Act places great emphasis on clarifying accountability and ensuring transparent processes so that key fiscal decisions have to be made public. The respective roles and responsibilities of mayors and municipal managers are clearly set out. Processes are stipulated for the drawing up of the budget, financial reporting, sound procurement practices, remuneration and performance contracts, the creation and governance of 'municipal entities'[6] and definitions of and sanctions for 'financial misconduct'. A significant section of the Act deals with borrowing, which *inter alia* states that municipalities may not borrow to finance operating expenditure other than for bridging purposes during the course of a fiscal year.[7]

A detailed chapter entitled 'Resolution of Financial Problems' sets out processes for identifying financial problems and regulating intervention by provincial and national governments in the event of 'financial emergencies'. The Act also provides for the creation of a Municipal Financial Recovery Service within the National Treasury. The purpose is to specify processes for liquidating and distributing these assets of municipalities not required for the provision of basic services in case of bankruptcy.

The New Municipal Infrastructure Grant

Over a three-year period beginning in 2003, the various conditional grants provided for financing the elimination of backlogs in capital infrastructure at the local level are being consolidated into a single Municipal Infrastructure Grant (MIG).

This is intended to make the system simpler and more direct, while also putting in place a stricter approach to ensuring financial sustainability. Municipalities are being given more flexibility in deciding how to allocate the capital resources, because the MIG will not fund projects; instead, it is designed to support the capital budgets of municipalities.

On the other hand, municipalities are now required to report to the national government on their whole capital budget, showing how the operations and maintenance of newly provided infrastructure will be funded. While the different national government departments will monitor different aspects, a single reporting process now replaces the plethora of different reporting processes under the previous approach.

Based on their capacity, the MIG categorizes municipalities into three groups. The 50 or so high-capacity municipalities are those able to produce sufficiently rigorous medium-term capital and operating budgets. They receive the MIG grants directly into their budgets, while others receive the funds less directly and are provided with support for capacity building.

The MIG is intended to place a greater emphasis on the achievement of outputs as opposed to inputs. It is focused on achieving a number of output conditions, including the achievement of service coverage targets, employment creation and the linkage of integrated development plans to budgets.

Over the next three years, most of the grants will be directed at addressing backlogs in water and sanitation, with significant amounts also intended for roads.

Borrowing Patterns

Borrowing by Metropolitan and Other Municipal Governments

Table 5.4 shows the total external borrowings by metropolitan governments as of March 2004.

Table 5.4
Municipal Governments' Borrowings

Municipality	*Total external borrowings (R millions)*
Cape Town	2,653.3
Johannesburg	3,842.8
Tshwane (Pretoria)	1.539.9
eThekwini (Durban)	3,085.4
Ekurhuleni (East Rand)	1,068.4
Nelson Mandela (Port Elizabeth)	296.9
TOTAL	12,486.7

Source: National Treasury, South Africa 2004b.
Note: These figures exclude the bond issues in 2004 by Johannesburg, totaling R 2 billion.

The key lenders have been the Development Bank of Southern Africa (DBSA), with loans totalling to a little over R 5 billion, and a private sector lender, the Infrastructure Finance Corporation (INCA), with loans of just under R 3 billion. Other private banks account for most of the remaining amounts.

Loans to metropolitan governments represent approximately two-thirds of all loans to municipalities by the DBSA, and just under three-quarters of all loans by INCA.

The Role of Borrowing in the Financing of the Capital Budgets of Metropolitan Councils

Cape Town

Tables 5.5 shows the revenue sources of the Cape Town metropolitan municipality, together with the funding sources for the capital budget.

Table 5.5
Cape Town Metropolitan Municipality

2004–05 Budgeted Income (R millions)	
Property taxes	2,299.0
Business levies	850.2
User charges	4,376.0
Grants and subsidies (including capital grants)	1,193.5
Other external income (including rents, fines, asset sales, etc.)	820.4
Internal income (including bulk charges, internal transfers, etc.)	1,786.4
TOTAL	11,325.5
2004–05 Budgeted Capital Sources (R millions)	
Capital grants and subsidies	630.6
Asset financing fund	258.3
External financing fund (i.e., borrowing)	685.0
Revenue	11.7
TOTAL	1,586.6

Source: City of Cape Town budget.
Note: US$1: R 5.70.

Municipalities in South Africa are in the process of introducing more modern and nationally standardized accrual accounting systems.[8] The Cape Town figures are presented on the basis of the new definitions.

In terms of this approach, municipalities are required to establish an external financing fund. This fund borrows from lenders such as DBSA, INCA and the private banks, and lends to the various departments of the municipality.

The capital grants include housing grants, which are received via the province and implemented by the municipality.

Cape Town will need to borrow in the near future and is considering, as are a number of other municipalities, the possibility of floating municipal bonds.

Cape Town, like most South African municipalities, is currently emerging from two hugely complex rounds of boundary changes and other institutional reforms. More than 30 municipalities in the metropolitan area which existed in 1994 were first reorganized into a two-tier system with a metropolitan level and six sub-structures. In line with new legislation, this was replaced from early 2001 by a single metropolitan council. It is understood that the new amalgamated council is about to receive an unqualified audit from the Auditor-General for the 2003–04 financial year, the first after many years of restructuring. This is likely to be followed by the city seeking an independent credit rating, and depending on the outcome of this, the city may decide to go the bond route.

Johannesburg

Table 5.6 shows the relative importance of the different sources of funding in Johannesburg's capital budget. As can be seen from the table, in 2004, Johannesburg successfully floated two bonds of R 1 billion each. In the late 1990s, Johannesburg experienced serious financial problems. Much of this was related to the institutional changes and complexity of the two-tier system that was initially introduced. Indeed, the Johannesburg experience was probably the crucial factor in the country deciding to create single-tier metropolitan governments from 2000.

Table 5.6
Share of Various Sources of Capital Financing for the City of Johannesburg

Loan funding	60%
Developers' contributions	7%
Provincial housing grants	25%
National infrastructure grants	8%

Source: Hunter 2004.

The successful floating of the bonds was significant in that it not only confirmed Johannesburg's recovery, but also served to demonstrate the scope for municipalities to raise finance in this way.

The first bond was a six-year unenhanced bond and carried a spread of 230 basis points over the rate for the equivalent national bond. The second is a 12-year bond and is enhanced by a 40 per cent guarantee by the IFC and INCA. It carried a spread of 164 basis points. Both bonds were over-subscribed.

The Scope for Further Bond Issues

South Africa has a relatively sophisticated financial sector, including an active bond market.

There are R 527.6 billion of outstanding bonds listed and traded on the Bond Exchange of South Africa (BESA).

Table 5.7
Share of Bonds Issued by Category of Public Sector Institution

Type of Institution	Share of total bonds issued by value
Central government	73.5%
Corporates	15.1%
Parastatals/utilities	7.5%
Water authorities	3.5%
Local authorities	0.4%

Source: Hunter 2004.

A municipal bond market did exist during the apartheid period, but this was in the context of prescribed asset requirements, whereby insurance companies and other major investors were required to hold a proportion of their assets in instruments such as municipal and other government bonds.

The new municipal bond market is emerging in the context of no pre-scribed asset requirements, no national guarantees and no tax benefits for municipal bonds. Indications are that it could become a very important source of future financing for local governments.

Further Realignment of Functions Related to Urban Infrastructure Provision

It was noted earlier that provincial governments are responsible for functions such as primary and secondary education and health, while munici-palities are responsible for services related to the provision of urban infrastructure.

This is somewhat of a simplification, because important aspects of urban infrastructure remain currently a responsibility of the national and provincial governments both. In particular, as in many other countries, national and provincial highways joining key national and provincial centres often constitute, in effect, a very significant part of intra-urban infrastructure. Furthermore, there are commuter rail systems in most of the major cities, which currently fall under Transnet, the national transport parastatal, which is in turn answerable to the national government rather than to municipal governments.

Similarly, provinces continue to play a key role in the social housing sector, including making decisions on the distribution of social housing grants originating from the centre.

During the apartheid period, when municipalities were geographically and racially fragmented, each serving only a portion of an urban area, it was necessary for higher tiers of government to play a significant role in the provision and management of citywide urban infrastructure. Now that municipalities have been created, incorporating the whole of the urban areas, including metropolitan areas (in the form of single-tier metropolitan councils), the conditions have been created whereby there is scope for greater devolution.

Some of the Constitutional provisions relating to the distribution of functions between different spheres of government have been noted earlier. A debate has begun to emerge as to how these provisions should be implemented in practical terms.

One possibility would be to regard provincial governments as the key locus of responsibility for functions related to investment in people. This would include the functions where provincial governments are already dominant, including health and education. Conversely, local governments would be acknowledged as the key locus of responsibility for functions related to the built environment. Again, this is where, for historic reasons, municipal governments tend to be dominant. National and provincial governments would always need to exercise some control over and responsibility for intracity national and provincial highways; however, this could be done within a framework that gave greater powers to city governments.

Making municipal governments, especially metropolitan and larger urban governments, responsible for these functions would make it possible for local governments to manage all issues related to urban form and urban space. In this way, linked functions can be dealt with by the same institutional entity and externalities more easily internalized.

One of the advantages of this approach is that it is broadly consistent with the current approach to financing of the two different spheres of government, whereby larger urban municipalities are financed primarily by local taxes and fees for services, whereas provinces are financed primarily by grants. Costs related to investment in people tend to be driven by population numbers, especially the size of the poor population. This places a limit on the extent to which provinces can be funded by provincial taxes, since there will tend to be a mismatch between revenue and expenditure needs. While this could be managed with equalization grants, the inequalities at a provincial level are very substantial, making this somewhat problematic.

On the other hand, the intensity and costs of services and infrastructure related to servicing the built environment tend to be driven by levels of economic activity. This makes it possible to finance these types of functions by means of locally raised revenues in a manner which does not result in such severe fiscal imbalance. The feasibility of increasing local responsibility in the areas of housing and transport, in particular, would depend to a significant degree on how the second general source of local tax revenue and grant flows are reformed.

Conclusion

Summary

Over the last decade, South Africa has succeeded in addressing significant urban services backlogs, while achieving macroeconomic balance from an initially precarious position.

This has been done through local borrowing and a combination of grants from the national government to the municipalities, particularly for provision of services to poor municipalities and neighbourhoods.

Following Constitutional provisions, the legislative framework excludes national guarantees of repayment of municipal borrowing. Policy makers and administrators have thus sought to create the conditions for borrowing within this context, to hasten the emergence of sound municipal finances while promoting autonomous local governments.

Indeed, given the relative ease with which the national government can currently raise revenue for infrastructure purposes, it could be argued that the system of local borrowing is more important as a means to ensure local fiscal rigour than as a means to raise capital. It offers one of the few instances where local leadership is required to demonstrate well-argued strategies and implementation plans well beyond the forthcoming elections to private lenders.

Key Risks

While there are grounds for optimism, a number of risks remain, which need to be managed.

First, the institutional changes that have been required of municipalities over the last decade have been hugely onerous. While most of the larger municipalities are finally bedding down the new systems and achieving a measure of administrative stability, a significant number of smaller municipalities have not by the end of 2004 been sufficiently successful. This requires sustained attention.

Second, until now the system has functioned reasonably successfully under relatively stable conditions and moderate economic growth. It may well be that the system is sufficiently stable to deal with much faster growth or recession. However, this is as yet unproven.

Third, South Africa needs to pay far more attention to the provision of mass urban transit systems. As indicated, how it is to be financed within the intergovernmental system has not yet been clarified. A failure to address this issue effectively is likely to lead to huge long-term urban inefficiencies.

Fourth, there is a danger that insufficient attention is being paid to the maintenance of existing infrastructure.

Fifth, the national government is currently reviewing the second general source of tax revenue to municipalities, with a view to reforming it. If this is not handled well (both effectively and efficiently), the system could be significantly undermined. It would be a significantly regressive step for the larger urban areas if the current RSC/JSB business levies were to be replaced by a central grant rather than a reformed local business tax—other than as a transitionary measure.

Sixth, there are processes underway to create independent electricity distributors. The major cities have all had large electricity distribution entities for many decades. While it is hoped that the restructuring can be undertaken in such a way so as not to undermine the municipalities, significant risks remain.

Seventh, the Constitution provides scope for increasing provincial autonomy. While municipal spending represents only about 6.5 per cent of GDP, provincial spending currently represents a further 12.5 per cent of GDP. As of now, the provinces do not borrow. Were they to do so, the task of ensuring that the financing of infrastructure occurs within a responsible fiscal framework may become more onerous and the risks greater. This needs to be carefully managed, drawing upon the lessons learned at the local level.

Finally, while it may take years to build trust in the rules of the game, a poor or populist response by the national government to a major subnational fiscal crisis has the potential to rapidly undermine this trust, despite carefully crafted legislation and other institutional arrangements. A system of the kind that South Africa is trying to establish needs to be constantly guarded and nurtured.

Notes

1. Of which the African National Congress (ANC) was by far the largest.
2. Approximately US\$ 230 billion at the exchange rate that existed at the time, of US\$ 1 = R 5.87.
3. Of the recipients, 49 per cent were women.
4. These figures are drawn from surveys by IDASA, quoted by GCIS (2003).
5. The author of this paper is involved in this research, together with Professor Richard Bird, Professor Emeritus of Economics and Co-Director of International Tax Program, Rotman School of Management, University of Toronto.
6. 'Municipal entities' are independent bodies created by municipalities, such as utilities.
7. There are provisions whereby lenders who knowingly lend to finance operating expenditures do not need to be repaid.
8. Accrual accounting has been used by municipalities in South Africa for more than two decades; however, new national standards are now being introduced, bringing the system as close as is feasible to current internationally recognized private sector accounting practice. Part of the motivation for this change has been the desire to improve transparency for prospective Private-Sector lenders, although there are far more substantial advantages for the municipal sector itself in improving the rigour and transparency of financial reporting on the basis of widely accepted standards.

References

GCIS. 2003. 'Towards a 10-year Review: Synthesis Report on Implementation of Government Programmes'. Discussion document published on behalf of the Presidency. Pretoria: GCIS.

Hunter, Roland. 2004. 'City of Johannesburg Municipal Bond Issue'. Presentation to IADF conference, 1 October, Washington.

Patel, Yusuf. 2004. 'New Urban Realities: Overview of Urban Challenges Facing South Africa'. Presentation at the World Urban Forum (WUF), 13 to 17 September, Barcelona.

National Treasury, South Africa. 2004a. *Budget Review*. Pretoria: Official Publication of the Government of the Republic of South Africa.

———. 2004b. *Trends in Inter-Governmental Finances: 2000/01–2006/07*. Pretoria: Official Publication of the Government of the Republic of South Africa.

PART II

Mobilizing Local Infrastructure Finance

The Financing Challenge

Local officials and their financial advisors have the job of mobilizing finance for urban infrastructure investment as effectively as possible within the fiscal policy framework that has been established. This section takes a practitioner's perspective in examining several of the financing strategies and institutional mechanisms that have been put together for this purpose, particularly innovations that have attempted to break new ground in mobilizing resources for local infrastructure investment. Understanding the nuts and bolts of how these efforts have worked in practice—often in ways quite different from the initial project design—should help others decide how institutional experience can best be applied to their own situations.

Discussion between fiscal policy experts and local practitioners at the conference allowed both parties to step back and consider the interaction between national development priorities, fiscal rules and local infrastructure financing options. The fiscal framework within which local practitioners work is more than a set of constraints on sub-national behaviour. It is a series of guidelines—well-defined or not, consistently applied or not—as to how responsibilities for building and financing urban infrastructure will be allocated among different levels of government and across the public and private sectors.

Local Governments' Investment Mission

National policy can assign local governments strikingly different missions in carrying out urban infrastructure investment. All five countries represented at the conference are pursuing 'decentralization' in the urban infrastructure sector, with the consequence that local institutions have taken on greater responsibility for implementing infrastructure projects. However, the scale of local government investment, its sectoral composition, and its priority in national development strategy are widely divergent. In this respect, the five countries are representative of a broader universe of countries working to define what it will mean in practice to decentralize urban infrastructure investment.

At one extreme of practice lies China. The People's Republic of China has adopted an explicit strategy of infrastructure-led growth. Responsibility for urban infrastructure investment has been assigned directly to municipalities and to municipally owned UDICs. It is common for infrastructure investment to account for 40 per cent of aggregate local public spending, and sometimes make up a higher share. Municipalities compete aggressively with one another to attract private investment to stimulate local economic growth. Foreign direct investment, the most mobile of the factors contributing to local economic growth, has been a special target of competition. The primary instrument for creating local competitive advantage has been infrastructure investment, primarily investments that contribute directly to Private-Sector productivity, but increasingly also environmental and other investments that contribute to quality of life. Local leaders who succeed in this municipal economic competition—as measured by growth in public fixed-asset formation, private investment attracted to the area, and public revenue generation—are rewarded not only by the satisfaction of higher economic growth rates but by promotion within the political party system. The distinctive mission that China has assigned to local governments, as the prime investors in national growth, profoundly affects their approach to mobilizing infrastructure finance.

Contrast this situation with the equally clear but very different investment priority that South Africa's policy and fiscal framework assigns to local government. The overwhelming driver of local government investment in South Africa is the national policy commitment to provide free basic services for all urban households. All households are to have free access to specified levels of water service delivery, solid waste collection and wastewater removal, electricity, and road access. All of these are services provided by local governments. Local governments' primary investment mission is to expand infrastructure networks so that the promised package of infrastructure services becomes available to households, mostly the poor, who are now without coverage. The commitment to provide a basic infrastructure service package to all households free of charge obviously shapes financing options.

The infrastructure financing choices of other countries similarly reflect national policy priorities for local investment. Poland is representative of a set of countries whose policy priority was gaining accession to the European Union, then meeting EU standards. Infrastructure investment needs have been skewed in particular toward bringing environmental standards up to EU levels with respect to safe water delivery, wastewater removal and treatment, and solid waste disposal. These are local responsibilities. The investment mission assigned to municipalities helps explain the importance for local infrastructure finance of such institutions as Poland's National Fund for Environmental Protection and the Environmental Protection Bank.

One can argue that the relative stalemate over urban infrastructure financing in Brazil and India reflects, as much as anything, lack of clear role assignment for local government investment. In both countries, an overlap of institutional responsibilities between state and local levels and between municipalities and parastatal agencies has clouded the role of local government in infrastructure investment and hampered the development of stable infrastructure financing strategies. In both countries, it is impossible to look at the Constitution or national legislation and say unequivocally what it is that local governments *should* be financing with their infrastructure budgets, or how the financing burden should be shared intergovernmentally.

Infrastructure Financing Options

Mobilizing finance for infrastructure investment is a two-step process. The papers in this volume concentrate primarily on capital financing—i.e., mobilizing the capital needed to finance initial investment and ensuring that, to the extent debt is incurred, it can be repaid by the borrower. However, responsible investment requires that adequate financing is also available for operations and maintenance (O&M) of capital facilities, once these are installed. Under some infrastructure development strategies, the challenge of long-term O&M financing weighs more heavily than the initial challenge of mobilizing investment capital. South Africa found this to be true of its pledge to provide free basic infrastructure access to all.

Tables II.1 and II.2 provide an overview of the array of financing sources that can, in principle, be tapped for local capital investment and O&M financing. They provide a reference point for considering the financing options that have been ruled in or ruled out by national fiscal policy and for assessing the components that go into the design of an overall financing strategy at the local level.

Table II.1
Potential Sources of Local Capital Financing

Intergovernmental grants
  Targeted capital grants for infrastructure investment
Local budget
  Operating budget surplus
  Dedicated taxes (e.g., betterment taxes) for capital projects
  Borrowing
    from market
    from higher-level governments or parastatals
Local balance sheet
  Asset sales
    municipally owned land
    other assets
Private sector investment in infrastructure
  Direct private investment
  Joint ventures
  Developer exactions (developer-installed infrastructure)

Table II.2
Potential Sources of O&M Financing

Intergovernmental grants
  Targeted grants for O&M of infrastructure networks
Local budget
  General operating revenues
  Dedicated (ring-fenced) user charges
    individual user charges scaled to consumption
    cross-subsidized user charges
  Dedicated (ring-fenced) taxes

A shorthand convention has emerged for describing the current urban infrastructure financing challenge. This 'conventional shorthand' holds that in an era of decentralization, national governments can no longer afford to be the primary financiers of urban infrastructure investment. Financing responsibility as well as management responsibility is being devolved on the local level. However, local budgets are inadequate to finance the high levels of investment needed to attack infrastructure backlogs and accommodate growth through a strategy of pay-as-you-go public financing. Therefore, local governments need to establish the capacity to access credit markets—long-term credit markets—if they are to install infrastructure on the scale demanded. They also need to reach outside public sector budgets to tap private investment. Finally, to be seen as creditworthy borrowers and viable partners in Private-Sector investment, local governments have to find ways to establish dedicated cost-recovery user fees for a wider range of urban services and ring-fence the resultant revenue streams to ensure that they are available for debt service or can be captured as reliable economic returns by private investors.

This capsule assessment underlies a large share of the infrastructure financing reforms launched in recent years in the urban sector, particularly those supported by international institutions. Although parts of the argument have been bolstered by efficiency claims—that private sector providers can operate services more efficiently than public providers or that borrowing from the market will force greater efficiency in local financial management—the main line of reasoning has been driven by financing considerations. Local governments are seen as needing large amounts of additional capital to meet their investment goals. In order to provide such capital, the market requires identifiable returns from project financing and legal assurance that it can capture these returns. If the national fiscal framework restricts local government debt issuance, more emphasis must be placed on attracting private sector partners as infrastructure investors.

The chapters in this section flesh out the institutional implications of this line of argument (where it has been followed) and offer some preliminary evidence regarding its impact on local infrastructure finance. They also point to a number of on-the-ground differences in policy approach. South Africa, for example, has a very strong policy of decentralization of urban service delivery and a remarkable rate of growth in urban infrastructure investment, yet it has financed the bulk of this growth through municipal infrastructure grants from the national level (see Chapter 9). Private sector investment in urban infrastructure has failed to materialize on the scale hoped for (Chapter 11), leading to debate as to whether expectations have been unrealistically high and should be permanently scaled downward, or whether government reform efforts have been inadequate and should be intensified. In some countries, land sales (Chapter 10) and other forms of extracting capital revenue from land-value gains have been able to finance a surprisingly large share of urban infrastructure budgets for a surprisingly long period, and may merit more policy emphasis than they usually receive.

The institutional experience discussed in this section also identifies different dimensions of risk trade-off. Fiscal framework design has concentrated on the risks associated with sub-national debt. However, as local governments seek out other forms of financing to substitute for borrowing, they can generate other types of risk that jeopardize stable financing arrangements. These include political rules associated with private infrastructure investment or the risk of turning municipalities into profit-maximizing land developers in the case of mobilizing infrastructure finance through land sales. The ramifications of these risks need to be weighed against the reduction in macroeconomic risk achieved by reducing local government borrowing.

One other dimension of institutional reality brought out by the papers is the complex role in infrastructure finance played by state or provincial governments—the middle tier—in federal systems or in systems like China's that approximate *de facto* federalism. It is tempting to think that national governments can dictate local policy for infrastructure finance. However, in federal systems, the last word often rests with the states, who have a large degree of freedom in deciding which investment responsibilities will be devolved to the local level and how investments will be financed.

Designing an Infrastructure Finance Strategy

The first pair of papers in this section tackles the question of designing a local infrastructure financing strategy.

Gao (Chapter 6) describes the infrastructure finance strategy applied in Shanghai and emulated by other cities in China. Shanghai became the world-class centre it now is through a deliberate policy of massive infrastructure-led investment. Over the period 1989 to 2004, roughly US$ 65 billion was invested in local infrastructure systems, helping to trigger rapid and sustained growth in complementary economic investment, economic growth and public sector revenue. In part because of the sheer scale of its infrastructure financing needs, Shanghai has adopted a 'diversified' financing strategy. It is the only city represented at the conference that has drawn upon *all* of the financing sources shown in Table II.1.

Three aspects of Shanghai's infrastructure financing strategy hold special interest for potential application elsewhere. First, Shanghai's economic assets and liabilities are now managed by specialized asset management companies (UDICs.) Gao is president of the largest Shanghai UDIC. Assets under UDIC management range from the city's subway system to its expressways, from water supply and distribution to wastewater collection and treatment, and to vacant land targeted for development. On the liability side of the UDICs' balance sheets are bank loans, bond issue debt and international debt obligations incurred to finance infrastructure projects. Specialized asset management companies of this kind have now been set up, by government decree, in all of China's municipalities. They are the only entities entitled to borrow on behalf of municipal governments. They have begun to introduce more professional standards in local asset management and finance, making it possible to gradually implement the government's announced goal of having municipalities rely less on politically captive branches of state-owned banks for their infrastructure financing.

Second, Shanghai has relied heavily on land leasing as a financing source. More than US$ 12 billion for investment has been generated directly by the upfront sale of land leasing rights, with the proceeds invested in urban infrastructure. Land also accounts for a large part of the balance-sheet asset value against which UDICs, as municipal agents, have borrowed.

Third, Shanghai's financing policy has called for modifying the mix of financing sources over time. Initial investment drew heavily from international lenders and the fiscal budget. As investment accelerated, incremental financing came largely from bank borrowing, supported by a general promise to pay from future revenues and assets and from the proceeds of land leasing. This strategy financed infrastructure to support urban growth by cashing in assets such as land inherited from the past and by borrowing against general revenues to be earned in the future. Now Shanghai is gradually shifting to a policy that requires current beneficiaries to pay for more of the costs of infrastructure investment—through higher user charges, polluter-pays charges and other devices. Joint venture capital has become a significant part of the financing mix for expressway construction and is planned to become a more important financing tool for other types of infrastructure, such as wastewater treatment plants. Shanghai, in short, illustrates the infrastructure-financing trajectory described by the 'conventional shorthand', with its own institutional modifications.

Cortines and Bondarovsky (Chapter 7) approach infrastructure-financing strategy from a sectoral perspective. They examine the evolution of Brazil's financing strategy for investment in water supply and sanitation. As in Shanghai, financing modes are deeply intertwined with institutional arrangements. In the face of rapidly accelerating urbanization in the 1970s, Brazil decided to abandon its traditional approach of municipally operated water supply and sanitation systems, which were seen as responding inadequately to investment demands for expanded coverage. A national policy was developed that financed water supply and sanitation investment through newly created public utilities at the state level.

The policy succeeded in boosting investment and rapidly expanding urban water and wastewater coverage rates. Investment financing was provided largely through borrowing from state banks. The programme, introduced at a time of strong economic growth and optimism about the future, was designed to be self-financing through user charges that included full cost recovery.

Financially, the system quickly came under pressure from runaway inflation and slowing economic growth. User charge adjustments failed to keep pace with inflation, partly because of government price controls. Over a longer period of time, municipal and public resentment mounted against the degree of centralization involved in state public utilities. A centralizing principle behind the state public utility design was that a single tariff rate for water use should apply to all municipal users in the state, regardless of actual local costs, and that local systems should be managed from the state level.

Today, the water supply and sanitation sector faces a financing challenge representative of all urban infrastructure investment in Brazil. Neither state public utilities nor municipalities have the funds to invest adequately in new infrastructure. As a result, the growth in water and sanitation coverage rates has slowed dramatically, with the remaining gap focused on those parts of the service universe—poor households and smaller, fiscally poor municipalities—that are most difficult to finance. Borrowing to finance public investment has been blocked by the Fiscal Responsibility Law.

Against this background, Brazil passed a new law on public–private partnership in December 2004. It was introduced in the hope that it would significantly solve the infrastructure-financing dilemma. Private-Sector equity capital and private borrowing would replace public borrowing as a financing source. It can be seen from the financing models elaborated by Cortines and Bondarovsky, however, that while the new institutional arrangements would *shift* financing risk from the public sector to the private sector, they would not reduce underlying risk. In one such model, the local government, instead of borrowing to build a public sanitary sewerage system, would contract with a private consortium to finance and build it, then lease the completed plant by pledging the revenue stream generated by user charges. In other words, the same revenue stream that would have secured public borrowing would now secure private borrowing and provide a return on private equity.

This relabelling of debt and revenue streams does not address any of the systemic risk involved in using politically sensitive and uncertain tariff revenues to support debt service. The strategy embodied in the Public–Private Partnership Act seems driven more by the extreme difficulty of mobilizing traditional revenue sources than by a realistic assessment of the probability of attracting private investment. At the time the Act was signed, it was projected that US$ 12 billion would be generated in private investment in infrastructure over the period 2005–07. However, more than a year after the Act was approved, not a single investment contract had been signed.

Municipal Development Funds

The second pair of papers in this section looks at variants of municipal development funds. Municipal development funds (MDFs) are wholesale financing intermediaries that lend to local governments. They are typically established by national governments or states, often under multi-lateral loan agreements, to support municipal investment. MDFs are a way to on-lend programme funds to individual municipalities without requiring the original supplier of funds to monitor each sub-loan.

One issue that has perplexed the design and implementation of MDFs is the sustainable impact that MDFs should have on municipal infrastructure finance. At the design stage, MDFs are typically envisioned as helping prepare the way for sustainable sub-national credit markets, by introducing municipal borrowers to market-like interest rates and standards of creditworthiness. Some MDF designs have gone further, to incorporate specific strategies for drawing Private-Sector banks or the domestic capital market into municipal lending via the MDF intermediary.

Kruger and Peterson (Chapter 9) examine the only 100 per cent Private-Sector specialized municipal credit intermediary in the developing world, the Infrastructure Finance Corporation of South Africa, or INCA. INCA has functioned as a pure intermediary. It issued bonds on the domestic market and used the proceeds to lend to municipal governments for infrastructure investment. Between 1987 (when INCA began operations) and 2004, INCA provided more than US$ 900 million of longer-term loans to South African local governments and allied institutions. It has been able to operate very profitably with a low spread between its own cost of funds and its on-lending rate. For the highest-rated credits, this spread has ranged between 50 and 70 basis points.

To designers of parastatal MDFs, INCA provides practical insight into what is required to make such intermediaries financially viable. INCA is a highly leveraged operation, whose targeted return on equity can be met only if loan loss provisioning does not exceed 0.25 per cent per year. Credit analysis and aggressive surveillance of outstanding loans therefore lie at the heart of INCA's activity. INCA lends only to an upper tier of South African municipalities (including all of the metropolitan regions) and charges higher interest rates for riskier credits. These policies stand in contrast to the typical parastatal MDF, which has spreads of 200–400 basis points, minimizes financial leverage, lends to all municipal borrowers at the same interest rate and experiences much higher loan default rates unless protected by indirect, higher-level government guarantees.

INCA's distinctive contribution to municipal infrastructure finance was to enter the municipal credit market at a time when traditional private lenders were exiting and to establish that market-rate borrowing was a feasible and sustainable component of investment financing for larger municipalities. INCA was founded at a time of great perceived risk in the local credit market. Formerly black townships had recently been amalgamated with formerly white townships amid vast uncertainty about the political and financial stability of the amalgamated municipalities. South Africa had not yet defined its intergovernmental grant or revenue-sharing systems. The national government had formally annulled the apartheid government's policy of guaranteeing Private-Sector loans to municipal governments.

In this context, INCA performed the classic intermediary function of delegated monitoring. It aggregated funds while specializing in assessment and control of the risks in municipal lending—a task that it was inefficient for individual banks to perform on their own. For a number of years, INCA was the sole private supplier of funds to municipalities. In the last year or two, however, as the budgetary situation of municipalities stabilized and intergovernmental financing policy was clarified, other financial institutions have returned to the municipal market. Banks and other lenders now compete vigorously for municipal loans. INCA's demonstration that the risks of municipal lending are manageable has helped develop credit as a reliable source of infrastructure finance at the local level.

Despite INCA's success as a municipal lender and the recent re-entry of other financial institutions into municipal lending, lending from all sources (public and private) has financed only 10–15 per cent of municipal infrastructure investment. Unlike national fiscal managers from several other countries represented at the conference, the South African National Treasury has argued that if future investment targets are to be met, municipal borrowing from the private sector will have to accelerate significantly. The treasury has estimated that the revenue flow to municipalities could responsibly support debt two or three times larger than current levels. Greater use of debt in the local financing mix will be necessary, especially for larger municipalities, since national infrastructure grants are planned to shift toward covering O&M costs in municipalities whose fiscal base is inadequate to finance the policy of free basic services for all households.

Krishnan (Chapter 8) examines an innovative MDF that stands out for incorporating an explicit strategy designed to promote Private-Sector participation in municipal infrastructure finance. The state of Tamil Nadu in southern India collaborated with the World Bank to set up the Tamil Nadu Urban Development Fund (TNUDF). TNUDF is the ultimate borrower under the World Bank programme agreement and on-lends to individual municipalities to finance infrastructure projects.

As pointed out in Section I, India has long had a low level of urban infrastructure investment. The principal innovation in TNUDF's design was to combine public (state of Tamil Nadu) and private ownership of the Fund and its management company. Three of India's largest financial institutions invested equity in TNUDF and are partners with the state in the management company. The project design anticipated that successful public–private collaboration would encourage the private partners to inject additional equity into the Fund and also attract private financing in other ways. For example, the private financing institutions were expected to co-finance infrastructure investment projects at the local level and help TNUDF launch domestic bond issues so that (like INCA) it could become a self-sustaining municipal credit intermediary.

In terms of the original financing goals, TNUDF's experience has been disappointing. The Private-Sector partners have not injected additional capital into TNUDF nor have they co-financed projects at the local level. TNUDF has not evolved into a financial intermediary that mobilizes financing on the domestic market for on-lending to municipalities.

The specific problems encountered by TNUDF are instructive for future MDF designs. As domestic interest rates fell, municipal demand for TNUDF loans evaporated. Other institutions undercut its lending rates and offered to re-finance TNUDF's outstanding loans. Ironically, these competing institutions were not direct Private-Sector lenders but other arms of the state of Tamil Nadu and the public sector.

There are alternative ways of interpreting TNUDF's experience. Krishnan faults the Private-Sector partners for not being more active in adjusting TNUDF lending to market realities. For their part, the private partners view TNUDF as being run as a *de facto* state agency, rather than a public–private partnership that pursues growth and profitability targets. All parties agree that if private-market principles are to be introduced into state MDFs, a common playing field must be established across state lending institutions so that these institutions do not cannibalize one another's loans merely because one institution is granted more favourable access to low-cost savings or tax advantages.

Despite its limitations in mobilizing domestic financing, the TNUDF model is widely viewed as having been successful in introducing governance reforms and enhancing implementation capacity for municipal investment. Accountability to a mixed public–private board of directors has increased the professionalism of project preparation and financing allocations. TNUDF's status outside of the government has allowed it to recruit staff from outside civil service and to pay compensation more competitive with the private sector. Early leadership in the Fund took an active role in assisting municipalities to experiment with alternative ways of securing direct financing for infrastructure projects, including pooled bond issues and private investment in infrastructure.

All of this suggests the need to define clearly the goals that are sought from public–private collaboration and to consider whether these are best served by joint ownership of a funding institution. Public goals for investment financing can conflict with the profit orientation of private owners. Performance management contracts may be a more appropriate way to enlist the professional skills of the private sector, while making explicit the exact performance goals that the state wants the MDF to pursue.

Other Strategies for Mobilizing Infrastructure Finance

Restrictions on municipal borrowing, coupled with municipal budget pressures, have caused governmental authorities to look beyond their regular budgets for sources of infrastructure finance. The final set of papers review comparative international experience with two of these financing options: sale of publicly held land and infrastructure investment by the private sector.

As Peterson (Chapter 10) points out, the sale of municipal land to finance infrastructure can be viewed as an exchange of assets on the municipal balance sheet. At this writing, much of the developing world has been experiencing an urban real-estate boom. Escalation of the value of land assets on municipal balance sheets raises the question of whether it makes sense to convert some of these land assets into infrastructure by selling land or land-use rights and using the proceeds to help finance the local capital budget.

The potential for municipal revenue mobilization is greatest when the public sector owns all land and economic rights have been assigned clearly to municipalities. This is the case in China. A number of Chinese cities have financed half or more of their very high investment in infrastructure directly from sale of land-use rights. Revenue generation on this scale is possible in part because of the high value of land (land-use rights in central Shanghai have sold for as much as US$ 9,000 per square metre) and in part because of the entrepreneurial manner in which Chinese municipalities approach the land market and urban land supply. Municipal governments aggressively 'create' marketable land by expanding urban boundaries at the rural fringe, taking up land in poverty zones for urban re-development, and even moving city hall and city administrative offices so that the vacated land in the city centre can be leased to developers. Within China's framework of competitive federalism, municipalities use the proceeds from land sales to finance fixed asset investment and stimulate local economic growth.

China is an exceptional case. However, Peterson shows that land leasing has become the largest source of municipal revenues and municipal investment financing in Ethiopia, at the other end of the development spectrum, and has the potential for substantial revenue mobilization in support of infrastructure investment in Indian cities, where the legal framework supports private ownership of land. Urban development authorities in India in particular have both land development and infrastructure financing responsibilities. The Mumbai Metropolitan Regional Development Authority, during January 2006, generated proceeds from land auctions at a single development complex that greatly exceeded annual infrastructure investment in the Mumbai region by all institutions of government.

Reliance on land sales for infrastructure finance creates a new set of fiscal risks that may need to be regulated by the intergovernmental fiscal framework. In financial terms, asset sales resemble borrowing. In both cases, up-front payment is received in exchange for a future revenue stream. The impulse by municipalities to generate cash by asset sales may require the same type of restraints in the name of fiscal responsibility as municipal borrowing. Such restrictions could include requiring that the proceeds of asset sales are invested in other forms of capital formation and not used to finance the operating budget, as well as other accountability rules to ensure that assets are not squandered.

Land prices have the advantage of long-term buoyancy with respect to economic growth and urbanization. However, they are extremely volatile. Dependence upon land sales for revenue creates a risk to fiscal stability exemplified in the recent past by the experience of Hong Kong, when the real estate market temporarily collapsed, driving revenues from land sales almost to zero. Vulnerability to real estate bubbles is compounded when land and property values become the primary basis for municipal borrowing. Intergovernmental rules may have to make special provisions to protect against municipal borrowing based upon speculative land-value gains that are expected to materialize after municipal infrastructure investment.

In the early and mid 1990s, expectations ran high among international donor institutions and governments that private investment in urban infrastructure could counterbalance the pressure on public budgets and significantly raise investment levels. Annez (Chapter 11) finds that private sector participation (or PPI) has fallen short of these expectations. Worldwide PPI spending for all types of infrastructure projects rose rapidly until the 1997–98 financial crisis, then plummeted and has not recovered. *Urban* infrastructure investment always has been a small part of total PPI, averaging only 10 per cent of total investment. It also peaked in 1997–98, and then declined precipitously. Even at its peak, PPI contributed only modestly to aggregate urban infrastructure investment levels. It was a more important source of finance in individual countries, such as Brazil, but even there PPI only moderated the decline in public infrastructure investment; it did not replace the loss of public-sector funding.

Experience with PPI has revealed that the risks associated with private investment are especially high in the urban services sector. Topping the list of risk factors are contract agreements regarding tariffs and investment in system expansion. No less than 76 per cent of all international PPI contracts in the water and sanitation sector had to be re-negotiated, on average within 1.6 years of contract signing. Contracts with price caps on user fees were especially vulnerable to renegotiation. Political sensitivities to rate hikes are part of the explanation for the failure to negotiate and implement stable tariff agreements, as is the absence of clearly defined and stable regulatory arrangements; but there are other factors as well. Water supply contracts have often required expansion of service delivery to poor households and repair of underground distribution networks. In retrospect, it is clear that both the companies bidding for contracts and the governments awarding them underestimated the difficulties of service expansion in poverty environments and the extent of deterioration in underground networks requiring repair. The notion that private businesses could straightforwardly apply customary business practices to collect water and sanitation charges also proved to be optimistic. Finally, the private companies involved in PPIs borrowed heavily on international markets for investment financing, exposing the projects to foreign exchange risk.

Looking forward, Annez predicts that PPI is likely to play a useful but limited role in future urban infrastructure investment. The revealed risks of the sector make it unlikely that private companies will be willing to assume both the capital risk of financing and the operating risks of system management. Governments therefore will have to examine more carefully what they want to gain from the private sector—mobilization of investment finance or potential operating efficiencies—and unbundle the institutional arrangements accordingly. To attract private investment, governments will have to lower project risk, which will require greater political and financial commitment—for example, by stabilizing regulatory procedures and refraining from fiscal capture of the rents that are produced when private managers succeed in improving the efficiency of local service monopolies.

The database examined in Chapter 11 covers primarily international investment in PPI. The next round of private investment in urban infrastructure may well come from domestic companies that are more familiar with the operating and political risks of urban services delivery and better able to manage these risks.

6

Urban Infrastructure Investment and Financing in Shanghai

Gao Guo Fu[*]

Introduction

Shanghai has a long history of seven centuries as a vibrant city with a distinctive culture of inclusion and diversity. But today's Shanghai is a youthful urban centre that is developing rapidly, as true urban modernization began only in the late 1980s.

Prior to the launch of this modernization drive, Shanghai's development had been hampered by insufficient investment in infrastructure, significant legacy issues and a poor investment climate. In 1990, on a per capita basis, road area was a mere 2.28 square metres; public green area was only 1.02 square metres; and housing space was only 6.6 square metres. In the late 1980s, there were almost 200,000 families struggling to live with housing space of less than 4 square metres per person. Traffic congestion, housing shortages and environmental pollution had become the three major obstacles constraining economic growth in Shanghai.

In addition, there were fiscal issues:

1. GDP growth hovered at around 4 per cent throughout the 1980s and early 1990s.
2. In 1990, the Shanghai government's fiscal receipts were only RMB 28.4 billion.[1]

[*] Gao Guo Fu is the President of the Shanghai Chengtou Corporation (Urban Development Investment Corporation).

3. Foreign direct investment was US$ 214 million.

Beginning in 1992, Shanghai seized the unprecedented opportunity of the development of the new Pudong District on the east side of the Huangpu River. A commitment was made to launch a new historical growth period, led by urban infrastructure development and the financing reforms that would support it. As a result, over 40 key projects have been completed, including four bridges and three tunnels crossing the Huangpu River, connecting the east and west parts of Shanghai; multiple expressways and an urban elevated road network; three railway transit lines, totalling 125 km in length; the Hongqiao Airport extension and the construction of Pudong International Airport; installation of an integrated sewerage system; upgrading of water supply facilities and water resource protection; and large-scale green area development. By the end of 2004, the per capita road area, public green area and net housing (living) space in Shanghai had risen dramatically compared with the situation in the 1990s (see Table 6.1).

Table 6.1
Comparison of Urban Infrastructure Development, 1990–2004

Item	1990	2004
Road area (m² per capita)	2.3	12.3 [2003]
Rail transit (km)	0	125
Living area (m² per capita)	6.6	14.2
Green area (m² per capita)	1.0	10
Wastewater treatment rate (%)	0	65.3

Source: Shanghai Statistical Yearbook 2004.

Shanghai has taken on an entirely new look. Moreover, Shanghai has adopted an explicit policy of using infrastructure transformation to generate economic growth. This has paid off in sustained double-digit growth for 13 consecutive years since 1992 (see Figure 6.1). Effective investment in infrastructure networks has not only directly improved the living standard and investment climate in Shanghai, but has contributed importantly to China's national economic growth.

By 2004, foreign direct investment (FDI) in Shanghai had risen to US$ 11.7 billion and the cumulative total of FDI between 1992 and 2004 had reached US$ 85 billion. The Shanghai government's fiscal receipts rose to RMB 359.2 billion by 2004, or more than 12 times what they were in 1990. Municipal own-source local revenues reached RMB 111.9 billion (see Figure 6.2).

Figure 6.1
GDP Growth Rate of Shanghai
In Percentage

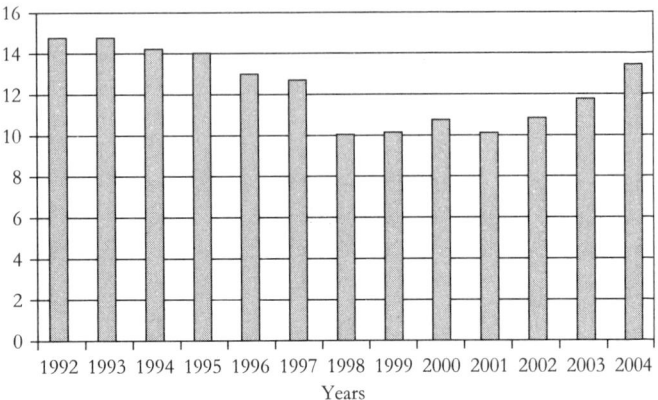

Source: Shanghai Statistical Yearbook 2004.

Figure 6.2
Foreign Direct Investment and Fiscal Revenue in Shanghai

Figure 6.2.1
Foreign Direct Investment in Shanghai
In US$ 100 Million

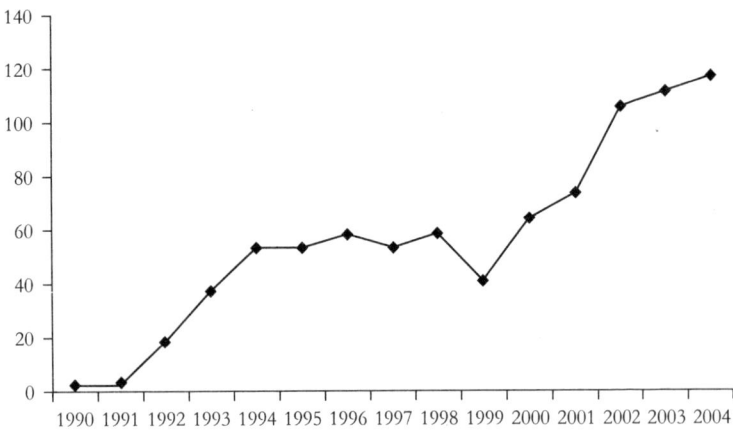

Figure 6.2.2
Fiscal Revenue in Shanghai
In RMB 100 Million

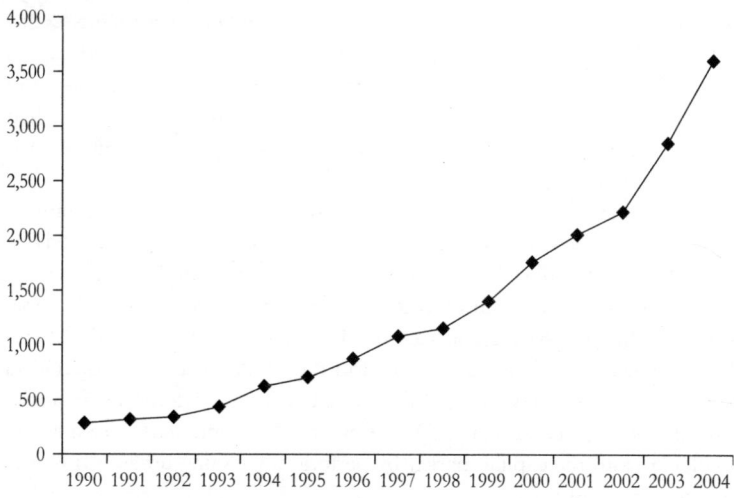

Source: *Shanghai Statistical Yearbook 2004.*

New Approaches to Urban Infrastructure Financing

The scale of urban infrastructure investment in Shanghai is very large and has required commensurate efforts to mobilize financing in a responsible way. During the 16 years from 1989 to 2004, a total of RMB 2,300 billion (approximately US$ 275 billion) was invested in all types of fixed asset formation in Shanghai. Of this total, almost a quarter (RMB 540 billion) was invested in urban infrastructure. It is expected that this rate of investment will be sustained. Accordingly, Shanghai Chengtou Corporation has been exploring new approaches to financing urban infrastructure construction, in line with the specific needs of Shanghai and the development characteristics of China in this new era. Specifically, the approaches adopted are as follows.

Diversification of Financing Sources

Under the planned economy, government fiscal input had been the only source of financing for urban infrastructure development. The first part of Shanghai's strategy for the diversification of infrastructure financing was the establishment of governmental investment corporations—such as the Shanghai Chengtou Corporation (an Urban Development and Investment Company [UDIC])—with a mandate to initiate new financing approaches, including bond issuance, concession management and capital market financing. As the biggest governmental investment corporation in Shanghai by the end of 2004, the Shanghai Chengtou Corporation had mobilized a total of more than RMB 140 billion (US$ 16.8 billion) for direct investment in urban infrastructure.

The second element of the financing strategy was to leverage limited governmental investments to attract loans from both international and domestic lenders. On the international front, loans from both multi-lateral and bilateral sources have been used to finance such projects as the Shanghai Sewerage Project Phase 1, the Yangpu Bridge, Metro Line #1 and #2, and the Hongqiao International Airport. On the domestic front, cooperation agreements have been successfully signed with large domestic financial institutions such as the China Development Bank and started mobilizing financing from the capital market by periodically issuing urban infrastructure construction bonds.

Through the above practices, the bottleneck effect has been eliminated under which the pace of development was constrained by the availability of government fiscal inputs, and have secured sufficient credit facilities for urban infrastructure development in the coming decade.

The unprecedented scale of investment in urban infrastructure in the 1990s might seem to involve 'pre-spending' future generations' earnings, but experience has demonstrated that in certain phases of development, it is more economical to invest early so as to take advantage of relatively low costs. Practice has proven that such investments can pay off handsomely.

Ending the Free Use of Land Resources and the Cheap Use of Infrastructure Facilities

In recent years, Shanghai has increasingly turned to financing strategies other than public borrowing. Since the 1990s, Shanghai has taken the lead in land leasing in China. More than 100 billion RMB (US$ 12 billion) has been generated from up-front payments for land leasing rights, all of which has been injected into urban infrastructure networks or infrastructure support for improvement of the city's housing condition. By leasing land at market values, the government has not only obtained a large amount of capital needed for upgrading urban infrastructure, but has also helped rationalize the spatial layout of the central city. Industrial sites, for example, have been moved out of the city centre and the vacated land leased to higher-value users who can take better advantage of the central location. It has thus been proven that land resources can be translated into capital in a market economy in which urban infrastructure is no longer treated as a 'charity' and payment is required for the use of scarce land resources and infrastructure access.

For revenue-generating infrastructure projects, such as expressways, urban water supply works, wastewater treatment facilities, etc., investments have been encouraged and attracted from international partners, domestic enterprises and private investors through concession contracts, joint ventures and competitive bidding. For example, the Pudong Water Works is a joint venture between Shanghai Chengtou and a French investor, Veolia Water, which successfully introduced an external investment of RMB 2.03 billion. The Zhuyuan Wastewater Treatment Plant is a BOT project won by a domestic investor, the Shanghai Youlian Consortium, which invested RMB 670 million of its own funds. Construction of expressways in Shanghai has been opened up to all kinds of investors, including private domestic and foreign investors, who have contributed RMB 44.8 billion, resulting in the substantial completion of the expressway network in Shanghai with a total length of 460 km.

In the early stages of attracting private capital for these projects, such as the Pudong Water Works, investors were guaranteed a specific rate of return and the city used other sources of income to supplement direct user tariffs. Now government guarantees have been greatly reduced or eliminated altogether, in favour of returns generated from tolls or user charges for projects where full cost recovery is appropriate. This policy both shifts more of the financial risk to investors and recognizes the economic value of infrastructure services to users.

For non-profit projects, which in Shanghai include bridges and tunnels, the rate of return on investment is determined and guaranteed by the government, while private investors are selected through market-based competition with open tenders, on the basis of project cost.

Development of diversified market-based financing has been accelerated by our strategy of opening up the infrastructure sector to market competition, in which the role of governmental investment corporations such as Chengtou is primarily to guide capital flows. This strategy is conducive to attracting more capital for investment in Shanghai's urban infrastructure from domestic enterprises, private businesses and international investors.

Reflecting on Shanghai's Experience

Looking back at our past experience, we believe that our modest success in infrastructure development over the past 13 years has been a result of four factors. First, it is very important to have a stable and sustainable master plan for urban infrastructure development, which should be in line with the overall city development strategy.

Second, Shanghai has had a major shift in mindset. Urban infrastructure investment is now at the centre of our city development strategy to improve the city's investment climate and to stimulate economic growth. This shift in orientation was particularly important at the initial development stage of the city.

Third, we have rationalized debt financing for urban infrastructure construction by effectively controlling associated risks. For a developing country, it is extremely important to control the scale of borrowing, as fiscal revenue may otherwise be insufficient for debt servicing. This is one of the primary reasons we have looked to the market for direct investment in infrastructure facilities.

Fourth, we have eliminated any monopoly in infrastructure investment and finance. The market should be opened and competition fostered, such that the private sector can participate in financing infrastructure development on a level playing field. The role of the government is to focus on implementation supervision, clarify and reinforce the policy framework, improve tariff collections and finance true public goods. To this end, we believe a certain amount of governmental financial input is still necessary in guiding urban infrastructure development.

The Future Agenda

If we look at Shanghai's pattern of urban infrastructure finance, we can broadly divide it into policies that use the money of previous generations, those that use the money of the next generation and those that use the money of the current generation.

Land leasing is a way of financing infrastructure that monetizes an inherited public asset (land) and the investment of past generations as reflected in urban land values. Borrowing places the burden of financing infrastructure on the next generation, when the loans that finance today's investments have to be repaid. As the economic development of Shanghai and China matures, it will be appropriate to place a greater share of the economic burden on the current generation. This will be achieved particularly by requiring that users of urban infrastructure facilities pay their full cost through user fees, highway tolls and rail charges, and tariffs for water supply and wastewater treatment. Shanghai is moving in this direction. We have a strong cost-recovery policy for highway usage and are gradually strengthening cost recovery through user charges and 'polluter-pays' charges for environmental services.

One other policy challenge that lies ahead involves the very concept of the metropolitan area. Shanghai is a 'province-level' municipality in China's governmental structure. It consists of a central municipal area and a number of surrounding districts that are part of the municipality. The urban centres of these outlying districts are quite large by international standards—sometimes exceeding 1 million in population. Moreover, most of the industrial growth in Shanghai is now occurring in these suburban districts, which also contain areas of intensive pig farming and other agricultural uses. From a metropolitan perspective, the most rapid growth in environmental pollution and corresponding need for environmental investment is found in the districts. For the most part, the districts also lie upstream of Shanghai's city centre, so that the pollution generated there directly impacts the central urban area.

In the past, Shanghai's fiscal system has been ill equipped to address the districts' financing needs. Shanghai, like other provincial capital cities, has viewed its investment financing obligation as extending primarily to the central area, the original 'municipality' at the core of the metropolitan region and the centre of the legal municipality. Outlying districts were left to finance infrastructure projects on their own, even though they typically lacked fiscal capacity or market access for financing.

In 2004–05, Shanghai fundamentally reformed its revenue assignment and tax-sharing policies. More revenue is now directed specifically to the districts, taking into account their environmental conditions and investment needs. Consistent with this reform, the Chengtou Corporation has developed a district financing vehicle (DFV) that will allow the Shanghai municipality to share its superior access to financing with district governments. Initially, the DFV will be used as a channel to finance district environmental projects, such as wastewater treatment plants, by sharing the proceeds of a World Bank loan to Shanghai. Repayment will be supported by project-level revenue streams and district guarantees. In the future, it is anticipated that the DFV, or an institutional variant of it, will be able to raise funds in the domestic capital market for on-lending to district projects and will be able to help organize joint-venture investment projects with Private-Sector investors for the districts' environmental facilities.

In this way, urban infrastructure investment can be extended into the outlying districts where, up to now, infrastructure investment has lagged behind the very rapid rate of population and industrial growth.

As a growing city, Shanghai will undoubtedly also face many new issues and challenges in the process of further urbanization. Given the objective of building Shanghai into an international economic, trade, financial and shipping centre and in view of the forthcoming World Expo 2010, there is much work that will need to be accomplished. Looking to the future, it is important to draw upon the valuable experience and best practice in infrastructure financing from around the world, in particular from other developing countries.

Note

1. Exchange rate throughout the period covered in this chapter was US$ 1 = RMB 8.35.

Reference

Shanghai Statistical Yearbook 2004. Beijing: China Statistics Press.

7

Mobilizing Financing for Urban Sanitation Infrastructure in Brazil

Aser Cortines and Sandra Bondarovsky[*]

Introduction

As pointed out earlier in this volume (Chapter 1), Brazil has imposed a number of restrictions on sub-national debt. These include the Fiscal Responsibility Law, which limits government deficits and borrowing, and prudential regulations that restrict financial institutions' exposure to government lending. The restrictions are part of a fiscal adjustment policy that, however necessary in macroeconomic terms, has contributed to a steep decline in sub-national infrastructure investment and has forced Brazil to search for alternative ways of financing infrastructure expenditures, especially at the local level.

This chapter focuses on the financing of investments in water supply and sanitary sewerage. The first section describes the institutional features of these services and their historical background in Brazil. The second section examines the current status of service provision and the magnitude of the urban investment backlog. The third section considers the new public–private partnership law that Brazil hopes will help generate direct private investment in urban infrastructure and outlines some of the ways this might be accomplished.

[*] Aser Cortines served as Vice President, Urban Development and Government Affairs, at Caixa Econômica Federal in Brazil.

Sandra Bondarovsky was an economist with Caixa Econômica Federal at the time of writing.

Brazil's Model for Urban Water Supply and Sanitation

Brazil began rapid urbanization around 1940. In that year, two-thirds of the country's population lived in rural areas. By 1980, 40 years later, the proportions had reversed: more than two-thirds of the population lived in urban areas. Figure 7.1 shows the dramatic rise in urbanization, which has continued since 1980, although at a slower rate.

Figure 7.1
Urban and Rural Population, 1940–2000
In Percentage of Total Population

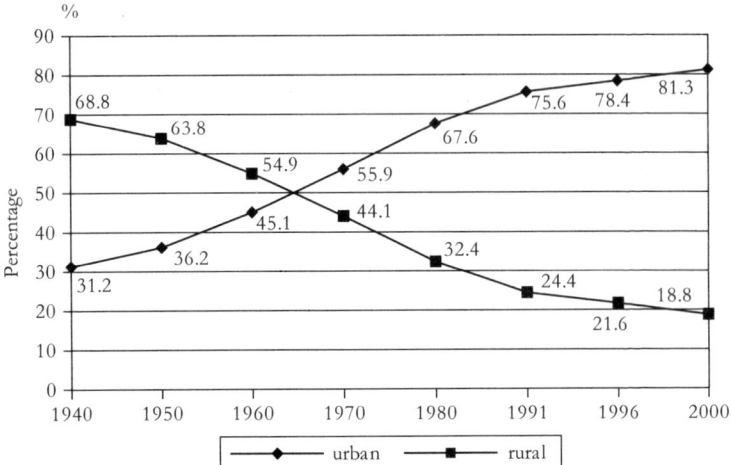

Source: IBGE, Demographic Censuses.

In 1967, Brazil's urban population was 43.3 million inhabitants. Out of these, 22.8 million—or just over half—were served by water supply services. Since water services were very expensive and irregular, only 35 per cent of the urban population was considered as having satisfactory access to supply. Concerning sewerage services, the situation was even worse. Only a few of the largest cities had sewerage services; when these were present, only part of the population was covered. Institutional responsibility for developing water supply and sewerage networks at the time was assigned to municipalities.

The quick urbanization process in Brazil and consequent need for investment in basic sanitation services led the government to establish a special financing and management system for the sector that replaced decentralized municipal management. The institutional model, named PLANASA, involved a national system of centralized planning, regulation, development and financing. It allowed the country to expand services at an extraordinary rate in the 1970s and 1980s—a period of strong population and urbanization growth.

The degree of success may be gauged by the quick expansion of the share of the urban population covered by water supply and sewerage. In 1970, 54 per cent of urban domiciles were served by water supply services. By 1980, the percentage had increased to 76 per cent and by 1990 to 88 per cent. Although reporting more modest results, sewerage system coverage increased from 22 per cent of urban domiciles in 1970, to 39 per cent in 1980 and 45 per cent in 1990. Because of the financial resources provided to the sector by state public utilities, municipalities started joining the PLANASA system. By 1984, it covered about 71 per cent of Brazilian municipalities.

Among the basic principles shaping PLANASA water and sanitation policy, the following were of particular importance:

1. A single basic sanitation public utility was established in each qualifying state. This concentration in a single public utility was intended, on the one hand, to reduce costs through economies of scale and, on the other hand, to provide comprehensive services to all urban areas, including the poorest ones, due to a system of cross-subsidization among urban areas.
2. A policy of self-financing through tariffs was established. Tariff rates were established for the public utility as a whole, regardless of the costs of each urban system's management. Tariff revenues were supposed to be sufficient to cover statewide operation and maintenance costs plus debt service (amortization of principal and loan interest).
3. Private participation was limited to consultants, contractors, materials and equipment suppliers.

The primary difficulty in implementing PLANASA involved the principle of financial self-sustainability. PLANASA was conceived in an environment of fast economic expansion. GDP growth over the period 1970–73 exceeded 10 per cent each year, reaching 14 per cent in 1973. In 1973, the real GDP was 90 per cent higher than in 1967. In the 1980s, however, the country encountered a period of macroeconomic instability, which hindered long-term plans and led to the indexing of tariffs to inflation. The extreme inflation rates of the 1980s created political pressure for price controls, including limits on tariffs and prices of goods produced by the public sector. Water and sewerage services fees were not able to keep pace with system costs, undermining the goal of financial self-sustainability.

If financial crisis was the most visible aspect of system breakdown, in political terms, emerging re-democratization also led to discontent with PLANASA. The government started discussing sanitation policy with broad segments of the civil population. The main criticism of PLANASA was its centralizing feature that excluded the participation of municipal local governments and consumers in addressing local problems. Concern was also expressed about the costs of state-level management.

The Brazilian institutional model for water and sanitation services still reflects this history. The sector is mainly organized at the regional level, with 25 mixed economy societies, controlled by the States, rendering services to 70 per cent of Brazilian municipalities and 77 per cent of the urban population in the country.

Current Situation of Sanitation Services

Today, Brazil faces a huge deficit of water and sewerage services. Besides the aggregate shortfall in coverage, the deficit is exacerbated by such factors as: concentration among the poorest population segments; concentration in less-developed regions and municipalities of the country; and severe financial deficits in sewerage services.

During the 1990s, the pace of expansion of sanitation services slowed considerably. Currently, Brazilian cities have 42.1 million permanent urban domiciles, out of which 4.4 million (10.4 per cent of domiciles) are not linked to public systems of drinkable water supply and 18.8 million (44.7 per cent of domiciles) are not served by sewerage networks (IBGE 2003). Most of the deficit is concentrated in lower-income populations. Among families with incomes up to five minimum wages (about US$ 430),[1] some 80 per cent lack public water supply and sewerage. Concerning territorial distribution, the deficit is concentrated in the smallest municipalities and less-developed regions of the country, as well as the quasi-rural areas surrounding major cities.

Another important aspect of the urban sanitation picture is the low level of sewerage treatment. Of the total sewerage collected, only 35.3 per cent is treated (IBGE 2000), while the remainder is directly launched into the environment with no treatment.

In brief, the remaining need for urban water and sewerage service is concentrated just where it is most difficult to pay for it—among low-income groups with the least ability to pay, in semi-arid regions where the cost of water supply is greatest, in small municipalities where fiscal capacity is lowest and in sewerage collection and treatment where investment costs are highest. The impacts of the cities' water supply and sanitation problems have reached beyond public health and citizen service quality to limit expansion of coastal tourism and affect business location decisions.

The Challenge of Universalizing Sanitation Services

It is estimated that to achieve universal urban sanitation service coverage in 10 years, considering annual population growth and standards appropriate to Brazil's developmental stage, would cost some US$ 41.3 billion—or an annual commitment of around 0.9 per cent of GDP. If the period for reaching this goal is expanded to 20 years, the estimated cost is US$ 59.3 billion[2], or the equivalent of about 0.6 per cent of GDP per year. In order to universalize service of solid waste collection, annually replace 20 per cent of the existing collection fleet, implement sanitary landfills at municipalities with populations under 1.5 million inhabitants, and replace unsafe municipal waste dumping sites would require another US$ 1.86 billion[3] per year for a decade.

By contrast, actual investment in the urban sanitation sector has been limited to roughly 0.25 per cent of GDP in recent years. Investment levels have been held back by the limits on public sector credit imposed since 1999, budgetary restraints, and lack of effective regulatory tools to impose environmental standards. The mismatch between investment need and identifiable financing has led to the search for new types of financing strategies that might close the gap.

Public–Private Partnerships (PPPs): What Is the Potential?

Brazilian policy has placed strong expectations on PPPs as a form of infrastructure investment that can avoid public-sector borrowing limitations and attract investment from the private sector. On 28 December 2004, the Brazilian National Congress approved and the President of the Republic signed the law that implements public–private partnerships.

The law is designed to encourage private initiative towards 'public' investments. In this kind of partnership, the private sector is in charge of totally financing the work and only after completion of the project, starts receiving payments for the investment it has made. In effect, the private partners advance the capital costs of construction, thereby avoiding the need for public borrowing. The public administration may set performance goals as a condition for releasing the remuneration to the private partner.

Under the law, public–private partnerships allow for a broad range of investments. There is no limitation concerning the nature of projects to be implemented. The partnership arrangement can be used to meet investment demands in fields such as public security, housing, basic sanitation, and roads or electric power infrastructure.

Among the main features of PPP contracts under the law are:

1. Contracts will be valid for no less than five years and may last up to 35 years. They shall establish legal arrangements to manage services and activities of public interest, where the private partner will be in charge of financing and executing the investment.
2. The minimum amount of a contract is set at US$ 6.7 million.
3. Government partners will contribute grants to assist financing. Grants may take innovative forms, such as dedicated revenues or special funds capitalized with federal real estates. A special fund having its own assets and governed by Private-Sector law will be established for the purpose of grant administration. The financial contribution of the federal government, state-owned enterprises and foundations to this fund will be limited to US$2 billion.
4. Payments shall be in cash, through non-tax credits or as a grants of rights.
5. Encumbrances may be liquidated in favour of the institution that financed the project as a guarantee of financial advances.
6. A management institution will be established at the national level and will be in charge of providing flexibility to PPP arrangements. It is intended to overcome bureaucratic barriers and reinforce transparency.
7. Private partners must finance at least 30 per cent of each project from their own (private) sources in order to prevent the undertaking from being fully financed by public institutions.
8. All projects are subject to approval by the Brazilian National Treasury, which must certify that the federal government's annual expenses with PPP do not exceed 1 per cent of its tax-related revenues. This limit is now roughly US$ 1.3 billion.

The programme expects to generate investments of approximately US$ 12 billion over the period 2005–07. A portfolio of projects of priority interest to the federal government was established, covering the fields of infrastructure and electric power. This portfolio has been presented to national and foreign investors. Other aspects of the law approved by the National Congress include a provision that contract payments under PPP shall be given legal priority and that financing will be facilitated by the National Bank for Economic and Social Development.

In spite of all the aspects mentioned above, only the methods of administration, control and supervision to implement partnerships were developed by the federal government in 2005; no project has been contracted. Besides, 2006 is expected to be a difficult year because there will be elections in Brazil. On the other hand, there are well-structured projects in some states and there is a strong conviction that they will be developed in 2006, mainly in the states of São Paulo, Bahia, Minas Gerais and Santa Catarina.

Models of PPP Developed by Caixa

Caixa Econômica has been elaborating models of how PPP financing might work in practice.

A Model of Asset Leasing

In one such model, the basic sanitation public utility conducts a bidding process, under which private partners agree to build infrastructure facilities and then lease them to the utility. The contract is awarded to the bidder that offers the lowest or most attractive leasing terms. In this model:

1. The successful bidder (which may be a consortium) establishes a specific-purpose society to be the owner of the asset to be leased to the public utility.
2. Lease payment is made by segregating receivables from the public utility, duly audited. The credit quality of the receivables would be rated by a credit agency.
3. The specific-purpose society obtains financing for its investment by pledging the receivable revenue stream.
4. Receivables (water bills) are provided by the utility as rental payment for the asset, through the intermediation of a financing agent.
5. The entire operation is continually monitored by a trustee with broad powers of financial management in the arrangement.

Such a model has been discussed by CAIXA for possible application in the financing of a sanitary sewerage system in a region of Campinas, a municipality of the state of São Paulo, to be operated by the municipal sanitation public utility. The specific-purpose society would be formed by five enterprises, with investment amounting to some US$ 11.7 million.

The model has also been discussed with the cities of Salvador and Lauro de Freitas (state of Bahia), where operations would be conducted by the state public utility on waters and sewerage. Expected investment would amount to US$ 50 million.

In each of these cases, the private investing group would obtain financing and build the project, using the public utility revenue stream as security. The model avoids public-sector borrowing. Its feasibility to private investors will depend on the reliability of the revenue stream, which in turns depends upon such critical issues as who will have responsibility and authority to collect water bills and what type of regulatory assurance can be obtained regarding the level of future water tariffs.

Other Types of Private Participation in Financing

CAIXA has supported the development and financing of other types of private participation in urban sanitation infrastructure. The governmental programme of financing to private sector concessionaires is aimed at financing private initiatives to improve sanitary conditions in urban areas, by increasing coverage and improving basic services. As an example, in December 2004, a BOT project was executed with the sanitation public utility of the municipality of Mauá, in the state of São Paulo. The investment, amounting to US$ 19 million, is for building a modern sewerage treatment plant, which will have as effluent water that can be reused by industrial consumers of the Petro-Chemical Pool.

The specific-purpose enterprise involved in this project received a partial grant for its investment, limited to sanitary sewerage and management of the commercial aspects of the municipal water system. The latter is an important feature of the grant, since the enterprise will handle management of water connections and billing for water provided by the municipal independent agency (*autarquia*) responsible for water supply.

Conclusion

As highlighted in the first section of this chapter, Brazil's urban sanitation sector got into trouble in the 1980s when state public utilities failed to adjust tariffs so as to maintain financial capacity in the face of inflation. In the years following Brazil's Real Plan, the public utilities attempted to recover their financial position and tariff levels, but most failed because of a lack of adequate regulatory framework that could simultaneously adjust tariffs and force greater cost-efficiency in service delivery.

Financial engineering on its own cannot solve the urban sanitation sector's problems. A comprehensive policy that sets clear rules for setting tariffs, identifying investment goals and controlling utility costs will be required. The process of formulating such a policy has begun. A series of regional workshops held in state capitals, culminating with a national seminar, has led to the outlines for a national sanitation system, coordinated by the Ministry of Cities. It is hoped that this effort will produce a regulatory framework that focuses on tariff policy and incentives to efficiency, while also producing the regulatory certainty that is necessary to support private investment in the sanitation sector.

Notes

1. US$ 1 = R$ 3.00. Exchange rate used throughout the chapter, corresponding to the average value of the dollar in 2004.
2. Data obtained from the Ministry of Cities.
3. Data obtained from the Ministry of Environment.

References

IBGE (Instituto Brasileiro de Geografia e Estatística). 2003. *National Survey of Domicile Samplings (PNAD—2003)*. Ministry of Planning, Budget and Management, Federal Government of Brazil.

————. 2001. *Demographic Censuses (1940–2000)*. Ministry of Planning, Budget and Management, Federal Government of Brazil.

————. 2000. *National Survey of Basic Sanitation (PNSB—2000)*. Ministry of Planning, Budget and Management, Federal Government of Brazil.

8

Tamil Nadu Urban Development Fund: Public–Private Partnership in an Infrastructure Finance Intermediary

Introduction

The Tamil Nadu Urban Development Fund (TNUDF) stands out as one of the first efforts in the developing world to establish public–private collaboration in the funding and management of a local urban-infrastructure financing intermediary. TNUDF had dual objectives in its design. As a financing vehicle, it was intended to attract private resources for on-lending to local governments and to support other forms of Private-Sector cofinancing of urban investment projects, thereby leveraging traditional resources, such as state government funding and multilateral donor loans, to help remedy a severe shortfall in urban infrastructure investment. As a management reform, TNUDF was designed to take urban infrastructure financing out of the realm of government budgetary allocations and regulations, and instill it with a business orientation that would accelerate financing decisions and encourage innovation.

It is an opportune time to take stock of TNUDF's accomplishments and shortfalls. The basic institutional design is being widely imitated in India and has been proposed by donor organizations for application in other countries. A similar structure is now being discussed in India as the basis

* L. Krishnan worked for the Government of India as Special Secretary to the Government of Tamil Nadu.

for an ambitious National Urban Investment Fund, which would have a core funding target of US$ 1 billion, besides additional project-level counterpart financing.

TNUDF has spawned a number of innovations in local infrastructure finance that provide potential models for future private financing. For a period, it successfully amplified the World Bank loan resources that formed the backbone of TNUDF's funds. The Tamil Nadu state government has judged this experiment—of taking many of the implementation decisions about local infrastructure finance and project investments outside the regular state machinery, to be executed by a separate institution, accountable to both private and public equity holders—to have been highly successful.

At the same time, several of the expectations about the impact of public–private collaboration through TNUDF have proved to be too optimistic. TNUDF has not been an especially effective vehicle for channelling Private-Sector funds into the local infrastructure sector. There have been no additions to Private-Sector equity investment in TNUDF since the institution's launch in 1997. On the contrary, the board of directors recommended in December 2005 that half of the outstanding capital contribution be returned to investors, on the ground that it was not needed to meet visible demand for TNUDF financing and because of unsatisfactory returns on equity. Part of the problem seems to have been the volatile movement of interest rates for debt financing in India over the last few years and less-than-optimal appreciation of portfolio management from the government side and the managers in the Fund. The Fund had to contend with a public-sector competitor who had access to grant funds from the federal government, the state government and reflows from municipal corporations and parastatals under various state-funded urban development initiatives. This led to some distortions in the urban financial market in the state. The financial institutions that are equity investors in TNUDF have not co-financed investment projects with TNUDF at the local level, as was foreseen in the original programme design. TNUDF has yet to regularly mobilize debt financing from the private capital market as an infrastructure-financing intermediary. Its one venture into debt issuance involved borrowing at a rate that exceeded the expectations of interest rate and tenor of urban local-body borrower institutions.

All of this is to say that TNUDF—like most institutions, when examined closely and even-handedly—has a mixed record of achievement and disappointment, both on its own and in its interaction with the state government and with the private sector. It is this mixed record that makes its experience instructive as a case study.

Local Government Context

The urban local bodies (ULBs) in Tamil Nadu—a major state in the southern part of India—comprise 6 municipal corporations, 102 municipalities and 43 intermediate urban centres recently upgraded to 'municipalities'. There are also roughly 565 rural Panchayats (also called Special Village Panchayats) which are in varying degrees of urbanization, going by the occupation and civic needs of the settlements. According to the most recent national census (Registrar General Census 2001), Tamil Nadu is considerably more urbanized than India as a whole. It has a 41 per cent urbanized population compared to 29 per cent for all of India. Except for the one metropolitan centre, Chennai, the urbanized population is spread more evenly over numerous small and mid-size urban locations than is true in other urbanized states.

Resources of Urban Local Bodies

The state government of Tamil Nadu contributes to the finances of urban bodies by way of revenue (operating) and capital expenditure grants from the budget, based on the revenue-sharing formula recommended by the State Finance Commission. The grant system, however, has not adequately addressed the infrastructure creation and maintenance issues of the urban local bodies. The Constitution of India was amended in 1994 (by the 74th Constitutional Amendment Act) to provide for elected local governments. It was also left to the states to provide for greater transfer of resources and functions to the urban local bodies. The revenues of the urban bodies now come from property taxes, profession tax, duty on registration, entertainment tax, and monies devolved from taxes collected by the state by means of statutory transfers. A user charge for water supply, which typically covers part of the operating costs, is collected in many urban local bodies. Own-source revenues, however, remain a small part of the budgets of urban local bodies. Most of their revenue comes from the state government, which also plays a large role in the determination of investment priorities.

ULB Expenditures

Aside from the personnel costs of general administration (establishment), the major expenditure items in the urban local bodies are for the operation and maintenance of civic assets and services. Many ULBs have contracted debt from institutions such as the Housing and Urban Development Corporation of India and the Life Insurance Corporation of India, as well as from the state government, for funding past investments in water supply and sanitation and solid waste management. Hence debt service is another significant item of expenditure.

In practice, investment in creation of new infrastructure assets was until a few years ago quite minimal, owing mainly to the paucity of grant funds from the state government, the reluctance of the private and public financing institutions to involve themselves in this line of activity, poor urban governance in some part, and the inability of ULBs to generate operating surpluses that could be devoted to capital formation. Maintenance and repair of existing assets also have been poor.

Urban Development Projects in Tamil Nadu

The government of Tamil Nadu has been successful in associating multilateral institutions such as the World Bank in development of the urban sector and for this purpose has been willing to put in place many reform measures both for service delivery and for attracting investments into the sector. The first Tamil Nadu Urban Development Project was a major effort at addressing infrastructure investment in terms of capacity enhancement for project execution in the local bodies, financing packages aimed at enhancing cost recovery, and the creation of a specialized financial intermediary to serve as a revolving fund for project finance.

It was a logical step for the government to scale up the experience gained in the first project and organize a much larger intervention in the urban sector through the Tamil Nadu Urban Development Project–II, which coincided with the national initiative on decentralization and democratization of the urban sector through the 74th Constitutional Amendment Act. The project has two distinct components—an institutional development component which looks at capacity building in urban local bodies and state institutions to support effective infrastructure investment and good governance, with a financing window for sub-projects aimed at improving urban infrastructure services and ensuring access for the poor to such services. The Tamil Nadu Urban Development Fund (TNUDF) is this financing window. A professional company called Tamil Nadu Urban Infrastructure and Financial Services Ltd (TNUIFSL) manages the Fund. Both the Fund (the Fund has a corporate trustee, i.e., the Tamil Nadu Urban Infrastructure Trustee Company Limited) and the management company have joint public–private equity ownership.

Urban Infrastructure Investment Needs in Tamil Nadu

The scale of the urban infrastructure investment backlog in Tamil Nadu can be gauged from recent reports of the State Finance Commissions. The TNUDF was set up in the hope that it would be able to address the backlog.

State Finance Commission (SFC) Estimates of Investment Needs

The Constitution of India mandates each state to establish a statutory finance commission every five years to recommend the revenue-sharing principles between the state and local bodies, including the urban local bodies. Two such commissions have been constituted and have submitted reports so far in Tamil Nadu. The first commission was constituted in 1994; its report was for application over the financial period 1997–2002. The report of the second commission, formed in 1999, covers the award period 2002–07. The third commission was constituted, with appropriate terms of reference, in December 2004, with a report due in mid-2006 for application in the next five-year period.

The finance commissions have not only come up with recommendations on revenue sharing between the state government and various tiers of local bodies, but also estimates of the investment requirements of local bodies to provide civic services based on standards arrived at in consultation with stakeholders. Table 8.1 summarizes the capital investment need projections prepared by the second finance commission. It estimated that investment of some Rs 81.2 billion (roughly US$ 2 billion)[1] would be required to meet the targeted infrastructure standards for all urban local bodies. A large part of this investment need was located in the urbanizing town Panchayats, where the cost of meeting water-delivery standards in particular was very large.

The Second State Finance Commission recognized that investment on this scale was beyond the realm of probable reality and that even if the capital

Table 8.1
Urban Investment Requirements as per the Second State Finance Commission
In Rs Million

Sl. No	Local bodies	Water supply	Sewerage & sanitation	Roads	Storm drains	Street lighting	Solid waste management	(Rs millions)	
								Others	Total
1	Chennai Municipal Corporation	1,756	956.6	1,147.2	3,124.9		502.2	1,430.9	8,917.8
2	Other municipal corporations	3,306	3,136.8	1,960.9	4,354.5	431.9	657.3	1,986.8	15,834.2
3	Municipalities	6,733.8	3,912.8	2,043.7	11,016.0	435.8	337.5	2,310.2	26,789.8
4	Town Panchayats	14,094.1	416.7	4,065.1	6,844.7	1253.0	204.8	2,829.1	29,707.5
	Total	25,889.9	8,422.9	9,216.9	25,340.1	2,120.7	1,701.8	8,557.0	81,249.6

Source: Government of Tamil Nadu (2001).

investment was made, local bodies would be unable to operate and maintain infrastructure service delivery, given the limitations of their operating budgets. The commission made an estimate of what it termed the 'sustainable' level of financing—i.e., the magnitude of infrastructure investment that was financially sustainable in terms of operations, maintenance and debt service, given local bodies' recurring revenues and the recommendations that the commission was making for changes in state support over the next five-year period. It put this sustainable investment level at about Rs 24.3 billion. As would be expected, a larger share of the 'sustainable' investment was concentrated in the larger urban local bodies, particularly the six municipal corporations, because of their stronger revenue bases and consequent greater ability to pay.

Estimates by TNUDF of Local Infrastructure 'Demand'

In 2004, as part of an analysis of future infrastructure financing demand, TNUDF carried out a similar study of local investment needs and financing capacity. The findings paralleled those of the Second Finance Commission. TNUDF estimated that some Rs 69 billion would be required over the next five years to meet physical investment standards for the urban population and that roughly two-fifths of this amount, or Rs 27 billion, constituted investment that could realistically be financed over a five-year period, based on the capacity of urban local bodies to tap their own tax revenues, the devolution of fiscal resources from the state government and the application of user charges at sustainable rates. One of the principal assumptions behind this estimate of financing capacity was the projection that the ULBs could borrow up to the point that annual debt service constituted 30 per cent of total revenue. This is the ceiling of debt-service-to-revenue-ratio allowed under TNUDF lending terms.

Of course, this estimate of financing 'capacity' is not the same thing as local 'demand' for infrastructure finance, since it does not take into account the extent of citizens' willingness to pay or the local governments' political willingness or ability to raise taxes and user fees for infrastructure investment purposes. Nor does it fully recognize constraints on the ability of governmental units at all levels to design and implement projects, notwithstanding the attempts to increase such capacities through the World Bank project. Nonetheless, the results of this estimate, reported in Table 8.2, provide a good picture of 'potential demand' for local infrastructure investment over the five-year period 2004–05 to 2008–09, as seen by the state government and TNUDF.

Table 8.2

TNUDF Estimates of Local Financing Capacity for Urban Investment Needs, Five-Year Period Starting 2004–05
Summary of Capital Investment Financing Capacity for Core Civic Services, 2004–05 to 2008–09
In Rs Millions

Particulars	Municipal corporations	Municipalities	Upgraded ULBs (erstwhile TPs)	Total	%
1. Water supply	4,539	7,634	4,214	16,387	24
2. Sewerage and sanitation	5,449	3,874	284	9,608	14
3. Storm water drainage	11,358	12,504	5,413	29,275	43
4. Solid waste management	55	98	39	192	0
5. Roads and other road infrastructure	2,274	2,012	1,467	5,753	8
6. Streetlights	393	458	470	1,321	2
7. Other services and infrastructure	2,407	2,658	1,189	6,254	9
Total	26,475	29,238	13,076	**68,789**	100
Percentage	38	43	19	100	
Capital investment estimate per capita—rupees					
1. Year 2003–04 population	3,130	3,350	6,410	3,578	
2. Year 2008–09 population	2,944	3,204	6,219	3,402	

Note: Norms for various civic services such as water supply and sanitation, storm water drainage, roads and culverts, etc., were arrived at after consultations with all stakeholders. For example, in the case of water supply, the norms vary between 90 litres per capita per day for municipal areas to 140 litres per capita in the Chennai Corporation area. Investment 'needs' estimated by this procedure were then reduced to take into account the portion of needs that could be realistically paid for by urban local bodies, given the revenue sources of different types of local bodies.

TP = town panchayats

One of the interesting features of Table 8.2 is the relative shift in sectoral needs estimates and implied sectoral priorities as compared to the State Finance Commission's report, summarized in Table 8.1. In TNUDF's projections, storm water drainage becomes the largest 'need' for ULB infrastructure financing. This reflects both a higher level of service norms, as established by state authorities, and a greater assumed ability to pay for investments in the sub-sector, given state support for such investment as part of its roads programme.

Design of the Tamil Nadu Urban Development Fund

Creation of a joint public–private financing intermediary was conceived as an institutional response to the magnitude of the ULB infrastructure financing gap and to the fact, as noted by the State Finance Commissions, that financing-as-usual was not making much headway in reducing the gap. This technical assessment was reinforced by the demand for better basic services exerted by citizens in the urban centres, as expressed through successive elections to councils. The government of Tamil Nadu was clearly searching for a mechanism to leverage the revenues of the ULBs so as to attract private capital and boost levels of investment in municipal infrastructure.

Underlying the TNUDF approach was the assumption that, because of the state's own budget difficulties, grants and shared revenues from the state could not meet local investment requirements. It was further assumed that there was unrealized potential for local revenue generation that, coupled with gradual increases in state revenue support, could produce revenue streams adequate to repay up-front local borrowing. Local government borrowing therefore became the critical element for responding to the investment financing gap. TNUDF was designed to be an efficient intermediary in the lending process, mobilizing capital from the domestic market and multilateral institutions on the one hand and on-lending to urban local bodies on the other.

Apart from enhancing capital flows by tapping Private-Sector resources, the government of Tamil Nadu sought to create in the TNUDF an arm's-length institution that could manage resource mobilization and allocation without the burden of governmental guarantees and which was insulated to a substantial degree from the pressures of everyday politics and the demands of bureaucracy. It was felt that such an institution would speed up decision making and establish more professional grounds for project development and financing. It was also expected to promote closer interaction with financial markets by improving the transparency of financial accounting and reporting in the local bodies, enhancing the cost effectiveness of project execution and ensuring that projects could be adequately operated and maintained once built.

Lessons Learnt from the Municipal Urban Development Fund

From June 1988 to September 1997, the state government implemented the first Tamil Nadu Urban Development Project. This was the largest urban finance project in India at that time and incorporated contemporary judgements about the reform measures needed for the urban sector in India. The project had an institutional development component and an on-lending component for municipal sub-projects. The on-lending component was administered through the Municipal Urban Development Fund (MUDF), which was a government-operated revolving fund. This was established to address the lack of long-term financing for urban infrastructure in India. A project management group was constituted to implement the project and act as the fund manager for the MUDF.

The MUDF financed about 500 sub-projects in Tamil Nadu, covering various components of urban infrastructure such as storm water drains, roads, bus stations and markets. It disbursed about Rs 1.65 billions. The fund established a good track record of lending procedures and well-defined rules for disbursements and loan recovery. Though conceived as an experimental operation, it exhibited the potential to become a good financial intermediary.

The MUDF had to contend with some shortcomings, which are understandable today in view of realities in the municipal financing sector at the time it was conceived. Its lending capacity was far too small compared with the scale of investment needed in the urban local bodies. It relied heavily on government grants. Fund mobilization was limited to public financing, especially IDA credit. It was administered by a project management group which was housed within the government set-up. This had adverse implications in terms of the efficiency of operations in view of the large turnover of officers and staff, rigid compensation rules for staff and the political risks associated with project selection and funding.

Nonetheless, the track record of the MUDF encouraged the government of Tamil Nadu to broaden the scope of the fund. The government agreed to a restructured public–private format for the fund, which was designed to attract private capital to leverage public funding contributions and to insulate the Fund management from day-to-day politics and bureaucracy.

Constitution of TNUDF

The Tamil Nadu Urban Development Fund (TNUDF) was established on 29 November 1996 as a trust under The Indian Trust Act 1882, with equity contributions from the government of Tamil Nadu, along with national financial institutions—ICICI Bank Limited (formerly ICICI Ltd), Housing Development Finance Corporation Limited (HDFC) and Infrastructure Leasing and Financial Services Limited (ILFS). TNUDF is the first public–private partnership providing long-term debt for civic infrastructure on a non-guarantee mode.[2]

The management structure of TNUDF was altered from that of MUDF in order to attract better talent into the fund management and to alleviate political influence on investment choices. Tamil Nadu Urban Infrastructure Financial Services Limited (TNUIFSL), a company registered under the Indian Companies Act, was established as the fund manager of TNUDF. The Fund and the management company were set up as separate legal bodies. The government of Tamil Nadu remains the majority equity contributor to TNUDF, contributing a little more than 70 per cent of the total equity (the state government did a valuation of the MUDF asset and liabilities and transferred the net worth of MUDF to TNUDF as its share in the corpus of the Fund, backed by government guarantee for repayment). However, the state government holds a minority (49 per cent) share of equity in the management company. The three all-India financial institutions hold majority equity in the management company. ICICI holds the largest non-governmental ownership share and has served as the lead organization in the management company.

The financial institutions contributed their equity in the form of cash investments. A grant-fund window funded by the government was established to fund technical assistance for sub-project preparation at the local-body level and for funding infrastructure investments that directly benefitted the poor in cities.

Attracting Private Capital to ULB Projects

Although some private financial institutions in India indicate their willingness to finance ULB projects off and on, none of them has been ready to enter this new market in a major way due to various perceptions about sub-national government financing. They cite substantial political economy risks associated with municipal governments and governance. They also cite the non-standard and less than credible accounting and financial reporting systems in local bodies. Moreover, urban local bodies still depend primarily on financial support from the state government, which creates uncertainties in revenue projections and realizations in tune with the fiscal ups and downs of the state.

A potentially greater deterrent to direct financial institution lending to ULBs has been the cost of municipal loan processing, credit assessment, lack of professional staff trained to understand municipal finance, and loan monitoring. Outside of Chennai, the potential scale of individual ULB borrowing is relatively small. This creates opportunities for economies of scale in loan management by an intermediary such as TNUDF, which can specialize in ULB lending. The advantages of delegated loan management are appealing to multi-lateral lenders as well as potentially attractive to domestic financing institutions. Moreover, given the fiscal and personnel constraints on ULBs, financial institutions consider the state of Tamil Nadu as the most suitable partner in urban-sector project financing. The state government has the power to implement reforms at sub-national levels and maintains control over most revenue flows. This provides the basic rationale for the government of Tamil Nadu's involvement in intermediation.

TNUDF's Track Record

The TNUDF's public–private design is reflected in the funds mobilization foreseen in the programme agreement signed with the World Bank. A World Bank line of credit provided a backbone of US$ 80 million in financing. Domestic bond issuance or other domestic-market borrowing by the TNUDF was planned to mobilize an additional US$ 25 million. The three financial institutions who are partners in the TNUDF were to contribute a minimum of US$ 10 million in equity to the TNUDF and to provide co-financing at the ULB project level for an additional US$ 25 million of investment.

Finally, the government of Tamil Nadu and the ULBs were to finance US$ 48 million from their own resources. In terms of Indian currency, the TNUDF was scheduled to participate in some Rs 7.5 billion of investment financing, or more than one-quarter of the sustainable ULB investment financing gap identified by the State Finance Commission and the TNUDF.

A Fast Start: Lending Volume and Financial Innovation

As can be seen from Table 8.3, the TNUDF got off to a fast start. Lending volumes ramped up quickly. Over the five-year period ending in 2002, the TNUDF approved 179 investment projects at a total project cost of Rs 6.7 billion and was able to disburse about Rs 3.4 billion in loans to ULBs and to joint public–private investment projects at the local level. The repayment performance of the Fund has been good, with project loan recoveries running close to 100 per cent (in fact, 99.75 per cent) of the scheduled repayments. TNUDF loan contracts with local governments have often called for a hierarchy of loan repayment methods, including (as a last resort) loan payments to be deducted at source by the state government—this facility was provided in the case of road projects that were financed in part by the state—and subtracted from ULB transfer amounts to the extent that ULB transfer entitlements were adequate to cover the amounts due. This indirect guarantee by the state, however limited, has strengthened the ULB repayment record, though it may have shielded ULBs from recognizing the full cost of debt service and thereby sometimes lessened local ownership of the financing choice.

Table 8.3
TNUDF Loan Disbursements and Approvals
In Rs Millions

	1997–99	1999–2000	2000–01	2001–02	2002–03	2003–04
Loan disbursements	200	560	2,190	440	25	509
Loan approvals	2,798	314	36	1	—	—
Loans outstanding	—	—	—	—	3,730[1]	852

Note: 1. includes loans carried forward from MUDF.

Perhaps more important than the volume of TNUDF lending was the catalytic role that TNUDF played in the early years in hiring consultants to prepare detailed project reports (over a period of five years, projects worth Rs 1500 crores were developed) and in putting together innovative financial structures that had potential as precedents for transforming local infrastructure financing practices. Other institutions—notably technical assistance and partial loan guarantees from USAID and a debt service reserve backup by the government of Tamil Nadu—also played an important role. However, TNUDF's participation was critical to developing these financing options, for which it sometimes also provided co-financing. Key examples of this activity include:

The First BOT Project by a ULB in India

The project involved construction of a toll bridge in Karur, at a cost of Rs 140 million. The TNUDF financed the private investor/operator to the extent of Rs 10 million. With TNUDF support, the enabling provisions of the Tamil Nadu State Toll Act were amended to allow ULBs to enter into BOT operations, thus offering investors a stable regulatory framework for projects of this kind.

The Madurai Inner Ring Road

This project involved construction of 27.2 km of road and overpasses. The Ring Road provides a time-saving bypass of congested urban roads and is operated by the ULB as a toll road. The TNUDF promoted and financed the project and, after the tolls stabilized, helped the local body to mobilize financing by accessing the capital market. It is to be noted that this bond issue was able to demonstrate that there is appetite for long-tenure municipal papers in India. This resulted in a savings in interest costs to the extent of Rs 6.5 million on a yearly basis.

Underground Sewerage Projects

Two ambitious sewerage projects, at Alandur and Coimbatore, were designed with TNUDF support and approved for financing. The Alandur project contained a BOT segment financed by a Private-Sector equity of Rs 66 million. Financing arrangements included up-front capital contributions of Rs 5,000 from each household connecting to the wastewater system, plus a five-year O&M contract at fixed annual fees and a proposed tariff rate that would cover O&M costs plus debt service.

Pooled Bond Financing

Twelve municipalities that had completed water and sanitation projects with TNUDF financing and had tariff mechanisms in place issued a pooled bond with TNUDF support. The bond was backed by (*a*) a debt service reserve fund, (*b*) a state government security back-up agreement to replenish the debt service reserve fund if it was depleted, and (*c*) a guarantee from USAID covering 50 per cent of the principal payments. The arrangement allowed the borrowers to refinance higher-cost outstanding loans. This experiment demonstrated that where a facilitator is willing to play a role between the local bodies, rating agencies, merchant banker and investors, local bodies can access the capital market. This bond also demonstrated that there was an appetite for long-tenure municipal paper from the investors on a pooled basis.

Financing initiatives such as these established new precedents for future financing in the urban infrastructure sector. As with any pilot programme, not all of the initiatives were fully successful. The Alandur sewerage project, for example, became mired in disputes between citizens, the municipality and the private operator due to the poor capacity of the city managers and the officials in charge at the directorate and also due to the differences between rival political parties. The elected council of the ULB did finally and satisfactorily resolve this. The Madurai Inner Ring Road has operated at less-than-projected traffic levels (the first year of operations achieved 60 per cent of projected traffic as compared to similar PPP facilities achieving 27 per cent elsewhere in India) for some time before picking up as per projections. Bond pooling was subsidized by international technical assistance (it is to be noted that the international guarantee was not seen as a major advantage by investors), and public authorities and market participants have not replicated it on their own. It remains to be seen to what extent the financing initiatives launched by TNUDF will actually become generalizable precedents for ULB infrastructure financing on a larger scale. The innovations promoted by the TNUDF are best seen as part of an important experiment—still in progress—to see how practicable it is, in the spirit of the 74th Constitutional Amendment Act, to push infrastructure financing options down to the ULB level.

Sustainability of the TNUDF Design

After 2001, TNUDF lending volumes declined even more precipitously than they had previously risen. Table 8.3 shows that loan disbursements dropped from Rs 2,190 million in 2000–01 to Rs 440 million in 2001–02 and a mere Rs 25 million in 2002–03. Loan approvals, a leading indicator of disbursements, fell earlier and still more steeply. Even these figures understate the total impact on TNUDF lending. The marked fall of new lending was accompanied by a rush of pre-payments on existing loans. The result was a piling up of cash in the TNUDF's hands that could not be placed with investors, either ULBs or public–private ventures.

Understanding the reasons for the decline in TNUDF loan activity is crucial for the design of future programmes that draw on the TNUDF model.

The TNUDF was a victim of falling interest rates, but its vulnerability lay as much in its own programme design as in external market forces. Liberalization of the Indian financial sector, coupled with declining inflation expectations, caused all interest rates in India to experience a steep descent between 2001 and 2004. The TNUDF's design was too rigid to allow it to adjust to changing market conditions. The TNUDF borrowed funds from the government of Tamil Nadu (via the World Bank credit) at a fixed rate of interest for 20-year terms and on-lent to ULBs, also at a fixed interest rate, for 15-year terms. TNUDF borrowing from the state government was conducted through a series of tranches, as funds were needed. The interest rate for each tranche was fixed according to a formula pegged to the interest rate on Government of India 10-year securities issued over the previous year, plus a spread charged by the state. The TNUDF then added its own spread, which, for investment projects in most sub-sectors, was 300 basis points. Under this formula, TNUDF originally borrowed funds at 13.5 per cent interest (these were the loans contracted by the predecessor MUDF and passed on to TNUDF as part of the state government's contribution to the Fund) and on-lent to ULBs and others at 16–16.5 per cent.

When interest rates began their steep decline, the TNUDF and its borrowers were saddled with loans that substantially exceeded current market rates. By 2003–04, other institutions were lending to ULBs at 8.75 per cent to 9.5 per cent, and interest rates on municipal bonds issues had reached even lower levels. The TNUDF was able to borrow new tranches of debt from the state at successively lower rates of interest, but always with a substantial formula lag that left it out of phase with the market and without being able to adjust the interest rate payable on earlier debts that remained outstanding. When the TNUDF lost its interest-rate competitiveness, it also lost demand for its loans. Worse: TNUDF loan agreements with borrowers allowed them to pre-pay outstanding loans without penalty. ULBs rushed to refinance their TNUDF loans with other borrowers. (TNUDF used these reflows to retire its high-cost loans and reduced its cost of funds.)

Most of this adjustment by ULBs was a market phenomenon and desirable in the sense that it lowered the ULBs' cost of financing. The TNUDF found itself unable to compete in the marketplace because it offered only one type of loan product—a fixed-rate 15-year loan, whose pricing was rigidly based on the TNUDF's cost of funds from the government of Tamil Nadu (and lagged behind the market in an environment of declining interest rates) plus the TNUDF's fixed (and costly) margin of 300 basis points.[3]

Level Playing Field with Other Public-Sector Lenders

Apart from market competition, the TNUDF faced competition from other public or quasi-public institutions that had more favourable access to capital. The TNUDF lost market share to a wide variety of financial institutions, but substantially to the Tamil Nadu Urban Finance & Infrastructure Development Corporation Limited (TUFIDCO), another financing entity owned by the Tamil Nadu state government. TUFIDCO received grants from the Government of India and the government of Tamil Nadu for implementing various urban investment schemes. These lowered its overall cost of capital and, in effect, subsidized its rates of lending to ULBs. Moreover, TUFIDCO is registered as a non-banking finance company, which allows it to raise public deposits, a lower-cost source of funds, and it is eligible to claim income tax exemption under specific sections of the Income Tax Act for income from infrastructure lending activities. The TNUDF's organization structure did not make it eligible for either type of favourable treatment.

As a result, the TNUDF, majority-owned by the government of Tamil Nadu, was in the anomalous position of seeing its outstanding loans 'cannibalized' via refinancings provided by another institution, also owned by the government of Tamil Nadu. Multiple attempts to work out terms of agreement between the two institutions did not result in any agreement.

Lessons Learnt

Several lessons about future programme design, both for the TNUDF and for other institutions of its kind, emerge from this experience:

1. No financial intermediary should be limited to a single lending instrument (a fixed-rate, 15-year loan in the TNUDF's case). One of the values of intermediation lies in the ability to adjust lending instruments and lending terms to meet borrower demand. This means offering shorter-term loans, variable-rate loans (tied to variable-rate sources of funding) and other options as desired and can be afforded by borrowers.

2. Financial intermediation becomes a risky undertaking in either a falling or rising interest-rate environment. The exact linkage between sources of funds and uses of funds cannot be prescribed in detail in advance in a written programme agreement, because market conditions cannot be adequately anticipated. Rigidly specified formulas for borrowing and lending rates, rigidly specified margins for the intermediary's spreads, etc., are bound to become out of sync with market realities at some point during a 20-year borrowing agreement. The primary purpose of having Private-Sector financial expertise in fund management is defeated by defining how all of the critical financial choices must be made in advance. Making these decisions is a role better assumed by the fund management board.

3. The government should adopt a common policy regarding the cost of capital and the terms of sub-national borrowing that applies to all state-owned financial intermediaries operating in a particular sector. To create a new state-owned financial intermediary that competes directly with another state-owned financial intermediary lending to the same type of borrowers but subject to a different set of legal, regulatory and policy rules makes no sense.

Financial Sustainability of the TNUDF as an Institution

The impact of loss of loan demand and other market developments on the TNUDF's financial condition can be seen from the key financial ratios presented in Table 8.4.

Table 8.4
Key Financial Ratios for the TNUDF

	1999–2000	2000–01	2001–02	2002–03	2003–04	2005
Loans to assets (%)	54	66	61	47	15	–
Short-term investments (%)	41	29	35	45	76	–
Debt–equity ratio	1.17	2.28	2.18	2.62	1.36	0.73
Before-tax return on equity (%)	15.3	13.4	16.8	12.6	9.4	–
After-tax return on equity	–	–	–	–	–	2.4
Debt service coverage ratio	3.43	1.52	1.32	1.19	0.3	–

As ULBs rushed to refinance outstanding loans and new loan demand shrivelled, the first impact on the TNUDF was to reduce drastically the percentage of assets held in the form of infrastructure loans. The loan-to-asset ratio fell from 54 per cent in 1999–2000 to 15 per cent in 2003–04, the TNUDF's assets were increasingly invested in short-term financial instruments or held as cash rather than used to finance urban infrastructure projects.

Faced with superfluous liquidity and unable to undertake significant new lending, the TNUDF began to repay its higher-cost borrowings from the state government. As a result, TNUDF lost the gearing or leverage necessary for a successful financial institution. The debt-to-equity ratio fell from 2.28 in 2000–01 (still undesirably low for a financial institution) to only 0.73 in early 2005. That is, the equity invested in the TNUDF exceeded the TNUDF's total outstanding borrowings, which by that time consisted almost exclusively of drawdowns of the World Bank credit via borrowing from the government of Tamil Nadu.

The financial impact of the loss of loan activity and profitable gearing was compounded by the fact that the decline in interest rates also reduced the yield on TNUDF's short-term investments. This led to an accelerating decline in returns on equity. Equity returns were further impaired by tax liability. The TNUDF had been set up as a trust under the Trust Act, based on legal advice that under this structure income would not be taxable at the entity level. India's revenue authorities have taken a different position and have held the TNUDF fully liable for income taxes. (The TNUDF has appealed this decision, but without encouragement as to the outcome of an appeal.) By 2005, the after-tax return on equity for the year had been reduced to 2.44 per cent.[4]

Finally, the coverage ratio on TNUDF's remaining debt service has steadily declined, falling well below 1.0 in 2003–04. The poor level of debt service coverage, if uncorrected, will mar future credit ratings and impede the TNUDF's attempts to access the capital market through bond issuance.

Lessons Learnt

1. Perhaps the fundamental lesson to be gained from this review is that the financial performance of a financial institution must be taken seriously and literally, especially if the goal is to attract private capital. A sustainable financial intermediary, operating with private capital, must be a profitable intermediary as well as one that has the flexibility to withstand swings in market conditions.

2. For public–private financial partnerships in India, tax liability is an important factor. The legal framework that now exists does not easily accommodate joint public–private ventures in the sector. If this form of partnership is to be encouraged, tax laws will have to be changed or a way found to insulate investors from taxation at the entity level.

3. Under most foreseeable conditions, private equity investment in public–private infrastructure intermediaries is likely to have limited appeal. The risk–reward balance is less favourable than in most other investment opportunities. This judgement appears to have been made by Indian financial institutions, as no new equity investments in intermediaries of this type have been made, either in the TNUDF or in other institutions. In the design of public–private lending intermediaries that is now under discussion in India, financial institutions have focused on fee-based management contracts or on providing funds through loans that have quasi-equity characteristics by retaining an upside that is based on financial performance. In this structure, financial institutions retain their priority claims on return of principal, unlike equity investors, whose capital is at risk as a first level of debt protection.

4. The public and private partners in a joint financing venture may well have different and conflicting values. One example: The TNUDF treated its development of innovative financing models as a 'public good'. It did not charge ULBs for the large amounts of executive time spent assembling such financing packages. In the case of pooled bond financing, the pooled bond issue that the TNUDF helped generate was actually used to pre-pay TNUDF loans made at a much higher rate. As the private partners pointed out, they would have preferred to find ways to capture the benefits of financial innovation for the TNUDF.

5. All of this suggests that there may be preferable designs for implementing public–private partnerships in the financial sector. In one alternative, the public sector would retain fund ownership and enter into a clearly defined performance-based management contract with a private fund manager. A performance contract has the advantage of forcing the public sector to identify clearly the goals of the intermediary (which may include development of 'public good' financing innovations) and to scale management compensation according to the achievement of these goals. Alternatively, an individual company can be allowed to develop and 'own' an infrastructure fund (if history of private infrastructure funds in India is taken as benchmark, government support in some form is a prerequisite for the success of the fund) subject to

public regulation and subject to open entry for other companies that want to form similar funds, as well as competition from commercial banks and other existing financial institutions. Public infrastructure grants would be made to ULBs based on project criteria, regardless of the source of complementary debt financing.

Conclusion: Reconsidering Public–Private Partnership in an Infrastructure Finance Intermediary

What sets the TNUDF apart from other finance intermediaries is the public–private partnership in ownership of both the Fund and its management company. Private participation is further distinguished by the involvement of three large financial institutions as equity contributors rather than a single private partner. After eight years of its operation, it is fitting to take stock of the advantages and disadvantages of this design.

Management Company Partnership

The establishment of a separate management company, led by ICICI but accountable to other equity contributors, both public and private, has produced several positive outcomes. It brought professional and self-motivated staff into fund management. The Fund's legal set-up outside of the government made it possible to incorporate incentives based on performance, a welcome change from the personnel and compensation arrangements in government departments. The management company accelerated project development at the local level, provided advisory services to ULBs on overall infrastructure financing, introduced innovative financing packages and compiled a good debt repayment record. The presence of three financial institutions on the Board of Trustees avoided the perception as well as the reality of a preferential relationship between the government and a single private party.

Still, the potential benefits of private fund management were not fully realized. Most of the policies that prevented the TNUDF from becoming more market-oriented in its intermediary operations were either self-imposed by the Fund and its management company or were elements of the pro-gramme agreement with the World Bank and government of Tamil Nadu (which could have been changed and eventually were changed). The private partners could have been expected to take more initiative in asserting the need to maintain market competitiveness. Their failure to do so probably reflects, first, the fact that TNUDF was a minor venture for them and its business development potential was seen as limited, reducing the incentive to 'push' the government of Tamil Nadu or the World Bank on policy mat-ters. Second, the management contract with the TNUIFSL was not a true performance contract. Management compensation was not tied to typical performance indicators, such as profitability, volume of lending or ULB investment levels, but rather to the TNUDF's loan approval volume, whether or not the loans eventually were consummated.

Attracting Private Capital

The TNUDF was designed with the idea that participation of Private-Sector financial institutions as equity partners would create the necessary edge for raising counterpart financing from the domestic private sector. The rationale most emphasized in the TNUDF design was the need to attract private capital into the urban infrastructure sector. The actual goals for Private-Sector capital mobilization, however, were relatively modest, and the results achieved were more modest. It was expected at the outset that, in one form or another, about US$ 60 million would be mobilized from the private sector with TNUDF participation, or in the range of 7–8 per cent of what the State Finance Commission had identified as the feasible financing gap.

The financial institutions contributed US$ 10 million of equity at the time of the programme's launch. One expectation was that they would boost this equity investment over time. However, the institutions have shown no desire to invest further in the TNUDF or the management company, and in December 2005, all of the equity partners voted to withdraw 50 per cent of the accumulated capital in the TNUDF in light of the unsatisfactory returns on equity and the TNUDF's low debt–equity ratio.

A covenant in the World Bank loan agreement required the TNUDF to raise US$ 25 million through a domestic bond issue in order to establish itself as a viable intermediary in the domestic market. The TNUDF did issue such a bond to satisfy the covenant. However, the five-year bond raised funds at a higher interest cost than the TNUDF could recover through on-lending, with a maturity far shorter than the 15-year term of its ULB loans and at a time when it could not fully place with ULBs the funds it already had access to. The TNUDF has not returned to the domestic market to raise financing.

The TNUDF's ability to operate as a domestic finance intermediary in the future is, at best, unclear. Most of the financial institutions that would purchase TNUDF bonds or make loans to the TNUDF, including large financial institutions and commercial banks, are now also willing to lend directly to larger ULBs (however, the willingness is more for take-over financing and refinancing and at a time when the substantial repayment period has expired—typically for a tenure of less than five years) or to public–private investment projects of scale that have sound financial prospects. To fill a domestic financing niche not already filled by the market, the TNUDF will have to develop a strategy for pooling smaller loans while also establishing risk-protection measures that make it a more creditworthy borrower in the eyes of the market.

The third leg of the original strategy for mobilizing private capital was reflected in a second covenant of the World Bank agreement. According to this covenant, the financial institutions investing in the TNUDF were obligated to finance an additional US$ 25 million at the ULB project level as counterpart financing for TNUDF loans.[5] This local financing on the part of the three financial institutions never materialized and the covenant was eventually waived. Various explanations have been put forth as to why this co-financing did not occur, but the principal reason is that the financial institutions simply did not see attractive investment opportunities at the local level (basically due to the presence of public-sector institutions such as the state-owned TUFIDCO and the federal government-owned HUDCO, which distorted the market, and also due to the fact that in many projects, such as water supply and sewerage systems, the user charges were not adequate even to cover O&M expenses due to regulatory restrictions on pricing) and did not find that the prospect of co-financing project investments with the TNUDF changed their evaluation.

Reconsidering Public–Private Partnerships

Public–private cooperation no doubt remains necessary to meet urban infrastructure investment needs in India. 'Public' infrastructure projects and 'public' rules for revenue generation have to be made more compatible with the profit objectives and risk-management requirements of private suppliers of capital — whether private capital is invested directly in projects, lent to local borrowers or lent to a specialized intermediary for on-lending to ULBs. Private institutions in turn will have to do a better job of understanding local governments' financial conditions to adequately assess the risk–reward balance of financing local infrastructure investment.

The TNUDF can be viewed as an experiment as to whether the most effective way to achieve this cooperation is by compressing public and private interests into a single, jointly owned institution. It is tempting to think that public–private partnerships will join the most attractive features of the public and private sectors, and that Private-Sector initiative and financing capacity therefore can be harnessed to public-sector investment goals without more fundamental reforms in ULB financing or the active cooperation of the state government (especially in competition in the same sector). The experience of the TNUDF, however, suggests that joint ownership of a financing intermediary by itself does not fully bring together the objectives of private and public partners or assure greater access to private capital markets.

The TNUDF's experience does, however, highlight the governance advantages of hiring professional managers of infrastructure funds as well as the potential advantages of having management report to a board composed of representatives of both private financial institutions and the government. It highlights the advantages of creating a new institutional mechanism for assisting the urban local bodies in India to plan rightly to fulfil their role as providers of civic services in a financially sustainable framework and to obtain the capacity to implement and continue to manage such civic services to the satisfaction of the citizenry. It also highlights a transition methodology for urban local institutions to migrate from a government-dependent system to a strong and healthy business partnership with a financial-cum-development intermediary dedicated to the growth of the sector.

Notes

1. The exchange rate in 2004 was roughly US$ 1 = Rs 44.
2. The term 'private sector' is used somewhat loosely to describe financial institutions in India. At the time TNUDF was created, all three of the participating 'private' financial institutions had a degree of public ownership.

3. Eventually, the TNUDF did lower its margin. However, the agreement with the World Bank specified that it must charge a minimum margin of 150 basis points over its cost of funds.

4. Ironically, it is the Government of Tamil Nadu that suffers the most from this tax liability. The financial institutions holding equity in the TNUDF would have to pay income tax at the company level even if earnings were not taxable at the trust level. The state government, though, as a tax-exempt entity, would not otherwise pay income taxes.

5. The second covenant actually stated that this US$ 25 million could take the form of counterpart financing at the local project level *or* additional equity investments in the TNUDF itself.

Reference

Government of Tamil Nadu. 2001. 'Report of the Second State Finance Commission'.

9

INCA: A South African Private-Sector Intermediary

Johan Kruger and George E. Peterson[*]

Introduction

INCA (Infrastructure Finance Corporation Limited) is the developing world's first privately owned, privately managed intermediary specializing in the financing of local infrastructure. INCA raises financing for municipal lending, primarily from the private capital market. It was established in South Africa at a time when the perceived risks of municipal lending had driven commercial banks and other private lenders out of sub-national financing, yet it has competed successfully with partially subsidized lending from the state-owned Development Bank of Southern Africa.

This chapter examines INCA's design and the practical implementation of that design, as well the institution's impact on local infrastructure finance in South Africa.

[*] Johan Kruger founded and served as Chief Executive Officer of the Infrastructure Finance Corporation Ltd of South Africa. George E. Peterson served as Senior Fellow in international public finance at the Urban Institute in Washington, D.C.

The South African Context:
High Investment Needs, High Perceived Risk

INCA was established in 1996 and began operations early in 1997. The rationale for its creation parallels the theme of this book: the need to mobilize new sources of financing for urban infrastructure investment within the framework of responsible national fiscal policy. In the words of INCA's initial prospectus (INCA 1997):

> The legacy of past [apartheid] policies and practices has left South Africa with the major challenge of reducing infrastructure backlogs in a period where macro financial discipline and resulting budget constraints are the order of the day. The public sector has always played a major role in the provision of infrastructure financing and will continue to do so, but the magnitude of the infrastructure development requirement is such that it can only be addressed successfully if the full participation of the private sector ... is obtained.

A national Infrastructure Investment Conference held in Cape Town in March 1996 as part of the government's Reconstruction and Development Programme set a target of R 34 billion (at the time, some US$ 4 billion) for municipal infrastructure investment over the next five years, with R 19 billion coming from the municipalities' own resources, as opposed to central government transfers. A large share of this investment was aimed at providing formerly black townships with basic services, such as water supply, drainage and local roads, which, under the Constitution, are municipal responsibilities.

In addition to large investment needs, South Africa faced special circumstances that made lending to local governments appear to carry a high risk. The country was still in the process of completing the amalgamation of formerly black and formerly white local authorities. The newly established Transitional Local Governments were supposed to consolidate the strong economic bases of white municipalities with the far weaker municipal economies of the majority black population.[1] How well municipal amalgamation would work in practice was the subject of much speculation.

Another element of risk was the lack of a well-defined intergovernmental financing system. At the time INCA was founded, South Africa had yet to establish either its general revenue support grant (equitable share) or its municipal infrastructure grant, but rather relied on more *ad hoc* central funding of local needs. Black local authorities did not have a history of financial self-governance. Rather, they had a tradition of using non-payment, in the form of rent and service-payment strikes, as a political weapon during the apartheid era. These background facts raised questions about the ability and willingness of local authorities to repay municipal debt in the future.

South Africa did have a history of municipal borrowing and issuance of municipal bonds by white local authorities. However, this system was backed by implicit central government guarantees that removed lenders' credit risk and all but eliminated the need to scrutinize local creditworthiness. One of the first acts of the new government formed by the African National Congress was to announce that in the future there would be no government guarantees for Private-Sector lending to public authorities. This explicit prohibition was written into the new Constitution.

As a result of the financial and political uncertainty, commercial banks and other traditional lenders and purchasers of municipal bonds withdrew from the municipal credit market. Local authorities had no access to Private-Sector credit. On the contrary: commercial banks and other institutions holding previously issued municipal bonds that no longer carried central government guarantees nervously sought ways to reduce their risk exposure.

It was in this environment that INCA was established to act as an intermediary by issuing corporate bonds and on-lending to local authorities. Its mission was to augment the infrastructure financing provided by the government and its agencies.

INCA's Business Plan

INCA's business plan may be divided into two parts: the internal plan that has allowed it to generate high returns on equity, despite on-lending to top credits at rates only 50–70 basis points over its own cost of borrowing, and the assessment of external factors that led INCA to conclude that external risks were manageable and in fact created a distinctive opportunity for INCA to add (and capture) value. INCA was created as a for-profit venture without direct or indirect government subsidy. Therefore, a viable business plan lies at the heart of its operation.

Internal Business Plan

The general business case for INCA is the classic intermediary role: borrow wholesale, lend retail after adding value and operate with small margins at high volumes. The value added by INCA also reflects classic intermediation.

INCA performs the role of delegated risk assessment and monitoring. As a specialized intermediary, INCA undertakes to identify, monitor and limit the risk involved in retail lending to municipalities. For the purchasers of INCA debt, the costs of assessing and monitoring the creditworthiness of individual municipalities in the new legal and financial circumstances of local government would have been too high to justify, even if these institutions had the capacity to perform the function. Delegation of risk-assessment and risk-management responsibilities to a specialized intermediary made financial sense.

Critical to INCA's success—and that of any market-oriented local infra-structure finance intermediary—is the fact that the market views the risks of INCA's bonds as better defined, more transparent, easier to assess and lower than the risks inherent in municipal bonds or retail loans to municipalities.

In order to generate its targeted returns on equity, INCA operates with a high degree of financial leverage. Its financial structure is constructed as an inverted pyramid (see Figure 9.1). At the base is a small amount of equity. Above this is provisioning for bad loans and reserves. A third tier consists of subordinated, junior debt. At the top is a large amount of senior bonds (supplemented in recent years by international loans.) Financial claims are recognized from the top down. Bondholders and other senior lenders have first claim on all payments. Holders of junior debt are paid only if and when senior debt obligations are met in full. Provisions and reserves are drawn upon to make good amounts owed to both classes of debt holders.

Figure 9.1
INCA's Capital Structure

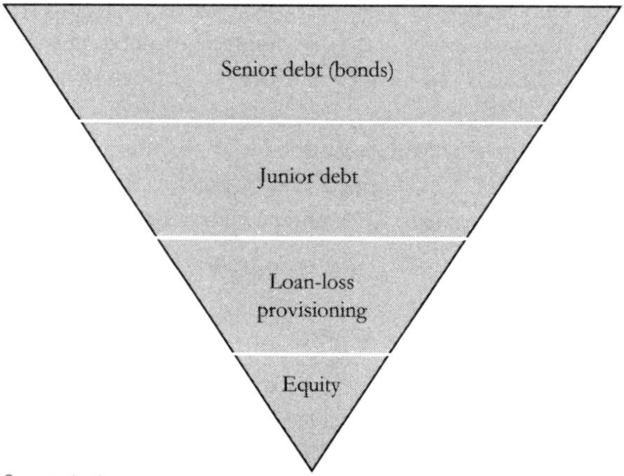

Source: Authors.

Equity holders are paid from residual earnings; returns to equity take the first hit from any non-performing loans.

Over its lifetime, INCA has operated with an average ratio of retail loans outstanding to shareholder equity of approximately 20:1. Its capital adequacy ratio (defined as total capital advances) has averaged between 6 per cent and 7 per cent (INCA 2004). In this highly leveraged structure, equity holders can earn a good return if the business model functions as designed. Relatively small variations in loan repayment performance or spreads, however, translate into greatly magnified variations in equity returns. Between 2000 and 2004, INCA's reported annual returns on equity ranged from 19.5 per cent to 40.4 per cent.

External Factors Supporting the Business Plan

Despite the perceived and real risks of the municipal credit market in 1996, INCA's founders determined that several factors in the external environment, coupled with good institutional design, could reduce risk to acceptable levels. First, South Africa had a well-developed capital market and an active secondary bond market, although bond transactions at the time were totally dominated by government issues (98 per cent). If INCA could successfully market its bonds as having high credit quality, it could count upon accessing an active capital market. This would make part of the task of intermediation—obtaining wholesale credit—relatively straightforward, even though the type of specialized intermediary it was putting forward was innovative.

Second, INCA selected its shareholders strategically. They represented major South African financial institutions—commercial banks, development banks and insurance companies—as well as black empowerment and women's groups, plus the international development finance community. The Commonwealth Development Fund took an initial equity stake, as did Credit Local de France (now Dexia). This mix of organizations was tapped not so much for the equity itself, which was of relatively modest size, as for the credibility that the different equity holders provided to the financial sector, especially in marketing INCA's bonds.

A critical step in INCA's business development was taken in February 1997, when, as its initial financial transaction, INCA sold bonds with a face value of R 1.2 billion (at the time some US$ 150 million). The bonds were listed on the Johannesburg Stock Exchange for secondary trading and INCA eventually became the Exchange's second most active issuer in trading volume. INCA had pre-arranged lending to municipalities for most of the initial financing it mobilized. It disbursed these loan funds to local authorities shortly after its bond sale.

INCA's bonds were rated AA by a domestic credit rating agency prior to issuance. Its intermediate-term, 6-and 10-year bonds have traded around 100 basis points above similarly dated government Treasury bonds, while the 15-year bonds have fluctuated around 110 basis points above similarly dated treasuries. INCA's original design, as specified in its prospectus, was to on-lend to top-rated local authorities at 50–70 basis points above its own cost of borrowing. Actual practice has approximated this target. This margin has covered INCA's costs of operation and, because of the leveraged financial structure, met financial targets for return on equity.

Equally fundamental to INCA's business design was its assessment of underlying risk and the municipal market for credit. At the time and for most of the period since its founding, the only other supplier of local authority credit of any scale was the Development Bank of Southern Africa (DBSA), a government-owned institution benefitting from below-market access to funds. INCA's business plan was premised on the assumption that INCA would not have to out-compete DBSA on lending rates; but that municipal demand for its credits would be strong, even at modestly higher interest rates than DBSA offered, if INCA could establish a reputation for customer service and rapid response to loan applications. The average turnaround time for a loan from INCA has been three weeks.

South Africa also enjoyed a legal environment that provided for clear and speedy enforcement of financial contracts. As described in the next section, INCA sought to reduce credit risk through a variety of strategies, including pledging of municipal collateral and ring-fencing (dedicated pledging) of project revenue streams. Legal clarity was crucial for enforcement of these provisions. South Africa's legal system both recognized financial contracts and acted swiftly to execute collateral. Well-defined procedures for obtaining court enforcement orders have lessened the risk of lengthy legal delays. Such delays have plagued the operations of financial intermediaries in other countries.

Finally, although South Africa's intergovernmental financing framework was still being defined, it was clear that municipal governments had unusually broad powers to raise revenues at the local level (see Chapter 5 in this volume). Besides a local property tax, municipalities had the authority and institutional practice of recovering from users the full cost of delivering basic services, such as water supply and distribution or solid waste collection, and had the power to establish cost-recovery tariffs for new undertakings.[2] This allocation of revenue-raising authority to the local level made municipalities, or at least those municipalities operating in strong economic markets, capable of repaying debt from locally generated revenue streams without dependence upon transfers or new legislative authority to impose taxes.

The Core Function:
Risk Assessment and Credit Monitoring

The value-added core of INCA's activity consists of its initial assessment and continual monitoring of credit risk, coupled with measures to reduce risk. Orientation towards credit risk is built into INCA's entire structure— from its dealings with local authority borrowers to the internal discipline that ties capital adequacy to loan risk levels. INCA's primary contribution to municipal credit market development in South Africa has been the explicit treatment of risk. The centrality of risk measurement and risk mitigation in INCA's own business plan can be seen from the fact that its baseline business plan called for provisioning only 0.25 per cent of outstanding loans per annum to cover non-performing loans. The business plan was viewed as viable up to the point that a 0.70 per cent per annum charge for non-performing loans was required. Beyond that, returns to equity became unacceptably low, or negative.[3]

Evaluating and Pricing Credit Risk

Risk management begins with an internal credit rating for each potential borrower. INCA lends to a universe that consists of municipalities, district councils, water authorities, utilities, development corporations, educational institutions, private infrastructure companies and public–private partnerships. It rates all loans according to a standardized credit model that takes into account financial position (emphasizing cash flow), economic base, management and institutional capacity, and underlying socio-economic factors (including payment history of the customer base). The model generates flags for deviations from preset norms and produces *pro forma* future balance sheets and income statements for each borrower.

INCA's deed of trust requires that loan risk be tied to capital adequacy. That is, at higher levels of underlying loan risk, INCA is required by its internal rules to maintain higher levels of capital as protection for INCA's bondholders. As an unregulated financial institution, INCA was not required to adhere to regulatory capital adequacy ratios, but adopted the capital requirement matrix shown in Table 9.1 for its own governance. In one respect, INCA's approach to capital adequacy went beyond the regulatory rules then in effect for banks. Bank regulations in South Africa required that a uniform risk premium (10 per cent risk weighting) be assigned for capital adequacy purposes to all loans made to the sub-national sector.[4] As appropriate for an institution specializing in sub-national lending, INCA went further to differentiate minimum capital requirements according to the estimated credit risk of individual loans. The required capital ratios range from 1.6 per cent for top-quality credits to 24 per cent for the poorest credits. In addition, INCA has set maximum exposure levels to individual borrowers within each category of internal credit rating (see Table 9.1).[5] The internal credit rating performed by INCA also dictates the conditionality and security requirements written into INCA loans. Riskier credits require stronger collateral or other security.

Table 9.1
Capital Requirement Matrix

	Credit rating equivalent[1]	Minimum capital requirement[2](%)	Maximum borrower exposure[3](%)
Category 1	AAA to AA–	1.6	80
Category 2	A+ to A–	3.2	20
Category 3	BBB+ to BBB–	4.8	13.5
Category 4	BB+ to BB–	15	4.0
Category 5	B+ to B–	24	2.0

Source: INCA (1997).
Notes: 1. Equivalent IBCA-Fitch-Global Credit Rating category.
　　　2. Percentage of capital held against loans in each category.
　　　3. Percentage of total capital that can be lent to one borrower in category.

The capital requirement matrix also serves as a pricing guide for credits carrying different risk profiles. In order to generate comparable returns on equity, loans carrying higher credit risks have to be charged higher interest rates in order to offset the higher capital requirements. This systematic approach to loan pricing also distinguishes INCA from most government-operated municipal credit intermediaries, which tend to lend at uniform rates to all borrowers, regardless of credit risk.

Credit Monitoring

Initial evaluation of credit risk is only part of the task of risk management. INCA undertakes a periodic review of the credit quality of its asset base—

at least annually, and more frequently if problems are identified. This review is conducted in collaboration with an external credit rating agency.

In the event that the credit review reveals the need to re-categorize outstanding loans as having higher risk profiles than originally evaluated, INCA—according to its deed of trust—is constrained to take certain actions:

1. It is required to build up its capital (by issuing additional junior bonds or shares or from retained earnings) before making further loans or issuing new unsubordinated bonds.
2. No dividend can be paid to shareholders until the minimum capital requirement is restored under the new categorization.
3. Payment of interest on junior bonds is deferred until the minimum capital requirement is restored.

These requirements are intended to protect the interests of senior bondholders and therefore allow INCA to access the capital market via bond issuance at lower interest rates.

INCA maintains a 'rating watch list' identifying all borrowers that need to be monitored more closely. The financial position of these borrowers is tracked regularly and contact is maintained with local officials regarding loan payment obligations. INCA also created a non-profit company called the INCA Capacity Building Fund to support local authorities in need of assistance. It has a 100 per cent subsidiary created to warehouse bonds or loans in distress as an intensive care unit.[6]

Credit Enhancement and Workouts

Credit enhancements and workout arrangements are designed to reduce the underlying loan risk and to accelerate remedies in the case of non-performing loans.

Almost all INCA loans are backed by collateral. Most are balance-sheet loans, supported by the borrower's general assets. Particular loans may contain specific pledges of collateral. Loans may also be supported by pledges of ring-fenced revenue streams. In this case, the loan is not treated as project financing, backed solely by the revenue stream, but as a balance-sheet loan, backed by the general ability to pay of the borrower, strengthened by the pledge of an identifiable and legally separable revenue source.

INCA's own risk exposure often is reduced through co-financing with the government. Many of its loans are used to help finance projects that also receive grant funding from the government. In other cases, INCA co-finances municipal loans with the Development Bank of Southern Africa. INCA's market-rate financing sometimes has been blended with below-market financing from DBSA when loan funds are targeted for special investment purposes.

INCA has adopted a pragmatic style of working with financially stressed municipalities to assure debt repayment. Formal loan-contract provisions are used as the entry point for negotiating more flexible workout arrangements. In a first step, INCA typically participates in stabilization and rehabilitation plans for borrowers facing financial difficulty. In the past, INCA sometimes worked independently with municipalities in need of this kind of help or collaborated with the government on a case-by-case basis. South African law now calls for provincial-level stabilization teams to intervene whenever a municipality cannot pay its debts or other financial obligations. These teams have the power to reduce local expenditures or raise special revenues in order to restore solvency.

If a municipality reaches the stage where it misses a debt payment, INCA's first action is to go to court to get an enforcement order, which typically allows it to seize municipal property that has been pledged as collateral. In the South African legal system, court orders of this kind can be obtained promptly. Armed with a court order, INCA approaches the municipality to negotiate workout terms. INCA uses even the threat of property seizure very selectively. In one case, it threatened to seize the mayor's cell phone as foreclosed collateral. The threat sufficed to restore prompt payment of debt service.

The combination of initial credit assessment, monitoring and potential execution of collateral has enabled INCA to operate at a very low rate of non-performing loans. Since its establishment, INCA has had a record of no capital write-offs and interest in default remaining below 0.1 per cent. Non-performing loan rates have remained below 1 per cent.

As an intermediary specializing in credit risk management within the municipal sector, INCA gained a reputation for efficient oversight. In addition to direct lending to finance new municipal infrastructure investment, INCA eventually purchased, at a discount, the outstanding municipal loan books of other financial institutions, both in the private and the public sector. These transactions enabled traditional lenders to cash out their holdings of debt instruments that now required much more active management. From INCA's perspective, the transactions were profitable because its management was able to reduce non-performing loan rates, thereby enhancing the value of the loan portfolios it acquired.

INCA's Impact on Local Infrastructure Finance

On its own terms, INCA has been a market success. The company has been regularly profitable. By June 2004, it had grown to the point that it had assets—mostly loan advances to municipalities—of R 5.5 billion, or more than US$ 900 million (at that time). INCA is able to access the domestic capital market for additional wholesale loans as needed at approximately 100 basis points above the rates on government bonds of comparable maturities.

In its initial years of operation, INCA clearly augmented the supply of loan funds to the municipal sector and indirectly helped augment municipal investment. Total new lending to the municipal sector jumped in 1997–98 when INCA entered the market. INCA's entry reversed what had been a steep decline in municipal debt held by the private sector, as outstanding bonds matured and were not replaced by new Private-Sector lending. The hypothesis of a supply-constrained credit market, where mobilization of private capital through a specialized intermediary would (*a*) increase total private sector lending to the municipal sector, (*b*) increase total lending, public and private, to the sector, and (*c*) support additional municipal investment, was vindicated.

The picture since 2001–02 has been less clear. Completion of the intergovernmental fiscal framework for municipalities, an improved economy and maturation of the municipal credit market, due in part to INCA's demonstration that the risks involved in municipal lending are manageable, all have combined to increase the willingness of the private sector to lend to municipalities. The increased availability of funds for municipal lending, however, has not translated into additional borrowing. Table 9.2 summarizes budgeted sources of municipal capital financing as reported by the

Table 9.2
Budgeted Sources of Finance for Municipal Capital Expenditure
In Rand millions

Source of financing	2001–02	2002–03	2003–04
National transfers	3,947	5,160	7,522
Internal advances	4,935	4,908	5,680
Other financing, provincial contributions	1,166	1,361	1,842
External loans	1,725	1,692	1,694
TOTAL	11,773	13,120	16,738

Source: South Africa National Treasury (2004).

South Africa National Treasury. Although there are complications with the data that will most likely lead to some under-reporting of external loans, the general trend is clear and somewhat surprising: there was very rapid growth in municipal capital investment between 2001–02 and 2003–04, but the surge in investment was financed primarily by national grants. Loan financing is a small proportion of total investment and did not grow.

The National Treasury, in fact, has argued that municipal budgets could support a tripling of outstanding debt and that debt must become a more important component of the capital financing mix if future investment targets are to be met.

At the least, Table 9.2 raises questions as to why debt financing has not grown with municipal capital spending. One explanation is simply that municipalities prefer, and have available to them, other sources of financing. With national capital grants growing so rapidly, municipalities would be foolish not to use these grants first rather than resort to borrowing. The category 'Internal advances' refers primarily to a South African carryover structure of accumulated past capital charges that have been pooled in a municipality's internal capital development fund and accumulated past external loans that have been pooled in a consolidated loan fund, from which internal advances are made to finance municipal departments' capital spending. It is quite plausible that municipalities have preferred to draw down these accumulated balances rather than enter into new borrowing. 'Internal advances' also contain an element of pay-as-you-go financing that may indicate a broader reluctance on the part of municipalities to borrow.

A second explanation, not inconsistent with the first, is that only a relatively narrow range of municipalities are creditworthy and that lending has been constrained by this narrow creditworthiness rather than by supply limitations. The six metropolitan governments account for upwards of 60 per cent of outstanding municipal debt. The remaining debt is highly concentrated in another 30 municipalities.

The fact that only an upper tier of local governments meets creditworthiness standards undoubtedly is part of the explanation for relatively low shares of debt financing of capital investment. However, even in the six metros—which are the strongest credits—external loans in 2003–04 accounted for only 12 per cent of budgeted capital financing. Clearly, local governments that are capable of more borrowing, permitted to borrow by law and deemed creditworthy by lenders have chosen not to borrow. The explanation appears to lie in limited demand for credit rather than supply constraints.

The need to tap private capital markets to help finance local infrastructure investment is likely to strengthen in the future. The government's Medium Term Expenditure Framework calls for a substantial rise in fixed capital formation as a percentage of GDP, with much of the investment responsibility vested in local governments. Municipalities are slated for a 50 per cent increase in real investment levels between 2004–05 and 2007–08 as the government gives priority to infrastructure investment to fulfill the Constitutional commitment of universal, free basic services (South Africa National Treasury 2005). Municipal borrowing is planned to be a larger part of the incremental financing mix. Greater reliance on borrowing will be necessitated in part by the depletion of municipalities' internal capital accumulations. However, central-level grant policy will continue to be a primary driver of loan demand. As long as grant funding is made available for capital investment, demand for debt as a capital-financing instrument will be subdued.

The Role of Private Lenders and the DBSA

Future demand for credit from the private sector also will depend in part on policy decisions that define the financing role of the state-owned DBSA. A policy debate, still unresolved, has been going on for several years regarding the appropriate policy posture for the DBSA and appropriate use of its ample resources. In its lending to the local government sector, should the DBSA concentrate on development lending to higher-risk municipalities, either on its own or as a co-financer with private credit suppliers? Should the DBSA go even farther and sell off to the private sector its stock of high credit-quality municipal loans to concentrate on development lending? Either step would greatly enlarge Private-Sector participation in the municipal credit market. It would also increase the share of loan financing in overall municipal infrastructure finance as a middle tier of municipalities is drawn into the loan market.

At present, the DBSA pursues a dual track. It provides developmental finance on below-market terms (either by lending at lower interest rates or accepting greater risk), but also lends to the top tier of municipalities in competition with Private-Sector lenders. In fact, as of 2004 the DBSA's municipal loan portfolio was more highly concentrated in the six metros than was INCA's loan portfolio, although this situation may subsequently have changed.

Partitioning of the municipal credit market would allow Private-Sector and public-sector lenders to specialize in different segments of the market, utilizing their comparative advantages while meeting the Treasury's goal of greater use of credit in the overall infrastructure financing strategy.

Municipal Infrastructure Grant Policy

Running parallel to the debate over the DBSA's role in the credit market is a debate over the best role for grants in the infrastructure financing picture—a debate that will also impact demand for Private-Sector credit. As suggested by Table 9.2, much of the increase in municipal infrastructure investment in recent years has been financed by grants, particularly the Municipal Infrastructure Grant (MIG).[7] The MIG is designed roughly to compensate local governments for the costs of expanding infrastructure coverage to service poor neighborhoods, in order to fulfill the Constitutional commitment to universal, free basic services.

One policy option that has been discussed is to focus MIG allocations more tightly on municipalities without the capacity to access debt markets. At present, for example, 24 per cent of MIG allocations go to the six metros. If MIG resources were redirected to focus a larger share of allocations on small, rural municipalities, where the ability to finance capital investment from own resources or borrowing is virtually nil, and to allocate a lesser share of MIG funding to metros, the latter would be obliged to rely more heavily on borrowing. This strategy would recognize three broad categories of local governments. At one end of the financing spectrum, a large number of smaller municipalities are unlikely to be creditworthy in the short-to-intermediate term, and thus will be dependent almost entirely upon grants to finance infrastructure investment. At the other end of the spectrum, the six metropolitan governments and a number of larger municipalities will have the financial ability to borrow from the private market at market rates of interest. National grants policy now dictates that even for these municipalities, the MIG should cover most of the capital costs of extending basic service provision to the unserved poor. National policy also calls for national grants to assist in the financing of major investments designed to stimulate national economic growth and employment. However, for other elements of the capital budget, these municipalities are capable of borrowing from the private market and could be asked to do so for a greater share of basic services investment.

In the middle of the spectrum lies a broad range of municipalities that could finance part of their capital needs from borrowing, but are marginally creditworthy. These municipalities are logical targets for developmental lending, either from the DBSA or from a combination of DBSA and private credit suppliers.

Of potentially greater impact is a policy decision about how future national assistance to the municipal infrastructure sector will be divided between capital grants and operating assistance. Detailed analysis makes clear that the greatest cost created by the policy of universal, free basic services is the operating and maintenance (O&M) cost of the newly built infrastructure, given that the overwhelming majority of new service recipients (in some smaller municipalities, almost 100 per cent) will not pay anything for service provision. A shift in the overall grant structure to cover a greater part of O&M costs, especially in small municipalities, and to cover a lesser share of capital costs, especially in metros and larger municipalities, would also necessitate greater use of debt financing to meet investment coverage targets.

The re-entry of commercial banks, insurance companies and other financial institutions into the municipal credit market since 2004 means that the private sector is capable of a larger credit financing role within a competitive framework than would have been possible even in the recent past. (To a significant degree, the re-entry of financial institutions into the market probably has been driven by the financial charter as agreed between the government and the financial sector. The financial charter requires all financial institutions to invest in previously disadvantaged areas to gain points, which in turn are used in the award of government tenders over a wide spectrum.)

One conclusion to emerge from INCA's experience and its impact on local infrastructure finance in South Africa is that even when municipalities undertake ambitious investment programmes and are creditworthy, it cannot be assumed that supply limitations in the credit market are the effective constraint on borrowing or investment. Municipal demand for market-based credit is a derived, residual demand—based on the need for financing after preferred sources of funds, such as intergovernmental grants, accumulated internal funds and subsidized credit, have been fully utilized. During the early part of INCA's life, demand for its credit was high and its ability to mobilize capital from the private sector was crucial as it was the sole institution performing this function. More recently, INCA has faced weaker demand from municipal customers. In part, the slowdown in demand is the result of a national grant policy leading to stagnation in overall municipal borrowing and in part it is the result of the expanded availability of private market capital from other financial institutions with which INCA must compete.

Recent Developments:
Is INCA's Role Transitional?

Both South Africa's intergovernmental fiscal system and its municipal credit market have matured rapidly. Fiscal stability and economic growth have reduced the risks of municipal lending. Individual credit risks now can be identified more readily through standard credit analysis. As a result, private financial institutions such as banks and insurance companies have returned to the municipal credit market.

These developments raise the question: 'Is a specialized intermediary like INCA still needed, or should INCA be viewed as a transitional institution whose job has been completed?' After all, INCA's key elements of value addition—the ability to assess and manage municipal credit risk and to mobilize capital from the private sector—now can be performed by others. INCA can legitimately claim credit for accelerating development of the local credit market, but it may no longer be able to capture substantial value from its traditional comparative advantage.

The new competitive environment in municipal lending may be illustrated by two events. In the spring of 2005, the municipality of Nelspruit issued a competitive tender for a loan to finance expansion of its water distribution system. Four private lenders, including INCA, responded with bids. For a 15-year loan carrying identically specified loan terms, all four Private-Sector respondents offered interest rates within a band of less than 10 basis points differential.

Competition within the loan market now has been expanded to competition between loans and municipal bonds. Johannesburg in 2003 issued the first in the new generation of municipal bonds. The issue came as part of a re-structuring triggered by Johannesburg's financial crisis and followed upon national and provincial intervention in Johannesburg's finances. This initial bond issue was perceived as risky, both because of Johannesburg's precarious finances and the lack of recent precedent for bond issues. The Johannesburg bond issue carried a large interest-rate premium over government bond issues and INCA's cost of capital through the bond market. INCA purchased 25 per cent of the issue. However, within 18 months, as Johannesburg's finances stabilized and its prospects improved, the municipality went back to the market with a second bond issue, supported by a partial IFC guarantee, the proceeds of which were used in part for refinancing. This time the bond issue was greatly over-subscribed by private investors at a much lower interest-rate premium, which made it unprofitable for INCA to participate as a purchaser.

Other large municipalities are now exploring the bond market to determine whether direct access to the capital market is a more cost effective way of raising funds than loans through intermediaries, whether specialized intermediaries such as INCA or traditional intermediaries such as commercial banks. The prospective revival of the municipal bond market is a further indication that the need and financial reward for delegated risk monitoring and risk management in the municipal sector has been reduced.[8]

Competition of this kind is excellent news for credit market development and for municipalities' cost of capital. For a specialized institution such as INCA, however, competition squeezes the margins that can be covered from its intermediation. Margins also have been squeezed by a very pronounced decline in overall interest rates.

INCA's Response to the New Environment

INCA has had to adjust to the new market realities. It has done so by redefining its role in the marketplace. The original majority shareholders of INCA sold their shares in the company as part of a black economic empowerment initiative. The original founders left the company, believing that it had largely completed its greenfield mission.

In its redesign, INCA has become a more diversified financial institution, one which—ironically—more closely resembles a traditional parastatal financing intermediary. It has identified lending to State-Owned Enterprises as a primary growth target. (In the fiscal year 2004, INCA's largest loan was to South African Airways.) INCA has reduced its domestic intermediation role, raising significantly less capital through domestic bond issues. Instead, it has taken on the role of managing loan funds provided by international financing institutions. The largest municipal lending activity entered into by INCA in 2005 has been the pass-through of two Euro 30 million loans from the European Investment Bank to Tshwane (Pretoria) and eThekwini (Durban) respectively. As the European Investment Bank's press release states, 'Lending through INCA will facilitate the monitoring of investments' and assure compliance with the cities' approved multi-sector investment programmes.'

One reason that INCA has backed away from a pure intermediation role is the exposure to term-intermediation risk. Interest rates have declined dramatically in South Africa. INCA's initial 15-year bonds, which mature in

2011, were issued at an effective yield of 16 per cent. In today's environment, retail loans to highly rated municipalities carry interest rates in the range of 9.5 per cent. Although INCA has sought to match the term structure of its assets and liabilities and has protected itself from early settlement through pre-payment penalties, falling interest rates have squeezed its margins. In addition, the differential between the rate at which INCA can raise new funds in the bond market and the rate at which it can on-lend to municipalities has been pressured by municipalities' improved creditworthiness and competition with other credit suppliers.

In its original design, INCA is best viewed as a transitional institution. It filled a critical niche when no other intermediary was willing to take on the task of risk evaluation, risk monitoring and risk management for the municipal infrastructure sector. Now that this task has been commoditized, there is less need and less reward for INCA's specialization. Its developmental role has been substantially completed.

Conclusion: Learning from INCA's Experience

The 'lessons' of INCA's experience are best considered against the backdrop of two realities. First, many proposals have been put forward in the developing world to establish infrastructure financing intermediaries that will tap private capital and channel it into municipal infrastructure investment, but few of these proposals have come to fruition. Even fewer institutions in this business, if any, have been privately owned. Second, many donor-supported intermediaries have set the goal of becoming self-sustaining from the domestic market once weaned from donor funds, but very few have actually made the transition.

INCA's experience does not provide a blueprint for duplication elsewhere, but the design and implementation choices it made provide a useful reference for other initiatives, given that INCA did succeed as a business model and fulfilled its original mission.

Institutional Design and Implementation

Ownership Structure

INCA had a variety of strategically placed equity owners, but its design expressly excluded government agencies as shareholders. The rationale:

government participation in ownership would jeopardize the fundamental power of a credit supplier—the ability to say 'No' to loan requests.

Aligning Risk with Reward

INCA's structure assigns risk to the equity holders, along with the potential for high returns on equity. In alternative models of Private-Sector participation, a private company often is responsible for fund management and earns a fixed management fee. This low-risk arrangement provides little incentive for performance and fails to take advantage of the private sector's comparative advantage in assuming and managing risk.

High Debt–Equity Ratio

To generate a high return for equity holders while maintaining low spreads for municipal borrowers, INCA operated with a high debt–equity ratio. Its capital adequacy ratio ranged between 6 per cent and 7 per cent. Intermediaries supported by international donor institutions are often steered in the direction of much higher equity levels. This forces the institution either to widen its on-lending spread, raising the cost of funds to ultimate borrowers, or to accept below-market equity returns, discouraging private investment in the intermediary.

Credit Risk Management

To be viable, an intermediary institution must add value. INCA's value addition has resided in its ability to evaluate, monitor, reduce and price municipal credit risk. These are the critical functions of any intermediary operating in this field. Well-defined, effective risk management is also the feature that allows an intermediary such as INCA to operate with a high debt–equity ratio. In contrast, most municipal infrastructure financing intermediaries in the developing world do not systematically price, monitor or provision for risk. Low debt–equity ratios in effect substitute, in the eyes of lenders, for poor control of the underlying risk of municipal on-lending.

Broader Policy Lessons

Is Access to Private Capital the Limiting Constraint on Municipal Investment?

INCA's experience illustrates that the answer to this question is very much case-specific. Even within INCA's eight-year lifetime, the answer has varied greatly. At its launch, INCA's infusion of Private-Sector capital into municipal lending was highly additive, both to aggregate municipal lending and aggregate municipal infrastructure financing. In later years, even as INCA continued to maintain profitable operations, its sectoral impact was more complex. For a time, its loans essentially replaced part of the private sector's reduction of lending through bond redemptions. In the most recent period, the capacity and willingness of the private sector (including INCA) to lend to municipalities at market rates has exceeded municipalities' desire to borrow. Municipal demand for Private-Sector credit is always a derived, residual demand. It depends on the desired level of investment by creditworthy municipalities (or creditworthy projects) *after* other, more favourable sources of financing, such as grants and below-market loans from public institutions, have been exhausted.

Specialized Municipal Infrastructure Financing Intermediaries Most Likely Are Transitional Institutions

The desired end state is a competitive municipal credit market, in which multiple private lenders compete with one another for municipal lending and with municipalities' direct access to capital markets through bond issuance. The costs and benefits of different financing arrangements are then a matter for the market to sort out. A specialized intermediary such as INCA performs its primary development role by accelerating the transition to a fully competitive, private-sector market. Whether municipal borrowers and Private-Sector suppliers of capital continue to see substantial advantages to having a specialized institution such as INCA serve as intermediary within a competitive market and whether the intermediary's role justifies its necessary on-lending margins are also matters for the market to resolve. It is likely that the intermediary's role will cover a smaller, more targeted segment of the market, where specialized risk identification and risk reduction continue to be important contributions.

Notes

1. As a result of amalgamation and reorganization, more than 840 municipalities have been reduced to 231 municipalities, 6 metros and 47 district governments.
2. In the South African system, service costs are not recovered from individual users, but rather from the entire user group in the aggregate. There is a great deal of cross-subsidization. Policy now calls for free basic services—e.g., a minimum amount of monthly

water consumption provided free of charge to all consumer units. The costs of free basic service provision are covered by higher charges for higher consumption levels.

3. In most years, INCA has not had specific provisioning for non-performing loans. Instead, it purchased insurance from Swiss Re that covered the first R 40 billion of loan losses and paid for this insurance through annual premiums. The insurance coverage has the same effect on financial structure as a reserve for bad loans.

4. This followed Bank of International Settlement rules establishing so-called BIS ratios, in which each country's bank regulator established risk weightings for different classes of borrowers, grouping sub-national borrowers as a single class.

5. As of 30 June 2004, the actual distribution of loan credit risk (as a percentage of loan advances) by the categories in Table 9.1 was:

Category 1: 36.3%
Category 2: 32.2%
Category 3: 27.5%
Category 4: 4.0%

6. The subsidiary is capitalized at 25 per cent and has a USAID Development Credit Assistance guarantee of 50 per cent of principal.

7. The other large source of capital grants for municipal infrastructure is the housing grant. It covers the costs of extending network connections to new housing and is especially important in municipalities with rapidly growing populations, primarily the metros.

8. Until the 2004 Johannesburg bond issue, the volume of capital market securities outstanding had been in persistent, rapid decline. The value of municipal bonds outstanding fell from R 11.6 billion in March 1997 to R 3.1 billion in March 2004. Long-term loans (almost entirely through INCA and DBSA) over the same period rose from R 3.9 billion to R 13.8 billion, essentially replacing the decline in bonds outstanding with very modest overall growth in total private credit supply after the initial impact of INCA's entry into the market in February 1997.

References

INCA. 1997. *Prospectus.* Johannesburg: INCA.

———. 2004. *INCA 2004 Annual Report.* Johannesburg: INCA.

Peterson, George E. 2006. 'Re-considering Municipal Development Funds'. Paper presented at Urban Learning Week, 22 March, Washington, DC.

South Africa National Treasury. 2004. *Trends in Intergovernmental Finances: 2000/1–2006/7.* Pretoria: Government Printer.

———. 2005. *Budget Review.* Pretoria: Government Printer.

10

Land Leasing and Land Sale as an Infrastructure Financing Option

George E. Peterson[*]

Introduction

In searching for infrastructure financing options, local governments can look to their balance sheets as well as their budgets. Municipalities often have a wide array of assets on their balance sheets, ranging from infrastructure networks to public buildings, from housing to municipally owned enterprises, as well as municipally owned land. Active asset management involves deciding what to do with these assets. Should they be held and operated in their present form? Should they be re-priced so that users pay true economic costs? Or should a municipality sell some assets, marginal to basic service delivery, and re-invest the proceeds in core urban infrastructure facilities?[1]

Asset sales have some attraction as a way to mobilize investment resources. From a local perspective, local governments often have more flexibility in managing their assets than they do in adjusting tax rates, introducing new taxes, increasing user fees or borrowing funds for investment—all of which may require higher-level governmental approval or be prohibited altogether by the intergovernmental fiscal framework. From the perspective of macro fiscal management, if local governments truly are disposing of assets tangential

[*] George E. Peterson served as Senior Fellow in international public finance at the Urban Institute in Washington, D.C.

to their core mission and using the proceeds to invest in basic infrastructure, this tightening of governmental focus without incurring debt is to be applauded.

Local governments, of course, have recognized the possibility of financing infrastructure investment through asset sales. For a period in the mid-1990s, the city of Bratislava, Slovakia, for example, financed roughly 15 per cent of its annual capital budget from privatization proceeds. As a general rule, however, asset sales of this kind have been viewed as a temporary financing expedient, made possible by the government's decision to exit certain activities, such as provision of public housing or operation of economic enterprises that compete with the private sector. Fiscal experts have warned cities not to become dependent upon asset sales as a significant or continuing source of capital financing.

Sale of municipally owned land may be a partial exception, in that it can sustain infrastructure finance for a longer period of time. In countries where all urban land is owned by the public sector, land is by far the most valuable asset on the municipal balance sheet. It is often the most valuable municipal asset under other landholding regimes. Urban land values are created in part by public investment. They reflect the capitalized value of access to road networks, water supply, schools and other services made possible by municipal investment. It is economically appropriate, therefore, for municipalities to capture part of the land-value increment they create through their investment. There are various ways that increases in urban land values can be captured, but the sale of land or land rights has the advantage of producing revenue quickly and being easier to administer than betterment taxes, land readjustment schemes or universal property taxation.

Moreover, municipally owned urban land is not a static asset. It can be 'created' by expanding the urban area into rural zones at the urban fringe. A legally empowered, active asset manager can also acquire additional land from current users for urban redevelopment or for highway and airport construction. It can then resell part of the land after its value has been enhanced by public investment. Even without public improvements, urbanization and economic growth tend to drive up land prices, adding to the value of land held on local balance sheets and raising the question of whether the municipal asset base would be more effectively deployed if some of the landholdings were exchanged for infrastructure.

This chapter examines the potential of land sales as an infrastructure financing tool. The first section looks at the land leasing process and its implementation in China, which has made the largest-scale commitment to converting land assets into infrastructure. Many cities in China have financed half or more of their very high urban infrastructure investment levels directly from land leasing, while borrowing against the value of land on their balance sheets to finance much of the remainder. The second section places China's experience in perspective, by looking briefly at Hong Kong, from which mainland China adapted its land-leasing framework; Ethiopia, a country at the other end of the prosperity spectrum, that recently introduced land leasing as a financing device for cities; and India. Land in India is not generally owned by the public sector, but the urban development authorities that have responsibility for much of urban infrastructure investment often have extensive landholdings, as do other governmental institutions. These institutions have begun to turn to land development and land sales as an infrastructure financing strategy. In all of these countries, land sales either are financing or have the potential for financing a surprisingly large share of urban infrastructure investment.

The final section weighs the policy issues and risks associated with land sales on this scale. Monetizing publicly held land may, for a period, generate an abundant source of revenue for local governments, but it also introduces a new set of risks that can profoundly affect fiscal management. In fact, as more countries are tempted to take advantage of the boom in urban land values to finance local budgets, the type of prudential restrictions built into fiscal responsibility laws may have to be broadened to deal with these risks.

Land Leasing and Urban Infrastructure Finance: The Case of China

Land leasing in China involves the up-front sale of long-term occupancy and development rights. The practice was introduced on an experimental basis in 1987 in Shenzhen and other coastal cities as part of the *de facto* decentralization of China's fiscal system. Up to that time, public authorities allocated land administratively and land use was free. The land-leasing reforms were intended in part to stimulate locally led economic development by allowing cities to attract foreign investment by providing stable land occupancy rights to investors. From the start, land leasing was tied to infrastructure investment. Land leasing provided a potentially large source of income, whose revenues were to be invested primarily in infrastructure systems, further enhancing cities' competitive position for economic growth.

In 1988, China's Constitution, which previously had prohibited all types of land transfer, was amended to permit land leasing while retaining public ownership of land. In 1990, the State Council formally affirmed land leasing as public policy. By 1992, Shanghai and Beijing had adopted land leasing as local practice, and it began to spread.[2] Like most of China's economic development and fiscal reforms, the wave of land leasing moved from coastal experimental cities to Shanghai and the capital, then westward to the rest of the country.

Land leasing has been a key element of China's fiscal decentralization. In China, the central government retains all tax-policy authority over local governments. Municipalities cannot change tax rates, introduce new taxes of their own design or scrap dysfunctional local taxes. They need higher-level governmental approval for adjustments in user charges. As initiated in Shenzhen and applied elsewhere, land leasing was an attempt by municipalities to gain control over a revenue source genuinely within their control. Until very recently, municipal governments have been free to assemble and sell land at their discretion, constrained only by the expansion of urban boundaries approved in their master plans.

Whereas China's 1994 fiscal framework reforms (see Chapter 2) have been described as a form of fiscal recentralization, due to the increase in central government's share of shared taxes, revenue-sharing arrangements for land leasing moved in the opposite direction. Originally, the central government's share of land-leasing revenues was set at 60 per cent. The split subsequently was modified to 40:60 for central and local governments respectively, then to 32:68 and 5:95 before all land-leasing revenues were assigned to municipal governments as part of the 1994 fiscal reforms (Chan 1997).[3] Much of the emphasis that cities place on land leasing in China's competitive federalism framework stems from the fact that fiscal rules allow them to keep the land-leasing revenues that they mobilize and grant municipalities a great deal of freedom to act as entrepreneurs in the local land market.

The purchaser of a land lease acquires land rights for a period of 40–70 years, depending upon the type of property development. Land that is 'sold' and approved for development can be reclaimed by the government if not developed within a specified time period. Originally, municipalities transferred land rights to developers primarily by private negotiation. In the mid 1990s, a review by the Ministry of Land and Resources found that more than 95 per cent of all transfers had taken this form (Sun 1995). Private negotiations with developers, however, provided a fertile ground for corruption, with consequent revenue loss to government. In 2002, the central authorities promulgated a new circular instructing municipalities to conduct all land leasing through public bidding at auction. Municipalities were slow to accept the new limitations (Beijing issued its order to conduct all municipal land transfers through public competition only in 2004). However, according to central statistics, the percentage of municipal land transfers occurring through auction or public bidding rose from 15 per cent in 2002 to 33 per cent in 2003 (*China Daily* 2004b), and has continued to rise, becoming the primary form of conveyance in economically advanced cities.

Revenue Generated from Land Sales

Because comprehensive municipal budgets are not released to the public, it is difficult to put together reliable data on the magnitude of land leasing except through case studies. Table 10.1 summarizes information from several different case studies regarding land-leasing revenues and their size, relative to total local spending or the local capital budget. Although land leasing is viewed as an infrastructure financing tool by Chinese municipalities, there is no legal requirement to dedicate revenues to the capital budget.

Table 10.1
Revenue from Land Leasing in Selected Cities

City	Period	Revenue raised
Shanghai[1]	1992–2004	More than RMB 100 billion, used for capital spending
Shenzhen[2]	Throughout the 1990s	Approximately 80% of total local government revenues
Beijing[3]	1995–96	RMB 6.9 billion (approximately 60% of local capital spending)
Chengdu[4]	2002–03	RMB 4.7 billion (approximately 45% of local capital spending)
Hangzhou[5]	2002	RMB 6 billion (more than 20% of total government revenues)
Guangdong province[6]	1992	RMB 9.4 billion (45% of total revenue of provincial government and municipalities)

Sources: 1. Gao (chapter 6, this volume)
2. Chan (1997)
3. Deng (2003)
4. Author's interviews. Chengdu is capital of Sichuan Province
5. Ding (2005) Hangzhou is capital of Zhejiang Province
6. Sun, Y. (1995)
Note: RMB 8.35 = US$ 1.00 during period covered.

The studies underlying these data suggest that direct revenues from land leasing can generate a substantial part of the municipal capital budget for a period of 10–15 years, even when investment levels are as high as they have been in China. Urban land values in China have risen at a frantic pace. The potential for revenue mobilization is indicated by two individual land-auction transactions consummated in Shanghai: one at the end of 2005, the other in January 2006. Sale of lease rights to two land plots in downtown Shanghai generated more than RMB 6.5 billion (roughly US$ 810 million), with leasing rights selling at US$ 9,300 per square metre in one transaction and US$ 7,500 in the other. As an indication of the volume of land leasing, Shanghai, in the third quarter of 2003, leased at auction 805 hectares (8.05 million square metres) of land, mostly in the new development area of Pudong. The real-estate boom has spread to western China. Chengdu, capital of Sichuan province, sold a single mixed commercial–residential site outside the central zone for the equivalent of US$ 97 million, or roughly $1,350 per square metre. The municipality has been actively auctioning large blocks of land in new development zones in order to finance its ambitious infrastructure programme.

The role of publicly owned land in urban infrastructure finance extends well beyond direct proceeds from land-leasing sales. Borrowing from state-owned commercial and development banks has financed much of the remaining urban infrastructure investment. This borrowing takes the form of balance-sheet debt, typically secured by municipally owned land. Debt service often is paid by selling off the leasing rights to parcels of land whose value has been enhanced by the debt-financed infrastructure projects.

The interaction between land leasing, debt and infrastructure investment is illustrated by the construction of the outer-ring circumferential highway in Changsha, capital of Hunan province in central China.[4] To finance the project, the municipality transferred to a public–private agency, the Ring Road Investment Corporation, leasing rights for strips of land 200 metres wide on both sides of the highway that was to be built, totalling 33 square kilometres of land in all, of which 12 square kilometres was finished land, possessing infrastructure access and development approvals. In its original state, without access to roads or infrastructure, the remaining land had very little market value. However, the plan was to sell off land parcels once the highway was built. The total cost of the second stage of the highway project was estimated at RMB 6 billion (at the time, some US$ 730 million). Approximately half of this amount was financed directly from sale of leasing rights to the land already having infrastructure service. The other half was financed through borrowing. The Ring Road Investment Corporation was able to borrow against the *future* anticipated value of the improved land to obtain financing from the China Development Bank and commercial banks, pledging to sell off land parcels in the future, after the highway was completed, to meet debt service.

Cities as Land Entrepreneurs

The importance of land-leasing revenues to cities' fiscal capacity and infrastructure investment has turned municipal governments into land-market entrepreneurs. Municipalities try to acquire as much land as possible, as cheaply as possible, then either sell it at market rates, or use it as collateral for infrastructure loans, or provide it at below-market rates to strategic (mostly foreign) investors for industrial development.

Municipalities acquire land in various ways. They can move municipal State-Owned Enterprises (SOEs) from central locations to the urban outskirts, where the companies have better transportation access but where land is cheaper, and then sell the vacated land to developers. This relocation is part of a broad rationalization of land use created by land pricing. In the first years of land-leasing, before the regulatory framework was clarified, SOEs tried to capture all the proceeds of land-leasing sales for themselves through direct transactions with developers. Municipalities fought successfully for control of the supply of land-leasing rights and land revenues. Such transactions must now proceed through the municipal Land Resource Center, subject to municipal decision making, with the municipal government receiving a prescribed share of sales revenue.

Municipalities can expand the urbanized area by acquiring land from rural communes and converting it to urban use. The municipality's sale price for leasing land for urban use has vastly exceeded the purchase price it pays farmers, often by a factor as large as 10 times.[5] The scramble by municipalities to acquire land for urbanization—dubbed China's version of the 'enclosure movement'—has led municipalities to stockpile land by taking advantage of (and abusing) exceptions to urban land-use limitations in their authorized development plans. One exception involves land acquired for approved economic development zones and industrial parks. The Ministry of Land and Resources found in 2004 that 6,015 development zones had been established by municipalities, of which only 1,251 had received the requisite approval of the State Council or provincial governments. In total, these municipalities had declared development zones and industrial parks covering an astounding 35,400 square kilometres of formerly rural land, most of which was serving as a land reserve for potential future development and municipal land leasing (*China Daily* 2004b).

A municipality or its development agency can also designate centrally located areas of rundown housing or small-scale businesses for redevelopment and acquire land from traditional users under a plan that involves mandatory resettlement. The municipality upgrades infrastructure, then sells land-leasing rights for redevelopment.

Perhaps the most novel form of freeing up land for resale involves moving the city hall and all of the municipality's administrative buildings to a new location outside the urban centre, then auctioning off the vacated central land to developers. As a strategy for generating land-leasing revenues and infrastructure investment, this approach has twin advantages. It creates a new urban centre where municipal offices can relocate, enhancing the value of the surrounding land, which the municipality can lease, while it frees up for competitive leasing and commercial redevelopment the very highly valued land at the existing urban centre. All six of the municipalities examined in the World Bank's City Development Strategies II programme had either moved their city hall and administrative offices in this way or were in the process of doing so (Chreod 2005).

In this type of land-market activity, municipalities act as aggressive, profit-maximizing monopolists. Local officials have formalized strategic guidelines as to how municipal governments should seek to gain control over all land-leasing transactions, so as to control the volume and location of land supply and maximize municipal revenues.[6] Municipalities are required to compensate land users who are resettled with cash and alternative housing. Analysis of the pattern of land leasing in Shanghai demonstrates that the areas leased for commercial development tended to maximize *net* leasing revenues after compensation costs, confirming the entrepreneurial mindset of the municipality (Fu et al. 1999).

Despite municipalities' ability to create new supplies of urban land, land leasing is a transitional infrastructure-financing strategy. The supply of land available for leasing eventually will run out. Shenzhen, the pioneer in land leasing, aggressively expanded its urban boundaries for 15 years. By now, the potential for further expansion or new land leasing has almost been exhausted. Shenzhen's asset management company, in fact, has turned to buying and selling land-use rights in other urban areas of the interior of China as a way of continuing to use its entrepreneurial skills to generate revenues from land transactions. By contrast, land leasing as an infrastructure-financing tool is gathering speed in later-developing regions of western China and the rustbelt north-east.

In summary, China used land leasing as part of a strategy to jumpstart urban infrastructure investment after decades of neglect. The 'marketization' of land in effect converted land that was generating no economic or financial return under the old landholding system into urban infrastructure, which is the cornerstone of national economic growth. Chinese authorities recognize that land leasing monetizes a finite asset and cannot indefinitely play such a prominent role in urban infrastructure finance. As discussed by Gao (chapter 6), the cities that pioneered land leasing are now shifting strategy to rely more on the income streams provided by infrastructure assets to recover capital costs.

Land Leasing and Land Sale: Experiences Beyond China

China is a special case. The nation has experienced exceptional economic growth, driven by urbanization. Its land-leasing system places land assets unambiguously in municipal governments' hands and has not been tested by a significant economic downturn. Is the financing capacity of land leasing and land sales unique to China, or is there comparable scope for revenue impacts in other places?

Hong Kong

China drew its land-leasing model from Hong Kong, where it has been applied for more than a century and has been the underpinning of urban infrastructure investment. Hong Kong's experience bears out the ability of land leasing to generate large amounts of revenue over an extended period of time. Between 1970 and 2000, Hong Kong is estimated to have realized some US$ 71.1 billion (in constant 2000 dollars) from up-front sale of land leases (Hong 2003), including renegotiation at current market value of leases whose original term had expired—this for a jurisdiction with a population of approximately 6.8 million people. Most of the revenue has traditionally been used to pay for infrastructure investment and other public works, although there is no legal earmarking of land-sale proceeds.

Table 10.2 summarizes land-lease revenues and their relation to total public expenditure and expenditure on public works for the period 1996–2000. Over this period, land leasing generated proceeds that exceeded Hong Kong's total spending on infrastructure and other public works. However, revenue collection from land leasing has been highly volatile, reflecting extreme volatility in the underlying land and property market. Between 1990 and 1995, the average value per square foot of land leased at auction rose by a factor of more than four times in constant Hong Kong dollars. With

Table 10.2
Revenue from Land Leasing, Hong Kong

Land leasing as percentage of:	1996	1997	1998	1999	2000	Average
Expenditure on public works	101	229	82	133	105	130
Total expenditure	16	34	11	18	14	18

Source: Hong (2003).

the arrival of the Asian financial crisis and uncertainty about Hong Kong's future economic role, land prices fell by almost 50 per cent between 1998 and 2002. Land market demand declined so severely that Hong Kong suspended all sales of land for commercial development for more than three years. Over the period 2001–03, revenues from land sales plummeted to almost zero, contributing to steep fiscal deficits that at their peak reached 30 per cent of fiscal revenues.

With recovery in the real estate market, Hong Kong has resumed land leasing, but changed its role from supplier of pre-announced amounts of land in locations designated for development by planners to a more passive role intended to be consistent with market forces. It adopted an 'application list' system, under which the government provides land only in response to developer requests at acceptable prices. It was hoped that this change in procedure would also moderate the large swings in revenues, but through 2006, revenue stabilization has been less than hoped for. Hong Kong, in its medium-range forecast prepared in 2003, foresaw relatively stable revenues from leasing land assets, at 12–13 per cent of annual total government revenue. In the first year of the five-year planning period 2004–05, actual revenue from land leasing substantially exceeded the target at HK\$ 34 billion, but in the next fiscal year only HK\$ 4 billion was realized.

The government has now convened a public consultative process pre-paratory to introducing a goods and services tax, motivated in part by the desire to reduce the exposure of the general budget to the high volatility of revenue resulting from land leasing. This reform would allow land leasing to continue as a major contributor to the public-works budget, while partially insulating the operating budget from revenue fluctuations.[7]

Ethiopia

Ethiopia lies at the other end of the economic spectrum from China. It has one of the lowest per-capita income levels in the world, low levels of urbanization and economic performance that fluctuates with rainfall. Like some other African countries, Ethiopia has recently introduced land leasing into urban areas.[8]

Land leasing has become an integral part of Ethiopia's local decentralization efforts. Economic rights to the income from land leasing have been assigned to municipalities.[9] Except for water tariffs, which some regions now allow municipalities to adjust in light of service costs, land leasing is the only source of revenue over which municipalities have policy control. All other sources of municipal revenue are laid out in regional proclamations dating back a decade or more, which specify the exact amounts that municipalities can levy for each of dozens of individual taxes and service fees (Peterson 2005).

Ethiopia does not require full up-front payment of the land-lease amount. A portion of lease payment is due at contract signing. The remainder can be paid over the lifetime of the lease agreement. Interest may or may not be charged, depending upon the type of property involved and the region that is implementing the federal land-leasing proclamation. Ethiopia is converting its land occupancy system from a previous regime where occupants 'rented' land from the municipality on an annual basis, without formal legal protection of occupancy beyond the current year, to the 'leasing' system, which is designed to give longer-term rights to land occupancy without surrendering public ownership. During the early years of the new system, much of leasing activity has been concentrated on vacant land, commercial properties, and property owners wanting to occupy plots greater than the maximum parcel size they are legally entitled to rent.

Ethiopian policy attempts to tie land-leasing revenue directly to municipal infrastructure investment. The federal land-leasing proclamation states that a municipality shall earmark 90 per cent of all land-leasing proceeds for infrastructure investment (Ethiopia, 2002). Municipalities are candid enough to acknowledge that literal budgetary earmarking of this kind does not occur, and cannot occur because of the condition of municipal accounting. However, at least in a sample of municipalities empowered with land-leasing authority in Amhara and Tigray regional states, growth in municipal land-leasing revenues has coincided with a growth in total municipal revenues and an increase in the proportion of municipal expenditure spent on capital projects.

The revenue implications of land leasing are summarized in Table 10.3 for the two largest cities in Amhara and Tigray regions. The cities have populations ranging from 75,000 to 325,000. Land leasing has become the single largest source of municipal revenue, overtaking the traditionally largest source of revenue, the local fee and tax items covered in regional tariff

Table 10.3
Revenue from Land Leasing for Ethiopian Municipalities in
Amhara and Tigray, 2003–04

Municipality	Land leasing as percentage of total revenue	Land leasing as percentage of capital spending	Growth in land-leasing revenue from 2002–03
Bahir Dar (Amhara)	45.3	140	NA
Gondar (Amhara)	42.3	105	35.8
Adigrat (Tigray)	21.5	77	144.7
Mekele (Tigray)	24.2	81	8.1

Source: Peterson 2005.
Notes: a. Municipalities do not have separate capital budgets; amounts of capital spending are estimated from line item expenditures.

    b. The US$-to-Ethiopian Birr exchange rate was unchanged over 2002–03 and 2003–04.

proclamations. By international standards, of course, the revenue generated from land leasing in Ethiopia is meagre. The highest-valued land lease in Mekele, capital of the Tigray region, was sold at auction for approximately US$ 1.60 per square metre. The infrastructure investments being financed are equally basic: they consist of modest upgrades to water distribution, road surfacing and the like.

The potential exists for further revenue mobilization through land leasing in cities where the population is growing and municipal management has an entrepreneurial mindset. A new municipal administration in Mekele, for example, was able to more than double the land-leasing revenue in 2004–05 from the levels shown in Table 10.3 by implementing a policy that sold a larger share of land leases at public auction and more aggressively identified undeveloped land parcels for leasing. If Ethiopia should succeed in implementing its planned conversion of the annual land-rent system to up-front leasing, it would further accelerate revenue mobilization for a transitional period.

At the same time, land leasing has introduced an unprecedented degree of volatility in municipalities' own-source revenues, especially for mid-sized and smaller urban administrations with weaker land markets. Unable to obtain revenue growth from other sources, almost all municipalities have taken the fiscally risky course of building land-leasing revenues into their future recurrent budgets.

India

As noted in several places in this volume, India long has been troubled by a low rate of urban infrastructure investment. Despite the recognition of urban local bodies as a third tier of government by the 74th Constitutional Amendment, municipalities remain creatures of the states, with low revenue-generating capacity, no authority to initiate taxes and, with rare exceptions, no power to modify tax rates on their own. Responsibility for urban infrastructure investment is scattered among many institutions, in addition to municipal governments. Foremost among these in large urban areas are urban development authorities (UDAs), which are agencies of the states. Political conflicts at the state level, between rural and urban interests, have limited the volume of resources that state budgets can direct to urban infrastructure investment through the UDAs.

In this environment, institutions have searched for other sources of urban infrastructure finance that do not require tax increases or state budget allocations. Land resources always have been part of the budgetary picture in India's cities, but they are just beginning to emerge as an important element in infrastructure financing strategy.

UDAs are typically holders of substantial amounts of urban land, obtained as part of urban development and redevelopment projects. In new development areas, the UDAs notify land for development, acquire land under public-purpose regulation, develop an area by installing internal infrastructure networks, sell or rent the land to developers and end-users, and turn over responsibility for maintenance and operation of infrastructure facilities to the municipal government. In urban redevelopment zones, too, UDAs carry out similar activities. The high value of improved land in redevelopment projects makes it possible for UDAs to use proceeds from land sale and land rental to help finance general urban infrastructure network improvements as well as infrastructure specific to the redevelopment area.

The Mumbai Metropolitan Regional Development Authority (MMRDA) illustrates this process and the potential for mobilizing infrastructure finance through land sales. In the early 1990s, the MMRDA developed from marshland a new 553-acre commercial centre called the Bandra–Kurla complex. Proceeds from the development—mostly in the form of annual rent payments and development fees—have provided the MMRDA with a capital fund that it has used for a variety of initiatives, in addition to infrastructure support for the complex itself. These include co-financing a road construction programme in Greater Mumbai and setting up a revolving fund for subsidized infrastructure lending to other municipalities in Maharashtra, as well as undesignated contributions to other state initiatives.

A strategic initiative developed for Mumbai (Bombay First and McKinsey 2003) has called attention to the much greater revenue-generating potential of the MMRDA and other public landholders if, instead of renting land on an annual basis, they were to sell fee-simple ownership rights. The proceeds of land sales could then be used to finance citywide infrastructure as a key part of the strategy for building Mumbai into a world-class financial centre. *Vision Mumbai* identifies land sales as one of the most important elements in the public sector's contribution to infrastructure financing.

The potential for revenue mobilization through land sales has been heightened by India's urban real-estate boom. In January 2006, in two separate auctions, the MMRDA sold land parcels in the Bandra–Kurla complex for Rs 22.9 billion (about US$ 510 million), including the highest-valued urban land transaction recorded to date in India, at roughly US$ 7,330 per square metre. The MMRDA has said it will use the proceeds to finance infrastructure investment. Table 10.4 compares the revenue mobilization generated by the auction of a few land parcels within this single development complex to total annual infrastructure investment by the Mumbai municipality (the Mumbai Municipal Corporation) and other infrastructure financing initiatives, including the central government's first-year contribution to infrastructure investment in 63 of India's largest cities via the highly publicized National Urban Renewal Mission.

Table 10.4
Land Sale Revenues and Infrastructure Spending in Mumbai, India
In Rs Billion

Item	Amount
MMRDA land auctions, Bandra–Kurla complex, January 2006	23.0
Total MMRDA infrastructure investment, 2004–05	5.4
Total infrastructure investment by the Mumbai Municipal Corporation, 2004–2005	10.4
Pledge for Mumbai infrastructure investment by the state of Maharashtras as part of the Mumbai Strategic Development Initiative, 2005–06	10.0
Central government funding for infrastructure investment and services to the poor in 63 major cities, including Mumbai—National Urban Renewal Mission, 2005–06	55.0

Sources: Data for MMRDA infrastructure spending, Municipal Corporation infrastructure spending, and the state of Maharashtra's pledge: Pathak 2005. Other data from official statements.

Note: 'Infrastructure' investment excludes capital spending for education and health.

The MMRDA's revenue mobilization from land sales reflects both the market reality of a real-estate boom and a change in asset management strategy away from annual rental of land to up-front sale of land properties. Similar initiatives to realize land values and invest the proceeds in infrastructure are being undertaken in other parts of urban India. The poorer state of Rajasthan, for example, announced at the beginning of 2006 that it was turning over to the Jaipur Development Authority for sale at auction pieces of land having a minimum auction price of Rs 5.07 billion (roughly US$ 113 million), a sum that vastly exceeds annual infrastructure investment by all levels of government in the capital region of Jaipur.

As urban land sales are presently administered in India, most of the revenue proceeds accrue to agencies of state governments, especially the states' urban development authorities. Land sales thus have not been an instrument of fiscal decentralization to the local level or a significant contributor to municipalities' capital budgets. The large sums generated by land sales have not, in the past, been publicly accountable and often have been treated by the states as off-budget cash hoards that can be allocated for any politically attractive purpose. The new land-auctioning guidelines in Rajasthan represent a step forward in this regard. They require that the urban development authority transfer 15 per cent of its proceeds from land sales to the fiscally impoverished Jaipur Municipal Corporation. The proportions to be transferred to the state government budget and to be retained by the UDA for its investment purposes are also specified.

Land as a Source of Infrastructure Finance

The experience reviewed in this chapter suggests that urban land can, under a variety of conditions, generate significant amounts of revenue that can help finance local infrastructure budgets. In a growing economy that is urbanizing at a fast pace, urban land values will tend to rise strongly over time, although in a highly volatile fashion. Selling land and converting the proceeds into infrastructure assets can make sense if it is part of a deliberate policy to accelerate infrastructure investment, based on the assessment that infrastructure has become a key bottleneck to economic growth and urban service delivery. This was the strategic assessment made in China in the early 1990s and it is the strategy advocated by some analysts and policy makers in India today.

It would be wildly imprudent, of course, to think that urban land values can continue to increase at the torrid pace that China, India, and parts of Latin America and Africa have experienced from 2002 to 2006. Counting on further land-value gains as a major source of financing may also be unwise. From the perspective of strategic asset management, however, the current reality of a real-estate boom makes it possible to convert publicly held land into publicly valuable infrastructure at an especially favourable rate of exchange.

The impetus to convert land into infrastructure is further strengthened when municipalities have few other options for raising discretionary revenues. The countries surveyed here have fiscal frameworks that strictly limit or prohibit local tax increases. Intergovernmental rules and market conditions restrict municipal borrowing. It is understandable, then, that authorities should turn to urban land assets for financing. This phenomenon is not limited to the developing world. In the wake of Proposition 13 in the State of California (United States), which essentially froze local property tax assessments, as well as related propositions that restricted other forms of local tax increases and municipal borrowing, California's localities also turned to land assets as a way to finance infrastructure. New intergovernmental rules were adopted that allowed developers to issue land-based bonds to finance roads, sewer and water systems, and other basic infrastructure that no longer could be financed by the public budget. Land became the collateral for a good deal of new infrastructure financing. The debt service obligation that developers assumed in order to finance their infrastructure investment became a lien on the land, which purchasers of developed parcels acquired along with their property.[10] This lien was enforced by municipal governments and billed along with property taxes, but as a legally separate item that allowed local governments to circumvent the restrictions on new taxes or public borrowing.

Conclusion: Fiscal Risks and Policy Choices

Financing part of urban infrastructure budgets from land sales appears to be feasible in countries that either have public ownership of land or institutional arrangements that allow special development authorities to acquire and sell land associated with infrastructure development projects. Reliance on land sales for revenue, however, creates special risks that need to be taken into account in the intergovernmental fiscal framework.

Linkage between Land Sales and Infrastructure Investment

In financial terms, sale of an income-producing asset closely resembles borrowing. In both cases, up-front payment is received in exchange for a future revenue stream. The foregone revenue stream in the case of asset sales may take the form of recurring revenues from user fees, annual land rents or lost proceeds from the sale of land at a future date when it may be more valuable.

Municipal land and asset sales therefore raise many of the same inter-governmental fiscal concerns as municipal borrowing. One danger involves use of the proceeds of asset sales to finance the municipal operating budget. The review in this chapter suggests that some municipalities with access to land-sale revenues have come to depend upon these revenues for more than investment purposes and that receipts spill over to become part of the operating budget. The fiscal risk is that municipalities become dependent upon asset sales for covering recurring costs and, at a future date, when the assets are gone, face more severe budget shortfalls, which they want the national government to absorb.

In the case of borrowing, a common component of fiscal regulation requires municipalities to use long-term borrowing only to finance investment. This Golden Rule could similarly apply to asset sales: municipalities must use the proceeds of asset sales to finance investment. Ethiopia has attempted to follow this approach by introducing into its land-leasing proclamation the requirement that 90 per cent of the proceeds from municipal land leasing be used for urban infrastructure investment, and China for a time required that a portion of lease/sale revenue be dedicated to urban infrastructure construction. Local governments have not applied this rule literally in Ethiopia and given the fungibility of budgets, it is impossible to ensure that asset sales are used to fund incremental investment. However, the requirement to enter asset sales as capital revenue in the capital budget can help maintain the policy perspective that one type of asset is being exchanged for another on the municipal balance sheet and that land is not being sold to finance operating expenses.

Paradoxically, the Golden Rule limitation would not assist China in managing the principal fiscal risks that have arisen there from municipal land sales. National authorities fear that municipalities will be *too* aggressive in using land sales to finance investment and that excessive investment in urban fixed assets will contribute to overheating the economy. To limit such risks, the central government has resorted to more direct restrictions of the kind used to limit or prohibit municipal borrowing. For a six-month period in 2004, municipal land purchases for urban development were halted altogether by central regulation, partly as a fiscal measure to restrain excessive local investment. Central authorities have continued to ban municipalities from acquiring land to create new special economic zones or industrial parks, out of fear that the practice was stimulating inefficient investment and would require massive amounts of infrastructure spending to make the new zones functional.[11]

Risks of a Real-Estate Bubble

Land prices have the advantage of long-term buoyancy with respect to economic growth and urbanization. However, they are extremely volatile. Although at this writing land prices are rising at a rate of 30–40 per cent per annum in India's large cities, they declined over the period 1998–2002 in response to the Asian financial crisis and other factors. Hong Kong's experience illustrates the threat to overall fiscal stability that can result from revenue dependence on land sales at a time of decline in the real-estate market.

The greatest financial risk manifests itself when land and property values become the primary basis for borrowing. Municipal land is the principal collateral for borrowing by Chinese municipalities' UDICs. China's banking system, which has concentrated on cleaning up non-performing loans, many of them to municipal entities or local State-Owned Enterprises, would be placed at high risk in the event of a collapse in land or real-estate prices. In fact, many of China's infrastructure financing policies have depended upon continually *rising* land values for their viability.

Sound fiscal management may require intergovernmental rules that restrict the way land values can be used to support municipal borrowing. One of the first steps that China took (in 2003) to restrict land-based municipal borrowing was to require that banks making loans for municipal investment appraise land at its current market value rather than at its projected value after the completion of infrastructure facilities. Prior to adoption of these controls, it had been common for banks to lend against future land values. This exposed their lending both to project risk—the risk that the proposed new special economic zone or new urban centre would not be completed as proposed—and to political risk. The close ties between the local branches of state banks and local political authorities made it possible to incorporate highly optimistic or speculative projections of future land values as the basis for lending.

The state of California, in passing legislation that permitted municipalities to authorize developers to finance infrastructure through land-based bonds recognized the risk that developer projects would not be completed as proposed and required that land used to collateralize bonds have a current market-value appraisal of at least three times the principal amount of debt issued.

The Entrepreneurial Municipality: Incentives and Distortions

In the end, the greatest challenge to the intergovernmental fiscal system lies in deciding how much entrepreneurial freedom to grant municipalities as land market players and how much importance to assign to municipal infrastructure investment versus the claims of other potential beneficiaries of municipal land-value increases.

Mobilizing large amounts of infrastructure financing from land sales requires a motivated, entrepreneurial municipality that has the freedom of action to assemble land parcels, sell them at market prices and keep most of the profits for investment. The land market is not an ordinary competitive market, however. Municipalities have potential monopolistic power over land supply, and local governments and land development agencies are likely to have far more political power at their command than farmers, rural communes, poor households and small businesses from whom the municipality acquires land. This imbalance lies at the heart of intergovernmental regulatory rules that are needed to define and constrain municipal governments as players in the local land market. Rules not only define how far municipalities can go in generating land profits, but they indirectly define how far the intergovernmental system will go in making a priority of municipal infrastructure investment. The land-value gains that municipalities use to finance infrastructure investment are also claimed by farmers, who demand that they should receive market value for the land taken from them; by the poor, who demand adequate compensation and replacement housing in return for mandatory resettlement; as well as by private developers and others.

China and India represent different starting points in defining the intergovernmental rules that allocate benefits from land appreciation. China started by assigning virtually all power over land acquisition and land disposition to municipalities. This assignment of institutional power allowed municipalities to move virtually unchecked to convert land rights into infrastructure assets. More recently, resistance from farmers and the poor has forced the government—first individual municipalities (Zhu 2004), then the national government—to adopt regulations that increase compensation levels, introduce hearing procedures to strengthen the rights of parties whose land is being taken, and prohibit municipalities from acquiring or redeveloping certain types of land without express authorization of higher-level governmental authorities. These steps have slowed somewhat the pace of municipalities' land-to-infrastructure conversion, though many conflicts over municipal land acquisition remain unresolved.

India started with rules that placed more obstacles in the path of municipalities and development agencies that wanted to mobilize investment financing through land acquisition and land sale. In Mumbai, residents of Dharavi, the largest slum in east Asia, won the right, if registered before 1995, to have new housing provided for them free of charge in the same area as part of any redevelopment project. Newer residents have exerted political pressure for comparable compensation. This protection has meant that public profits from redevelopment and land sales in Dharavi will be channelled primarily to housing for the poor rather than citywide infrastructure. Other restrictions direct India's urban development authorities to provide land at the urban fringe to middle-class applicants at highly subsidized rates, not at market rates that would generate a profit available for investment. Such restrictions have made it difficult to mobilize surplus financing through land sales and target it to infrastructure improvements. In the last three years, however, Mumbai has, with great publicity, launched a redevelopment effort expressly designed to emulate Shanghai's development. The initiative focuses on redevelopment of publicly held land and proposes to generate financing for general infrastructure in part by claiming a greater share of the revenue generated by land sales for public investment.

As long as urban land prices continue to rise, institutional conflict over how to allocate the benefits of land value gains will continue, and likely intensify. Municipal infrastructure investment is one claimant for increased funding, but it must compete with the demands of social groups that have a stake in urban land and land values. Whenever large sums of money are generated by off-budget transactions, there is also the potential for political wastefulness and corruption. Clear institutional accounting for the revenues generated by land sales and the uses of funds, whether for infrastructure or other purposes, is the first step toward responsible management of increasingly valuable urban land assets.

Notes

1. For the role of balance sheet and asset management in municipal finance, see Peterson 2006.
2. The speed with which land leasing was adopted can be seen from Shanghai's records. Between 1988 and 1991, 12 land leases were granted in Shanghai. The total rose to 201 in 1992 and 3,000 in 1993 (Fu 1996).
3. The decision to assign all revenue from land leasing to municipalities in part recognized on-the-ground reality. The State Auditing Authority found that in 1991 and 1992, 80 per cent of the land-leasing revenues generated by sample municipalities were concealed from the local fiscal authority, and of the amount received by the fiscal authority, 90 per cent was assigned to the local discretionary budget rather than shared with the central government according to the rules then in effect.
4. This account is drawn from Peterson (2006: 163).
5. The minimum price that municipalities have to pay for rural land has been calculated as a multiple of a commune's actual annual income from agriculture, not 'market' value. In reality, there is no land market for farmers since they cannot own or lease land individually and the commune cannot sell land-use rights directly to developers or others.
6. For example, the Vice Mayor of Chengdu authored a volume (Sung Ping et al. 2003) emphasizing that (*a*) land leasing and land supply should be the exclusive responsibility of the government, (*b*) that therefore land transactions, including those by SOEs on the secondary market, should go through the municipality's Land Resource Center or be approved by it, (*c*) that the municipality should capture for itself at least 60 per cent of the net value gains resulting from the sale of leasing rights for land originally allocated to municipal SOEs, and (*d*) that land leasing proceeds should be used to finance municipal fixed-asset investment.
7. An IMF Mission in October 2005 emphasized the importance of broadening Hong Kong's tax base (IMF 2005): 'A substantial part of non-tax revenues accrues from land sales and investment income that are very volatile.'
8. Botswana and Mozambique are other nations that have variants of urban land leasing.
9. Local governments in Ethiopia are split into an 'urban administration' that acts as the local agent for the regional government in providing health and education and a 'municipal' government that provides basic services primarily from its own resources.
10. These are termed Mello-Roos bonds after the authors of the bill that established this mode of financing for new community infrastructure. See California Debt and Investment Advisory Commission (2002) and Chapman (1998).
11. The Vice-Director of the central government's Department of Land Use and Management estimated that RMB 200 million (US$ 25 million) of infrastructure was required to develop each square kilometre of an industrial zone. At that rate, more than RMB 600 billion (US$ 75 billion) would be required to develop only 10 per cent of the undeveloped areas municipalities had claimed for development zones in 2004. In the Vice-Director's words, the municipalities' excesses implied that 'large sums of money will be "buried" in the soil' (*China Daily* 2004c).

References

Ahmad, Ehtisham, Li Keping, Thomas Richardson and Raju Sing. 2003. 'Recentralization in China?' in Ehtisham Ahmad and Vito Tanzi (eds), *Managing Fiscal Decentralization*. London: Routledge.

Bombay First and McKinsey & Company. 2003. *Vision Mumbai: Transforming Mumbai into a World-Class City*. Mumbai: Bombay First.

California Debt and Investment Advisory Commission. 2002. *1999 Annual Report*. Sacramento: California.

Chan, Kam Wing. 1997. 'Urbanization and Urban Infrastructure Services in the PRC', in Christine P.W. Wong (ed.), *Financing Local Government in the People's Republic of China*, chapter 3. Hong Kong: Asian Development Bank and Oxford University Press.

Chapman, Jeffrey I. 1998. *Proposition 13: Some Unintended Consequences*. Berkeley, California: Public Policy Institute of California.

China Daily. 2004a. 'Land Auction Enthusiasm Still Missing'. www.chinadaily.com.cn/english/doc/2004-06/21/content_34128.htm.

———. 2004b. 'Nation Clamps Down on Land Abuses'. www.china.org.cn/english/china/88003.htm.

———. 2004c. 'China Cancels 4,800 Development Zones'. www.chinadaily.com.cn/english/doc/2004-08/24/content_368120.htm.

Chreod Ltd. 2005. *Report to World Bank on City Development Strategies II*. Ottawa, Canada: Chreod Ltd.

Deng, F. Frederic. 2003. 'Political Economy of Public Land Leasing in Beijing, China', in Stephen C. Bourassa and Yu-Hung Hong (eds), *Leasing Public Land: Policy Debates and International Experiences*, pp. 229–50. Cambridge, Massachusetts: Lincoln Institute of Land Policy.

———. 2005. 'Public Land Leasing and the Changing Roles of Local Government in Urban China', *Annals of Regional Science*, 39 (2): 353–73.

Ding, Chengri. 2005. 'Property Tax Developments in China', *Land Lines*, 17 (3). Cambridge, Massachusetts: Lincoln Institute of Land Policy.

Ethiopia, Federal Democratic Republic of. 2002. 'Proclamation No. 272/2002. A Proclamation to Provide for the Re-enactment of Lease Holding of Urban Lands. Federal Negrit Gazeta, 14 May, Addis Ababa.

Fu, Yu-Ming. 1996. 'Urban Land in China's Economic Reform', *City Economist*. Hong Kong: City University of Hong Kong. www.cityu.edu.hk/ef/english/ce96_8.htm.

Hong, Yu-Hung. 2003a. 'Policy Dilemma of Capturing Land Value under the Hong Kong Public Leasehold System', in Stephen C. Bourassa and Yu-Hung Hong (eds), *Leasing Public Land: Policy Debates and International Experiences*, pp. 151–78. Cambridge, Massachusetts: Lincoln Institute of Land Policy.

———. 2003b. 'Can Leasing Public Land be an Alternative Source of Public Finance', Working Paper WP96YH2. Cambridge, Massachusetts: Lincoln Institute of Land Policy.

IMF (International Monetary Fund). 2005. 'Hong Kong SAR: Preliminary Conclusions of the IMF Mission'. Washington, DC: IMF.

Pathak, Pushpa. 2005. 'Sub-National Government Expenditure: Mumbai'. Report prepared for DFID and World Bank, Washington DC.

Peterson, George E. 2005. 'Report and Recommendations on Municipal Finance Situation in Amhara and Tigray Regions'. Prepared for the Government of Ethiopia. Washington DC: The Urban Institute.

————. 2006. 'Municipal Asset Management: A Balance Sheet Approach', in Olga Kaganova and James MacKellar (eds), *Managing Government Property Assets: Inter-national Experiences*, pp. 145–70. Washington DC: The Urban Institute.

Sun, Ping et al. 2003. *Case Study for City Management in Chengdu* (Chinese). Chengdu: Chengdu Municipality.

Sun, Yinh-hui. 1995. 'China's Land Market: Current Situation, Problems, and Development Trends', Bangkok: Urban Management Programme for Asia-Pacific.

Zhu, Jieming. 2004. 'From Land Use Right to Land Development Right: Institutional Change in China's Urban Development', *Urban Studies*, 41 (7): 1249–68.

Zhu, Jieming and Loo-Lee Sim. 2005. 'A Transitional Institution of the Emerging Real Estate Market in Urban China', *Urban Studies*, 42 (8): 1369–90.

11

Urban Infrastructure Finance from Private Operators: What Have We Learned from Recent Experience?[1]

Patricia Clarke Annez[*]

Introduction

Ever since the mid 1990s, no discussion of urban infrastructure finance could be complete without discussing private participation in infrastructure[2] (PPI). This development represented a significant shift in attitude. For most of the period following World War II, much of network infrastructure was operated and financed by the state, both in developed and developing countries.[3] The economic contribution of these services, their linkage with broad public interest and concerns about the potential abuse of private market power in activities that offered limited, if any, scope for competition led governments to take a dominant role in their provision. The fall of the Soviet Union marked the acceleration of a trend that had started earlier in the decade, as reservations about private involvement in infrastructure were reconsidered and the scope for productive involvement of the state in any economic activity was fundamentally questioned, although evidence to confirm the superiority of private involvement in network infrastructure was scant, given the preponderance of the government in infrastructure provision. New approaches were attempted in developed countries first, most

[*] Patricia Clarke Annez is Urban Advisor at the World Bank in Washington, D.C.

notably in the UK, propelled in part by technical changes in such sectors as telecommunications and electric power that offered scope for efficiency improvements that could best be seized by private operators and financiers (Jamasb 2005). These technical changes also offered more scope for competition in certain segments such as electricity generation.[4] In the case of the UK, privatization of infrastructure was also part of a much broader withdrawal of the state from economic activity and privatization of assets held in an array of productive sectors, such as airlines, automobile production and coal mining. While the budgetary payoffs of divestiture were significant at certain points in time, fiscal pressure did not play a dominant role (Parker 2004).

In many developing countries, the fiscal pressures were more intense and the prospect of shifting investment responsibility to private infrastructure providers played a more significant role in the increased acceptance of Srivate-Sector involvement in infrastructure. In Latin America, many countries adapted to the need for fiscal retrenchment by cutting infrastructure investment (Fay and Morrison 2005). PPI held out the hope of expanding and improving services without further burdening the fiscal accounts, while sale of assets brought welcome revenues. In east Asia, rapid economic growth, urbanization and the demands for more and better infrastructure—urban rapid transport in Thailand, highways in China and power generation in the Philippines, to name a few—led to a spate of transactions in the early 1990s.

Concurrent with the trend toward greater PPI, decentralization expanded rapidly in the 1990s, touching all regions, albeit in different forms specific to each country. Decentralization added to the fiscal pressures to find alternative sources of finance for urban infrastructure. A common occurrence in the early phase of decentralization has been to delegate functional responsibilities to local governments without shifting tax or other revenue bases, leaving a vertical imbalance to be managed with transfers.[5] Many cities were faced with rapidly expanding infrastructure demands. Newly elected local governments were under pressure to expand and improve services, and were open to reaping the fiscal benefits of shifting some investment responsibilities to private operators. Dissatisfaction with the quality and reliability of service and the inefficiencies and suspected corruption of public-sector operators made Private-Sector participation attractive. Thus the two concerns, fiscal and operational, merged in developing countries in a way they did not in developed countries. The expectations that PPI would play an important role in addressing these concerns were high. (See, for example, an analysis for India by the Expert Group on the Commercialization of Infrastructure Projects 1996 [Mohan report].)

In this regard, however, PPI has disappointed, playing a far less significant role in financing infrastructure in cities than was hoped for and which might be expected, given the attention it has received and continues to receive in strategies to mobilize financing for infrastructure. This paper seeks to understand better the experience in developing countries thus far and to understand some of the reasons behind these outcomes. The experience examined here is a specific subset of the broader PPI trends across all infrastructure sectors whose successes and shortcomings have been documented at length elsewhere. (See, for example, Harris 2003 and Kessides 2004.) Also, our focus is on the role of PPI in mobilizing finance. Other benefits of bringing in private operators, such as more efficient operations, are not explicitly examined here.

In this review, we find that, in terms of the numbers, PPI for urban infrastructure has mobilized little private finance. Examining the experiences in more detail, we also find that there are good reasons—practical, political, economic and institutional—for this outcome. Recommending that cities in developing countries try harder is not likely to relieve all these constraints. Indeed, experience shows that there are a number of features that raise the risk profile of urban infrastructure for private investors, which has meant that the bulk of the transactions that have taken place have been exceptions rather than harbingers of a growing trend. Many of the measures that could reduce the risk profile are outside the control of many cities, others are unlikely to change, and yet another group of steps has to be taken that would improve prospects for urban service provision, whether in the hands of public or private operators. These findings suggest a more pragmatic and selective approach to the focus on PPI as a source of finance and more focus on some of the array of fundamental steps required to make urban infrastructure investments viable propositions.

Trends in PPI in Urban Infrastructure for Developing Countries

First, let us consider the trends in urban infrastructure investment in developing countries in the context of overall PPI over the last several years. These data are drawn from the World Bank's PPI database. We constructed a database covering urban infrastructure as a subset of all infrastructure by identifying specific transactions in sectors in the database that can reasonably be characterized as urban services (water and sanitation and a subset of transport projects). We calculated flows of finance by using the investment figures in the database and excluded revenues from the acquisition of assets. (See Annexure 11.1 for details on the sources and construction of the dataset.) While it is the only source of statistical data on PPI, the database is not without its limitations, particularly for urban infrastructure. Unfortunately, the World Bank PPI database does not cover an important element of urban infrastructure—solid waste management and disposal, which is a potentially significant source of PPI transactions. Moreover, the database covers primarily transactions involving international investors, whereas local private investors could possibly have played a more important role in urban infrastructure sectors.[6]

Figure 11.1 shows both total PPI investment in infrastructure and in urban infrastructure for the entire period 1983–2004, over which data has been collected. It shows that urban infrastructure investment has only had a very minor share in total PPI throughout the period, 10 per cent in total. Urban infrastructure was slower to take off, with the first transactions captured in the database taking place in 1989. Investments peaked at roughly the same time as the total, in the later half of the1990s, just as the optimism for PPI began to take hold.

Figure 11.1
Total PPI and Urban PPI

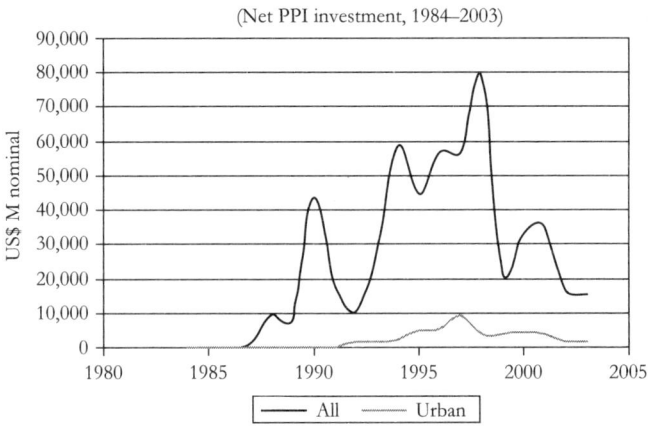

Source: World Bank PPI database. See Annexure for further details.

The regional breakdown of total PPI, as shown in Table 11.1, illustrates what has already been noted elsewhere, that is, the concentration of private investment in two regions, in Latin America and in east Asia and the Pacific.

Table 11.1
Regional Breakdown of Total PPI and Urban PPI, 1984–2003

US$M nominal	EAP	ECA	LAC	MENA	SAR	SSA	Total
All PPI	157,867.1	77,502.8	273,678.4	22,473.5	37,943.4	28,468.5	597,933.7
Percentage of total by region	26	13	46	4	6	5	–
Urban	26,492.9	2,795.7	24,580.8	5,373.3	423	1,600.4	61,266.1
Urban as a percentage of regional total	17	4	9	24	1	6	10

Source: World Bank PPI database. See Annexure for further details.
Note: EAP = East Asia and Pacific; ECA = Europe and Central Asia; LAC = Latin America and the Caribbean; MENA = Middle East and North Africa; SAR = South Asia Region; SSA = sub-Saharan Africa

These two regions also dominate the urban PPI, and to a more significant extent, accounting for 83 per cent of the total. The amounts of urban PPI in all other regions are virtually insignificant in relation to the size of their economies, with less than 1 billion dollars in south Asia and barely more than that in sub-Saharan Africa. Urban PPI is quite concentrated in a few countries, with 64 per cent of the total investment flows accounted for by the top five countries. There is much less concentration in the transactions for total PPI, where the top 10 countries account for a comparable percentage (67 per cent) of the investment.

Because the database reports all PPI transactions, including those that were cancelled, distressed or otherwise compromised, we netted out these problem transactions to get a better, albeit imperfect measure of actual investment flows from urban PPI.[7] (See Annexure 11.1 for definitions of these categories.) As shown in Table 11.2, this netting out has a considerable impact for urban PPI, with 25 per cent of total transactions classified as problem transactions. Here there are also very clear differences between

Table 11.2
Problem Projects in Urban PPI, 1984–2003

Urban PPI $ M Nominal Project status	Energy	Transport	WSS	Total
Regular transactions	5,734.7	18,746.5	21,532.07	46,013.27
Problem transactions	11	1,999	13,243	15,253
Total by sector	5,745.6	20,745.1	34,775.37	61,266.07
Problem transactions as percentage of total	0	10	38	25

Source: World Bank PPI database. See Annexure for further details.

the urban PPI and the total PPI transactions, where the total problem transaction component is only 10 per cent. Water supply and sanitation transactions clearly drive this outcome, with nearly 40 per cent classified as problem projects.

Thus, we conclude from this overview of the trends in private participation in infrastructure that investments in urban infrastructure have played a relatively minor role in the overall PPI flows generated even during the peak period in the mid-1990s. PPI for urban infrastructure has been more concentrated in a few countries than overall investment flows, and is often quite insignificant in countries such as Brazil and South Africa, which within their regions attracted quite significant flows of PPI overall. This last point suggests that even for countries that appear to have been well disposed to PPI in general, attracting significant flows of funds for urban infrastructure PPI turned out to be more difficult. Analysis of problem projects in the database also points to this finding. There were significantly more problem projects in the urban sectors than in the others, with a total of 25 per cent compromised by problems as opposed to 10 per cent in total.

PPI in Urban and Total Infrastructure Investment

Having examined the overall trends in urban PPI, we now look at them in relation to total urban infrastructure investments, a significant indicator of the potential role of PPI in an investment strategy. This ratio can only be measured roughly, since very few countries specifically measure their urban infrastructure investments separately. It was impossible to prepare such estimations on an aggregated regional or global basis because the data is so sparse and is rarely comparable across countries. Instead, we examined each of the countries featured at the conference and sought to obtain the best approximate measure of the significance of PPI for financing urban infrastructure.

Looking first at Brazil, we have some indications from work by Calderon and Serven (2004b). Using a number of different data sources, they have estimated the share of both public and private investment in the entire infrastructure as a share of GDP for Brazil. These shares are published for two different periods, 1980–85 and 1996–2001. For the period 1996–2001, the share of PPI in total infrastructure investment is over 57 per cent, up from 30 per cent in 1980–85. In spite of this dramatic increase in the share of PPI in total investment, PPI in Brazil as a percent of GDP stays roughly the same, declining somewhat from 1.5 per cent to 1.4 per cent. Thus the increased share of PPI results from a dramatic reduction in public-sector spending, declining from 3.6 per cent of GDP to 1.0 per cent. Thus the increase in the private investment share is largely as a result of the decline in public-sector activity, not a major increase in PPI. Turning our focus to urban infrastructure, we note that PPI investment is dominated in both periods by both telecommunications and power, accounting for three-quarters of the PPI in the early 1980s and over 90 per cent from 1996 to 2001. Based on our estimates of urban PPI from 1996–2001 from the PPI database, urban PPI accounts for about 0.07 per cent of GDP or 3 per cent of total infrastructure investment. While we have no precise estimate of what the urban infrastructure spending is in relation to the total,[8] it seems quite likely that 3 per cent of total covers only a fraction of urban infrastructure needs. The World Bank (2001) cites a government estimate of about R$ 7 billion per annum for municipal infrastructure investment needs or about US$ 3.5 billion (at the exchange rate prevailing in early 2001). Average annual urban PPI over this period was roughly US$ 465 million per annum, and hence covers only a fraction of these estimated needs. Considering that most of those transactions took place prior to 2001, the potential appears even less promising. Thus, while Brazil mobilized a good deal of PPI, and its share in total infrastructure investment has been significant, in aggregate, PPI did not fully substitute for public spending on infrastructure; instead, it only attenuated a dramatic decline. Moreover, the information available indicates that the role of PPI in financing urban infrastructure is even less important, in spite of the considerable financial constraints placed on cities in the wake of the sub-national financing crisis and the implementation of the Fiscal Responsibility Law.

China has experienced trends in infrastructure investment that are quite different from those of Brazil, with rapid increases in infrastructure spending attracting attention worldwide. The indicators of service increases give a flavour of the massive investment flows involved. Between 1991 and 1999, city-based domestic water use has increased by over 75 per cent, municipal wastewater treatment capacity by nearly 250 per cent, and city sewer-network length by nearly 225 per cent (Bellier and Zhou 2003). Interestingly, however, PPI has not as yet played a major role. According to Bellier and Zhou, between 1992 and 1998, less than 4 per cent of total investment in water supply and sanitation had been financed by PPI. The share of PPI in the total fell from 7.5 per cent to only 3 per cent in 2002. According to the PPI database, the total PPI in urban water and sanitation in China for the entire 25 years covered by the database amounts to about US$ 2 billion, close to the amount of total annual (estimated) investment by the State-Owned Enterprises (SOEs) in the water and sanitation sector in 2002 (Asian Development Bank et al. 2005). The authors of this study note that SOEs account for only a small share of total water investment, since most of this investment is handled by local governments, for which they were not able to locate aggregate data. In relation to the projected investment needs for the 10th Five-Year Plan from 2001–05, PPI in WSS from 2001 to 2003 in China thus far amounts to about 4 per cent of estimated needs (pro-rated because the PPI data covers only 60 per cent of the plan period). Put otherwise, Bellier and Zhou underscore that the planned investments in water alone amounts to over 100 Chengdu BOT water projects, the Chengdu project being the largest PPI on record at the time of writing their paper.

Transportation PPI appears to have fared somewhat better in terms of the total investment in China, at least for a period. Bellier and Zhou (2003) cite estimates that about 10 per cent of the total transport investment (not exclusively urban) has been financed by PPI. However, they also note that a significant share of those investments, around 80 per cent, has been for expansion or rehabilitation of existing expressways. In those projects, the government has already taken most of the construction and traffic risks. It appears that the role of PPI in urban transportation overall has not been so significant. According to the Asian Development Bank et al. (2005), local governments are estimated to have spent over US\$ 37 billion on urban transport in 2003. This is about 12 times the amount raised in all urban transport transactions captured in the PPI database over several years. The trend for urban transport PPI in China is also disturbing. The PPI database indicates no projects concluded since 1999. This coincides with the change in central government policy regarding guaranteed returns in expressway projects (Bellier and Zhou 2003). Thus, although the sector appears somewhat less problematic than water, the share of PPI in total urban transport investment remains quite limited. While China has shown itself a world leader in attracting FDI and has concluded a number of PPI transactions towards infrastructure, the evidence indicates that PPI remains a minor source of urban infrastructure investment funding.

PPI in India has been limited and disappointing in comparison to the great hopes in the mid-1990s that accompanied economy-wide reforms and worldwide interest in PPI. India accounts for only 5 per cent of total PPI transactions in the World Bank database and only 1 per cent of the total urban infrastructure transactions. PPI has not succeeded in making any significant impact on the low level of infrastructure investment in cities. There is very little data available measuring actual infrastructure investment spending in Indian cities. Nonetheless, it is estimated that total spending in cities has not increased from about 0.5 per cent of GDP over the 15-year period since the 74th Constitutional Amendment Act that started the decentralization process in India. While the states and the centre may spend on urban infrastructure in India (see Chapter 3 of this volume), there is little evidence of service improvements to indicate that there has been a significant upsurge in infrastructure investment as the Indian economy has taken off more broadly. In a very influential volume, the Expert Group on the Commercialization of Infrastructure Projects (1996) (also known as the Mohan report) estimated urban infrastructure investment requirements in India both to meet the existing service gap and to satisfy incremental needs as the urban population grows. They estimated annual urban infrastructure investment requirements phased over 10 years at around Rs 280 billion (in 1994–95 prices). By contrast, total urban PPI from the World Bank database amounts to about US$ 420 million in total, or about Rs 19 billion, representing an average of a little over Rs 2 billion per annum, less than 1 per cent of the total urban infrastructure investment requirements.[9] Particularly given the sense of opportunity perceived in the Indian markets at the time of publication of the Expert Group report and the capabilities of the private sector and financial sector in India, this outcome is very disappointing.

As noted in Chapter 4 of this volume, Poland faces both a tight fiscal constraint as it seeks to meet EU fiscal management requirements and a strong demand for urban infrastructure investment to meet EU environmental standards. Nonetheless, the evidence suggests that PPI has made a *de minimus* contribution thus far to meeting infrastructure investment needs. Noel and Brzeski (2005) cite estimates of investment requirements for urban wastewater treatment in Poland amounting to over Euro 6.5 billion. The PPI database indicates that only US$ 16 million, far less than 1 per cent of this estimated requirement, has actually been mobilized for wastewater investments through PPI. This figure is also quite low in relation to the estimate of total local investment spending in 2003 of about US$ 3.5 billion (Chapter 4).

As discussed earlier, South Africa was one of the African countries most successful in attracting PPI. There was significant demand for infrastructure investment over the 1990s, as considerable catching-up was needed in terms of improving infrastructure in the newly amalgamated local governments that now included the under-served black townships, and government spending has been quite substantial. Chapter 5 in this volume, on South Africa, provides us with an estimate of total spending by local governments, net of interest payments in 2003–04. This amounts to roughly US$ 11 billion, or roughly about 6 per cent of GDP. By comparison, however, urban PPI in total over the period covered by the database has been quite insignificant, at about US$ 80 million, or much less than 1 per cent of one year's local government spending.

Thus, across the wide range of different countries featured in the conference, certain similar patterns emerge. For all of these countries excepting Brazil, PPI for urban infrastructure has not emerged as a major contributor to investment funding, certainly not substituting in a significant fashion for government funds. Its contribution in Brazil, in percentage terms appears to be the most significant, where urban PPI accounts for about 3 per cent of total infrastructure investment spending and a larger share of urban investment spending. While in Brazil and the rest of Latin America policy makers in the 1990s hoped that increased PPI could fill the spending gap created by fiscal discipline, spending declined overall as a share in GDP. As indicated in Chapter 3 of this volume, Indian cities have both very limited budgets and very pressing needs for infrastructure improvements, but urban PPI has been nearly insignificant there. While Brazil and India faced harsh fiscal constraints, China's government spending was expanding rapidly, as was the economy. Apparently, however, the contribution of PPI to urban infrastructure remains limited, less than 5 per cent. Moreover, it appears that the PPI on urban toll roads was short-lived and disappeared when government guarantees were withdrawn. Poland and South Africa's local governments appear well resourced and many are quite well managed, but PPI has also made insignificant contributions to the total urban infrastructure financing needs. It is worth mentioning here that the data available in the PPI database overstates to some extent the net investment provided from private sources because the transactions often include government contributions to the investment, amounting to about 10–15 per cent of the total (Ettinger et al. 2005).

Why Private Participation in Infrastructure Has Provided So Little Urban Infrastructure Finance

This section explores experience in the last several years to understand the reasons why—while a number of transactions took place and great efforts were made to promote PPI in urban infrastructure—so little finance was actually mobilized across a wide range of countries. A sector such as water supply and sanitation (WSS) is largely excludable[10] and user charges can, at least in theory, be used to recover costs. These conditions offer the possibility of attracting private finance and a number of WSS PPIs were concluded, even if WSS projects represent a small fraction of the total PPI. These projects suffered from a number of difficulties, as evidence by the high incidence (25 per cent) of problem projects, indicating considerable risks to both sides that could not be managed within the original contract arrangements.

One reason for this is that in practice, it has proven much harder to achieve full cost recovery (even in water supply) across a very wide range of countries and in spite of a decade of serious reform efforts and, in many places, fiscal pressures. Komives et al. (2005) and Foster and Yepes (2005) document in detail the state of cost recovery in the water sector. What is particularly striking about their findings is how very widespread subsidies are for the water sector, notwithstanding substantial reform efforts in many countries. As shown in Table 11.3, 42 per cent of High Income Countries are estimated to subsidize O&M costs of water provision for residential users. While many countries recover more from commercial users and hence improve overall cost recovery from these low levels, that bifur-cation of the market introduces complexities and risks for any Private-Sector investor, especially if they are being asked to expand coverage for residential users as part of the investment plan. Luque (2005) notes, for example, that the São Pãulo state water utility (SABESP), while recovering costs through a cross-subsidy from commercial users, has been losing its commercial customer base.

Table 11.3
Overview of Average Residential Water Tariffs

	Percentage of utilities which are:		
	Too low to cover basic O&M	*Enough to cover most O&M*	*Enough for O&M and partial capital*
By income			
HIC	8	42	50
UMIC	39	22	39
LMIC	37	41	22
LIC	89	9	3
By region			
OECD	6	43	51
LAC	13	39	48
MEENA	58	25	17
EAP	53	32	16
ECA	100	0	0
SAS	100	0	0

Source: Adapted from Komives et al. (2005).

This evidence suggests strongly that no matter how desirable the objective of full cost recovery may be for water, its practicability is questionable. Adding sanitation to the package of services provided—as many utilities do, although coverage is typically lower in developing countries—makes cost recovery less feasible or even desirable. The externalities associated with sanitation services imply that some subsidization funded out of general tax revenues is efficient. Clearly, the presence of significant subsidies on current operations substantially reduces the prospects for attracting long-term private finance for the necessary investments in the expansion of water and sanitation services.

While political will and populist politics have often been cited as reasons for the persistent poor performance in cost recovery, problems of affordability in low-income countries may also account for the inertia in reducing subsidies for residential water. The impact will vary from country to country, depending on water and sanitation coverage among the poorest households (which in regions such as Africa is quite low), the costs consumers bear to cope with poor service, and the scope (often unexplored) to restructure tariffs to cross-subsidize poor consumers. Recent estimates for Delhi indicate that substantial increases in water tariffs may still be affordable for poor households, especially if the coping costs, sometimes two or three times what is paid to the utility, can be reduced. (World Bank 2006). South Africa has achieved cost recovery, yet subsidizes basic consumption levels for rich and poor alike, with stiff tariff increases.[11] Overall, Komives et al. (2005) estimate, based on a review of a number of studies, that subsidies for electricity and WSS are equivalent to roughly 3–4 per cent of the household expenditure or income of poor households that receive them. This relatively modest number nonetheless indicates that there is substance to the concern that lower-income groups may suffer should full-cost recovery tariffs be adopted and if tariffs are not restructured to protect poor consumers. Thus, in many developing countries, two significant reforms of tariffs may be needed to achieve cost recovery that is both socially acceptable and makes water operations a viable proposition to private operators. Even with political will, it is likely that many countries will face a lengthy period of transition in which some form of public funding supports provision of these services, especially if coverage is to be extended to those not currently served.

Evidence on Chile's relatively successful privatization efforts in the water sector shows, in some ways, that they are the exception that proves the rule. Fischer and Serra (2004) discuss privatization of electricity, telecommunications and WSS. Of the three, WSS was the most problematic. Nonetheless, the programme registered successes in mobilizing finance for wastewater treatment programmes, one of the important motivations for privatization. The initial conditions are of interest, however. At the time of the privatization, 98 per cent of the urban population had access to the urban water network and 89 per cent to sanitation (Fischer and Serra 2004). As part of the programme, subsidies were restructured and government subsidies were re-oriented to the rural sector, doubtless facilitated by the fiscal space freed up by private investments in urban wastewater treatment. Some other countries in Latin America sought to mobilize private financing while expanding water system coverage. Experience has been quite mixed, as is well summarized by Kessides (2004). Barja and Urquiola (2001) note that in Bolivia, as in the case of Chile, the water privatization programme was the most difficult and limited in scope, although the El Alto private water programme increased coverage at about the same pace at which it increased in other urban areas. Kessides (2004) also discusses the distinct contrast of experience between the El Alto and the Cochamba water privatizations in Bolivia. The experience in Latin America indicates that recovering costs for new water connections adds a substantial layer of complexity to an already difficult transaction. In El Alto, this challenge led to an innovation in standards, while in Argentina, the private contract for Buenos Aires had to be renegotiated to soften the impacts on poor neighborhoods, but this renegotiation also lowered the expansion targets. In any case, mobilizing private operators to finance new connections adds a significant level of risk, which impedes the flow of capital or raises the costs if borne by the private sector alone.

WSS, and more particularly piped water supply, offer in many respects some of the most favourable conditions for private entry into urban infrastructure because it has most of the features of a private good; and yet, PPI has not been easy to encourage. It has been recognized for some time that municipal solid waste management (MSWM) is very much amenable to private participation (Cointreau 1994). The operational efficiencies that private operators can bring lower the cost structure. If proper fee structures are in place, sanitary landfills can be viable investments for private providers. However, in order to assume the significant investment risks involved, private operators need to be able to rely on a steady flow of revenues. This revenue flow in turn relies on the system of charging for garbage collection. These fees are typically managed by the local government and must address issues of local acceptance by the public and affordability. Cointreau (2005) points out that solid waste management has many aspects of a public good because it involves waste removal from public spaces and safe disposal, not just removal from the neighbourhood. Moreover, the tariff structure typically involves some level of cross-subsidy, because it is more costly to provide waste removal in poorer, more crowded neighbourhoods. Local governments that have not addressed these issues and that do not have some flow of general revenues to cover additions to direct service charges will be in a poor position to negotiate with private providers to make major investments. Urban transport has benefitted from a considerable shift away from public provision of services such as buses, and this move to private provision brings with it private investment. Nonetheless, considerable investment needs remain. Some urban transport infrastructure projects, such as dedicated expressways, have mobilized investment, as the earlier discussion showed. Apparently, however, this investment involved very little assumption of market risk by the private sector. Both in China and India, the focus on private sector investment for expressways has been on improvement and rehabilitation, and in China, the flow of transactions dried up when guaranteed returns were not provided (Bellier and Zhou 2003).

An example of a planned urban transport investment in Mumbai, India, illustrates a part of the problem. Buckley (2005) cites a feasibility study for a harbour bridge project in Mumbai. Such a development would have a high value for the local economy by relieving a tightly binding land constraint. The government is seeking private investors, and has estimated a toll of Rs 100 to make the project financially attractive to private investors. However, the average daily income in the city in only Rs 125 and is thus likely to exclude many whose use of the bridge would much increase its overall economic value. Were the government to be in a position to tax the properties on the other side of the bridge in accordance with the increase in value that these properties would experience as a result of the bridge construction, the tolls needed to make the project a viable proposition could be reduced and usage most likely improved. This preferable public finance option could improve the prospect of private finance by lowering both traffic risks and the risks of protests and judicial challenges to the tolls. Thus, focusing only on private finance in this case could raise the risk of successful project implementation, raise the cost of the project and hence the finance, while lowering the economic and social returns of the investment. The presence of declining marginal costs per user, low incomes and weak public finances combine to offer this difficult prospect for a PPI transaction.

These features, while perhaps uniquely acute in Mumbai, are not unique to many of the infrastructure demands in cities. Luque (2005) illustrates the relative difficulties of achieving cost recovery in sectors other than water in São Pāulo state. Urban rapid transit is seen as a key public service and helps to reduce congestion, but requires a substantial subsidy.[12] For a variety of reasons, ranging from impracticability of charging to externalities to affordability, much of urban infrastructure cannot be financed through direct user charges. As such, it will thus not be readily amenable to finance through PPI. Published estimates of total investment requirements for urban infrastructure are relatively few, but the Expert Group on Commercialisation of Infrastructure Projects (1996) compiled an assessment of the costs of investment for core urban infrastructure in Indian cities.[13] Based on their estimates of the different types of infrastructure requirements for urban India and if we assume (somewhat optimistically) that all of water supply, 50 per cent of sewerage and 25 per cent of urban road investments can be recouped through user charges, then only about 45 per cent of those investments identified are even likely to have the basic elements to attract the private sector. Thus cities must have a strong public finance base to implement a reasonably balanced infrastructure investment programme. Relying on PPI alone would limit very strongly investments in important areas of urban services.

In a historical discussion of municipal franchising in North America in the late 19th and early 20th Centuries, Gómez-Ibáñez (2003)[14] provides an interesting example regarding the extent to which full user benefits can be captured in user charges. In discussing the decline of the municipal franchising movement, he explains that those services where the utility provided benefits beyond those captured in the user charges for private beneficiaries tended to be taken over and run by the municipalities. He says:

'For example, fighting fires requires considerably larger mains and higher pressures than are needed for normal household consumption. Nineteenth century households were not always willing to pay a fee for a domestic connection that was sufficient to finance a system capable of fighting fires. And the household that chose not to connect would still be connected by the fire hydrants in its neighborhood. The cities might have solved the problem by compelling households to subscribe to the water system by subsidizing the extra costs out of tax revenues. Compulsory subscription or public subsidies seem to have been politically less acceptable as long as the water company remained in private hands. Piped sewage collection systems didn't become widespread until the late 19th century, but the need to compel or subsidize subscriptions to prevent the spread of disease was so obvious that most sewage systems were built by municipalities from the start.'

In the case of electricity and gas, the public uses for these services were far less significant and, unlike firefighting for water companies, did not impose unusual technical requirements and costs. Moreover, the rate of technical improvement in municipal infrastructure sectors such as water and public transport was slow in relation to gas and electricity supply. In the latter sectors, these technological gains forestalled conflicts between regulators and the private companies because it was possible to reduce costs and prices more frequently. Thus, the companies for electricity and gas more often stayed private and regulation, for various reasons, shifted to the state level, while most of the private providers of water and public transport were taken over by municipalities. These features, so decisive in the United States in that period, continue to be relevant in many ways for the core municipal services today.

Many of the features of urban infrastructure sectors make them sensitive politically and socially, as this discussion has shown. The infrastructure services that cities need to provide are essential to life and livelihood. When existing subsidies are deep, shifting to cost recovery is not a simple matter. Because urban infrastructure involves politically sensitive sectors providing basic services, the risks to the government in offering the private sector a role in supply are, in principle, significant. Likewise, the risks to private providers are also significant. While this reasoning perhaps became an excuse for avoiding reform of public provision, experience with PPI in the last several years also shows that these risks to both sides of the transaction are not as easy to mitigate as was once hoped in the context of concluding a PPI transaction. As a result, even when it became more acceptable to seek out such transactions, relatively few were concluded and a relatively high percentage of these transactions unwound.

Some cases from developed countries, where urban PPI ran into difficulties, illustrates the risks of these transactions and the costs that are incurred when PPI's go wrong. In the US, 94 per cent of water systems are publicly controlled.[15] Atlanta, Georgia, explored a different approach by signing a 20-year water concession with a subsidiary of Suez in 1999, the largest of a wave of concession arrangements made in recent years as municipalities sought to access private capital for the extensive repair and rehabilitation of local water systems. In the case of Atlanta, the concessionaire was to make US$ 800 million in repairs over five years. Three years into the contract, in January 2003, both parties agreed to cancel the contract. The concessionaire argued that the system's infrastructure was in much worse shape than it had been led to believe on signing and that they were making losses close to 50 per cent of total annual revenues. Meanwhile, city residents and officials complained that service was poor and unresponsive. As a result of the contract cancellation, the municipality has had to resume management of the utility. Because of the contract cancellation, many of the expected financial savings to the government did not materialize, in addition to the costs to the concessionaire.

In 1999, the state government of Victoria in Australia acted to involve the private sector in provision of urban transport services in Melbourne.[16] The state-owned corporation providing services on an extensive network of trams and trains made substantial annual losses, covered by a recurrent subsidy. In addition, users were dissatisfied with service quality. The service was divided across five franchises and contracts were awarded through competitive bids. The government did not wish to raise fares; operators were to include the subsidy requirement in their bids and this would be an important factor in evaluation. Operators were required to maintain minimum equity levels and post performance bonds. The contract did not require the operators to invest in or build significant new infrastructure assets. Bidding was strong and when the contracts were awarded, the government expected savings of A$ 1.8 billion over the 15-year life of the contract. Within a few years, the franchisees hit financial difficulties. Demand growth, projected at 3.6 per cent per annum on average by the successful bidders (as contrasted with the historical average of 1 per cent) did not materialize and costs were not reduced as expected. The financial position of the operators was highly sensitive to this assumption, since the performance bond and equity combined amounted to only one year's losses if demand growth were zero. Two years into the contract, the franchisees requested a negotiation with the government. The options open to the government by that time were limited. In the intervening two years, the appetite for international franchises had diminished, making retendering the contracts a difficult option. Taking a hard line on the contracts would only exacerbate the problem of finding bidders at competitive subsidy rates. Moreover, there was considerable concern about the possibility of service disruption. Ultimately, the contracts were mostly restructured, although one operator, who unsuccessfully demanded a cap on future losses, ultimately pulled out and the government had to operate the franchises through a receiver. The result for the government was that for the system to remain viable, A$ 1 million would be required over five years, thus negating much of the expected fiscal advantage to the government.

This case is interesting and illustrative for municipal PPI in developing countries because, in nearly all respects, it represents a 'better than best case' scenario. The investment climate and capacity of the government of Victoria would be the envy of most LDC sub-national governments. The franchising operation involved only operations risks and did not require any investment finance from operators. Moreover, the contract was well structured on the whole and the process of awarding the contract competitive. Vulnerabilities were there, but these hinged primarily on two features:

first, the sensitivity to demand growth and the optimism embodied in the winning bids; and second, the meagre equity and performance bond in relation to the risks. With regard to the latter, while Irwin and Earhardt (2004) quite rightly note that assessing these features *ex ante* is essential to structuring contracts, it is quite probable that the outcome of the bidding would have been less favourable should the equity or performance requirements be increased. The bidders were able to compete using optimistic demand projections, which were apparently (and quite understandably) overlooked with the prospect of large subsidy savings to be realized. Nonetheless, given the importance of the service being tendered and the thinness of the market in the face of a retender, the government arguably bore more risk than did the operators should the winning bidder's projection prove to be wrong — as it did. While Victoria may ultimately reduce the subsidy substantially through repeated contracting, the gains likely to be achieved and the risk profile hardly constitute a major source of finance. It is interesting to note that high debt-to-equity ratios have been typical of urban PPIs to the extent they are documented. For example, Haarmeyer and Mody (1998) show that this was the case in a number of water projects in developed and developing countries.[17]

Moving to developing countries, a number of studies show that the concession contracts for water in Latin America in the 1990s proved to be quite fragile. While many of these contracts were negotiated on tight contractual terms, they ended up being particularly subject to contract renegotiation risks (see, for example, Estache et al. 2003; Guasch et al. 2000; and Guasch et al. 2003); Guasch et al. (2003) shows that water had the highest incidence of renegotiation, at 75 per cent of all contracts, on an average of 1.6 years after contract signing—66 per cent of these requests were initiated by the operator. Guasch et al. (2003) show that firm-initiated renegotiations are also positively related to contracts that involve private investment funding. Estache et al. (2003) also note that the high renegotiation rate is linked closely to the practice of price cap regulation. Price cap is a regulatory arrangement embodied in a private contract and considered better adapted to environments with weak institutions not able to manage the information and analytical requirements of rate-of-return regulation, because all it requires is a price resetting about once every five years. Price caps turned out to be highly vulnerable to contract renegotiations: 88 per cent of the price-capped water contracts concluded in the Latin America region were renegotiated. Estache et al. (2003) note too that a common outcome of these renegotiations under price caps was to agree to decrease the level and pace of investment. Some 85 per cent of the water projects with investment obligations were renegotiated (Guasch and Spiller 1999, cited in Estache et al. 2003). This experience with price caps illustrates well the limitations of the Private-Sector's appetite for risk and the repercussions this may have on finance mobilized through PPI. The price caps were brought in as a means of compensating for the weak institutional capacity to regulate private monopolies to achieve efficiencies and, in this respect, addressed an important need, one that is particularly acute at the municipal level. In the process, however, risks were shifted to the Private-Sector. The high rate of renegotiations illustrated how the limited appetite for Private-Sector risk taking combined with limited regulatory capacity. The impacts on investment were unfortunate and suggest caution in using PPIs if expanding finance for infrastructure is the primary objective of such transactions.

These difficulties are to be expected in these risky sectors and risky environments, and do not necessarily nullify the benefits of private participation. Many studies have described the benefits of these experiments of private participation. See, for example, Harris (2003) and Kessides (2004) for particularly comprehensive reviews of this experience. However, there are important lessons from this experience for sub-national governments seeking to use such transactions for *finance*. The risks to the financing stream derived from the concession arrangements are substantial, and achieving efficiency conflicts with mobilizing investment finance. As Guasch et al. (2003) note:

> The fact that [the price cap regulatory regime] induced a higher cost of capital because they tended to pass on to the operators a larger share of the project risks was very seldom considered. Also the fact that the regime was associated with a risk of under-investment (which has happened) was surprisingly seldom addressed in a region in which one of the main reasons to try to reform and privatize was to attract private investment to compensate for reduction in public investment.

This Latin American experience, which is the richest among all regions in terms of PPI in water, offers a sobering prospect for PPI for financing urban water needs around the world.

Water is a 'difficult' sector, and the risks involved for both sides are significant enough to make it difficult to mobilize substantial finance for water supply investments. Estache and Pinglo (2004) analyze returns to equity and volatility in several sectors, including water supply, in relation to the cost of capital in the period following the East Asian crisis (1998–2002). They find that water averaged a small negative return on equity, one of the lowest in the sample covering railways, energy and ports, in relation to a cost of capital exceeding 10 per cent. Moreover, the volatility of the return on equity was the highest in the water sector.

The Malaysian programme for private participation in sewerage also illustrates some of the disappointments that can occur when an aggressive private participation plan is put in place to mobilize finance and accelerate investments (see Mody 2002). After a few successful water and sanitation BOT projects in Malaysia, the government chose to support a national sewerage project, the Indah Water Konsortium (IWK). This project arose from concerns over local governments' weak technical and financial capability in the face of poorly maintained facilities and rising demands for better sewerage services. An unsolicited proposal was brought to the government and was approved rapidly in 1994. Investments and the level of service improved dramatically in the immediate term. However, even before the economic crisis in 1997, consumers objected to the tariffs imposed. The tariff structure originally stipulated in the agreements was suspended without compensation for the private contractors and a new tariff structure was only established in 1997. The economic crisis then prompted further reductions while the IWK discovered that the rehabilitation needed involved more investment than anticipated. As a result, the government felt obliged to provide substantial financial support to IWK, including long-term soft loans amounting to MYR 450 million.[18] As Mody points out, this transaction could have been designed better in many respects. However, as a transaction designed to mobilize substantial finance for new capacity in a short time, with plenty of incentives to private participants, it is not atypical. The economic crisis multiplied the difficulties tremendously, but the problems had already emerged before devaluation aggravated them. While private participation doubtless brought considerable implementation capacity to the task, they did not resolve the fundamental impediments to making provision of sanitation services a viable financial proposition. The government succeeded in attracting private involvement, but the structure of guarantees provided and the nature of the risks involved in the project were such that both the capital mobilized and the physical achievements of the projects were much less than originally expected.

The Malaysia example is interesting in that the sanitation programme, while providing a core urban infrastructure service, did so through a national programme. Many other PPIs for core urban services, especially water concessions in Latin America, have involved municipalities. Experience indicates that working with local rather than national governments brings with it an additional layer of risk for the private supplier, for a variety of reasons. The first of these may be political alliances and election calendars. Guasch and Straub's (2005) evidence for Latin America indicates that changes of government at the local level help to explain the frequency of government-initiated contract negotiations in a number of water concession contracts. They also cite several examples of contract renegotiations for water concessions subsequent to a change in elected local government. Likewise Galiani et al. (2005) analysis indicates that in Argentina, when water companies were either controlled by the federal government or if the local government was the same as the ruling federal party, a privatization transaction was more probable. Private investors or operators thus ran the risk that political shifts in either the local government or the federal government could endanger their contractual arrangements.

A second risk of working with local governments is their limited scope of authority. Kessides (2004) and Gómez-Ibáñez (2006) cite numerous examples of confusion across different levels of government in water concessions, leading to a murky relationship with the regulator or simply bypassing of the regulator altogether. Local governments may be subject to various pressures or to direct intervention from higher levels of government, and thus may be less predictable, less capable of making credible commitments than national governments. For similar reasons, regulatory opportunism is less costly for local governments than for a national government in that the repercussions of arbitrary behaviour especially with foreign private investors, are less costly to local governments than to a national government. The impact on FDI, for example, is likely to be felt nationwide if a major contract is not honoured, even if the contractor is only a municipal government. Private investors are likely to view contracts with sub-national governments as particularly risky for this reason.

The experience of the Argentinean water concessions illustrates how different levels of government may interact so as to complicate the relationship between local governments and private concessionaires. As Kessides (2004) has pointed out, a service such as water involves a local monopoly, with large fixed investments that create long-lived assets that generate rents. The parties to a concession contract are intent on extracting their share of the rents, the private operators on compensating their efforts and risk and the government on ensuring that rate payers do not bear an excessive burden. The contracts are typically long-term, with strong negotiation over adjustment clauses so that rents are properly distributed over time as efficiency improvements and cost shifts come into play. Estache et al. (2003) hypothesize an interesting twist in this relationship in the case of the Argentinean water concessions. While the private water operators were able to achieve substantial efficiency gains—from 3 to 6 per cent per annum under a price cap regime[19]—tariff rates did not decline and there were still a number of contract renegotiations. Estache et al. (2003) argue that the government captured the rents generated by the more efficient private water operators through indirect tax increases, thereby increasing the tax revenue derived from the privatized infrastructure sectors about 4–5 times across all levels of government. This fiscal capture of the efficiency gains did not prove sustainable, because it provoked a number of contract renegotiations and rising public discontent with privatization, again understandable because the *quid pro quo* for the higher water rates was far from evident to the public. With a local service such as water, the temptation for the tax authorities at different levels of government to appropriate some of the improving rents is great. Yet the government that is getting the tax benefit is not necessarily the same government—for example, a province or municipality—that will be faced with a difficult contract negotiation as a result.

A final point worthy of mention in terms of the risks facing international investors for concessions is the exchange-rate risk. Infrastructure projects are especially vulnerable, since providers of core urban services do not typically earn foreign exchange. Unquestionably, devaluations during the Asia crisis affected the viability of a number of projects through a variety of channels, as outlined by Baietti (2001), and led to a number of renegotiations. Likewise Guasch, Laffont and Straub's analysis (2003) has shown that the timing of renegotiations of private investment contracts in a number of infrastructure sectors was affected by the devaluations in Latin America. As Baietti discusses, the impacts of a major macroeconomic disruption such as the east Asian crisis are not only limited to international investors. A strong devaluation can have a substantial impact on demand and willingness to pay for services as well. Moreover, an increase in the cost of imported inputs due to a devaluation or an oil price shock can raise the cost profile for a local utility in an environment where rate increases will be particularly unwelcome. Thus macroeconomic shocks are a threat to urban infrastructure PPIs. On the other hand, local governments do not manage the macro policy and are much less able to offer comfort to a private investor when these difficulties arise. This is one more factor making municipal investment less attractive than other potential private investment transactions managed nationally, such as telecommunications.

This discussion has covered several different factors, that make assets that provide urban infrastructure services risky financial propositions and thus less attractive to private investors than other uses for their money and capabilities. These factors limit the supply of private funding for owning and operating urban infrastructure, whether or not governments are inclined to seek out this funding. In the 1990s, governments did seek out more private participation for a number of reasons. As this strategy evolved, they sought methods to reduce the risk to private parties and to make these investments more attractive. One means of achieving this was through structuring transactions that would securitize revenues such as taxes or user charges. Such methods are helpful, but limited in scope. Ravi (2005) provides a useful illustration for India, listing the wide range of potential structuring instruments that could be used while recognizing the fundamental limitations imposed by weak urban local-government finances. Essentially, while securitization can use the revenue streams available to local governments in ways that are more attractive to private investors, it does not overcome the strong revenue limitations that local governments in countries such as India face (see also Chapter 3). Securitizing user charges, for example, cannot make up for a political unwillingness to set and collect them. Moreover, the costs of securitizing revenue streams and structuring risk mitigation measures more generally can come at a high cost in relation to the funds mobilized. This is especially so when the basic revenue base is low or when intergovernmental relations are complex due to low local autonomy. Often subsidized by donors or governments, these costs are not properly accounted for in weighing funding options. Given the confidential nature of transactional arrangements, they are also not reported or widely scrutinized.

Often the argument made for subsidizing structuring is that as the market becomes more familiar with the transactions, these costs will go down. This result does not necessarily follow, however, when the structuring is used when the market potential is very limited. Arguably, the municipal bond issues in India started in the 1990s fit this profile. As the World Bank (2003) notes:

> In 2002, interest rates on municipal bonds had fallen from the 14.5 percent required for the first bond to 8.5 percent. Yet the total volume of debt issued yearly has never reached the levels achieved in 1998, the year of the first bond issue.

Thus, structuring is a useful tool for improving the prospects of PPI, but given the financial condition of many developing country cities, it is by itself quite limited. Accordingly, the subsidization of transaction structuring should be made more transparent and its impact scrutinized to avoid distorting financing choices for the sole purpose of promoting PPI in markets with limited potential.

In seeking to attract private investors, governments have also sought to lower the operational risk profile of PPI projects. This typically involves assuming some form of contingent liability or guaranteed returns. The literature on PPI offers many examples in which these project-contingent liabilities were assumed by the government. There are two costs associated with these risk-mitigating measures: they dampen the incentives to private operators to achieve efficiency gains and they can have a high fiscal cost. Neither cost is easy to measure *ex ante* when the financing decision is made. Perhaps the best known is the Mexican toll road programme that, subsequent to a devaluation and macroeconomic crisis, is estimated to have cost the government somewhere between 1 and 2 per cent of GDP (Serven and Irwin 2005). In the case of China, for example, some private water concessions and urban expressway concessions have included rate-of-return guarantees. Hungary's contingent liabilities for PPI are currently estimated at about 2 per cent of GDP (World Bank 2005). In assessing PPI as an option for infrastructure finance, it is essential to take into account these contingent liabilities because they have fiscal impacts.

A disadvantage of these contingent liabilities is that these impacts are far from transparent or predictable. Moreover, if not managed correctly, they will tend to suffer from adverse selection bias. PPI can create fiscal space in the short term, so governments in need are likely to pursue it. These are just the governments that have the least capacity to take on these responsibilities. As noted by Schwarz (2006) and World Bank (2005), the fiscal impacts of contingent liabilities are not as readily or easily scrutinized as are the direct budgetary outlays, and there is no agreed methodology for measuring this government assumption of risk. The danger this poses is already significant at the national level. At the sub-national level, ensuring consistent reporting and monitoring liabilities is an even more difficult task.

Experience thus far indicates that the private operators, even during the favourable phase of the market in the 1990s, have tended to limit their risks either by maintaining limited equity stakes and using special purpose vehicle (SPV) arrangements to shelter the sponsor's credit rating from project risks or by requesting governments to assume contingent liabilities (Irwin and Ehrhardt 2004). Ultimately, the need to provide a critical public service leaves the risk with the government, and expanding investment through PPI may well take these to unsustainable levels. Of course, under purely public provision, the government and the public share the risks of bad developments through some combination of deteriorating service delivery and fiscal costs; but budget constraints will tend to limit the fiscal impacts. As local governments assess their financing strategies and national governments set a policy framework for urban finance, they should take into account the relative attractiveness of these different risk profiles.

Concluding Remarks: Public and Private Urban Infrastructure Finance— Complements or Substitutes?

This paper has explored the experience with PPI for urban infrastructure finance over the last decade with a view to understanding its potential role in a strategy for expanding infrastructure finance while respecting government budget constraints. The private financing mobilized for urban PPI has been quite limited and undeniably disappointing in relation to the high expectations prevailing in the 1990s. At that time, donors strongly promoted the concept, governments became more open to sharing responsibilities for public service delivery through the private sector, and international providers actively sought to expand their presence in developing countries. But experience shows that financing urban infrastructure through PPI has not proven to be 'low-hanging fruit'. Indeed, it appears to be a fairly unpredictable source of finance, given the number of problems encountered with even the relatively limited number of transactions completed. Those local governments strapped for funding and keen to expand their investments would be wise to recognize these limitations. Federal governments encouraging local governments to use PPI to support their investment programmes need to recognize that PPI financing entails important fiscal risks as well. Because the future fiscal obligations taken on by local governments in PPI don't show up in traditional accounting frameworks, federal governments would be well advised to put in place safeguards to ensure that those local governments with fragile finances don't take on more risk than they can bear in the interest of mobilizing funding through PPI in the short run. Finally, PPI is inherently limited in scope for financing urban infrastructure for the wide array of non-commercial infrastructure services cities need. Even for commercial services such as water supply, subsidies are prevalent all over the world and in many of the poorest, most rapidly urbanizing countries, it will be difficult to attract private finance for necessary expansions of the water network while restructuring subsidies to make them financially sustainable and socially acceptable. Local governments need good sources of public finance to fund those services, and some form of government borrowing is needed for major investments in these areas to avoid inter-generational inequities.

Notwithstanding these caveats with respect to the role of PPI in finance, PPI can play a useful, if limited, role in a strategy to improve urban service delivery. Experience thus far suggests that PPI has more potential to improve efficiency than to mobilize new finance. Private suppliers have limited their financial exposure in urban PPI even in financially strong, developed-country cities. It is highly unlikely that in developing-country cities, they will be willing to put substantial capital or borrowing headroom at risk while also taking on an operating risk, which is the best means of achieving the efficiencies that are the potential comparative advantage of the private sector. Lowering the risk profile of the private sector to attract their participation involves mobilizing more public finance, be it in user charges or taxes, to give the private sector the assurance they need to get involved in private provision of services. Private finance cannot be a substitute for sound public finance in developing-country cities.

Annexure 11.1: Collection of Data on Urban PPI

Unless otherwise noted, figures quoted on investment in infrastructure projects with private participation have been taken from the World Bank's Private Participation in Infrastructure Project Database (http://ppi.worldbank.org/). Investment figures are investment in facilities (as provided in the database) and thus do not include divestiture transactions or any other transfer of assets (all figures are in units of US$ million). Figures are gross of government investment contributions. While these are not quantified consistently in the database, some studies indicate the 10–15 per cent of total investment captured in the database is actually provided by the government (PPIAF: 2005). Projects are considered to have private participation if a private company or investor bears a share of the project's operating risk. The information in the database is updated yearly through a comprehensive review of activity in each of the low- and middle-income economies, using commercial news databases, specialized and industry publications, and internet resources such as web sites of developers, sponsors and regulatory agencies. If necessary, information is also requested from or verified with project companies, developers and sponsors, and regulatory agencies.

Method for Identifying Urban PPI within the PPI Database

We created an urban subset that consisted of all the projects in the PPI database that cover urban infrastructure—water and sanitation,

Annexure 11.1 continued

Annexure 11.1 continued

urban transport, municipal solid waste, street lighting, etc. Excluded are sectors such as telecommunications and power, which while used widely in urban areas, are not local city-based infrastructure services. Unfortunately, there is no coverage of municipal solid waste in the database, and while this omission could be material, it is beyond the scope of this paper to address it.

We examined sectors such as water and transportation in more detail, because these sectors may include a mix of both urban and other infrastructure. To do this, we obtained detailed descriptions for each project in the water and transport sectors. Within transport, we excluded ports and airports and focused on the road and rail sub-sectors. For water projects, we searched for rural projects—and found very few references to rural water and no self-standing rural projects. Hence all water projects were included as urban. For urban transport, we excluded any projects that appeared to be inter-city or long-haul rail. We also excluded inter-city highway projects and focused only on roads such as expressways and ring roads that served urban areas. We included city bypasses, even when these were managed by a higher level national or provincial authority, on the grounds that these substantively serviced urban traffic, even if inter-city traffic also benefitted. When the information was not complete enough to determine whether road projects fell into one or the other category, we assumed that highway projects with capacity (provided in kilometres) less than 50 kilometres would be classified as urban. Some of the transactions recorded in the database involve two different sectors, such as power and water. In some of these cases, the primary sector would be power, but water investments would be included. We were able to access these transactions by identifying the water sub-sector or the transport sub-sector through a special search by sub-sector performed by the database managers. Because the database cannot disaggregate the investment by sector in combined projects, we assumed the entire value of the investment was for the respective sub-sector we are searching. Thus, the 'urban' PPI investment is unavoidably overstated.

Investment figures in the database are provided in terms of the estimated total for the entire project at the time when the contract is signed. However, since the contract period for the project can extend for up to 60 years, to annualize the investment figures, we assumed that the bulk of the investment was going to occur over the next five years, commencing from the year the contract is signed.

Notes

1. The views expressed in this paper are those of the author and do not necessarily reflect those of the World Bank. The author is indebted to Robert Buckley, Jonathan Halpern, Sonia Hammam, Ioannes Kessides and George Peterson for comments and discussions on this paper. All errors and omissions are the responsibility of the author.
2. When we refer to finance through PPI, we are referring to a bundled transaction that brings in private entities as operators that finance, or mobilize finance for, infrastructure. Mobilizing private finance for publicly operated infrastructure—for example, through municipal bond issues—or tapping private savings through the intermediation system is a different type of financing strategy, which countries such as the United States, among others, have very successfully pursued, and is not treated in this paper.
3. Private infrastructure operations were common in Latin America in the late 19th and early 20th centuries, but most were nationalized by the end of Second World War.
4. Note, however, that the evidence on the impacts of private ownership in power in developed countries is still ambiguous. See Kwoka (1996) and Jamasb (2005).
5. The vertical imbalance facing local governments derives from the advantages enjoyed by central governments in levying relatively easier-to-administer and less distortionary taxes. See, for example, Broadway (2001). Peterson (2005) provides an interesting case study of China, illustrating an alternative approach which shifts taxing power to local governments.
6. The database is being upgraded to include local investors to some extent; however, these data were not available at the time of writing this paper (early 2006).
7. Some transactions may have been cancelled after major investments were made, in which case our adjusted figures may understate the investment. However, this is not likely to be a material error, given that most problems in water projects, for example, were encountered early in the project cycle (Guasch et al. 2003 and Guasch et al. 2005). On the other hand, the database does not measure the costs the government may have incurred as a result of contract termination. These numbers are not necessarily insignificant: it is estimated that the Mexican toll road bail-out, probably one of the largest, cost over 1 per cent of GDP (World Bank 2005 in Serven and Irwin 2005).
8. Bremacker (1997), cited by the World Bank (2001), estimates municipal expenditures on housing and urban at 82 per cent of public expenditures in those sectors. If investment follows the pattern of total spending, then municipalities account for the bulk of urban infrastructure investment. Bremacker's study covers the period prior to the sub-national fiscal contraction and these ratios may also have changed since that time.
9. Dollar amounts from the PPI database were converted at the annual average exchange rate in the year of the transaction closure. Since transactions started in 1996, we counted an eight year period. The figures from the Mohan report are in real terms and the data in the PPI database are in nominal terms. Since all the nominal figures are from the years after the base year (1994–95) for the investment requirements, this low percentage share is biased somewhat upward.
10. Publicly provided services are said to be 'excludable' if access to the service can be denied to those who do not pay for it. Piped water can, in principle, be cut off if users do not pay their bills. This contrasts, for example, with public services such as national defence or city streets, where it is impracticable to bill directly those who use the service or prevent those who do not pay from benefitting.

11. Although, as mentioned, this does not lead to a high volume of PPI transactions, water charges do offer a revenue stream that can be capitalized on to mobilize finance in capital markets.

12. At the time of writing this paper, in the spring of 2006, financing the extension of the São Pãulo metro is being considered one of the first candidates for usign the new law implementing public–private partnerships, but no agreement has been successfully concluded (see Chapter 7).

13. Core urban services, in this case, include water supply, sewerage, solid waste disposal, drainage, roads and streetlights.

14. At the turn of the 20th century, the US income per capita was roughly US$ 5,000 in constant US$ 2,000. This compares with constant US$ 2,000 Purchasing Power Parity adjusted per capita income in 2004 of US$ 2,100 in low-income countries and US$ 6,200 in middle-income countries, indicating a broadly similar level of development to many of the countries now contemplating PPI.

15. Discussion of this case is drawn from Jehl (2003), cited in Kessides (2004).

16. Discussion of this case is drawn from Irwin and Ehrhardt (2004) and Earhardt (2006).

17. They note the exception of the UK where a debt write down accompanied privatization of the utilities.

18. This Malaysian Ringit being roughly equivalent to US$ 180 million at the pre-crisis exchange rates.

19. Price cap regimes are an alternative to the more classic rate of return regulation for public service monopolies, used widely in Latin America in the 1990s. Since they require concessionaires to compete on pricing and offer much less leeway for price adjustment, they are considered to provide superior incentives for efficiency gains. See Estache et al. (2003) for further details.

References

Asian Development Bank, Japan Bank for International Development and the World Bank. 2005. *Connecting East Asia: A New Framework for Infrastructure*. Manila, Tokyo and Washington, DC.

Baietti, Aldo. 2001. 'Private Infrastructure in East Asia: Lessons Learned in the Aftermath of the Crisis'. World Bank Technical Paper No. 50. Washington, DC.

Barja, Gover, and Miguel Irquiola. 2001. *Capitalization, Regulation and the Poor: Access to Basic Services in Bolivia*. World Institute for Development Economics Research Discussion Paper No. 2001/34.

Bayliss, Kate, David Hall and Emanuele Lobina. 2001. 'Has Liberalisation Gone Too Far?— A Review of the Issues in Water and Energy'. London: Public Services International Research Unit (PSIRU).

Bellier, Michel and Maggie Zhou. 2003. "Private Participation in Infrastructure in China" World Bank Working Paper No. 2.Washington, DC: World Bank.

Boix, Carles. 2005. 'Privatization and Public Discontent in Latin America'. Paper presented at the Conference on Joint World Bank Inter-American Bank Conference on Diagnosis and Challenges in Infrastructure Economic in Latin America and the Caribbean, 6–7 June, Washington, DC.

Broadway, Robin. 2001. 'Intergovernmental Fiscal Relations: The Facilitator of Fiscal Decentralization', *Constitutional Political Economy*, 12: 93–121.

Bremacker, Francois. 1997. 'Evolucao dos Municipios no Periodo 1989/1995', Working paper of the Instituto Brasileiro de Administracao Municipal, Rio de Janeiro: Instituto Brasileiro de Administracao Municipal.

Buckley, Robert. 2005. 'Reforming Mumbai's Real Estate Raj: A Prelude to a Business Plan'. World Bank. Unpublished manuscript.

Calderon, Cesar, and Luis Serven. 2004a. 'The Effects of Infrastructure on Growth and Income Distribution', World Bank Policy Research Working Paper 3400. Washington, DC: World Bank.

————. 2004b. 'Trends in Infrastructure in Latin America 1980–2001', Central Bank of Chile Working Paper No. 269. Santiago: Central Bank of Chile.

Cohen, Remy. 2005. 'Diagnosis and Challenges of Economic Infrastructure in Latin America'. Paper presented at a conference of the World Bank and the Inter-American Development Bank on Diagnosis and Challenges of Economic Infrastructure in Latin America, 6–7 June, Washington DC.

Cointreau, Sandra. 1994. 'Private Sector Participation in Municipal Solid Waste Services in Developing Countries (Vol. 1)', Urban Management Programme Discussion Paper No. 13. Washington, DC: World Bank.

————. 2005. 'Solid Waste Sector in Developing Countries: Some Thoughts on Finance, Cost Recovery and Subsidies'. Mimeograph, August 2005.

DFID (Department for International Development). 2002. *Making Connections: Infrastructure for Poverty Reduction*. London: Department for International Development.

Earhardt, David. 2006. 'The Dark Side of PPI'. Paper presented at the World Bank's Urban Learning Week, 22–23 March, Washington, DC.

Estache, Antonio, Jose Luis Guasch and Lourdes Trujillo. 2003. 'Price Caps, Efficiency Payoffs, and Infrastructure Contract Renegotiations in Latin America', World Bank Policy Research Working Paper 3129. Washington, DC: World Bank.

Estache, Antonio, and Maria Elena Pinglo. 2004. 'Are Returns to Private Infrastructure in Developing Countries Consistent with Risks since the Asian Crisis?' World Bank Policy Research Working Paper 3373. Washington, DC: World Bank.

Ettinger, Stephen, Shelly Hahn and Georgine Dellache. 2005. 'Developing Country Investors and Operators in Infrastructure: Global Overview of the Emergence of Developing Country Investors and Operators in Infrastructure Provision in Emerging Markets.' PPIAF Phase I Report. Unpublished manuscript.

Expert Group on the Commercialization of Infrastructure Projects. 1996. *The India Infrastructure Report: Policy Imperatives for Growth and Welfare*. New Delhi: India National Council of Applied Economic Research.

Fay, Marianne, and Mary Morrison. 2005. 'Infrastructure in Latin America and the Caribbean: Recent Developments and Key Challenges'. Washington, DC: World Bank Finance Private Sector and Infrastructure Unit, Latin America and Caribbean Region.

Fischer, Ronald, and Pablo Serra. 2004. *Efectos de la Privatizacion de Servicios Publicos en Chile: Casos Sanitario, Electricidad y Telecommunicaciones*. Banco Interamericano de Desarrollo, Serie de Estudios Economicos y Sociales, RE1-04-017. Washington, DC: Inter-American Development Bank.

Foster, Vivien, and Tito Yepes. 2005. 'Latin America Regional Study on Infrastructure: Is Cost Recovery a Feasible Objective for Water and Electricity?' Paper presented at the Joint World Bank Inter-American Bank Conference on Diagnosis and Challenges in Infrastructure Economic in Latin America and the Caribbean, 6–7 June, Washington, DC.

Galiani, Sebastian, Paul Gertler and Ernesto Schargrodsky. 2005. 'Water for Life: The Impact of Privatization of Water Services on Child Mortality', *Journal of Political Economy*, 113 (1): 83–120.

Gómez-Ibáñez, Jose Antonio. 2003. *Regulating Infrastructure: Monopoly, Contracts, and Discretion.* Cambridge, Massachusetts: Harvard University Press.

————. 2006. 'Alternative Regulatory Strategies'. Paper presented to the Municipal Finance Thematic Group, World Bank, 17 May, Washington, DC.

Guasch, Jose Luis and Pablo Spiller. 1999. 'Managing the Regulatory Process: Design, Concepts, Issues and the LDC Story'. Washington, DC: World Bank.

Guasch, Jose Luis, A. Kartacheva and Stefane Straub. 2000. *Contract Renegotiations and Concessions in the Latin America and Caribbean Region: An Economic Analysis and Empirical Implications.* Washington DC: World Bank.

Guasch, Jose Luis, J.J. Laffont and Stefane Straub. 2003. 'Renegotiation of Concession Contracts in Latin America', World Bank Policy Research Working Paper 3011.

Guasch, Jose Luis, and Stefane Straub. 2005. 'Infrastructure Concessions in Latin America: Government-Led Renegotiations'. World Bank Policy Research Working Paper 3749.

Haarmeyer, David, and Ashoka Mody. 1998. 'Tapping the Private Sector: Approaches to Managing Risk in Water and Sanitation', *Journal of Project Finance*, 4(2): 7–23.

Hall, David. 1997. *Public Partnership and Private Control—Ownership Control and Regulation in Water Concessions in Central Europe.* London: Public Services International Research Unit (PSIRU).

Harris, Clive. 2003. 'Private Participation in Infrastructure in Developing Countries: Trends, Impacts and Policy Lessons', World Bank Working Paper No. 5. Washington, DC: World Bank.

Irwin, Timothy, and David Ehrhardt. 2004. 'Avoiding Customer and Taxpayer Bailouts in Private Infrastructure Projects: Policy Toward Leverage, Risk Allocation and Bankruptcy', World Bank Policy Research Working Paper 3274. Washington, DC: World Bank.

Jamasb, Tooraj, Rafaella Mota, David Newbery and Michael Pollitt. 2005. 'Electricity Sector Reform in Developing Countries: A Survey of Empirical Evidence on Determinants and Performance', World Bank Policy Research Working Paper 3549. Washington, DC: World Bank.

Jehl, Douglas. 2003. 'As Cities Move to Privatize Water, Atlanta Steps Back', *New York Times*, 10 February.

Kessides, Iohannes. 2004. *Reforming Infrastructure: Privatization, Regulation, and Competition.* Washington, DC: International Bank for Reconstruction and Development and Oxford University Press.

Komives, Kristin, Vivien Foster, Jonathan Halpern and Quentin Wodon. 2005. *Water, Electricity and the Poor: Who Benefits from Utility Subsidies?* Washington DC: World Bank.

Kwoka, John E. 1996. *Power Structure: Integration and Competition in the US Electricity Industry.* Boston: Kluwer Academic Publishers.

Luque, Carlos Antonio. 2005. 'Improving Infrastructure Offer at the State of São Paulo'. Paper presented to the Conference on Mobilizing Finance in a Fiscally Responsible Framework, 6–8 January, Jaipur. http://www.worldbank.org/uifconference

Martimort, David, and Stephen Straub. 2005. 'The Political Economy of Private Participation, Social Discontent and Regulatory Governance'. Paper presented at the Joint World Bank Inter-American Bank Conference on Diagnosis and Challenges in Infrastructure Economic in Latin America and the Caribbean, 6–7 June, Washington, DC.

Montgomery, Mark (ed.). 2003. 'Cities Transformed: Demographic Change and its Implications in the Developing World'. Panel on Urban Population Dynamics, Committee on Population, Division of Behavioral and Social Sciences and Education, National Research Council, Washington, DC.

Mody, Ashoka. 2002. 'Contingent Liabilities in Infrastructure: Lessons from the East Asia Financial Crisis', in Hana Polackova Brixi and Allen Shick (eds), *Government at Risk: Contingent Liabilities and Fiscal Risk*. New York: World Bank and Oxford University Press.

Noel, Michel and W. Jan Brezeski. 2005. 'Mobilizing Private Finance for Local Infrastructure in Europe and Central Asia: An Alternative Public Private Partnership Framework Model'. World Bank Working Paper Number 46. Washington, D.C.: World Bank.

Parker, David. 2004. 'The UK's Privatization Experiment: The Passage of Time Permits a Sober Assessment', CESifo Working Paper No. 1126, Category 9: Industrial Organization, February. Presented at the CESifo Conference on Privatization Experiences in the EU in Munich, November 2003.

Peterson, George E. 2005. 'Intergovernmental Fiscal Systems and Sub-National Growth: China.' Unpublished manuscript. World Bank and the Department for International Development.

Ravi, P.V. 2005. 'Urban Infrastructure Investment in India: Mechanisms, Possibilities and Special Financing Vehicles'. Paper presented to the Conference on Mobilizing Finance in a Fiscally Responsible Framework, 6–8 January, Jaipur. http://www.worldbank.org/uifconference

Schwarz, Gerd. 2006. 'Fiscal Space, Fiscal Risk, and Municipal Investments: Is PPI the Solution?'. Paper presented at the World Bank's Urban Learning Week, 22–23 March, Washington, DC.

Serven, Luis, and Timothy Irwin. 2005. 'Fiscal Space: LAC Regional Study: Summary'. Unpublished manuscript. World Bank.

World Bank. 2001. 'Brazil Financing Municipal Investment: Issues and Options', Brazil Country Management Unit, Finance Private Sector and Infrastructure Management Unit Latin America and Caribbean Region, 20 April. Washington, DC: World Bank.

———. 2003. 'Real Estate Reforms: Bringing India's Cities into the Economic Liberalization Program', South Asia Energy and Infrastructure Unit. World Bank. Unpublished manuscript.

———. 2005. 'Part III. Special Topic: PPPs—Fiscal Risks and Institutions', *World Bank EU8 Quarterly Report*, Washington, DC.

———. 2006. 'Delhi Water Supply: Willingness to Pay, Coping Costs and Affordability'. Manuscript, South Asia Energy and Infrastructure Unit (Smita Misra Task Leader).

About the Editors and Contributors

Editors

George E. Peterson is Senior Fellow at the Urban Institute, Washington, D.C., working on international public finance and intergovernmental relations. Previously he has been Director of Public Finance Center at the Urban Institute, where he directed the institute's programme in intergovernmental finance in the United States. He is also the recipient of the Donald C. Stone Award for intergovernmental management and research from the American Society for Public Management. He has published *Decentralisation in Asia and Latin America: A Political and Economic Comparison* (co-edited, 2006).

Patricia Clarke Annez is Urban Advisor at the World Bank, responsible for strategy development, policy analysis, review of performance and new product development Bank-wide. She has extensive operational experience in South Asia, Europe, the Middle East and Latin America. She has also worked as an economic and financial advisor for ABB in Canada and for US corporate clients in PricewaterhouseCoopers in New York.

Contributors

Sandra Bondarovsky was an economist with Caixa Econômica Federal in Brazil.

Aser Cortines Peixoto Filho was Vice-President of Caixa Econômica Federal, Urban Development and Government Affairs, in Brazil at the time of the conference. He has also been Caixa representative and Director of the BIAPE International Bank Ltd; Director of Urban Development and Government; Superintendent of Institutional Businesses in the state of Rio de Janeiro; Advisor, Staff of the Presidency and Coordinator in Chief of Research Advisory of the Banco Nacional da Habitaçao (BNH). Mr Cortines is currently Deputy Professor in the School of Economics and Business Management and Professor in the Center for Research and Post-Graduation at the Rio de Janeiro Federal University.

Luiz de Mello is Head of the Brazil/South America Desk of the Economics Department of the OECD. Prior to joining the OECD, he held a lectureship at the Economics Department of the University of Kent, UK, and was a Senior Economist at the Fiscal Affairs Department of the International Monetary Fund. His main interests are public finances and international finance, with emphasis on emerging market economies.

Gao Guo Fu is the President of the Shanghai Chengtou Corporation (Urban Development and Investment Company—UDIC). The Shanghai Chengtou Corporation was established in 1992 as a governmental investment corporation. It mainly invests in major urban infrastructure projects in Shanghai, such as highways, urban water supply and sewage system, and gas supply.

Subhash Chandra Garg is currently serving as Secretary of Finance, Government of Rajashtan. Previously, he was Joint Secretary (State Finances) in the Ministry of Finance, Government of India. Mr Garg has had extensive experience working with governments in India at the local, state and national levels in various capacities. In these positions, he has become deeply involved with state governments and finances. In particular, he has focused on infrastructure development, intergovernmental transfers and the restructuring of state finances.

Vijay Kelkar is Chairman, India Development Foundation and Chairman of IDFC Private Equity Co. Ltd. Dr Kelkar has held a number of high level positions in the government of India. Most recently, he was advisor to the Minister of Finance of India, and Executive Director for India, Sri Lanka, Bangladesh and Bhutan at the International Monetary Fund.

Prior to that, Dr Kelkar was Finance Secretary; Chairman of the Tariff Commission; Secretary, Ministry of Petroleum and Natural Gas and Chairman, Bureau of Industrial Costs and Prices. He has also served as the Chairman of the Task Force for Implementation of the Fiscal Responsibility and Budget Management Act in the Ministry of Finance.

L. Krishnan has worked for the Government of India for many years, most recently as Special Secretary to the Government of Tamil Nadu, India. He is currently working as an advisor to the Infrastructure Leasing and Finance Services Company of India.

Johan Kruger is Founder and former Chief Executive Officer of the Infrastructure Finance Corporation Ltd (INCA). Under his leadership, INCA grew to a more than $1 billion company in eight years. INCA, which won an award for the best non-listed company in 2001 after being a finalist in 1999 and 2000, has been described as proof that development can be bankable in emerging economies. Mr Kruger has also worked at the Development Bank of Southern Africa (DBSA) with varying responsibilities including human resources, infrastructure, urban and southern region. He was responsible for starting the urban section in DBSA.

Su Ming is a teacher and researcher at the Research Institute for Fiscal Science (RIFS) under the Ministry of Finance of China. He is also Vice Chancellor and member of the Standing Council, China's Institute for Agricultural Finance; Chancellor and member of the Standing Council, China's Institute for Urban Finance; member of the Standing Committee, China's Academy for Public Finance; member of the Standing Council, China's Investment Institute; and Vice Editor-in-Chief for the magazines, *Finance Research* and *China Financial and Economic Data*. He has also published extensively on Chinese fiscal issues.

Krzysztof Ners was Vice-Governor, Council of Europe Development Bank at the time of the conference. From 1990 to 1998, he was a member of various teams of experts at the Institute for Eastern and Western Studies (New York), UN, OECD and World Bank. From 1998 to 2001, he was Alternate Governor of the IMF and the World Bank. As Deputy Minister of Finance, Government Plenipotentiary for EU Funds, he was responsible for public debt management, management of European Union funds to

Poland, including domestic co-financing, as well as bilateral cooperation in the field of finance, in particular with the central and eastern European countries.

Philip van Ryneveld is an independent consultant and the South African National Treasury is one of his main clients. His work has included local budget reform; an ongoing assessment of city strategies in the context of the National Treasury's Local Government Restructuring Grant programme, which was established after the Johannesburg financial crisis of 1999; and a project to further develop the Local Government Fiscal Framework. He has been Chief Financial Officer of the Cape Town Municipality from 1997 to 2001. Mr van Ryneveld was Commissioner of South Africa's Financial and Fiscal Commission from 1997 to 2002, and has recently been appointed as a non-executive director to the first board of Johannesburg's newly created Revenue Shared Services Centre.

Zhao Quanhou is a researcher at the Research Institute for Fiscal Science (RIFS) under the Ministry of Finance of China. He has published in the areas of China's fiscal policy, agricultural and infrastructure pricing frameworks, and public sector resource management.

Index

Accelerated Urban Water Supply Programme (AUWSP), 155–56

Ahmedabad Municipal Corporation, municipal bonds issue, 134

Andhra Pradesh Urban Infrastructure and Finance Development Corporation (APUIFDC), 154

AP Housing Development Corporation (APHDC), 114

Asian Development Bank, 133, 314

Auditor and Comptroller General of India, 120

Balcerowicz economic reform package, Poland, 164

Bangalore Municipal Corporation, 125; municipal bonds issue, 134

banking sector, finance mobilization from, 30

Brazil, budget balance in per cent of GDP, 42–43; challenge of universalizing sanitation services, 233; debt sustainability in, 42–46; decentralization in, 33–34; evolution of fiscal institutions over time in, 49–51; ceilings on personnel spending, 50–51; debt restructuring, 49–50; financial markets use for subnational fiscal discipline in, 35; fiscal adjustment in, 40–68; fiscal responsibility legislation role, 47–54; trends in, 42–46; fiscal performance during 1990–2003, 43–45;—central government outlays on Pensions and discretionary programmes, 45;—central government revenue and expenditure, 44;—fiscal stance over business cycle, 44;—indebtedness and fiscal stance, 43; infrastructure investment, municipal finances and, 56–66; public–private partnerships, 67; local government: constraints to finance, 66;—spending and economic performance, 54–56;—model for urban water supply and sanitation, 230–37; municipal finances and infrastructure investment, 56–66; municipal government expenditure: current expenditure, 59–61;—on debt service, 60;—on healthcare and sanitation, 60;—on housing and urbanization, 61;—on interest and amortization, 60; on investment, 59;—as percentage of GDP, 37;—on personnel, 59;—on transport, 60;—trends in, 59–61;— municipal indebtedness and primary budget balance, 65; municipal revenue, 61–63; compensatory transfers, 63;— composition of, 64;—constitutional transfers, 63;—intergovernmental transfers, 63;—municipal taxes, 61–62; —non-constitutional transfers, 63;— sharing, 63;—nationalhealth system, 56; PLANASA water and sanitation policy, 231–32; PPI in, 312–13, 316;